# The Collected Plays of Theodore Dreiser

# The Collected Plays of Theodore Dreiser

edited by

Keith Newlin & Frederic E. Rusch

Whitston Publishing Company, Inc.
Albany, New York
2000

Copyright © 2000
Keith Newlin & Frederic E. Rusch

Library of Congress Catalog Card Number 99-73842

ISBN 0-87875-510-1

Printed in the United States of America

**Contents**

List of Illustrations.................................................................................vi
Acknowledgements............................................................................. vii
Introduction........................................................................................... ix
The Plays
   1.   *The Girl in the Coffin* ............................................................1
   2.   *The Blue Sphere* ....................................................................25
   3.   *Laughing Gas* ........................................................................38
   4.   *In the Dark* ............................................................................55
   5.   *The Spring Recital* ................................................................69
   6.   *The Light in the Window*....................................................82
   7.   *"Old Ragpicker"* ...................................................................95
   8.   *The Dream* ...........................................................................109
   9.   *Phantasmagoria* ...................................................................122
  10.   *The Court of Progress* .........................................................138
  11.   *The Voice* .............................................................................172
  12.   *The Hand of the Potter* ......................................................188
Textual Commentary.........................................................................283
Emendations in the Copy-Texts......................................................290
Appendices
   1.   The Anæsthetic Revelation ...............................................317
   2.   Textual Changes in the Revised Second Edition
        of *The Hand of the Potter*..................................................324
   3.   Productions of Dreiser's Plays...........................................331

## List of Illustrations

1 Theodore Dreiser
2 Kirah Markham
3 Estelle Kubitz
4 First leaf of *The Voice*
5 Photo of *The Girl in the Coffin* production
6 Sketch of *Laughing Gas* set
7 Photo of *Laughing Gas* production
8 *New York World* source for suicide notes in *The Hand of the Potter*
9 *New York Herald* headline quoted in *The Hand of the Potter*
10 Sketch of the characters in *The Hand of the Potter*, appearing in the *New York Call*

# ACKNOWLEDGEMENTS

We are indebted to the Trustees of the University of Pennsylvania for permission to publish *The Voice*, to reprint photos, and for allowing us to quote from letters and manuscripts in the Theodore Dreiser Papers, Rare Book and Manuscript Library. We would like especially to thank Nancy Shawcross, Curator of Manuscripts, who made our job much easier by offering us assistance throughout this project. For permission to quote from a letter from Dreiser to Willard Dillman, we are grateful to the Clifton Waller Barrett Library, Special Collections Department, University of Virginia Library. And for permission to quote from the manuscript of *The Hand of the Potter*, we are indebted to the Manuscripts and Archives Division, The New York Public Library, Astor, Lenox and Tilden Foundations.

Portions of the Introduction and Appendix 3: Productions of Dreiser's Plays have previously appeared in journals. We would like to thank the editors of those journals for permission to include portions of the following: Frederic E. Rusch, "Dreiser's Other Tragedy," *Modern Fiction Studies* 23 (1977): 449-456; Keith Newlin, "Dreiser's 'The Girl in the Coffin' in the Little Theatre," *Dreiser Studies* 25.1 (1994): 31-50; and Keith Newlin, "Expressionism Takes the Stage: Dreiser's 'Laughing Gas,'" *Journal of American Drama and Theatre* 4.1 (1992): 5-22.

We are grateful to our universities for financial support of this volume: to the University of North Carolina at Wilmington, College of Arts and Science Summer Initiative Program, for a grant to Newlin; and to Indiana State University for a grant to Rusch.

Keith Newlin owes a special debt to Peter L. Shillingsburg, who generously gave him a copy of his textual editing program PC-CASE, which was tremendously helpful in collating variants among the versions of the one act-plays. He thanks also Jacinda

Nettik, his student assistant, for help at various stages of this project. And to Robin, who patiently listened to the details of variant comparison without too many complaints, his appreciation for her indulgence and good humor.

Frederic Rusch thanks Tammy South for her secretarial assistance, Professors Charles Hoffman and Paul Hightower for preparing the photographic reproductions of the newspaper drawings and the illustrations of Kirah Markham, and Indiana State University Provost Richard Wells for allowing him time for the project. Above all, he is grateful to his wife, Yvonne, for her support and encouragement throughout the project, her companionship during research trips, and her tolerance when his work on this collection left her without companionship during many weekends over the past year.

# INTRODUCTION

Like many writers, Theodore Dreiser nourished a long-standing attraction to the stage, beginning in 1893 when he was offered a position as the dramatic critic for the *St. Louis Globe-Democrat*. Dreaming of success on the boards, he drafted a comic opera called *Jeremiah I*, about an Indiana farmer who is magically transported to Aztec Mexico and becomes a despot.[1] Although he was a frequent theater-goer, his dramatic ambitions appeared to languish until late December 1912, when he traveled to Chicago to gather material about Charles Yerkes for *The Titan*. Accompanied by Edgar Lee Masters, Floyd Dell, and William Lengel, he went to Maurice Browne's Chicago Little Theater in January and saw Euripides' *The Trojan Women*, its first production in the United States. Dreiser was immensely attracted to Elaine Hyman (who later took the stage name Kirah Markham), a 21-year-old actress who was playing Andromache. Markham was involved with the 26-year-old Dell, but soon the 41-year-old Dreiser diverted her attentions to him, and in the summer Markham followed Dreiser to New York where she lived with him until 1916.[2]

Although his infatuation with Markham was perhaps the initial reason for Dreiser's interest in the Chicago Little Theater, he was impressed enough by its goals and staging methods to become active in promoting it. To Mary Elizabeth Titzel, the Theater's secretary, he wrote that the Theater and its company "seem to me to be truly leading in dramatic effort in America."[3] He acquainted his friend and champion, the critic H. L. Mencken, with his delight in the theater and asked him for help in publicizing the Theater's activities in *Smart Set*, of which Mencken was co-editor, and for assistance in arranging playhouses for the Theater's tour to eastern cities. Dreiser also was on the watch for plays for Browne's troupe to produce. On 17 February 1913 he wrote to Mencken, enclosed a program from the Little Theater, and asked, "If you have a radical one act play—something remote from the courage of the average stage send it to me & I'll get Browne to read it. He's the real thing."[4] Mencken declined, explaining that he was too busy, but he did help Dreiser and Browne schedule performances in Baltimore for *The Trojan Women* when it went on tour.

Dreiser greatly admired Browne's effort to form an "art" theater in rebellion against the usual fare of musical comedies and melodramas offered at commercial theaters. Founded in the fall of 1912 in response to a recent visit by Dublin's Abbey Players, the theater was, in Browne's words,

> a repertory and experimental art theatre producing classical and modern plays, both tragedy and comedy, at popular prices. Preference is given in its productions to poetic and imaginative plays, dealing primarily whether as tragedy or comedy with character in action.... The Chicago Little Theatre has for its object the creation of a new plastic and rhythmic drama in America.[5]

A poet himself, Browne wanted to foster poetic drama (which in 1912 meant a Maeterlinckian symbolism), for only through poetry, he believed, could an artist fully engage his audience's emotional and intellectual attention. As Dell, one of Browne's most enthusiastic supporters, explained,

> The theater of today, it may be said, engages to take a citizen, slightly flushed with dinner, to coax and cajole him, tickle and fascinate him—and then, when it has him fully under its spell, to raise his soul for a moment to the height of crisis. But for a moment only! The tension is relaxed, the dénouement arrives swiftly.... But the poetic play, which neither amuses nor cajoles ... requires of the audience from beginning to end a sustained intensity of attention.[6]

Browne was one of the first American directors to adopt Gordon Craig's theories of stagecraft as a means of sustaining this intensity. Craig denounced realism in stage design, arguing that realistic sets distracted the audience's full attention from the play through the inevitable evaluation of their verisimilitude. Instead of realistic scenic design, Craig advocated a set expressive of the thought of the playwright, as interpreted by the director. The scene should harmonize with and focus attention to the play itself. As Kenneth Macgowan explains in his study of the new stagecraft, *The Theatre of Tomorrow* (1921), the set design should offer "a rounded and complete emotional interpretation of a play, analyzing the emotional values established by the dramatist, interpreting these values in the terms of human actors and stage atmosphere, in movements, lights, color, line, costume, and background."[7] The productions of plays at the Chicago Little Theater, and especially *The Trojan Women*, were characterized by a scenic design that created atmosphere through symbolism and suggestion. The set, for example, consisted of nothing more than a wall with a jagged gap in it and two steps leading up to it.[8] Browne himself argued that the new stagecraft should be a "rhythmic fusion of movement, light, and sound" and drew his inspiration from the Greek chorus and pantomime.[9] This new impressionism in stagecraft, as articulated by Craig and practiced by Browne, was thus an early forerunner of the later expressionist sets constructed by the Theater Guild.

Dreiser was enchanted with the simplicity, dignity, sensitivity, and beauty of the production of *The Trojan Women*. Browne's use of suggestive and symbolic sets, his theories of "plastic and rhythmic drama," and his selection of avant-garde plays undoubtedly sparked in Dreiser an awareness of the possibilities of dramatic form as a means of expression. But Dreiser was equally enchanted with Markham, and if one can trust Dreiser's fictional treatment of her as Stephanie Platow in *The Titan* and as Sidonie Platow in "This Madness: The Book of Sidonie," it's clear that part of Dreiser's enthusiasm for the little theater stemmed from his desire to be near Markham, who would be with *The Trojan Women* when it went on tour in the spring.[10]

## I. The Composition of the One-Act Plays

In the late spring or early summer of 1913, Dreiser interrupted his composition of *The Titan* to write a one-act play about a strike leader's conflict between his personal grief over the death of his daughter and his larger duty to lead the strike. Entitled *The Girl in the Coffin*, the play was likely inspired by an event which occurred on 7 June 1913. An audience of 15,000 gathered at Madison Square Garden to watch a cast of about 1,500 strikers from Paterson, New Jersey, re-enact the principal events of the textile strike then being waged at Paterson. Written by John Reed and with scenery painted by Robert Edmund Jones (who would become a distinguished scene designer for the Provincetown Players), *The Paterson Strike Pageant* attracted wide coverage by the press and therefore succeeded in publicizing the strikers' grievances.[11]

The strike had begun on 27 January 1913 after 800 workers of the Henry Dougherty Silk Co. walked out over the firing of four labor leaders. By 3 March, the strike had spread to include 25,000 silk workers, many of whom were Italian and Jewish immigrants, and on 7 March "Big" Bill Haywood, the renowned I.W.W. organizer, had arrived in Paterson to coordinate strike efforts as chairman of the general strike committee. The resulting turmoil quickly dominated local and New York papers, and the plight of the workers became a *cause célèbre* for the New York intelligentsia. Strikers regularly had their rights to free speech abrogated; the Paterson press, police, and community leaders tried every means at their disposal to break the strike by arresting hundreds on trumped-up charges and by waging a vicious propaganda battle in the newspapers. Bill Haywood commuted between Paterson and New York's Greenwich Village, where he lived and regularly addressed sympathetic listeners at the Liberal Club, a popular meeting place for writers, artists, and radicals, and at Mabel Dodge Luhan's salon, where her weekly "Evenings" brought together an assortment of socialists, writers, journalists, artists, feminists, and others for animated discussion.

The events of the strike were inherently dramatic and Dreiser, with his sympathy for the labor movement, likely knew of the pageant if he did not actually attend it. He was certainly aware of the strike itself and describes his impressions in *A Hoosier Holiday* (1916): "I could not help thinking, as I stood looking at [the mills], of the great strike that occurred two years before, in which all sorts of nameless brutalities had occurred, brutalities practised by judges, manufacturers and the police no less than by the eager workers themselves."[12]

In *The Girl in the Coffin*, Dreiser does not dramatize the Paterson Silk Strike but rather incorporates the strike as the backdrop for his study of the conflict between duty and desire. Events in the play loosely match those of the strike. On 7 March

1913 Haywood arrived in Paterson to address the ribbon-silk weavers at Helvetia Hall and was met by several hundred strikers.[13] (To underscore the importance of his arrival during the *Pageant*, the cast sings the *Marseillaise* at the opening and close.) When Ferguson arrives at the train depot, he is met by a crowd singing the *Marseillaise*; he has come to convince the recalcitrant workers at the Tabitha Mill, the lone holdouts who are preventing the strikers from prevailing, to join in the strike. Since many of the workers Haywood addressed spoke only Italian, he relied on Carlo Tresca, another I.W.W. leader, to interpret, just as Ferguson relies on Magnet to interpret for him. Dreiser also based his characterization of Ferguson upon Haywood. Both are large men noted for their oratorical prowess, and their early histories are a close match. After the death of his father Haywood worked in Nevada mines at fifteen, joined the I.W.W. and organized strikes in various parts of the country. Ferguson tells Magnet that, after the death of his mother, he began work at age ten in Colorado mines; he has won previous strikes in Montana, Oregon, North Carolina, and New Jersey. Finally, the single-most dramatic element of the strike and the pageant—the death and funeral of Valentino Modestino—may have influenced Dreiser's decision to place Mary Magnet's coffin in center stage.

The most realistic of Dreiser's one-act plays, *The Girl in the Coffin* enjoyed an immediate success. Mencken snapped it up for the October *Smart Set* in its original form—a feat rare for a Dreiser manuscript.[14] And when the play appeared, it immediately attracted the attention of producers. Dixie Hines, an agent for the International Press Bureau and "The Broadway Feuilletonist" for the *Chicago Saturday Evening Telegraph*, wrote to Dreiser on 1 October 1913 to say that he would like to offer it to B. Iden Payne, who had recently arrived in Chicago to direct a new company of players sponsored by the Chicago Theater Society. Dreiser's play would be in good company, for the other playwrights included Stanley Houghton, Arnold Bennett, Shaw and Strindberg. Hines and Payne agreed to produce the play but negotiations stalled over the question of royalties. Dreiser, naive about the amount of royalty he could reasonably request, at first set too high a price. After Hines informed him that "we are paying less, very much less," for plays by Shaw, Galsworthy and others, Dreiser agreed to a lower fee, and Hines asked him to bring parts for assignment to actors.[15] The play, however, was not produced by Hines and Payne; the extant correspondence does not reveal the reason.

By 1914 Dreiser was growing discouraged by the poor sales of his novels and he began to explore other markets and other genres. He wrote to Mencken that "I have various plans—books etc in mind—a new philosophic interpretation of Earthly life for one thing."[16] As part of these "plans," Dreiser returned to the drama, no doubt encouraged by the positive response he had received to *The Girl in the Coffin*. During the negotiations with Dixie Hines, Dreiser had written about his hopes to Kirah Markham, then an understudy on her first tour with a Shubert Company. She had replied that "Your last letter held such wonderful dreams of the artistic theatre, but it seems so nearly impossible when I look around now."[17] Dreiser was not discouraged by this guarded assessment from a professional actress and promptly cranked out three one-act "reading plays" in July 1914 and sent them to Mencken for appraisal.

These three plays—*The Blue Sphere*, *In the Dark*, and *Laughing Gas*—were markedly different from anything Dreiser had previously written. Unlike *The Girl in the Coffin*, the plays ignore the dramatic unities of space and time through a cinematic technique of intercutting. Their characters are abstract representations of the motive forces of behavior, and their dominant tone is of mystery, despair and wonder at the omnipresence of death. Since Dreiser had enjoyed a measure of approval with the realism of *The Girl in the Coffin*, what prompted him to risk criticism with the strange form of these plays of the "supernatural"?

The answer appears to be a nearly fatal operation for carbuncles in March 1914 that reacquainted him with the tenuousness of life. In early March, Dreiser returned to Chicago for additional research for his third volume on Charles Yerkes. There he rejoined Kirah Markham, who had left Dreiser in New York after learning that he was still spending time with his wife. Between the 6th and 16th of March, Dreiser underwent surgery while anesthetized with nitrous oxide. Markham's account of the surgery, although no doubt embellished, both reveals the source of Dreiser's later treatment of that experience in *Laughing Gas* and suggests that this near brush with death reconfirmed his sense of the transience of man and his essential helplessness before the "forces" of life. "While we were there," Markham wrote to William Swanberg, Dreiser's biographer, he developed a carbuncle on the back of his neck. We were having tea with the wonderful doctor, Dr. Julia Strong, who had brought me through all of my childhood diseases, and when she realized how he was suffering she loaded us into her little car and took us to Hanniman Hospital, ordered an operating room, and went to work on him. She said "It's trivial, we'll just use gas." In the midst of the operation things grew serious. You may not know, but a carbuncle, unlike a boil, has roots, and in Theo's case they were wound around the jugular vein. Working with laughing gas Dr. Julia realized it was going to take longer than she had anticipated and ordered oxygen. A nurse went to the store room and found it locked and no one had a key. In the end it was brought from another building and by that time Theo was turning blue and we were all, doctor, nurses and I, chaffing his hands and feet to restore circulation. When a tank of oxygen was finally brought and administered he rose up on the operating table roaring with gargantuan laughter. "I've got it, I've got it on you all, the secret of the universe, the same thing over and over, God damned rep[et]ition!"

It was almost a year later that he handed me the first draft of the one act play, "Laughing Gas." I had never told him of what happened, of how nearly he had died, yet it is all in the play.[18]

Readers familiar with *Laughing Gas* will readily see that the foregoing account describes exactly the plot of the play, in which a patient undergoing surgery for a neck tumor nearly dies when the oxygen supply runs out. It is, of course, difficult to determine how accurate Markham's account is, given the 50 years' lapse between the event and the memoir and the fact that she favored *Laughing Gas* over Dreiser's other plays (she also errs by one year in dating the play's composition). But Dreiser's letters to Mencken also confirm the importance of this experience to his imagination. Immediately following the operation he acquainted Mencken of his surgery and mentioned that he was planning "a new philosophic interpretation of Earthly life."[19] Moreover, his letters are peppered with cryptic references to health and luck—an indication of his introspection as he pondered his own transience. As he wrote 22 June 1914: "The ills that affect man are truly mental and not material. Mostly they are damned theories that blow like diseases on every wind."[20] Knowing of Mencken's preference for realism, when he sent him the plays on 29 July, Dreiser warned him, "I am not turning esoteric, metaphysical or spiritualistic. These are merely an effort at drama outside the ordinary limits of dramatic interpretation."[21]

It is not surprising that, as Dreiser's interests turned to drama, he should have wanted to expand "the ordinary limits of dramatic interpretation." Greenwich Village in the summer of 1914 was the focus of an intense literary renascence. Dreiser's friends and acquaintances included such journalists as Floyd Dell, Hutchins Hapgood, and John Reed, who would later write some of the more important memoirs of the period as well as novels based on their experiences in the Village. Dreiser formed friendships with Max Eastman and Waldo Frank, the editors of the radical *Masses* and *The Seven Arts*, who actively sought and published work that stretched the boundaries of conventional propriety. He was also acquainted with such theater personages as Lawrence Langner, the future founder of the Washington Square Players, and George Cram Cook and Susan Glaspell, who later patterned their Provincetown Players after both the Washington Square Players and the Chicago Little Theater.[22]

The center of Village social life was the Liberal Club on Macdougal Street; its motto—"A Meeting Place for Those Interested in New Ideas." Through the efforts of Floyd Dell, Dreiser was elected a member and was often seen either at the Club or at Polly Holladay's restaurant, conveniently located in its basement. As the social gathering point of Greenwich Village, the Liberal Club offered a stimulating atmosphere for discussion of the latest ideas. Composed of novelists and poets, artists and journalists, feminists and socialists, its members heard lectures by such luminaries as Horace Traubel on Walt Whitman, Jacques Loeb on sex determinism by chromosomes, "Big" Bill Haywood on socialism, and Christabel Pankhurst on the English Suffrage movement. Although Swanberg writes that Dreiser "remained on the periphery rather than at the center of this neighborhood circle of rebels,"[23] memoirists frequently place Dreiser at many of the Club's meetings. Moreover, Dreiser was deeply interested in Village dramatic activities. He was asked to be "the guest of honor" at a meeting of the amateur Playwrights Club, and he became a member of the Poetry Theater League.[24]

Dreiser was especially interested in the Liberal Club Dramatic Group. His friend Floyd Dell wrote the first play for the newly-formed club—eventually entitled *St. George in Greenwich Village*—which Dell describes as "a satire upon everything in which the Village believed."[25] The play was well-received and inaugurated a regular series of one-act satires, most of them written by Dell and produced every two or three months.

Dreiser was well aware of his friend Dell's plays. Kirah Markham acted in several of them, and Dell dedicated the published version of *Legend: A Romance* to her and *Enigma: A Domestic Conversation* to Dreiser.[26] Moreover, Dell's dramas may have suggested dramatic form as a medium through which to explore his ideas about human frailty and man's place in the cosmos, which began to preoccupy him as he pondered his own financial failure as a novelist. One play in particular—*A Five Minute Problem Play*—bears striking similarities to Dreiser's supernatural dramas. Set in "Boundless blue space," "Two Celestial Figures" discuss earth's "one curious feature": the coyness of its mating rituals, known as "human nature."[27] Dreiser may have been drawn to symbolistic rather than realistic drama because symbolistic staging methods were especially suitable to his subject of inquiry—the rhythmic cycle of life and death. The stylized pantomime and the creation of mood through the rhythmic play of light and shadow, which he had witnessed employed in Maurice Browne's staging of *The Trojan Women*, may also have seemed an effective means through which to dramatize the psychic forces Dreiser believed responsible for human behavior. Given the success of Dell's satires among the Greenwich Village crowd, Dreiser may have felt that the closet drama—what he variously refers to as "skits" and "stunts" in his letters to Mencken—would afford him a new market for his ideas in the little theater.

By July 1914 Dreiser was planning to collect his plays into a volume entitled *Plays of the Natural and Supernatural*, which was published by John Lane on 18 February 1916. Of the seven dramas in the volume, only *The Girl in the Coffin* and "*Old Ragpicker*" observe any fidelity to realism; the latter play enlists realistic detail to delineate the pathos of an old street scavenger's decline. The other five plays exhibit various dramatizations of the supernatural and "chemical" forces that Dreiser believed to be responsible for human behavior and action. *The Blue Sphere* violates unity of time and place as a mysterious Shadow, the embodiment of its parents' wishes, lures a deformed child to its death under the wheels of a train; *Laughing Gas* depicts a surgical patient's dream vision in which the leading characters are The Rhythm of the Universe, the gas nitrous oxide, and "Alcepheron, an element of physics." *In the Dark* conveys the melodrama of guilt and vengeance as a murderer is pursued by spirits and demons; *The Spring Recital* portrays an organist playing for various human and spectral entities; and *The Light in the Window*, a study in the irony of envy, depicts the poor's images of the wealthy through a kaleidoscopic montage that violates dramatic space.

Reviews of the book were generally good. Nearly all singled out *The Girl in the Coffin* as the most accomplished, with the socialist *Appeal to Reason* calling it "one of the best one-act labor plays we have ever read."[28] Reviewers were, however, a bit baffled by the fanciful structure of the supernatural plays, with the *San Francisco Chronicle* dismissing them as "absolutely unplayable."[29] But most were more enthusiastic. The *Outlook* suggested that Dreiser "invents an entirely new technic, whereby he shifts his scene from one point to another as rapidly as motion pictures do; and further complicates his surprise by introducing a strong undercurrent of mysticism of an unclassifiable sort."[30] The *Pittsburgh Dispatch* observed, "In the 'supernatural' plays Mr. Dreiser has co-ordinated the real and the unreal, the physical and the metaphysical, making their interdependence visible and coherent."[31] What interested these reviewers was Dreiser's innovative attempt to dramatize the spiritual and material forces responsible for human action and perception. The *Boston Evening Transcript* suggested that the volume "opens up a new vista in American play writing," for through Dreiser's art "we have been enabled to grasp a little more clearly the inner meanings of life and the subtle dependence of the material on the immaterial."[32] And the *American Review of Reviews* concluded that "Everyone who is interested in the progress of the American drama will welcome this new departure in the field of dramatics."[33]

After *Plays of the Natural and Supernatural* appeared in 1916, Dreiser completed four more "supernatural" plays. *The Voice*—a brief drama about the spirit of a jealous lover who cannot quite let go—exists only in manuscript. A woman, grieving for a dead lover, marries another man but cannot forget her dead love, who appears as an objectification of her conscience to force her to choose which lover to remain faithful to. *The Dream*, completed by June 1917 and published in *The Seven Arts* in July, was prompted by a bizarre theory of "autogeneic orthgenesis," proposed by Dreiser's friend Charles Fort. In July 1915 Fort sent Dreiser the manuscript of "X," a book which, according to Dreiser, demonstrated that human beings and the world they inhabit were nothing more than the emanations of some cosmic mind. "And it did this," Dreiser writes in an unpublished memoir,

> quite as we, by the means of light and photography, throw a moving picture on a screen, the sensitive chemicals of a photographic film and the light that causes the film first to receive an impression of something and later to retransmit it as seemingly the very substance of reality. Only to X, the earth is the sensitive film and its speeding rays the light of the modern camera film.[34]

*The Dream* is a dramatization of "X," written, Dreiser says in his memoir, as the result of a dream "which seemed in no indefinite way to confirm it. And arising from that dream, some months or weeks after I had read the book, I immediately sat down and wrote out a one-act interpretation of it, using Fort's theory as the thesis or backbone of the action." *The Dream* is interesting not because it reflects Dreiser's credulity but because in the process of dramatizing "X" Dreiser incorporated elements of Freudian dream analysis that transformed a lunatic theory into a compelling dramatic experiment. Dreiser structures the play along lines suggested by Freud's dream theory, with which he probably became acquainted indirectly through Floyd Dell, Max Eastman, and other Liberal Club habitués who were earnest enthusiasts and popularizers of Freud.

In 1918 Dreiser completed two plays that reflect his battles with the censors and his struggle to earn a living through his writing. In February he finished *Phantasmagoria*, a fantasy about the Lord of the Universe and his despair as he attempts to mediate conflict between Ambition and Beauty. And by July he had completed *The Court of Progress*, a lengthy and overdone satire attacking the various forms of censorship through caricature. He was unable to find a magazine willing to publish them—not because of their content but because of their loose, indulgent form—and in 1920 they appeared in his collection of philosophical essays, *Hey Rub-A-Dub-Dub*. Most reviewers of the book confined their comments to general remarks about

Dreiser's philosophy rather than evaluation of specific essays, but in a review for the *New York Times Book Review*, Benjamin Casseres selected *The Court of Progress* as one of the collection's best pieces. "In 'The Court of Progress' Mr. Dreiser has written one of the most drastic satires ever written in this country," Casseres opined. "This ought to be printed separately and distributed by the million. All the stupidities of the present time are doused in vitriol in this burlesque on 'progress.'" The play "is a tremendous piece of satiric buffoonery . . . worth all the rest of the iterations of the obvious that precede it."[35]

## II. The Composition of *The Hand of the Potter*

In *My Life With Dreiser*, Helen Richardson Dreiser notes that "with all [Dreiser's] novels, the ideas were carried in his mind for years before he ever sat down to work them out."[36] Helen's comment is equally applicable to *The Hand of the Potter*, Dreiser's only four-act play. Dreiser began work on the play in the fall of 1916, but the idea of writing about a sex crime that destroys a family must have come to him in the summer of 1912 when he read newspaper accounts of the suffering of the Nathan Swartz family following the murder of 12-year-old Julia Connors by their son.[37] At the time that the crime was being reported in the New York papers, Dreiser was working hard at completing the manuscript of *The Financier*, the first volume in his "trilogy of desire" based on the life of Charles T. Yerkes. He must have added clippings of newspaper accounts of the case to his files of potential story ideas, however, for these accounts became his primary source for most of the action and many of the characters in *The Hand of the Potter*.

On the morning of Sunday, 7 July 1912, the nude body of Julia Connors was discovered heaped in a wooden box in a vacant lot next to the apartment building where the Connors lived. Three pieces of old oilcloth partially covered her; her clothes and locks of hair that had been hacked from her head were found nearby, also covered by strips of the same oilcloth. Julia had obviously been tortured. Her body was covered with 41 knife wounds, and her lips were burned, suggesting she had been drugged by her assailant. Yet, when found, she was still alive and revived enough to whisper her name and the words "a man, a man" when asked who had attacked her. She then lapsed into unconsciousness and died at Fordham hospital a few hours later. Shortly after Julia was found, police investigators discovered that the actual scene of the crime had been a vacant flat in an apartment building next to the one she lived in. The strips of oilcloth that covered her body and her clothes had been ripped from the floor of this flat.

Police arrested several suspects before narrowing their inquiry to Nathan Swartz, who had been paroled from the juvenile prison at Harts Island after serving 18 months of a 3-year sentence for "imperiling the morals" of a 14-year-old girl in the office of a dentist he worked for in 1910. Swartz had dropped from sight shortly after the crime, and while the police searched for him, the District Attorney decided to seek an indictment against him from the Grand Jury.

Prior to the Grand Jury hearing on 16 July, the Connors, the Swartzes, and other witnesses met in the office of the Assistant District Attorney who was to present the case. Julia's clothes and hair were laid out on a table for the various witnesses to see when they entered the office. As reported in the *New York Herald*,

> the detectives waited to observe the effect the grewsome reminders of the tragedy would have on Mr. and Mrs. Swartz. . . . As they entered the room, Mr. Swartz was the first to notice the red stained dress and locks of hair. He quickly placed his hand in front of his eyes and groped his way to a chair, facing the opposite direction.

Then, following testimony by Julia's sister and a number of detectives, Mr. Swartz was called to testify. "He was pale as he arose," wrote the *Herald* reporter, "and had hardly assumed an erect posture when he suddenly cried:—'My son did it!' and sank back again into his chair."[38]

Following this disclosure to the Assistant District Attorney, Mr. Swartz repeated his testimony before the Grand Jury, which subsequently brought an indictment against Nathan. During the next two days a warrant was issued for Nathan's arrest, and bulletins giving his description were sent around the country. Yet despite these efforts, Nathan remained at large until, on the morning of 18 July, his body was found in a room of a tenement house on the east side of New York that was next door to one the Swartz family had lived in a few years before. He had committed suicide by attaching one end of a tube to a gas burner in the center of the room and placing the other end in his mouth. Scattered throughout the room were numerous notes to members of his family written on pieces of newspaper plus one on a soiled collar stating: "I'm guilty & I'm insane—Caused by the beautiful make up's of women that has set me very passionate."

Dreiser may have reflected on and perhaps even discussed the Swartz-Connors case during the next four years, particularly when he read about so-called "Jack-the-Ripper" murders that were reported at various times in the New York papers or when he followed the national attention given to the Leo Frank case in Georgia between 1913 and 1915, but there is no evidence in his extant diaries or his correspondence to show that he did any writing on the case.[39] One reason he probably did not do so is suggested in a letter Dreiser wrote to Willard Dillman, an admirer of his work living in Minneapolis, Minnesota, on 31 July 1916. Responding to a letter he had received from Dillman about the recently published *Plays of the Natural and Supernatural,* Dreiser stated: "I liked your letter about the plays, not because I agreed with it exactly but because you were so forthright about the whole affair. I have always intended to do a few three or four act plays but have never arranged my themes just right."[40]

If Dreiser had not "arranged his themes just right" at the time he wrote Dillman, he must have done so shortly thereafter, for in the fall of 1916 he outlined *The Hand of the Potter* to Edgar Lee Masters, Hutchins Hapgood, Estelle Kubitz, and Rella Abell Armstrong.[41] Precisely why Dreiser began thinking about the Swartz-Connors case at this time is unknown, but the case lent itself to the development of two themes he had been considering for a number of years. One might be called the "inscrutability of life" theme. By the time he began writing his play, Dreiser had come to believe in the idea that nature was constantly working toward an "equation" or balance in the world. In the spring of 1916, while he was writing *A Hoosier Holiday,* he expressed this idea of a balance, particularly as it relates to man's moral behavior:

> The moralists and religionists and those who are saintly minded and believe that nature seeks only a conservative or coolly virtuous state have these questions to answer:

(1) How is it that for every saint born into the world there is also a cruel or evil minded genius born practically at the same time? The twain are ever present.
(2) That for every virtuous maid there is one who has no trace of virtue?—possibly many?
(3) That while an evil minded person may be reforming, or an immoral person becoming moral, nature itself (which religion is supposed to be reforming) is breeding others constantly, fresh and fresh, new types of those who, sex hungry or wealth hungry or adventure hungry, have no part or parcel with morality? The best religion or morals appear to be able to do is to contend with nature, which is constantly breeding the un-or immoral and generating blood lusts which result in all the crimes we know, and by the same token, all the religions. How is that?[42]

In his own attempts to answer "how is that," Dreiser had turned to the study of physics and chemistry. In time this study would lead him to embrace the "mechanistic" doctrine of man espoused by Jacques Loeb, although the manuscript of *The Hand of the Potter* does not indicate that he had fully arrived at this point in his thinking in the fall of 1916. What his studies had led him to, however, was the belief that man's chemistry or chemical make-up was the cause of his behavior and not free will. Again, *A Hoosier Holiday* provides an illustration of Dreiser's thought in 1916. In a long passage dealing with "the natural chemical action and reaction between the sexes," Dreiser concluded,

It is the all mother who schemes the Circe and Hellenic temperaments—the fox, the wolf, the lion. A raging, destroying bull, which insists on gormandizing all the females of a herd, is the product of nature, not of man. Man did not make the bull or the stallion, nor did they make themselves. Is nature to be controlled, made over, by man, according to some secret theory which man, a product of nature, has discovered?[43]

Working within the framework of these beliefs, Dreiser saw in the crime of Nathan Swartz yet another example of the "inscrutability of life" caused by the workings of nature. The weakness in Swartz's temperament that caused him to attack Julia Connors was something he neither created or controlled. Its source lay in nature as the all mother sought to provide some kind of equation or balance in the world.

It was not only the "inscrutability of life" theme that attracted Dreiser to the Swartz-Connors case, however. In thinking about the case, he also noticed how it served as an illustration of another theme that interested him, one that might be called "The suffering of a good man." Dreiser had been developing this theme in *The Bulwark*, which he began writing in 1914. Based on a story that Anna Tatum, one of Dreiser's lovers, had told him about her father, the novel focuses on a good and religious man who suffers greatly because of the actions of his children. One of the central events of the novel concerns the involvement of Stewart, the young son of the protagonist, Solon Barnes, in a sex crime that brings shame to his family. Stewart, as Dreiser depicts him in the novel, "was cursed with an overwhelming hunger for physical sex gratification."[44] This hunger, combined with Stewart's resentment at the restrictions placed on him by his father, leads him into a series of weekend escapades with two boys at the school he attends. In one of these escapades, a young girl dies after one of Stewart's friends gives her a drug in an attempt to make her more responsive to his demands. Stewart and his friends are soon arrested and imprisoned, and, in his remorse over the shame he has brought his parents, Stewart commits suicide. Stewart's death, occurring on top of his involvement in the death of a young girl, throws Solon Barnes into "deep spiritual uncertainty," so that, "almost like Jesus on the Cross, he was ready to cry, 'My God, my God, why hast thou forsaken me?'"[45]

Although Dreiser did not complete *The Bulwark* until 1944, he wrote a synopsis of it in 1914 that indicated he had this event in mind at that time.[46] In fact, he told Marguerite Tjader, one of his friends who helped him complete the novel, that he wrote the scene where Solon is alone with the body of his son after Stewart has committed suicide "when I first thought of the idea of *The Bulwark*, to see if it had the germ of a great tragedy in it. After I wrote this, I felt that it did."[47] As Dreiser studied newspaper accounts of Nathan Swartz's father at the indictment hearing, he must have been struck by the similarity between him and Solon Barnes. Like Solon, Samuel Swartz was a good man, who, along with his family, was suffering deep sorrow and despair over the actions of his son. Here, too, was a tragedy. It was not only the causes of Nathan Swartz's crime that presented a theme to Dreiser therefore; the effects of his crime presented a theme as well.

Dreiser began writing *The Hand of the Potter* in late October or early November of 1916. Estelle Kubitz, with whom Dreiser lived sporadically between 1916 and 1919, completed a typescript of Dreiser's manuscript on 8 December, and on the 13th Dreiser sent a copy of the typescript to H. L. Mencken.[48] Knowing that Mencken was busy making preparations for a trip to Europe at the end of the month, Dreiser also mailed Mencken a separate letter, in which he stated, "I hope among the many things you are compelled to do before 'getting off' you will find time to examine [the play] leisurely. The one thing I am concerned about is to have little inaccuracies of dialect corrected. In the case of Daubenspeck, act III [,] I would be grateful if you would look after his broken German."[49]

Mencken was horrified. "Frankly, the play seems to me to be hopeless," he wrote Dreiser on 16 December 1916. "The whole thing is loose, elephantine and devoid of sting. It has no more dramatic structure than a jelly-fish." Mencken went on to dissect the play at great length, pointing out its dramatic weaknesses and inappropriate subject matter but focusing his objection primarily on what he perceived as Dreiser's deplorable timing:

> I say the subject is forbidden on the stage, and mean it. It is all very well to talk of artistic freedom, but it must be plain that there must be a limit in the theatre, as in books. . . . If the thing were possible, I'd advocate absolutely unlimited freedom in speech, written and spoken. I think the world would be better off . . . if the stage could be used to set up a more humane attitude toward sexual perverts, who are helpless and unhappy folks—if novels and other books could describe the precise process of reproduction, beginning with the handshake and ending with lactation, and so show the young what a bore it is. But these things are forbidden. The overwhelming weight of opinion is against them. . . . Surely you don't want to get into the position of a mere bad boy of letters—shocking the numskulls for the mere sake of shocking them. Consider the politics of the situation. Imagine the play printed tomorrow. The moralists would pounce upon it with cheers. And remember that

not only your own artistic freedom, but also the freedom of many other men depends upon the issue.[50]

Dreiser sought to defend his play in a reply to Mencken written on the 18th. "For the life of me," he began,

> I cannot discover what there is in the subject *matter* of this play to have evoked this tirade—all this denunciation and elucidation of the limits of the stage. Admittedly the idea may be badly worked out—a botch. But the subject! A poor weak pervert, defended or tolerated and half concealed by a family for social reasons, commits a sex crime—not shown on the stage—and thereby entails a chain of disaster which destroys the home and breaks the spirits of the father and mother. What pray is there about this that is so low and vulgar? . . . You speak of the text failing to illuminate the central matter. I wonder really what you assume *the central matter* of this play to be. You write as if you thought I were entering on a defense of perversion—trying to make it plausible or customary. If you would look at the title page you would see it is labeled *a tragedy*. What has a tragedy ever illuminated—unless it is the inscrutability of life and its forces and its accidents[?] What has one ever sought to teach or inculcate.

Adding that he did "not care to argue this further, now or in the future," Dreiser concluded by asking Mencken not to speak to J. Jefferson Jones of the John Lane Company (Dreiser's publishers at the time) about it and, if Dreiser published it, not to condemn it in writing before other reviews were out.[51]

Judged in the light of his source for the play, Dreiser's hurt and anger are understandable. Instead of sensationalizing the crime as the newspapers had, he had played down many of its repulsive features. In accordance with his themes, his emphasis was on causes and effects rather than the deed itself. Yet Mencken, too, had a good reason for his point of view. In July 1916, John S. Sumner of the New York Society for the Suppression of Vice read Dreiser's novel *The "Genius"* and, finding what he regarded as 17 profane and 75 lewd passages in it, he managed to intimidate the John Lane Company, the novel's publisher, into withdrawing it from circulation. Dreiser sought Mencken's help in fighting this censorship, and throughout the fall Mencken spent many hours convincing members of the Authors League of America to sign a protest in Dreiser's behalf. Since a considerable number of the better-known authors did not think much of Dreiser and thought even less of the novel, it was no easy task. To Mencken, therefore, the issue was not really the quality of the play but rather the effect the play's publication would have on the protest over the suppression of *The "Genius."* For this reason, he decided to ignore Dreiser's request not to "argue this further," and replied on 20 December 1916:

> Despite all your honeyed eloquence, I still think it rotten politics to come out with a play on sexual perversion at such a time. . . . Fully half of the signers of the Protest, painfully seduced into signing by all sorts of artifices, will demand that their names be taken off. You fill me with ire. I damn you in every European language. You have a positive genius for doing foolish things. . . . The play is a piece of pish—clumsy, banal, unnatural, almost idiotic. Its publication would lose you your case, forfeit the respect of all intelligent persons, and make every man who has labored on the protest look like an ass.[52]

Mencken continued his onslaught in even harsher and more sarcastic tones in letters he sent on the 21st, the 22nd and the 23rd, but as he must have feared, Dreiser refused to accept his objections. As far as Dreiser was concerned, Mencken was wrong about the play, and consequently, perhaps mindful of the season, on Christmas day he again proposed that the argument be set aside "for the time being anyhow."[53]

One of Mencken's problems in changing Dreiser's mind was that the author was receiving favorable reactions from others to whom he showed the play. After he received Mencken's letter of the 16th, for instance, he took a copy to the lawyers he had hired to fight the suppression of *The "Genius,"* John B. Stanchfield and Louis Levy. Dreiser described their reaction in a letter to Mencken dated 21 December 1916: "Levy, after passing it on to Stanchfield and a leading movie producer whose name slips me for the moment returned it with the statement that he thought it a great play, ditto Stanchfield, ditto the movie producer and the latter 'is crazy to produce it.'"[54] In the same letter Dreiser indicated that he gave a copy to John Cowper Powys and sent another copy to Edgar Lee Masters. Even after Mencken left for Europe, Dreiser continued to seek the reactions of others. In early January 1917 he gave a copy to William C. Lengel, a magazine editor and Dreiser's former secretary at *The Delineator*. After Lengel read the play, he wrote Dreiser a critique in which he stated, "You have a big idea for this play and it is developed strongly in the first two acts. Then it slumps!"[55]

If Dreiser was disappointed by Lengel's lukewarm response, his disappointment didn't last long, for a few days later he received a call from Arthur Hopkins, then producing Clare Kummer's *A Successful Calamity*. Hopkins was perhaps the foremost producer of serious drama on Broadway at the time, and he actively sought to engage his audience's intelligence in the dramas he produced: "I want people to leave my theatre actually quarrelling about what they have seen," he once said.[56] In May he asked Dreiser "to hold off the publication" of *The Hand of the Potter* and paid $1000 for an option. The proposed production languished. In July Hopkins wrote, "I have hopes of doing the play" but wouldn't set a date,[57] in the meantime producing *The Deluge* (20 August 1917), *Barbara* (5 November 1917), and *Madame Sand* (19 November 1917).

Finally, Dreiser received word that Hopkins, then producing *Gipsy Trail* (begun 4 December 1917 for 111 performances), would stage the play in a "special performance" at the Friars Club, apparently as consolation for his decision not to produce it on Broadway. But Hopkins never did stage *The Hand of the Potter*, either at the Friars Club or on Broadway, and Dreiser attributed this failure to "the noisy interference and criticism of Mencken and Nathan talking to Hopkins behind my back."[58] A more likely explanation, however, is that, still smarting from Mencken's criticisms and his battles with the *"Genius"* censors, Dreiser apparently refused to agree to the script changes necessary for the production of a new play. George Jean Nathan, in his review of Dreiser's play, quotes Hopkins' explanation for the delay: "It is the best American play that has been submitted to me, and I would eagerly have produced it had not Dreiser imposed on me so many bulls, caveats, and salvos."[59] Of the two accounts, one is inclined to believe Nathan's rather than Dreiser's, particularly since, unlike Mencken, Nathan was not opposed to the play and seems to have admired Hopkins for wanting to stage it.[60]

During these negotiations with Hopkins, Dreiser was busy exploring other markets. He sent the manuscript to J. Jefferson

Jones, the managing director of the John Lane Co., with whom Dreiser was growing increasingly impatient because of his timidity in dealing with the impending suit against *The "Genius."* Jones refused to publish such an inflammatory play and wrote to "urge you again, not only as your publisher, but as a friend, not to put this play out in book form, as, in my opinion, it would do you immeasurable harm."[61] Dreiser then sent the script to Sewell Haggard of *Hearst's Magazine*, who rejected the play for serialization. At last, in January 1918, the new firm of Boni & Liveright agreed to publish the play to convince Dreiser that it was serious in its desire to become his publisher.[62]

Boni & Liveright received galley proofs of the play from the printers on 26 and 27 February 1918 and promptly forwarded them to Dreiser. Dreiser took the proofs to Estelle Kubitz "for examination" and then revised them himself on 1 March.[63] The revised galley proofs are not extant, but a comparison of an extant salesman's dummy, which was made up from type set for the galleys, to extant page proofs provides some clues to his revisions. For instance, the "Cast of Characters" in the dummy includes the names of Assistant District Attorney Balch and three jurors who do not appear in the page proofs, which suggests that Dreiser changed the opening to the courtroom scene in Act III. It may have been in this stage of revision, also, that Dreiser decided to add the discovery of a child's slipper in the Berchansky apartment to the action in Act II.[64]

The revised galleys were returned to the printers, J. J. Little & Ives, who delivered page proofs to Dreiser on 17 April. A few days later Dreiser sent a set of the proofs to Edward H. Smith, a friend who worked for the *New York World*, and Smith, in turn, asked for and received Dreiser's permission to show the set he received to a friend of his and Dreiser's, Edith DeLong.[65] Dreiser's decision to show the proofs to Smith and DeLong is important, for they were almost certainly the source of two significant revisions in Act IV. The first appears at the beginning of Quinn's argument where Dreiser added:

> I've been reading up on these cases for some time, an' from what I can make out they're no more guilty than any other person with a disease. Did ye know, ayther ave ye, that there's something they've called *harmones* which the body manufactures an' which is poured into the blood streams of every waan ave us which excites us to the m'aning ave

> beauty an' thim things—"sensitizes" is the word they use. Now if a felly is so constituted that he has more ave that an' less ave somethin' else—somethin' which balances him a little an' makes him less sensitive to the beauty of women or girls—he's likely to be like that. He can't help it. There's something in him that pushes him on in spite of himself.[66]

These lines must have been suggested to Dreiser by Edward H. Smith, who had become interested in the theories of a Dr. Max Schlapp, head of the Department of Neuropathology at the Cornell Medical School in New York City. In an article entitled "An Enemy at the Gate," Schlapp discussed the function of hormones to explain how the tensions of life in industrialized societies were causing "a disturbance in the chemical balance of the body." To Schlapp this disturbance was the reason for a decrease in the birth rate and an increase in the number of imbeciles and criminals.[67] Perhaps Smith showed this article to Dreiser, but he could have simply outlined Schlapp's theories to him. In either case, Dreiser would have been impressed with how endocrinology gave scientific support to Quinn's arguments about nature and the notion of free-will.

The second revision comes near the conclusion of Quinn's argument. In place of a statement about love and the power of the "sex-instinct," Dreiser substituted the following passage:

> If ye'd ever made a study ave the passion ave love in the sense that Freud an' some others have ye'd understand it well enough. It's a great force about which we know naathing as yet an' which we're just beginning to look into—what it manes, how it affects people.[68]

The revision is significant not only because it marks the first time in his writings that Dreiser refers to Freud, but also because it gives support to Dreiser's assertion that Edith DeLong introduced him to Freud's works.[69] Scholars have usually dismissed Dreiser's version of his introduction to Freud because they assumed the reference to him appeared in the manuscript of the play.

A new set of page proofs incorporating the corrections in Act IV was sent to Dreiser in August, and apparently, he finally was satisfied with the text of his play. Now, instead of making further changes, he requested that Boni & Liveright delay publication, for he was in the process of making arrangements with a new producer for a stage production.

Actually Dreiser had never stopped looking for someone to stage his play after he severed his relationship with Arthur Hopkins. In the spring of 1918 he sent copies of the revised galleys to the noted actor Arnold Daly and to another producer John D. Williams. Neither took an option on it. Daly praised the play but did not see a role in it for him, and Williams, it seems from extant correspondence, wanted to make too many changes.[70] Then sometime in the summer, Dreiser got a copy to Charles D. Coburn, who along with his wife had formed a production company in New York. After reading the play, Coburn asked Dreiser to delay publication, and in September, he and Dreiser agreed to a contract for a production.[71]

At the time the contract was signed, the Coburns were in rehearsal for a play entitled *The Better 'Ole* to be staged at the Greenwich Village Theatre. But Charles Coburn must have told Dreiser that he would launch a production of *The Hand of the Potter* after *The Better 'Ole* completed its run, for Dreiser wrote Smith that the play was scheduled for the Greenwich Village Theatre in December. Unfortunately for Dreiser, after it opened in New York on 19 October, *The Better 'Ole* became the smash hit of the season. Because of the success of *The Better 'Ole*—the play was to run for 353 performances over two seasons—the Coburns did not attempt a production of *The Hand of the Potter* in December.[72]

In January, after it became clear that the Coburns had changed their plans, Dreiser sought to have them relinquish their option on it. In answer to his request, Charles Coburn wrote on 3 February 1919 that he would be willing to do so "upon payment of $500" from Dreiser.[73] There is no record that Dreiser made this payment, but he could have used an advance of $500 on *Twelve Men* he received from Boni & Liveright on 11 February.[74] Certainly, he had reason for doing so, since he had now been asked by Rollo Peters whether he would consider letting the recently organized Theatre Guild do a production on a royalty basis.[75] Since Peters and many of the others who formed the group had previously been associated with the Washington Square Players, which had successfully produced *The Girl in the*

*Coffin* in 1917, there was justification for Dreiser's hoping they would select his play.

As it turned out, the Theatre Guild finally chose St. John Ervine's *John Ferguson* for its second play, but the decision was not made until sometime in April, and by then Boni & Liveright had just published Dreiser's *Twelve Men*.[76] Thus, even though there was no longer any reason to delay publication, the publishers decided to wait until the fall to release the book to the public.

The official publication date of *The Hand of the Potter* was 20 September 1919, although reviews began to appear in the press as early as 6 September. Predictably, they were mixed. Nearly every reviewer faulted the play for its undramatic and unnecessary fourth act. As Alexander Woollcott noted in the *New York Times Review of Books*, "The publishers of 'The Hand of the Potter' bill it somewhat meretriciously as 'Stark naked and unashamed'; but it really ought to be ashamed of its last act."[77] Others, expectedly, condemned it on moral grounds. The *Indianapolis News* claimed that "Several scenes in it are so revolting that if presented with the vividness of stage projection they would horrify and physically sicken any audience."[78] And John T. Stone, debating the issue of an artist's choice of material in the *Detroit Sunday News*, called the book "potentially harmful" because "The power of suggestion on ill-balanced minds is not a force to be trifled with." But because Dreiser's play is so badly written, he concluded, "Probably it will accomplish less harm than many a salacious best seller."[79]

Dreiser's champions, however, found much to praise despite the weakness of the fourth act. Writing in the *Nation*, Ludwig Lewisohn, who had read the play in manuscript, lauded Dreiser's ability to reify tragic guilt, to depict in Isadore the concerns of the age. Isadore's "guilt is merged into social and, in the last analysis, into cosmic forces; his importance is in his character as representative of the tragic consequence of ignorance, poverty, and oppression." Isadore therefore becomes important as an emblem of "the fundamental change in thinking about human life which is the very soul of the age in which we live."[80] In a perceptive review in the *Chicago Tribune*, Burton Rascoe confessed his astonishment that Dreiser had "written so dignified and impressive a drama upon so treacherous a theme." While praising Dreiser for his "superb restraint, convincing sincerity, and no little technical art," he faulted him for being "so tiresomely and uninterestingly moral. . . . He cannot resist a temptation to preach, to advise, to comment."[81] And in the *Smart Set* George Jean Nathan found himself "between the two camps": while condemning the play's melodrama and its pandering to the audience's desire for sensationalism, he praised its ability to evoke "a poignant and tragic pity . . . [which] Dreiser can strike as few other Americans can strike it." Interestingly, he concluded by predicting the play would achieve "financial success if handled with a sufficiently cunning showmanship."[82]

NOTES

[1] Richard Lingeman discovered a fragment of *Jeremiah I* and published it as "Dreiser's 'Jeremiah I': Found at Last," *Dreiser Studies* 20.2 (1989): 2-8.

[2] For fuller discussion of the Dreiser-Markham relationship, see W. A. Swanberg, *Dreiser* (New York: Scribner, 1965), *passim*; Dale Kramer, *Chicago Renaissance: The Literary Life in the Midwest, 1900-1930* (New York: Appleton, 1966), pp. 192-99; and Dreiser, *American Diaries, 1902-1926*, ed. Thomas P. Riggio (Philadelphia: University of Pennsylvania Press, 1983), pp. 117-44, 207.

[3] Dreiser to Mary Elizabeth Titzel, 20 February 1913; qtd. in Bernard Dukore, "Maurice Browne and the Chicago Little Theatre" (Diss., University of Illinois, 1957), p. 1.

[4] Thomas P. Riggio, ed., *Dreiser-Mencken Letters: The Correspondence of Theodore Dreiser and H. L. Mencken, 1907-1945*, 2 vols. (Philadelphia: University of Pennsylvania Press, 1986), 1: 115.

[5] Qtd. in Constance D'Arcy Mackay, *The Little Theatre in the United States* (New York: Holt, 1917), p. 104).

[6] Floyd Dell, "The Littlest Theater," *Harper's Weekly* 58 (29 November 1913): 22.

[7] Kenneth Macgowan, *The Theatre of Tomorrow* (New York: Boni & Liveright, 1921), p. 101.

[8] Dukore, p. 71.

[9] Maurice Browne, "The New Rhythmic Drama," *The Drama* 16 (1914): 617.

[10] For more extended discussion of Dreiser's fictional treatment of the Chicago Little Theater and Kirah Markham in *The Titan*, see Kramer, pp. 195-99. In "Sidonie," Dreiser writes that he helped schedule the Theater's Eastern visits so he could be near Sidonie (Markham). See "This Madness: The Book of Sidonie," *Hearst's International Cosmopolitan* 86 (June 1929): 166.

[11] For a fuller account of *The Girl and the Coffin*, its sources, and productions of the play, see Keith Newlin, "Dreiser's 'The Girl in the Coffin' in the Little Theatre," *Dreiser Studies* 25.1 (1994): 31-50. The Paterson Strike and the Paterson Strike Pageant have been the subject of many good studies. Among the best are Anne Huber Tripp, *The I.W.W. and the Paterson Silk Strike of 1913* (Urbana: University of Illinois Press, 1987); Martin Green, *New York 1913* (New York: Scribner's, 1988); and Linda Nochlin, "The Paterson Strike Pageant of

1913," in *Theatre for Working-Class Audiences in the United States, 1830-1980*, ed. Bruce A. McConachie and Daniel Friedman (Westport, Connecticut: Greenwood, 1985), pp. 87-95.

[12] *A Hoosier Holiday* (New York: John Lane, 1916), p. 27.

[13] Tripp, p. 75.

[14] Dreiser apparently paid "someone else $50 for work of various kinds" on the play, as he notes in a letter to Mencken, 22 August 1914; *Dreiser-Mencken Letters*, 1: 152. The identity of this person—or the extent of the work—remains unknown.

[15] See Hines to Dreiser, 1, 7, 11, 22 October 1913; and Lengel to Dreiser, 1 October 1913, Dreiser Collection, Van Pelt-Dietrich Library, University of Pennsylvania—hereafter cited as Dreiser Collection.

[16] Dreiser to Mencken, 16 March 1914; *Dreiser-Mencken Letters*, 1: 133.

[17] Markham to Dreiser, 25 January 1914; Dreiser Collection.

[18] Markham to Swanberg, 23 August 1964; Swanberg Collection, Van Pelt-Dietrich Library, University of Pennsylvania. For a more extended discussion of the composition and production of *Laughing Gas*, see Keith Newlin, "Expressionism Takes the Stage: Dreiser's 'Laughing Gas,'" *Journal of American Drama and Theatre* 4.1 (1992): 5-22.

[19] Dreiser to Mencken, 16 March 1914; *Dreiser-Mencken Letters*, 1: 133.

[20] Dreiser to Mencken, 29 July 1914; *Dreiser-Mencken Letters*, 1: 144.

[21] Dreiser to Mencken, 29 July 1914; *Dreiser-Mencken Letters*, 1: 146-47.

[22] Memoirs recounting Dreiser's involvement with the bohemians in Greenwich Village include Lawrence Langner, *The Magic Curtain* (New York: Dutton, 1951), pp. 67-73, 90-93; Floyd Dell, *Homecoming* (New York: Farrar and Rinehart, 1933), pp. 246-48, 268-71; and Hutchins Hapgood, *A Victorian in the Modern World* (New York: Harcourt, 1939), pp. 266-74. For discussion of the Liberal Club and the Greenwich Village bohemians, see Swanberg, pp.180-83; Arthur F. Wertheim, *The New York Little Renaissance* (New York: New York University Press, 1976); Robert E. Humphrey, *Children of Fantasy: The First Rebels of Greenwich Village* (New York: Wiley, 1978); and Keith Norton Richwine, "The Liberal Club: Bohemia and the Resurgence in Greenwich Village, 1912-1918" (Diss., University of Pennsylvania, 1968).

[23] Swanberg, p. 182.

[24] See Homer Croy to Dreiser [1913-14], and Alter Brody to Dreiser, 21 July 1917; Dreiser Collection.

[25] Dell, *Homecoming*, pp. 247, 250.

[26] Dreiser's apartment also provided the location for an interesting footnote to American theatrical history. In December 1914, during a rehearsal of *Legend*, which was to star Kirah Markham and Lawrence Langner as two Spanish lovers, Dell objected to Langner's diction. "Dreiser sat and watched us with ponderous amusement," Langner recalled, as the two disputed the propriety of Langner's British diction versus Dell's "harsh Middle-Western accents." Disgruntled with Dell's direction, Langner quit and with Ida Rauh and Albert Boni decided to form a rival dramatic group. Taking their inspiration from Maurice Browne's Chicago Little Theater, the three formed the Washington Square Players. "When the would-be actors of the Liberal Club Dramatic Group learned that we intended to produce real plays on a real stage," Langner recalled, "they rallied to our banner." The Liberal Club amateurs had at last

found a home. See Langner, pp. 91, 93. Langner confuses two separate events in his recollection, occurring at least a year apart, as Richwine notes (pp. 134-35). "Legend" starred Clement Wood (not Dell) and Kirah Markham; Langner apparently conflates the inaugural play—"St. George in Greenwich Village," in which Dell acted—with "Legend." See also Clement Wood, "The Story of Greenwich Village," *Haldeman-Julius Quarterly* 1 (1926): 169-85.

[27] *A Five Minute Problem Play* was later revised and printed as *Human Nature: A Very Short Morality Play* in Dell, *King Arthur's Socks and Other Village Plays* (New York: Knopf, 1922).

[28] "The Appeal Book Shelf: Seven One-Act Plays," [Girard, Kansas] *Appeal to Reason*, 15 April 1916, p. 5; rpt. in Jack Salzman, *Theodore Dreiser: The Critical Reception* (New York: David Lewis, 1972), p. 265.

[29] G[eorge] D[ouglas], "Fourth Dimensional Dramas," *San Francisco Chronicle*, 23 April 1916, Special Feature Section, p. 23; rpt. in Salzman, p. 261.

[30] Bruce Bliven, "Some Spooky Drama," *Outlook*, August 1916; rpt. in Salzman, p. 270.

[31] James Edward Leslie, rev. of *Plays*, *Pittsburgh Dispatch*, 26 February 1916, p. 11; rpt. in Salzman, p. 257.

[32] D. L. M., "With the Supernatural," *Boston Evening Transcript*, 18 March 1916, pt. 3, p. 9; rpt. in Salzman, p. 259.

[33] "Plays and Pageants," *American Review of Reviews* 53 (May 1916): 634; rpt. in Salzman, p. 265.

[34] A portion of this memoir has been published by Helen Dreiser in *My Life with Dreiser* (Cleveland: World, 1951), pp. 220-23, from which we have quoted. The unpublished memoir is entitled "Dreiser Interviewed on the Subject of Charles Fort"; the published section is heavily edited, probably by Helen Dreiser. For additional information about Fort, see Damon Knight, *Charles Fort: Prophet of the Unexplained* (London: Victor Gollancz, 1971). Fort's published writings have been collected in *The Complete Books of Charles Fort* (New York: Dover, 1974).

[35] "Mr. Dreiser Talks of Many Things," *New York Times Book Review*, 11 April 1920, p. 167; rpt. in Salzman, p. 377-78.

[36] Helen Dreiser, p. 80.

[37] The summary of these accounts that follows is based on stories that appeared in the *New York Times*, the *New York Herald*, and the *New York World* between 8 July 1912 and 19 July 1912. A fuller account of the genesis of the play appeared as Frederic E. Rusch, "Dreiser's Other Tragedy," *Modern Fiction Studies* 23 (1977): 449-56.

[38] "'My Son Did It!' Cries Swartz: Boy Confessed He Drugged and Slew Little Girl in Flat," *New York Herald*, 17 July 1912, p. 7.

[39] Two highly publicized "Ripper" cases were the mutilations and murders of five-year-old Lenora Cohn and four-and-a half-year-old Charles Murray on New York's east side in the spring of 1915. Leo Frank was convicted of murdering 13-year-old Mary Phagan in Atlanta in 1913. His case received national attention because of the anti-Semitism and apparent perjury at his trial. After the United States Supreme Court turned down Frank's appeal in 1915, the Governor of Georgia commuted his sentence from death to life imprisonment. A few months later, 25 men broke into the state prison farm, kidnapped Frank,

and lynched him near Mary Phagan's hometown. Dreiser commented on the case in *A Hoosier Holiday*, pp. 236-38.

[40] Dreiser to Dillman, 31 July 1916; Theodore Dreiser Collection (#6220), Clifton Waller Barrett Library, Special Collections Department, University of Virginia Library.

[41] Dreiser to Mencken, 21 December 1916, *Dreiser-Mencken Letters*, 1: 286.

[42] *A Hoosier Holiday*, pp. 364-65.

[43] *A Hoosier Holiday*, pp. 377-78.

[44] *The Bulwark* (Garden City, New York: Doubleday, 1946), p. 244.

[45] *The Bulwark*, pp. 298-99.

[46] For a description of the synopsis, see Donald Pizer, *The Novels of Theodore Dreiser* (Minneapolis: University of Minnesota Press, 1976), pp. 302-03.

[47] Marguerite Tjader, *Theodore Dreiser: A New Dimension* (Norwalk, Connecticut: Silvermine Publishers, 1965), p. 156.

[48] A fragment of a diary entry or letter by Estelle Kubitz dated 9 December 1916 in the Dreiser Collection reads: "Well, I had the last act of the play to write over yesterday. He insisted that I get it done by 2 o'clock. It was a terrible job, and I said I couldn't do it before three. But, to make an impression on him, I had it done by two, working like a dog to do it."

[49] Dreiser to Mencken, 13 December 1916; *Dreiser-Mencken Letters*, 1: 280.

[50] Mencken to Dreiser, 16 December 1916; *Dreiser-Mencken Letters*, 1: 281-83.

[51] Dreiser to Mencken, 18 December 1916; *Dreiser-Mencken Letters*, 1: 283-84.

[52] Mencken to Dreiser, 20 December 1916; *Dreiser-Mencken Letters*, 1: 284-85.

[53] Dreiser to Mencken, 25 December 1916; *Dreiser-Mencken Letters*, 1: 291

[54] Dreiser to Mencken, 21 December 1916; *Dreiser-Mencken Letters*, 1: 286.

[55] Lengel to Dreiser, 13 January 1917; Dreiser Collection.

[56] Richard Moody, "American Actors, Managers, Producers, and Directors," in *The Revels History of Drama in English*, vol. 8: American Drama, ed. Travis Bogard, Richard Moody, and Walter J. Meserve (London: Methuen, 1977), p. 121.

[57] Hopkins to Dreiser, 23 May 1917 and 23 July 1917; Dreiser Collection.

[58] Dreiser to Edward H. Smith, 25 November 1920; Robert H Elias, ed., *Letters of Theodore Dreiser: A Selection*, 3 vols. (Philadelphia: University of Pennsylvania Press, 1959), 1: 302.

[59] "Dreiser's Play—And Some Others," *Smart Set* 60 (October 1919): 131-33; rpt. in Salzman, p. 351.

[60] In his Foreword to Hopkins' *How's Your Second Act?* (New York: Knopf, 1919), Nathan wrote: "Hopkins probably possesses to a greater degree than any other American producing manager—new or old—the editorial instinct so far as respectable dramatic manuscripts are concerned.... It is this instinct that has caused him to plan the production of a play by one of the fore-

most literary artists of the country, a play on which it is safe to assume no other producer would take a chance" (pp. 8-9).

[61] Jones to Dreiser, 14 September 1917; Dreiser Collection.

[62] See Haggard to Dreiser, 9 January 1918, and Liveright to Dreiser, 15 January 1918; Dreiser Collection.

[63] See Albert Boni to Dreiser, 26 February 1918 and 27 February 1918; Dreiser Collection; and *American Diaries*, pp. 251-53.

[64] See also Frederic E. Rusch, "The Dummy of *The Hand of the Potter*," *Papers on Language and Literature* 27 (1991): 288-99.

[65] See Albert Boni to Dreiser, 16 April 1918; Dreiser to Smith, 23 April 1918; Smith to Dreiser, 2 May 1918; all in the Dreiser Collection.

[66] Second page proofs, p. 193; Dreiser Collection (AC9/D8144/918h.1). The addition appears also in the first American edition, p. 193.

[67] Schlapp, "An Enemy at the Gate," *The Outlook* 100 (6 April 1912): 782-88.

[68] Second page proofs, p. 200. The revision appears also in the first American edition, p. 200.

[69] "Olive Brand," in *A Gallery of Women* (New York: Liveright, 1929), 1: 81-82. See also Frederic E. Rusch, "Dreiser's Introduction to Freudianism," *Dreiser Studies* 18.2 (1987): 34-38.

[70] *American Diaries*, pp. 254-55; excerpt from letter from Daly to Dreiser in advertising brochure, *The Hand of the Potter: A Tragedy in Four Acts* (New York: Boni & Liveright, [1920]), p. [8]; Williams to Dreiser, 23 March 1918; Dreiser Collection.

[71] Coburn to Dreiser, 21 August 1918 and 12 September 1918; Dreiser Collection.

[72] Dreiser to Smith, 1 October 1918; Dreiser Collection. *The Best Plays of 1909-1919*, ed. Burns Mantle and Garrison P. Sherwood (New York: Dodd, Mead, 1933), p. 641.

[73] Coburn to Dreiser, 3 February 1918; Dreiser Collection.

[74] Liveright to Dreiser, 11 February 1918; Dreiser Collection.

[75] Dreiser to Smith, 25 November 1920; *Letters of Theodore Dreiser*, 1: 302.

[76] Walter Prichard Eaton, "The History of the Theatre Guild," in *The Theatre Guild: The First Ten Years*, ed. Walter Prichard Eaton (1929; Freeport, New York: Books for Libraries Press, 1970), pp. 30-37.

[77] "Hand of the Potter," *New York Times Review of Books*, 26 October 1919, p. 598; rpt. in Salzman, p. 361.

[78] "Notes and News on Plays and Players," *Indianapolis News*, 13 September 1919, p. 16; rpt. in Salzman, p. 349.

[79] "Choice of Material Spoils Play," *Detroit Sunday News*, 12 October 1919, Magazine Section, p. 15; rpt. in Salzman, p. 359.

[80] "Tragedy and Trifles," *Nation* 109 (6 September 1919): 340; rpt. in Salzman, p. 347.

[81] "Dreiser Shakes the Potter's Hand," *Chicago Daily Tribune*, 11 October 1919, p. 13; rpt. in Salzman, p. 356-57.

[82] "Dreiser's Play—And Some Others," *Smart Set* 60 (October 1919): 131-33; rpt. in Salzman, pp. 351-53.

# THE GIRL IN THE COFFIN

## CHARACTERS

WILLIAM MAGNET, *a foreman of loom workers.*
JOHN FERGUSON, *a strike leader.*
MRS. MAMIE SHAEFER, *a striker's wife.*
MRS. MARGARET RICKERT, *another striker's wife.*
MRS. HANNAH LITTIG, *an old woman.*
NICHOLAS BLUNDY, *a young mill worker.*
TIMOTHY MCGRATH, *a member of the strikers' executive committee.*

## TIME

*Between seven and eight o'clock of an early spring evening.*

## PLACE

*A large mill town.*

## SCENE

The parlor *of* WILLIAM MAGNET'S *house, which is that of a well-to-do workingman. At the left is a door leading outside to the porch. On either side of the door is a window, with blinds drawn and heavy coarse white lace curtains. To the right is a wooden mantel with a plush lambrequin, an ornamental clock, a gilded plaster cast and a photograph in a celluloid frame. Over the mantel hangs a large "crayon portrait" of a woman in a heavy silvered frame. Toward the rear is a door leading to the dining room and the kitchen. In one corner stands a cheap "mahogany" upright piano with silk drapery hung over one corner. A large majolica vase and a chromo under glass representing St. Cecelia playing to the angels (this picture supported by a bracket) ornament the top of the piano. To the right of it is a standing lamp (unlighted when the curtain rises). Near this are three tiers of section bookcases filled with "sets." Under the window at the left is a small upholstered plush sofa with a sofa cushion made of cigar ribbons. In the middle of the back wall hangs a large framed lithograph portrait of* JOHN FERGUSON, *strike leader, standing in an oratorical attitude. A real silk flag with gilt lettering and gilt fringe is draped over one corner of this portrait. On the floor directly below this picture—far enough out so that there is room to pass between it and the wall—stands a black coffin on trestles. The pallid profile and thick dark hair of a dead woman are barely visible.*

*To the right of the stage toward the front stands a small oak table with a lace cover and a large oil lamp with a painted china shade giving a dim light.*

MRS. MAMIE SHAEFER *is discovered seated to the left of the table in a straight chair, crocheting lace edging. She is stout, neat, vigorous, red-cheeked, her hair brushed tightly back. She is dressed in tight-fitting black merino. To her left,* MRS. MARGARET RICKERT *occupies a cane-seated rocker. She also is stout and rosy, but of a more placid type. She wears a brown shawl and over her* head a knitted scarf of pink wool. While MRS. RICKERT rocks and MRS. SHAEFER crochets, enter from the dining room door MRS. LITTIG, a little, thin, pale, vapid-looking old woman with scraggly gray hair, a gray calico dress and a small woolen shawl over her shoulders. She walks across the stage and lights the lamp by the piano.*

MRS. SHAEFER: [*Looking up from her crocheting.*] Has Magnet come in yet, Mrs. Littig?

MRS. LITTIG: [*Busy with the lamp-lighting.*] No, he ain't come in. [*She speaks in a mild, high, patient voice.*]

MRS. SHAEFER: Where'd he say he was goin'?

MRS. LITTIG: He didn't say. Most like he went to the cemetery.

MRS. SHAEFER: It's queer he wouldn't be back by now.

MRS. RICKERT: He might be at the depot to meet Ferguson's train. A quarter past seven he gets here. The crowds was thick already when I come up the street.

MRS. SHAEFER: To be sure, that's where he is. Are you gettin' somethin' to eat, Mrs. Littig? Magnet'll need a good hot bite in case he goes to the hall.

MRS. LITTIG: There's coffee made and ham and eggs ready to fry ef he'll eat.

MRS. RICKERT: [*To* MRS. LITTIG.] Poor man, he ain't much appetite, I expect.

MRS. LITTIG: No, he don't eat very good. [*When* MRS. LITTIG *has finished lighting the lamp, she walks to the coffin and stands, facing the audience, stroking her cheek and wiping her eyes now and then with her hand. She is disregarded by the others, who go on talking. After a moment or two she goes out by the dining room door.*]

MRS. RICKERT: I understand he takes it terrible hard, Mrs. Shaefer. My Jim met him on the street last night, and he says to him: "Magnet," he says, "I'm sorry trouble should 'a' come to you of all men in this town just at this time," he says, "when so many looks to you for help." And with that Magnet just give him a nod and walked on without a word to say. Jim was tellin' me he had a terrible look on his face like he was near to lose his senses. "It was a bad day for the workers o' this town, Maggie," Jim says to me, "when Magnet's girl took sick. You want to remember," he says, "let the Tabitha run another week an' this strike's lost; an' run it will," he says, "as sure as I'm alive, without Magnet sticks on the job. Ferguson's a wonder," he says, "but he can't do everything alone. It's a shame for Magnet to draw out just now—there ain't nothin' ought to make him do it," he says.

MRS. SHAEFER: I heard say they got a message last night from Ferguson, one o' them secret telegrams. "The Tabitha walks out at noon Saturday," he says, "or the game's up. Drive them damn scabs"—that's what he says right in the telegram—"drive them damn scabs into Murray Hall at half past eight and look for me on the seven fifteen train. *Have Magnet there*," he says. [*A slight pause.*] Ferguson—ain't it surprising, now what he's done in this town? Ain't he got a terrible strong will? "He's a great man"—that's what Tim McGrath says to a crowd down there one night. "Talk about your kings and your emperors and your presidents and your millionaires," he says—"there ain't one of 'em all with the brains and the fists could stand up alone against Ferguson."

MRS. RICKERT: It's little Ferguson can do without others to help him. What do them nine-dollar-a-week scabs at the Tabitha know or care who Ferguson is? He can't talk no Eyetalian. He ain't never run no loom. It needs somebody can speak their own tongue and has lived in the same place and worked on the same job. Magnet's the man to talk to them men. Do you think he'll go to the meetin' tonight, Mrs. Shaefer?

MRS. SHAEFER: I don't know, I'm sure, Mrs. Rickert. I'm here to do what I can. "It's his duty," that's what my Joe says to me this mornin'—"it's his duty, an' no man ain't got no right to go against his duty, no matter how black his trouble may be. Do you want we should 'a' starved and scraped ten weeks for nothin'?" he says. "Mill after mill will shut down," he says—"the Excelsior down a month since, the Maxwell down a fortnight this coming Wednesday, the Junta down three weeks past—My God, think o' that!" Joe says to me, "the Junta—that miserable pesthouse o' poor, chatterin' Dago apes that you wouldn't 'a' thought would 'a' ever knowed the difference between a strike and a bunch o' spaghetti; and here they are a holdin' together like human men, an' who's done it?" Joe says to me. "Why, old Magnet's done it. Ferguson never could 'a' brought this strike to where it is today without Magnet to back him. When the Tabitha shuts down," he says, "we've got the best o' them bloodsuckers that's tryin' to live off our carcasses, an' there's only one man can put a little reason an' backbone into them cowardly sponges o' furren scabs, an' that man's Magnet. Magnet's in a bad place," he says, "with nobuddy but that one pore foolish old woman"—[*she lowers her voice and motions toward the dining room door*]—"to look after him. She'd 'a' been in the almshouse long ago ef it hadn't 'a' been for Magnet's good heart. She's nobuddy to put nerve into a man. Now for God's sake," Joe says to me, "you go down there tonight, Mamie, and see he gets a good meal an' turns up at the hall an' gives his talk accordin' to the timetable. It's a great pity," he says, "*for more reasons than one*, that Magnet's wife is no more alive. That house would 'a' been better this long time past for a good, strong woman in it," he says.

MRS. RICKERT: Seemed like he was terrible devoted to Mary.

MRS. SHAEFER: He made a great mistake to indulge her the way he did, Mrs. Rickert, a great mistake.

MRS. RICKERT: Seems queer she wouldn't 'a' got a man of her own before now—a bright, stylish girl like Mary. There was plenty courted her. They say as young Nick Blundy, that's foreman of the warpers and twisters down to the Waverly, was after her to marry him this long time.

MRS. SHAEFER: [*Severely.*] She would never 'a' been content to be a mill worker's wife—Mary Magnet wouldn't. She'd too many notions for that. It takes a hard jolt to bring some off their high horse. [*Significantly.*]

MRS. RICKERT: [*Leaning forward confidentially.*] Ain't it surprising now that she should 'a' gone so quick? A strong, lively girl like that—she did look the very picture o' health. What did *you* understand was the cause of her sickness, Mrs. Shaefer? I heard say the doctors wasn't able to give any satisfaction whatever.

[*A sudden knock at the door intercepts the reply to this query.* MRS. RICKERT *rocks in silence, while* MRS. SHAEFER *opens the door and admits* NICK BLUNDY, *a tall, good-looking young workingman in a dark gray suit and flannel shirt. He carries a large pasteboard box under his arm, and enters nervously, quickly removing his soft felt hat.*]

MRS. SHAEFER: [*In a subdued voice and with great solemnity.*] Good evening, Mr. Blundy. You come to view the corpse?

[*She makes an impressive gesture toward the coffin and resumes her seat. The rocking and crocheting continue, while* NICK *stands for a moment or two by the coffin. The women glance furtively at him. When he moves* MRS. SHAEFER *speaks.*]

MRS. SHAEFER: Won't you set down a minute, Mr. Blundy?

[*She places a chair to the left of* MRS. RICKERT. NICK *seats himself gingerly on the edge of the chair, propping his package against it and turning his hat in his hand. The woman assume attitudes and expressions of renewed gravity and importance.* MRS. RICKERT *almost ceases to rock.*]

NICK: [*In a subdued, nervous voice.*] It's a terrible thing about Mary, ain't it?

[*Appropriately lugubrious sighs and murmurs come from the women.*]

WOMEN: It is indeed, Mr. Blundy. Terrible. Yes, it's very sad.

NICK: [*After a slight pause.*] Where's the old man?

MRS. SHAEFER: We're expectin' him in any minute.

NICK: They say he grieves very bitter.

MRS. SHAEFER: Yes, he takes on a good bit.

NICK: Ain't he goin' down to the hall tonight?

MRS. SHAEFER: [*With much gravity.*] I can't say positive, Mr. Bundy. It's his *duty* to go. There's hopes he may be made to feel that.

NICK: [*Spasmodically, after another slight pause.*] I didn't know there was anything ailed Mary. I seed her only a week or two ago walkin' down Grant Street one night, an' she says to me: "Nick," she says, "it's slow times these days, ain't it, with the girls and the fellows; but," she says, "what'll you bet when we win this strike we don't have more coin in our pockets than ever we did—and then for the good old Saturday nights!" Why, she was laughin' and carryin' on as lively as a kitten.

MRS. RICKERT: [*Nodding.*] She did enjoy a good time as much as any girl, Mary did.

NICK: [*Shaking his head mournfully.*] She must 'a' been tuck awful sudden. I heard she died Wednesday night down in the St. Francis. Is that right?

MRS. SHAEFER: Yes, Mr. Blundy, them's the facts.

NICK: Have you heard say what it was that ailed her?

[MRS. RICKERT *stops rocking entirely and looks expectantly at* MRS. SHAEFER, *who draws herself up with portentous dignity.*]

MRS. SHAEFER: She was took very sudden, and they had need to operate to cure her. There's great danger in them operations.

[*A pause.* MRS. RICKERT *resumes rocking, folds her hands and looks wise.* NICK *gazes silently at the floor.*]

NICK: [*Sadly reflective.*] She sure did have the ginger in her, that girl. There was few fellows could do with a loom what she could.

MRS. RICKERT: Mary was smart all right. I guess there ain't nobody question that.

NICK: [*Lost in his own recollections.*] Why, I seed her one day on a bet run six looms, at onct—seventy picks to the inch, mind you—and not a snarl on one o' them six machines. While we was standin' there watchin' the boss come by, an' he says: "Mary Magnet," he says, "ef I could get the rest o' these chaps to work the way you kin work," he says, "I'd git a damn big raise to me wages," he says; an' quick as a flash Mary says back: "Well just because me and the boys *kin* make human shuttlecocks out o' ourselves, that ain't no reason why we're a goin' to *do* it," she says, "just to raise *your* pay. We know darn well we'd never raise our own," she says, all the time jumpin' around from one loom to another as springy as a cricket. [*A pause.*] Gee! [*He shakes his head.*] It sure is hard to believe she'd 'a' been took like this so soon.

[*He fumbles after the box on the floor and lifts it to his knees, hesitates awkwardly and then removes the cover, displaying a white pillow of immortelles with the word "Asleep" formed upon it in large purple letters and tied across one corner with an elaborate bow of purple satin ribbon. There is a chorus of appreciative murmurs from the women.* MRS. SHAEFER *rises and takes the box, holding it up to full view.*]

MRS. SHAEFER: Now, ain't that a beautiful thing?

MRS. RICKERT: Oh, that is *handsome*.

MRS. SHAEFER: Wait till I fix it on the coffin.

[*She walks across the room and props the pillow (which has a fixture for this purpose) on the lower half of the coffin which is closed, then backs away admiringly to get the effect. The others rise for the same purpose. At this moment the sound of shouts and band music, faintly audible outside in the distance for some few moments previous, becomes more distinct.* MRS. SHAEFER *lifts her hand.*]

MRS. SHAEFER: It's Ferguson.

MRS. RICKERT: Yes, that's who it is. They're bringin' him up from the depot.

MRS. SHAEFER: Most like there'll be trouble with the police down here by the mill at the corner.

[*A sudden loud knock comes. All walk toward the door, and* MRS. SHAEFER *opens it, admitting* TIMOTHY MCGRATH, *a stocky, sandy-haired, smooth-shaven man in a black suit with a striker's button and ribbon conspicuous in his buttonhole. At the sound of the knock* MRS. LITTIG *creeps timidly in from the kitchen and stands in the background with one hand on the coffin.*]

MCGRATH: [*Standing in the doorway.*] Where's Magnet?

MRS. SHAEFER: He ain't come in yet.

MRS. RICKERT: Wasn't he at the depot?

MCGRATH: [*Rapidly and excitedly.*] No, he was not, and Ferguson's been raisin' hell down there. "Where's Magnet?" he says the first thing he steps off the train. "Take away the band, take away the parade, take away that carriage," he says, "and get me Magnet. Why ain't Magnet here?" he says. "I told you to have Magnet here." Jack Flaven spoke up and says: "Mr. Ferguson, we done our best but we can't locate Magnet. You may not 'a' heard," he says, "but Magnet's had trouble. His girl's dead. He won't talk tonight," and Ferguson says: [*he lowers his voice*] "I don't give a damn who's dead; I'll have no words with anybody till I've seen Magnet," he says. Can't none of you tell me where he is? When was he last home?

MRS. SHAEFER: I understand he ain't been home since noon, Mr. McGrath.

MCGRATH: Well, for Christ's sake, any time he gets in send him down to the hall.

[NICK BLUNDY *and* MCGRATH *go out.* MRS. SHAEFER *and* MRS. RICKERT *remain standing just inside the open door.* MRS. LITTIG *moves aimlessly back and forth behind the coffin, her arms folded, gazing at the dead and now and then wiping her eyes. The band is now distinctly heard at the end of the street playing the "Marseillaise," and cheers, "Hurrah for Ferguson!" mingled with shouts.*]

MRS. RICKERT: [*Pointing excitedly.*] There's Ferguson! See him there walkin' behind the band! Oh, he's a grand man! There ain't nothin' this town can do that's too good for Ferguson—that's what my Jim says.

[*They stand for a moment looking and listening, then close the outside door.* MRS. LITTIG *furtively leaves her stand by the coffin and starts toward the dining room door, but is intercepted by* MRS. RICKERT, *who crosses the stage and seats herself near* MRS. SHAEFER, *who has resumed her crocheting.*]

MRS. RICKERT: Mis' Littig, you was at the hospital when Mary died, wasn't you? I heard tell she suffered a good bit.

MRS. LITTIG: [*Turning reluctantly on her way to the door.*] She died very quiet, Mary did.

MRS. RICKERT: [*Persistently.*] Ain't you heard the doctors say what was the matter with her?

MRS. LITTIG: No, I ain't heard.

MRS. RICKERT: Ain't they told her father?

MRS. LITTIG: I ain't heard him say.

MRS. RICKERT: I heard tell Mary was to be married in the summer, Mrs. Littig. Is that a fact?

MRS. LITTIG: I ain't never heard Mary was to be married.

MRS. SHAEFER: [*Addressing* MRS. RICKERT *in a contemptuous whisper.*] She don't know nothin'.

*The Girl in the Coffin*

[*Exit* MRS. LITTIG *by the dining room door.* MRS. RICKERT *looks around to make sure that she has gone, then draws her chair close to* MRS. SHAEFER *and whispers a question. The latter responds by a very slow and preternaturally solemn nodding of the head, accompanied by a sideward glance full of the direst meaning.*]

MRS. RICKERT: Oh, ain't that terrible now! [*Parenthetically.*] I had my suspicions! [*She leans forward eagerly and whispers another question.*]

MRS. SHAEFER: [*Very impressively.*] That I don't know, Mrs. Rickert. As far as I can make out there ain't *nobody* knows. "You can be sure o' one thing," Joe says to me this morning: "whoever it is, *Magnet has still to learn his name*. It's a short lease o' life for the man that wronged Mary Magnet, once her father finds out the truth. That's what ails Magnet," Joe says to me. "*He can't find out.* Ef somethin' don't happen to take his mind off it he'll brood hisself crazy."

MRS. RICKERT: [*Shaking her head and clicking her tongue.*] Tck! Tck! tck! It certainly is awful. Now whoever do you suppose?

MRS. SHAEFER: In *my* belief it's some rich fellow she met up to the city. Many a Saturday night when work was over she's been seen to take the train. I understand she spread round the report she was goin' to business college up there. I guess, if truth be told, it was the gay life she was after.—Well, she's not the first girl foolishness has brought to her grave. [*She nods wisely.*] Them rich ones knows how to cover their tracks.

MRS. RICKERT: Ain't it a terrible shame now for a man like Magnet, a man as has worked hard and lived an honest life and everybody respects, that his girl should make a common woman of herself and his name be made a shame in the town?

MRS. SHAEFER: There's very few knows the real truth, Mrs. Rickert. "Whatever you do, Mamie," Joe says to me, "*don't talk.* It would be a bad thing just at this time," he says, "if many was to get the straight of how Magnet's girl come to her death. I wouldn't want Ferguson to know of it," he says; "why, Ferguson thinks the sun rises and sets in old Magnet," he says.

MRS. RICKERT: Mary always did seem like a right well behaved, sensible girl, too—for all her free ways and smart talk. It's queer about them things.

MRS. SHAEFER: She looked too high, Mrs. Rickert—she looked too high. That's the way with them smart, good-lookin' girls. They ain't never content with enough. That's what I says to Joe this mornin'. "Now there was a girl," I says, "that wanted to own the earth." Why, I used to see her go down to work in the mornin', her head way up in the air, swingin' her arms and steppin' along as proud as a peacock. You might 'a' thought she was some fine lady instead of a mill girl. An' now look what she's come to. A bitter dose she's had to take for her pride.

[*There is a sound of voices and footsteps on the porch outside. The women rise. The door opens and* WILLIAM MAGNET *enters. He is a tall, spare man of over fifty, with plentiful gray hair, dressed in a dark suit and flannel shirt. He is pale and harassed-looking, and almost savagely grim and abrupt in manner. He holds open the door, admitting* TIMOTHY MCGRATH.]

MAGNET: [*Abruptly, closing the door.*] Take a seat, Tim. I'll be with you in a minute. [*To* MRS. SHAEFER, *politely but sternly.*] What is there I can do for *you*, Mrs. Shaefer?

MRS. SHAEFER: [*Ingratiatingly.*] Put it the other way round, Mr. Magnet. Ain't there nothin' we can do for *you*? That's what we're here for. Won't you come out in the kitchen and have a bite of somethin' before you talk to Mr. McGrath? It'll do you a sight o' good, Mr. Magnet. There's coffee right on the stove.

MAGNET: [*Maintaining his direct and forbidding manner.*] Thank you very kindly, but I ain't hungry just at present. There's one thing you *can* do, if you'll excuse my speaking very plain, Mrs. Shaefer.

MRS. SHAEFER: [*Somewhat awed.*] Well, now, what's that, Mr. Magnet?

MAGNET: You can leave me to myself for this evening if you'll be so kind. I'm willing those that wants to should come in during the daytime, but at nights it suits me better to be alone.

MRS. SHAEFER: [*Swelling with offended dignity.*] Why, certainly, Mr. Magnet, just as you say. I've no wish to thrust in my company anywhere I ain't wanted.

[*She goes out promptly by the dining room door, followed by* MRS. RICKERT. MAGNET, *quite unmoved, draws up a chair and seats himself in front of* MCGRATH. *He speaks restlessly, and with a harsh, detached manner.*]

MAGNET: Now, Tim, whatever you've got to say, make it as short as you can. This is no time and place to waste words. [*He motions vaguely toward the coffin.*] That ought to be plain.

MCGRATH: [*Leaning forward and placing his hand on* MAGNET'S *knee.*] You have us all wrong, Magnet, if you think you ain't got our sympathy. You've *got* it. But, man alive—[*straightening slightly and shaking both hands in front of him*]—we can't stop tonight to think of our feelings. We gotta think of the proposition we're up against. Inside of an hour that hall down there'll be chock full o' workers from the Tabitha. We've sweat blood to get 'em there. If they go back to work tomorrow morning, this strike's on the blink. Who's goin' to hold that crowd, Magnet? Ferguson can't do it. He don't know the language.

MAGNET: [*Impatiently.*] What's the matter with Bruno Bastido? He can make a speech all right.

MCGRATH: They're jealous of Bastido. They think he's got a graft. Magnet, do you remember what you says to us down at the hotel that night last January when Ferguson first come to town? You says: "Boys, it ain't no use tryin' to stir up the warpers an' the twisters an' the loom workers—they're organized so tight already they can hardly move. If you want to see a real strike in this town, there's just one way to do it, and that is to *stop the looms*. Begin at the bottom of the ladder and get the dyers and the weavers out. Stop wastin' your breath on these gentlemen of labor that's enjoyin' good union wages, and talk to them poor devils that's starved so long they don't know they're hungry. Get out them at the bottom and the others'll follow fast enough."—Wasn't that the advice you give, Magnet?

MAGNET: [*Indifferently.*] I guess it was, Tim.

MCGRATH: Ain't we stuck pretty close to them tactics you proposed? Ain't that the way the Maxwell was shut down, an' the Junta? Wasn't you personally pretty much responsible for bringin' about them two walkouts?

MAGNET: [*Wearily.*] Well, suppose I was, Tim. What's that to do with it?

MCGRATH: [*With renewed earnestness.*] Why, just this, Magnet. You *got* the men out, but there's some of the rest of us has had the devil's own time tryin' to *keep* 'em out. You know what the trouble is. Up to the middle o' last week we ain't never been able to get as much as a look-in on the Tabitha. That G— d— Vito Toccati they've got for a foreman up there has double-crossed us from the start. It's pretty hard on them poor devils from the Maxwell and the Junta that's livin' along from day to day on bread and potatoes from the relief station to see the Tabitha hands goin' to work an' know they're gettin' double pay and the promise of a big raise when the strike's over. They won't stick it out that way much longer. You can't put *too* big a strain on human nature. We've got to shut down the Tabitha. Why, Magnet, you was the first to say it. For two weeks we've kept a hundred pickets round that mill. It's been a grim game. Every day now there's been as many as thirty out of the hundred arrested or sent to the hospital with a shot through the arm or a broken head, and every time the next morning we've had thirty new ones there to take their places. Well, we've made some progress. Out of the 425 that works in that mill there was only one hundred got through the picket lines this mornin'. But, my

God, the fight's only just begun! We gotta get 'em *all* out an' we gotta *keep* 'em out. We gotta clinch this thing, and tonight's the time. Ferguson's come down a' purpose. If this meeting falls flat the whole strike may go for nothing. You wouldn't want that to happen, would you, Magnet? Don't you feel like you ought to come down and help us put it through?

[*A pause.* MAGNET *rises abruptly and faces* MCGRATH *squarely.*]

MAGNET: Well, now, Tim, if you've said your say and feel satisfied, you can have my answer. It's the same I give you before we come in a few minutes ago. I can't do what you want me to do. [*Hastily, as* MCGRATH *starts to interrupt.*] At least, I *won't* do it. There's no more chance of my goin' down to Murray Hall tonight than there would be if it was me instead of my girl lyin' in that coffin. Now that's all I have to say. I hope it's enough. I wish you'd go now and leave me to myself.

MCGRATH: Do you mean that, Magnet?

MAGNET: [*Savagely.*] Do I *mean* it? O' course I mean it. Did you ever know me say anything I didn't mean? [*He turns his back.*]

MCGRATH: [*Rising.*] Do you think you're doin' the square thing by Ferguson, Magnet? He's staked pretty heavy on you.

MAGNET: [*Desperately.*] Square or crooked, Tim, have it as you please. I ain't goin' down to Murray Hall tonight. And what's more, I ain't goin' to argue about it any further. Now I wish you'd go.

MCGRATH: [*Shaking his head.*] I'm sorry about this, Magnet. I don't think you're doin' the thing that will give you the most satisfaction in the end.

[MCGRATH *goes out.* MAGNET *closes the door and stands for a moment stretching his arms back and forth with a weary movement of mental suffering and physical exhaustion. He walks to the coffin for a moment, shakes his head, moans a little and swears under his breath, then sinks into a rocking chair near the table, stretches out his feet, throws back his head, closes his eyes and lets his hands rest limply one above the other in an attitude of utter weariness and dejection.* MRS. LITTIG *looks in from the dining room, retreats for a moment, and then reappears, carrying a pair of shoes, which she places on the floor beside him. He stirs a little, but otherwise pays no attention.* MRS. LITTIG *returns to the kitchen and brings back a large bottle, cup and spoon. She pours from the bottle into the cup and touches* MAGNET *on the arm.*]

MRS. LITTIG: Take a sup o' this.

MAGNET: [*Rousing.*] What is it?

MRS. LITTIG: It's hot spirits and Jamaicy ginger.

MAGNET: [*Motioning her away impatiently.*] No, no. I don't want it.

[MRS. LITTIG *places the cup on the table near him and starts toward the door.*]

MAGNET: [*Moving uneasily.*] Mis' Littig!

[MRS. LITTIG *turns and walks slowly back.*]

MAGNET: Mis' Littig! Come set here a minute. I want to ask you somethin'.

[MRS. LITTIG *seats herself in a nearby chair and rocks timidly with folded arms.* MAGNET, *with eyes still closed, twists about in great distress.*]

What did you say was the last thing Mary said to you?

MRS. LITTIG: She says: "Tell pap it's all right. Tell him he ain't to worry."

MAGNET: Didn't she never leave a message for anybody else?

MRS. LITTIG: Not as I heard.

MAGNET: That night you was settin' by her when her fever was so high— Ain't she never mentioned anybody's name?

MRS. LITTIG: [*Shaking her head.*] No, she ain't.

MAGNET: Didn't you never hear the nurse or the doctor say there was somebody she was talkin' about?

MRS. LITTIG: No, I didn't hear.

MAGNET: [*Reaching shakily over to the table for his cup and taking a long drink, then replacing the cup on the table and slowly beginning to unlace his boots and put on dry ones.*] What ever become o' that ring Mary used to wear?

MRS. LITTIG: What ring?

MAGNET: Why, that gold ring with a little blue stone in it. You've seed her wear it. She told me she bought it out of her savings. It ain't on her finger now. What become of it?

MRS. LITTIG: I dunno, Mr. Magnet, I never noticed what she done with it.

MAGNET: I was upstairs this mornin' lookin' through all her things, and I couldn't find it. It ain't on her finger now. [*A pause.*] Them times last winter, Mrs. Littig, when Mary went up to the city so often, didn't she ever tell you nothing about where she went and what she done?

MRS. LITTIG: [*Reflectively.*] She wasn't ever much to tell.

MAGNET: Can't you recall she ever mentioned anybody she met up there, anybody that took her round and acted nice to her?

MRS. LITTIG: [*Mildly.*] Don't seem like I can remember she ever did. [*A pause.* MRS. LITTIG *rises, takes the bottle and cup from the table and moves toward the kitchen. She turns as she reaches the dining room door.*] Mebbe you would eat a little after a while. I got some supper in the stove. [*She goes out.*]

MAGNET: [*Groaning despairingly and turning in his chair.*] Her mother would 'a' knew! Her mother would 'a' knew! [*There is a knock.* MAGNET *does not move.*] Somebody else after me, damn it! Why can't they leave me alone? [*The knock is repeated.* MAGNET *rises and goes savagely toward the door.*] I'll teach 'em to stay out o' here for one night! [*He opens and admits* JOHN FERGUSON—*a large man, tall, heavily built, smooth-shaven. He enters in silence.* MAGNET *succumbs a little under his steady eye.*] Oh, why, good evening, Mr. Ferguson, good evening. [*He holds out his hand, which* FERGUSON *takes silently.*]

FERGUSON: I'm sorry to find you in trouble, Magnet.

MAGNET: [*Walking toward the opposite side of the room. For the first time he speaks a little tremulously.*] Yes, I'm in a bad way, Mr. Ferguson, a bad way. It's my girl, Mary. [*He motions toward the coffin.*] She's all I had.

[*While* MAGNET'S *back is turned,* FERGUSON *glances swiftly about the room and in the direction of the open coffin with a look that is peculiarly painful, apprehensive and significant. Then he walks toward* MAGNET *and puts a hand on his shoulder.*]

FERGUSON: I know you've had a hard blow, Magnet, but there's only one way to meet it. Pull yourself together. You have work to do. You're lucky there. Not every man has that comfort in his trouble.

MAGNET: [*Half turning away.*] It don't seem like I can take any comfort from that, Mr. Ferguson. I'd be glad to if I could. I wish I *could* talk to the boys tonight. I can't do it. I can't do nothing for a while but set here an' think. I can't believe Mary's gone. I can't get used to it. She was all I had. I'd better be dead myself. [*Passionately.*] My god, I wish I was!

FERGUSON: [*Very quiet and repressed.*] That's no thought for you to hold tonight, Magnet. If a man's no good to the world and he knows it, let him get out of it if he wants to. It don't stand that way with you. You've got a big responsibility. Why don't you be worthy of it? Why don't you stand up to it?

MAGNET: I can't think about that now, Mr. Ferguson. The way I see it I've got a right to be left alone with my own trouble. It's a privilege belongs to any man if he's a mind to claim it.

FERGUSON: [*With sudden intensity.*] Let me tell you, Magnet, it's a privilege no man ought to want to claim at the expense of fourteen thousand of his fellow workers. Things have got to a crisis, and you've had as much to do with that as anybody. If we can close out the Tabitha tomorrow and hold down it and the other mills till the end of next week, we're over the danger line. If we can't, we lose as sure as fate. If we lose, it'll take years, years—you know that, Magnet—to win back what we've gained. The outcome o' this strike don't rest on High, Magnet—[*he makes a sardonic upward gesture*]—it rests right here in this room with you and me. [*He pounds his fist softly on the table.*] Now what are you going to do about it? [MAGNET *shakes his head doubtfully.* FERGUSON *continues.*] You want to remember how much depends on a big fight like this. What made the workers of this town listen to me when I landed here? It was because they knew I'd won a miners' strike out in Montana and a lumber jacks' strike in Oregon and a cotton workers' strike in North Carolina and a glass blowers' strike in New Jersey. They thought if I'd helped others to better wages and shorter hours I could help them. If we lose here, the next town where I go they won't be quite so ready to listen, now will they? To every big strike lost there's a hundred others lost in future. I've been holding off from this town a long time. I thought they weren't ripe for it. I looked over the ground a good while before I made up my mind. Do you want to know what was the chief thing made me decide to come here this winter and stick it out? It was because I found you here. When I heard you talk to that crowd outside the Excelsior one night last year, I said to myself: "When the time comes, there's a man I can depend on." Well, I have depended on you. You don't want to give me cause to regret that, do you, Magnet? If it hadn't been for you, things here could never have come to a head the way they have. You know that. It's no time for you to desert me now. You can't do more to prove your sorrow than to meet it

the way a man ought. Come on down to the hall, Magnet.
The boys are waiting.

MAGNET: [*Painfully, after a pause.*] I'm sorry. I can't do it, Ferguson.

FERGUSON: Why can't you do it?

MAGNET: [*Moving away a little distance and speaking with great feeling.*] You're a big man, Ferguson. You've got a big mind. You've got a big power. You know how to fight, and you know how to put fight into other men. You put it into me. I shan't ever forget the day you come into this God-forsaken town. It give me a feeling I ain't had for a good many years—a feeling I'd clean forgot I ever could have. Well—I followed it. I've fought for you, Ferguson, every day and every night for these past two months, and I'd 'a' fought for you to the end for better or for worse if it hadn't been for this. There's something, Ferguson, a man's mind don't seem to have no power to make him understand. He's got to 'a' been there himself. You ain't got no children of your own, Ferguson. You can't understand there's some troubles comes first with a man. The whole world might be waiting for him to save it, but it'd have to wait. Nobody wouldn't have any right to interfere. You don't know what it is to a man, Ferguson, when somebody—when somebody—[MAGNET's *voice breaks. He pauses and looks about hopelessly as if driven into a corner. Then, with a sudden, desperate gesture, he breaks out fiercely.*] Damn it, there's some rotten coward, some beast, some low down scoundrel has ruined my girl. I don't know who he is. But I want to know! I want to find out! I want to find him! I want to kill him! It's the only thing I do want. Until I've done that, this strike can go to hell. You can go to hell. They all can go to hell.

[*He drops into a chair and covers his face with his hands.* FERGUSON *watches him steadily in silence, then as he quiets a little begins to pace up and down.*]

FERGUSON: This man you say has done your girl so much harm—how do you know but what she loved him?

MAGNET: [*In a savage tone, looking up swiftly.*] Loved him! Loved him! The damn dog! Suppose she *did* love him! What's that to do with it?

FERGUSON: [*Very quietly, still pacing up and down and looking at the floor.*] A whole lot. No man ever lived that ruined the woman that loved him. It can't be done. [*There is such deep conviction in* FERGUSON'S *tone that* MAGNET *gazes at him in silent astonishment.* FERGUSON *seats himself slowly, remaining silent a minute.*] There's something I might as well tell you, Magnet, if you have a mind to listen. [*A long pause follows,* FERGUSON *gazing at the floor. Then he speaks in a low voice.*] You're not the only man in this town tonight whose hopes are lying in a coffin.

MAGNET: [*Startled, looking closely at* FERGUSON.] You? [FERGUSON *nods.*] Somebody close?

FERGUSON: Yes, somebody close.

MAGNET: Dead?

FERGUSON: [*Heavily.*] Yes, dead.

MAGNET: [*After a pause, drawing closer.*] It ain't your wife?

FERGUSON: No, not my wife. [*He moves restlessly, and speaks, after a pause, in a changed tone.*] It's been some time since your girl's mother died, Magnet—isn't that so?

MAGNET: Fifteen years.

FERGUSON: I suppose you and her lived happy together, didn't you?

MAGNET: [*Solemnly.*] We did that.

FERGUSON: Well—I wasn't so lucky. My wife and I haven't lived together at all this many a day. If we had I'd never be here in a loom worker's cottage, fighting within an inch of my life to win a strike. I'd be sitting in some hotel parlor hobnobbing with a lot of bishops and politicians and college professors, trying to patch up a peace between the mill owners and the strikers. I'd wear a medal and have a good fat bank account. I'd kowtow to ladies and gentlemen. They wouldn't hate me the way they do now—they'd only snub me. I wouldn't stick out my tongue at the minister. When I drank champagne and ate at swell restaurants, I'd do it on the quiet. The newspapers wouldn't hound me—they'd praise me. I wouldn't be a scoundrel, an anarchist, a cut-throat revolutionist. I'd be a respectable labor leader—that's what I'd be if I'd stayed with my wife. Maybe you think I'd better have stayed with her. [*He laughs sneeringly.*] There's plenty would agree with you in that opinion. [MAGNET *makes a protesting gesture, but* FERGUSON *pays no attention.*] Well, I didn't stay with her, I left her. A good living is all she gets out of me. It's all she ever will get. Except my name. She hangs on to that. And my freedom. She's got that locked up safe enough, or she thinks she has. She claims I'm not good enough to marry any other woman. [*He laughs cynically.*] Maybe she's right about that. But I was good enough for another woman to love me just the same. [*With a touch of boyish pride.*] She did love me anyhow, this other woman, whether I was good enough or not. She didn't get a living out of me. She didn't get my name. She didn't get a right to blame me if I was unfaithful to her—and I wasn't always faithful to her. She didn't even get a right to tell anybody she loved me, and it seems like that's what a woman hankers after the most of all. I never told her I loved her. She just had a sort of an idea I was glad she loved me. I *was* glad—for a kind of a queer reason. She kept me from feeling lonely. I'll say that for her—she was the only human being I've ever known that could stand between me and mortal loneliness. Maybe that means I loved her. I don't know. I don't suppose I did. [*A pause.*] Well, tonight, just before I took the train to come down here, I heard that woman was dead. I didn't enjoy the trip down so very much. [*There is so much suppressed suffering in his voice that* MAGNET *instinctively reaches forward and lays a hand on his shoulder.* FERGUSON *shakes it off, rises and faces* MAGNET.] You said to me I don't know how it feels to be a father. You're right about that, Magnet, dead right. I don't know. Being the kind of man I am, nobody seems to think I'm entitled to any connection with a family. A courtroom or jail cell is supposed to be the place where my disposition thrives to the best advantage. The only kind of a father I've ever had a chance to be you wouldn't call a father at all. You'd call him a beast, a low-down scoundrel, a man that ruins other men's daughters. Since my mother died, when I was a ten-year-old kid working on the bunkers in a coal mine out in Colorado, I've never known but one home, and that's in a dead woman's heart. I'm alone now and likely to stay so. I haven't any more hope of happiness in this world than I have of going to heaven when I die, and that's none at all. [*With sudden, passionate emphasis.*] But there's one thing I don't ever forget, Magnet—unhappiness is a lot easier to bear when you've got clothes to cover your back and food enough to hold your body and soul together. When I come to a town in the dead of winter and find twenty-five thousand people on the edge of freezing and starvation, I remember the time when my own mother went cold and hungry, and it don't seem to make very much difference to me whether I'm happy or not. [*He takes up his hat as if to leave, and moves a little toward the door.*] As long as I can keep alive to fight for those poor devils, I'll fight for 'em. There was a while I expected others to feel the same way, but I've got over that. Nobody knows any better than I do how few men you're likely to run across in a lifetime that'll join the ranks to stay. I used to take it pretty hard when an old comrade fell out, but it don't make so much difference any more. I've swallowed that kind of disappointment with my daily bread for so many years now that it's got to be a pretty old story. There's one thing that always helps me to stand it. If there's nobody else in this world I can count on, I know I can always count on myself. As long as there's breath in my body I'll never lose heart and I'll never give up the game. A good part of the world seems to look on me as a kind of devil. Well, if that's the way they feel about it, let 'em think so. I don't mind being the kind of individual that can walk through hell without being scorched any so's you'd notice it. Life can kill and bury my happiness, but it can't kill and bury my courage. This strike that's on in this town is the biggest I've ever handled. Without you to help me, Magnet, maybe I'll lose it. Or maybe I won't lose it. Maybe I'll win it anyhow. This night may mean the beginning of the end for me or it may mean the beginning of the biggest success I've ever known. But whichever way it is, you can be sure of one thing—if ever I go down it'll be with every man's hand against me and my back shoved up against a hard high wall.

[*There is a knock.* FERGUSON *opens the door and* MCGRATH *steps just inside.*]

MCGRATH: Are you ready, Mr. Ferguson? Time's getting short.

FERGUSON: All ready, McGrath.

MAGNET: [*Rising suddenly.*] Hang on there a minute, Tim. [*He walks to the dining room door and calls to* MRS. LITTIG.] You needn't set the table till I get back, Mrs. Littig. I'm going down to the hall. [*He takes his hat and walks to the door.*]

FERGUSON: You take the machine and go on over, boys. I want to walk. I'll be with you in a few minutes.

[MAGNET *and* MCGRATH *go out.* FERGUSON *closes the door and leans against it, raising his head and laying one hand across his mouth. As he stands there,* MRS. LITTIG *enters hesitatingly, looking about to make sure* MAGNET *has gone. She walks over to* FERGUSON, *and standing before him, pulls from the neck of her dress a long ribbon and from it unties a gold ring which she hands to* FERGUSON. *She looks at him sadly and timidly but simply and quite without reproach.*]

MRS. LITTIG: She said I was to give you this. She said I was to say she died happy.

[*Without waiting for comment or reply,* MRS. LITTIG *leaves the room by the dining room door.* FERGUSON *slips the ring in his vest pocket and walks slowly to the coffin. He stands behind it and looks down.*]

# CURTAIN

# THE BLUE SPHERE

## CHARACTERS

JOSEPH DELEVAN, *a grocer.*
MRS. DELAVAN.
HARRY, *their son.*
EDDIE, *the monstrosity.*
THE SHADOW.
THE FAST MAIL.
MRS. MINTURN, *a neighbor.*
JOHN GALLOWAY, *an engineer.*
PETERSON, *a fireman.*
       Conductor, Postmen, Trainmen and Passengers.

### SCENE

*The kitchen of the Delavan home, one block from the tracks at the outskirts of Marydale. A solid board fence, unpainted, encloses the yard on three sides. In the front, a yellow picket fence with a gate caught by a string. From the gate to the front and rear doors, a moist, brick walk. Outside the kitchen window, vines and hollyhocks. Inside, a breakfast table on which dishes are spread, and at opposite sides of which sit* MR. *and* MRS. DELAVAN.

### TIME

*Seven-thirty* A.M.


JOSEPH DELAVAN: [*A short, stout man with brown hair and mustache, and brown-blue eyes, a grocery man by trade—rising and brushing the crumbs from his lap.*] Well, I'll be going. [*He takes down his coat and hat from a hook, and folds up his paper.*] See that the boy don't get out again today, will you? [*He glances toward the front room in an apprehensive, strained way, and goes out, leaving the door open, but carefully fastening the gate behind him.*]

MRS. DELAVAN: [*A blonde woman of thirty-three, clearing away the breakfast dishes and shaking her head dolefully.*] Ah, me! Oh, the day that it was born! It makes all the difference. Things have not been the same since it came—poor little thing that it is! And to think that I should have given birth to it! [*She brushes away the gathering tears with her hand.*] It would be a blessing almost—[*she pauses, terrified by her own thoughts*]—but God forgive me for thinkin' of it! It would be me that would suffer if any harm came to a single hair of its head. [*She wipes her eyes anew.*]

DELAVAN: [*Walking out Wood Street to his store, and sighing heavily.*] Dear, dear, dear, dear! That this should have befallen us! [*He sighs again.*] Three years old! Not walking, not talking, and never will! The years! The years! [*He renews his sigh.*]

THE SHADOW: [*A soft girlish figure, entering the Delavan kitchen, trailing clouds of diaphanous drapery, a pale blue sphere in her hands. She looks about, passes through the walls to the front bedroom, where Eddie,* THE MONSTROSITY, *lies, and bends over the crib.*] Eddie! Eddie! [*She holds up the sphere.*]

THE FAST MAIL: [*Passing Ellsworth, one hundred and sixty miles away.*] Ooooooo-ee! Ooo-ee! Ooh-ooh!

MRS. DELAVAN: [*Laying dishes in the dishpan.*] My, but the flowers smell sweet this morning. [*She pauses to examine the trumpet flowers.*]

THE MONSTROSITY: [*A child, with a head almost twice the size of a normal one, opening its large and unnaturally starey eyes, and for the first time perceiving the blue sphere.*] Urg-ubbla-da! Blub! Blub! [*It holds out its hands.*]

THE SHADOW: [*Smiling winsomely, and waving the sphere to and fro, and revealing the splendor of its clarity.*] See how beautiful it is! How blue, how light! [*It seems to float in her hands like a bubble as she turns it round and round, beckoning the child to follow.*]

THE MONSTROSITY: [*Its arms still aloft, kicking and crowing horribly.*] Ahda-da! Urg! Ahbublu!

MRS. DELAVAN: [*Hearing the sound of its voice, and opening the door.*] It's awake is it? My little pet. [*She suppresses an almost uncontrollable shudder as she views it.*] I thought I heard you kicking and crowing. Poor little dear! My loving, petty lamb! Come now! [*She lifts it up and fondles it on her breast and neck.*] Oh, the poor little sweetheart. Was it having to talk all to itself? Well, mother's been thinking of her pretty baby all the night long. [*To the lad of nine years who appears in the doorway.*] Come, Harry. Get your clothes on. I'll want you to go to the store. [*She smoothes the great head on her breast with a feeling of anguish.*] Sweety baby! Mother's little lamb. [*She begins to dress it.*]

THE FAST MAIL: [*Passing Ultona, one hundred and fifty miles away.*] Oooooo-ee! Oooooo-ee! Ooh-ooh!

DELAVAN: [*Arriving at his store, still thinking.*] It would be so much better if it should die—though I don't suppose I ought to wish it. It's unchristian. [*He unlocks the door and goes in.*]

THE SHADOW: [*Before the child and its mother, waving the blue ball.*] See! How wonderful! How lovely! Here are yellow and grey and green as I turn it. See the pink here—isn't it lovely? This soft, soft shade of pink! [*She holds the ball close.*]

THE MONSTROSITY: [*Staring, interested, allured.*] Ah-da! Eee! Oo-blub! [*It holds out its hands and kicks and struggles.* THE SHADOW *moves backward, then forward, then backward, then forward, luring the child by the motion.*]

MRS. DELAVAN: [*Carrying the child to the kitchen.*] Come now, I'll put you down here where mother can see you. That's right. Now here's a nice wooden rattle for baby to play with until mother gets it something to eat. [*She places a red and green rattle in the child's lap. He drops it to gaze at the blue sphere.*] And now here is something for the baby to eat. [*She brings a bowl with a spoon, from which she feeds it, sighing the while.* THE SHADOW *disappears.*]

MRS. MINTURN: [*A neighbor, looking out of her window at some sweet pea vines and smiling.*] What a perfect day! How nice Mrs. Arthur's trees look! I think—[*She is thinking of calling upon Mrs. Arthur.*]

THE SHADOW: [*At her elbow.*] You think you will call on Mrs. Delavan, don't you? She is so lonely!

MRS. MINTURN: [*Sympathetically but seemingly continuing her own thoughts.*] I will call on Mrs. Delavan; she is so lonely. I guess I'd better do my house work first, though.

MRS. DELAVAN: [*Ceasing to feed the child.*] Now then, will it play with its rattle like a nicey baby, while mama does the front room? [*She passes her hand over her forehead wearily, and turns to her work.*]

THE SHADOW: [*Reappearing to the child.*] See how wonderful! How beautiful! It floats and flies as you will float and fly if you come with me. [*She dances the sphere before it.*]

THE MONSTROSITY: Ugh! Blooble! [*It begins to propel itself across the floor toward the door, holding out its hands at times.*]

THE SHADOW: [*Waving the blue sphere.*] Come! Come!

THE FAST MAIL: [*Passing Ungers, one hundred and twenty miles away.*] Ooooo-ee! Ooooo-ee! Ooh-ooh!

MRS. MINTURN: [*Finishing her housework at eleven.*] Now I think I'll go. Mrs. Delavan's life with that child on her hands must be awful. [*She throws a light shawl about her shoulders and steps out.*]

THE SHADOW: [*Meeting her at the Delavan gate.*] Forget the gate! Forget the gate! [*Unconsciously* MRS. MINTURN *leaves the gate open.*]

MRS. DELAVAN: [*The spell of self-absorption broken by the sight of* MRS. MINTURN *nearing her window.*] Eddie! Eddie! Where *is* he? [*She hurries to the kitchen and out upon the walk, where she finds him. To* MRS. MINTURN, *without greeting.*] He always makes for the gate for some reason, and we're so afraid that if he gets out some time he'll get hurt. [*She picks him up and carries him back to the kitchen entrance with grieved thoughts.*] Now won't you play here, dearie? [*She puts him down.*]

MRS. MINTURN: [*A pale, slight woman with partially gray hair.*] It is such a lovely morning I thought I would run over and see how you are getting along. [*To herself.*] What an affliction! Horrible! What a dreadful thing it really is. [*She plunges into an exchange of friendly gossip.*]

THE SHADOW: [*Reappearing before the child, the blue sphere in her hands.*] See! How perfect! Green and violet, and this fleck of milky white all toned into one! [*She waves the blue sphere.*]

THE FAST MAIL: [*Passing Berham, eighty miles away.*] Ooooo-ee! Oooooo-ee! Ooh-ooh!

JOHN GALLOWAY: [*The engineer, stout and round, to* PETERSON, *the fireman, slender and smoky.*] This makes the fifteenth year I've been on this run; fifteen years tomorrow. If somethin' don't happen then it'll be fifteen years without a real, serious, big accident. I guess I'd better tap on wood. [*He smites the small window ledge of his window. The engine takes a great trestle.*]

PETERSON: [*Stopping in his shoveling to view a stream of water far below.*] This makes my fifth. [*The thunder of the wheels on the bridge drowns most of the sound, and the wind blows the rest away.*]

DELAVAN: [*Approaching the house at twelve-fifteen, a block distant.*] Well, if the gate isn't open and Eddie on the sidewalk! Ella ought to keep a better lookout than that. I told her about it this morning. [*He hurries forward.*] It's bad enough to have a child in this state, but to have it crawling all over the neighborhood. [*He stoops to pick it up.*]

THE SHADOW: [*The blue sphere in her hands.*] Forget the gate! Forget the gate! [*Passing her hand before his eyes.* DELAVAN *enters the gate, leaving it open, but returns after a little to close it.*]

MRS. DELAVAN: [*Appearing at the door, distressed and ashamed.*] Eddie! He has crawled out again! Oh, dear! Oh, dear! Whatever will I do with him! Why, he was right here only a moment ago. Where did you find him? [*She makes room for* MRS. MINTURN, *who comes forward to make her departure.*]

DELAVAN: [*With suppressed irritation.*] Outside the gate. He was half way down the street here. The gate was wide open.

MRS. MINTURN: [*Apologetically, sorry for* MRS. DELAVAN.] I may have left it open, though I thought I closed it. I must be going now. I'm sorry. I know how it is with children. They love to crawl. [*She greets* MR. DELAVAN.]

DELAVAN: [*To* MRS. DELAVAN, *after* MRS. MINTURN *has gone.*] Something is sure to happen one of these days if you don't keep that gate closed. It's bad enough as it is, seems to me, without making a spectacle of us. I—

MRS. DELAVAN: [*Wiping her eyes.*] There you go. As though I didn't have a hundred things to think of besides watching him. Heaven knows, I don't want him to get away any more than you do, but he seems possessed to do it. I didn't leave the gate open. Mrs. Minturn called a little while ago—

DELAVAN: [*Sympathetically.*] I know you've got a lot to do. I'm just ashamed to have him crawling around that way. [*He pats her shoulder.*]

THE MAILMAN: [*Whistling and calling.*] "Delavan!" [*He hands in a letter.*]

THE SHADOW: [*As he goes out the gate.*] Forget the gate! Forget the gate! [*He goes off, leaving it open.*]

THE FAST MAIL: [*Passing Tyndale, sixty miles away.*] Ooooo-ee! Oooo-ee! Ooh-ooh!

THE SHADOW: [*To the child, who is just inside the door.*] Grey! Green! Blue! Brown! See how smooth, how glistening, how round! [*She coaxes it with the sphere, waving it before her. The child begins to crawl.*]

DELAVAN: [*To his wife, who is putting food on the table.*] Mrs. MacMichaels was in this morning. She wanted me to give her more credit. But with that husband of hers I couldn't. I told her if she would pay half the old bill—but she can't, of course. I don't see why I should be called upon to trust them. [*He eats rapidly.*]

MRS. DELAVAN: [*Forgetful of* THE MONSTROSITY *for a moment.*] Nor I. I know it's too bad, and I'm sorry for her, but I don't see that you should be called upon to do it. I wonder what's keeping Harry so long? [*She goes to the door.*]

THE SHADOW: [*Before the child outside, waving the sphere in sinuous lines.*] Thus and so, right and left, round and round. [*The child rocks its head in time with the motion.*]

DELAVAN: [*Chancing to glance at the child and deeming the motion to be the result of idiocy.*] Tct! Tct! Tct! It's too bad. [*He hides his distress behind a grave face.*]

MRS. DELAVAN: [*Returning from looking for her son.*] I don't see him. [*She seats herself. They eat in silence.*]

THE SHADOW: [*The child following her.*] Round and round, round and round. Pale grey! Pale blue! Dark! Light! Light! Dark! Light! Dark! [*The child crawls eagerly after.*]

HARRY: [*Entering a few moments later with Eddie in his arms.*] Somebody's left the gate open again. The kid was right near it. Say, if we don't keep it closed he'll get out some day and right down on the tracks. He was just scramblin' along.

MRS. DELAVAN: [*Wearily.*] Now, who could have done that! It must have been the mailman. [*She puts the child beside her on the floor.*] I think I'll have to tie a string around him. He's getting awfully restless these days. I never saw anything like it. [*She contemplates the years of misery and discomfort and distress which he represents, but reproaches herself for it all at the same time.*] I don't know whatever I am to do with him. I can't lock him up in a room all day all by himself. [*She closes the door.*]

DELAVAN: That makes it pretty hot in here, don't it?

THE SHADOW: [*Hovering over the child.*] To hold this would be so wonderful—see round, blue, glistening! [*She waves it rhythmically. The child follows it with his eyes.*]

THE FAST MAIL: [*Passing Wheatlands, forty-five miles away.*] Ooooo-ee! Ooooo-ee! Ooh-ooh!

GALLOWAY: [*The engineer, wiping the dust out of the corners of his eyes and turning to* PETERSON.] Remember the cow we killed at Ellsworth two years ago?

PETERSON: [*Shoveling coal at his feet.*] Yay-o.

GALLOWAY: [*Proudly.*] They collected sixty dollars for that—so I understand—Utterson was telling me here a few days ago. [*He sticks his head out of a window and surveys the elbow of a stream that comes into view, then withdraws it.*] I never saw a cow tossed clean up in the air before. Her tail stood out as straight as a stick. [*He smiles and whistles for a crossing.*]

DELAVAN: [*Arising and shaking off the crumbs.*] Well, I'd better be going now, I guess. [*He takes down his hat and coat.*] I don't see why he shouldn't play in the yard if we can keep the gate shut. [*He goes out.*]

HARRY: [*Fifteen minutes later, hanging around his mother's skirt.*] Ma, I promised to pitch at a ball game at two o'clock. Can I go?

MRS. DELAVAN: [*Wearily, but sympathetically.*] If you'll promise me faithfully to be back at five. You know what your father told you the other day. You ought to really stay here and help me mind the baby. [*He takes his cap and goes.*]

THE SHADOW: [*Moving before him to the gate.*] Forget the gate! Forget the gate! [*He goes out, leaving the gate open.*]

THE FAST MAIL: [*Passing Hunterstown, thirty-five miles away.*] Oooo-ee! Ooooo-ee! Ooh-ooh!

MRS. DELAVAN: [*Entering the front room for a moment.*] And now I have that mending to do. And those pies. I think I'll do the mending first—no; I'll make the pies first. [*She returns to the kitchen.*]

THE SHADOW: [*Retreating before her.*] I'll watch the child! Forget him! Forget him! [MRS. DELAVAN *commences paring apples, all thought of the child passing from her.*]

THE SHADOW: [*Before the baby on the walk.*] Come! [THE MONSTROSITY *crawls eagerly after.*]

THE FAST MAIL: [*Passing Palmer's Station, fifteen miles away.*] Ooooo-ee! Oooo-ee! Ooh-ooh!

GALLOWAY: [*Watching a barn recede in the distance.*] Didjy see where Esposito got thirty days for that last shindig of his?

PETERSON: [*Manifesting a proper interest.*] No! You don't say! When did that happen?

GALLOWAY: [*Loftily.*] Oh, last Monday. He come around the roundhouse, talkin' his usual guff, and they just took an' locked him up. It's thirty days for him now.

PETERSON: [*Reverently and righteously.*] An' it serves him good and right, I say.

GALLOWAY: That's what *I* say, too. These dago wipers! What good are they? [*He blows for another crossing.*]

MRS. DELAVAN: [*Paring in her kitchen.*] These apples are not as good as bell-flowers for pies, but they'll do. [*She casts cores and peelings away, mixes flour and rolls her dough.*]

THE SHADOW: [*Half way down the street to the track, the child following.*] Such a pretty color. Blue! Blue as your mother's eyes! See how the light touches it here. See how clear it is. If you had this in your hands you would be happy, happy, happy! [*The child crawls, his eyes fixed on it.*]

MRS. DELAVAN: [*Spreading the dough for the third pie.*] This dough is really softer than it ought to be. It's so hard to get it just right. Those last pies—[*She sprinkles a little flour on it.*]

THE SHADOW: [*Returning for a second and holding a pink-flowered dress before her eyes.*] Do you remember this?

MRS. DELAVAN: [*A vision of the church door at Clarendon, a small town thirty miles away, and of herself entering it in this very dress, and Nate Saulsby passing her and looking at her admiringly, filling her eyes.*] That was such a pretty dress. It had such nice frilled collars and cuffs. I wonder how Nate is doing now. He was a nice, handsome, clever boy. [*Shadows of other girls and boys troop by—bits of crowds, country roads, country squares, a panorama of half-forgotten faces and places.*]

THE SHADOW: [*As* MRS. DELAVAN *dreams and the child crawls.*] This ball is so perfect that if you had it you would be happy for ever and ever. It is perpetual joy, the color of peace. No need to seek for happiness elsewhere. Follow this—but take it from my hands, you will be happy. See— [*She waves it near, then far, then near, then far.*]

THE MONSTROSITY: Ooogh! Bubblum!

THE FAST MAIL: [*Passing Rutland, five miles away.*] Ooooo-ee! Ooooo-ee! Ooh-ooh!

THE SHADOW: Just a little farther! Soon you will have it now. Soon I will give it to you. When we reach the corner, when we get there where the steel rails shine—I will give it to you. Isn't it perfect! Isn't it blue! See how the light falls through it—clear as water. [*She trips gaily backward, waving the sphere before her from side to side.*]

THE FAST MAIL: [*Entering the environs of Marydale at fifty miles an hour and only a mile away.*] Ooooo-ee! Oooooo-ee! Ooh-ooh!

THE SHADOW: [*Hovering above the tracks a few feet in front of the child.*] See, when you get here, right here, I will give it to you. The beautiful ball! The beautiful sphere! This you are to have when you get here—here! You will be so happy. [*She coaxes, smiles and pleads.* THE MONSTROSITY *follows.*]

PETERSON: [*To* GALLOWAY, *as he notes the outlying houses and ringing the bell.*] I see they haven't started on that siding yet here. They were to begin yesterday, so Jaycox said.

GALLOWAY: [*On his seat by the window, a look of serene content on his face.*] So I see. They couldn't get done at Linden, I suppose. [*He shifts his position for comfort and prepares to maintain silence as the train rounds a curve and the Wood Street crossing comes into view. Noting a wagon waiting at the minor crossing.*] They ought to put a gate or two more in this town. They need 'em. [*He blows the whistle.*]

THE SHADOW: [*Hovering above* THE MONSTROSITY, *the blue sphere in her hand.*] Just a little farther, dearest. Only a little more, and then—[*The child crawls out on the tracks as the engine rounds the curve, eight hundred feet away.*]

GALLOWAY: [*Stiffening.*] By God! I believe that's a child on the track! Shake down the sand, will you? It is, as I live. Oh, Jesus! [*He reverses the lever and throws on the air brakes.*]

PETERSON: [*Leaping to the sand box.*] Can't you stop her?

GALLOWAY: [*As the engine grinds and clanks, a frozen grip on the throttle.*] No, by God! It's *too* late!! [*The engine strikes.*]

THE SHADOW: [*Tossing the blue ball in the air.*] There, my sweet, it is yours! [*The ball falls into the child's hands.*]

MRS. DELAVAN: [*Hearing the whistle and shaking off her dreams.*] The express! The baby! Good gracious! Where is it? [*She runs to the door, the gate, the street.*] Eddie! Eddie! Where is he, anyway? [*She notes the train grinding to a stop at the corner and runs in that direction. A cold trembling seizes upon her.*]

GALLOWAY: [*Holding the air brake in a cutting grip, his face drawn and yellow.*] I saw its face! I saw its face! I tell you! A beautiful child! I can never forgive myself for this. Just a little baby, too. Not more than two or three years old. [*He drops down as the train stops and runs back—the conductor, trainmen and passengers join. A large crowd, gesticulating and exclaiming, gathers.*]

A SCORE OF PASSENGERS: How dreadful! How terrible! What a pity! [*Two women faint.*]

GALLOWAY: [*Explaining.*] I didn't see it until I was right on it. I have three little ones of my own.

MRS. DELAVAN: [*Frantically making her way forward and falling on her knees.*] My Eddie! My Eddie! [*She screams hysterically and bends over.*]

THE SHADOW: [*Appearing to the bereft mother as she weeps over the broken body.*] It is here, it is here, don't you see! [*The baby, holding the blue sphere, appears to the mother's eyes. It smiles.*]

THE CONDUCTOR: [*To a passenger, as the train moves slowly and then a little faster.*] Well, it's a God's blessing if a child had to be killed it was a deformed one, anyway.

THE PASSENGER: You're right there.

GALLOWAY: [*A heavy, weary look on his face.*] And I thought I was looking! The first child I ever killed in my fifteen years!

## CURTAIN

# LAUGHING GAS

## CHARACTERS

JASON JAMES VATABEEL, *an eminent physician.*
FENWAY BAIL, *a celebrated surgeon.*
ARTHUR GAILEY, *house physician of the Michael Slade Memorial Hospital.*
SLASON TUFTS, *his assistant.*
FRANKLIN DRYDEN, *an anesthetist.*
DEMYAPHON [*nitrous oxide*], *an element of chemistry.*
ALCEPHORAN, *a power of physics.*
    *Shadows and voices of the first, second, third and fourth planes. Nurses and internes of the Michael Slade Memorial Hospital. The Rhythm of the Universe.*

## SCENE

*The operating-room of the Michael Slade Memorial Hospital, a glistening chamber of white porcelain and white tile. Nickel operating table in the foreground. Racks of surgical instruments and supplies to either side. A strong, even light from the north French windows. Attendants in white bustling about preparatory to an operation. Enter* FENWAY BAIL, *an eminent surgeon, and* JASON JAMES VATABEEL, *his friend, a celebrated physician. They are followed by* ARTHUR GAILEY, *chief house physician;* SLASON TUFTS, *his assistant;* FRANKLIN DRYDEN, *the anesthetist; and two nurses.*

BAIL: [*A cool, sallow-faced, collected man of perhaps fifty-five, wise and incisive.*] Well, Jason, here you are, a victim of surgery after all!

VATABEEL: [*Tall, gaunt, all of fifty-eight, very distinguished, a little pale from recent suffering, a bandage about his neck, beginning to loosen his shirt in front.*] The last time I took ether I had a very strange experience or dream, one of the best of the etheric variety, I fancy. I am wondering whether it will repeat itself today.

BAIL: [*Examining a case of instruments, and busy with asides to* GAILEY *and others.*] I was thinking of using nitrous oxide, unless you would prefer ether. It seems to me a little too much for a minor operation. I doubt whether I shall be four or five minutes in all. Just as you say, however.

VATABEEL: [*With a dry, medical smile.*] Far be it from me to demand ether. I dislike the stuff intensely. [*He begins to take off his coat and waistcoat and adjusts an aseptic apron.*]

BAIL: [*To* GAILEY.] I shall want a retractor, clamps and thumb forceps. Are all the different ligatures here? Ah, yes, I see. [*To* VATABEEL.] Now, Doctor, if you will just make yourself comfortable. [*He indicates the operating table.*]

VATABEEL: [*Opening the neck of his undershirt and sitting down on the edge of the operating table.*] I never imagined a small tumor could be so troublesome. [*To* BAIL.] This is where Greek meets Greek, isn't it?

BAIL: [*When* GAILEY *has unfastened the bandage around* VATABEEL'S *neck, pressing the tumor lightly with his forefinger.*] But not bearing gifts, unfortunately—at least, not pleasant ones. This seems to be doing very well; no inflammation.

VATABEEL: [*Stretching himself comfortably, with, however, a sense of impending disaster or the possibility of it.*] At least this is the end of my bother with it. [*The gas tank is wheeled forward, the breathing cone adjusted.*]

DRYDEN: [*Taking his place at the doctor-patient's head.*] Now, Doctor, if you please. We are only using one-fourth strength to begin with. And don't forget the forefinger.

VATABEEL: [*Beginning to inhale and thinking of the mysteries of medicine and surgery and gases—to himself.*] Ah, yes, the forefinger. I must keep that going, or try to, until the gas overpowers me and I can no longer do it. When it drops of its own accord they will know I am unconscious. Marvelous progress medicine has made in these last few years! It hasn't been ten years since we had to administer ether and gas full strength because we didn't know how to dilute them. And there weren't any anesthetists. [*He begins to crook his finger.*]

DRYDEN: [*One finger on* VATABEEL'S *pulse, the other on the siphon regulator.*] That's very nice, Doctor, excellent. Breathe very deeply, please—as deep as possible.

VATABEEL: [*Continuing his thoughts, but taking a deep, full breath.*] How self-contained and executive these young beginners are—just as I was in my day! Thus the control of the world passes from generation to generation. [*His face and ears begin to tingle. The fumes of the gas reach his brain. A warm, delightful stupor overcomes him. He imagines he is moving his forefinger, but he is not.*]

GAILEY: [*Noting the change.*] Very full breath, Doctor, if you please. Keep the finger moving as long as you are conscious. [*The finger moves feebly once or twice; then ceases. The arms and legs become inert.*]

THE RHYTHM OF THE UNIVERSE: Om! Om! Om! Om! Om! Om! Om! Om! Om! Om! Om! Om! Om! Om! Om! Om! Om!

VATABEEL: [*Functioning through the spirit only, conscious of tremendous speed, tremendous space, and figures gathered around him in the gloom.*] Strange! Wonderful! Astounding! This is the same place I was in when I was operated on before. These are the same people. I hear voices. A most impressive company! [*The figures begin to converse.*] This is immensity—all space—that surrounds me. I am not alive, really, and yet I am. Am I so important as this? How dark, and yet how strangely light! [*Feels a sense of great heaviness and great speed.*] This operating table is moving like lightning! Who are these people about me, not Bail or Gailey? [*He thinks to see, but cannot.*] This is something else. I wonder if I shall come out of this! Oh, the terror! I really don't want to die! I can't! There are so many things I want to do. People *do* die under the influence of gas. [*The arc of his flight bisects the first of a series of astral planes.*]

ALCEPHORAN: [*A power of physics without form or substance, generating and superimposing ideas without let or hindrance. They come without word or form and take possession as a mood and as understanding without thought.*] Deep, deep and involute are the ways and the substance of things. Oh, endless reaches! Oh, endless order! Oh, endless disorder! Death without life! Life without death! A sinking! A rising! An endless sinking! An endless rising!

THE RHYTHM OF THE UNIVERSE: Om! Om! Om! Om! Om! Om!

BAIL: [*Turning from the examination of instruments and examining the eyes of* VATABEEL, *turning the lids up; to himself.*] A remarkable man, very. Such sacrifices for his profession! How persistently he has scorned money. Great, and poor—that is my idea of a physician. [*To* DRYDEN.] How is he now, Doctor?

DRYDEN: [*Who is holding* VATABEEL'S *left wrist.*] Very good, I think. [*He looks at* GAILEY *for confirmation.*] His pulse is one hundred and ten. His blood pressure seventy.

GAILEY: He is quite under.

BAIL: [*Lifting an arm and dropping it.*] Excellent! [*To* GAILEY *and* TUFTS.] Turn him on his right side, please. The scalpel and the retractor, please. [*He takes up a scalpel and makes an incision one and one-half inches long by one-half inch deep.* TUFTS *sponges the blood.*]

VATABEEL: [*An inert mass carried in the line of the earth's arc and becoming conscious of it, but unconscious of pain.*] Oh, wonderful, wonderful! They are talking! It is light! It is dark! What is it that they are saying? This rhythmic beat is so strange! [*The arc of the earth bisects a second plane.*]

THE RHYTHM OF THE UNIVERSE: Om! Om! Om! Om! Om! Om! Om! Om! Om! Om! Om! Om! Om! Om! Om! Om! Om!

FIRST SHADOW: [*Of the second astral plane; a tall, grave man, seemingly with heavy dark whiskers and hair and deep blue eyes, surveying* VATABEEL'S *body as it speeds onward and he with it.*] This man is of the greatest import, scientifically speaking, to his day. His trouble relates to Valerian, an element inimical to him. It is more serious than he thinks. It may be that he will not live. It may be that Valerian is unalterably opposed to him. [*The voice becomes confused with other voices. Shadows gather about as though in conference. The operating table sweeps on at limitless speed.*]

THE RHYTHM OF THE UNIVERSE: Om! Om! Om! Om!

SECOND SHADOW: [*Seemingly near; a surgeon in contact with the wound.*] Very serious! Very serious! It lies closer to the large artery than they think. In fact, it surrounds it. A separating shield may help. This man should not be permitted to end yet. He is of great import to life. [*Other figures gather about in the gloom and confer. The shadow increases. The voices cease.*]

ALCEPHORAN: No high, no low! Now low, no high! Time without measure, measure without time. A rising, a sinking! An endless rising, and an endless sinking!

VATABEEL: [*Experiencing a vast depression as of endless space and unutterable loneliness.*] Ah!!!

THE RHYTHM OF THE UNIVERSE: Om! Om! Om! Om!

[*The earth sweeps onward in its arc, bisecting a third plane.*]

BAIL: [*Inserting a surgical spoon and scraping out the wound.*] This thing is somewhat more serious than I thought. I believe the tumor surrounds the large artery. It has ramifications I hadn't thought were here. [*To* GAILEY *and one of the Nurses, bending over.*] Here are two side pockets to the left and one just below. And another! We'll have to tie up some of these veins before I can go any farther. This artery is abnormally near the surface, to begin with. How is his pulse? [*He talks as he works, holding a bit of tissue up to the light, catching vein ends with hemostats, while* GAILEY *ties the knots with silk thread and the Nurses pass thread and sponges.*]

DRYDEN: [*In charge of the tank and feeding cone.*] One hundred and ten.

BAIL: [*To himself.*] Excellent.

VATABEEL: [*Sensing the line of the arc of his flight to be upward as yet.*] Strange, I feel so comfortable, yet so helpless—Jason James Vatabeel, physician extraordinary, scientist. Of so much importance. Will I live? Will I die? Life is so treacherous, so sad!

FIRST SHADOW: [*Central figure of a new group and a surgeon—as the operating table rushes into a new realm.*] Difficult! Difficult! This man is in a very serious condition—much more serious than he imagines. The envy of elements! His services to life are in great danger. I am not sure that he can return to the world. [*He shakes his head with grave, oppressive solemnity while the other shadows seem to listen and articulate.*]

THE RHYTHM OF THE UNIVERSE: Om! Om! Om! Om! Om! Om! Om! Om!

ALCEPHORAN: Deep below deep! High above high! No high! No low! Space beyond space! Singleness without unity! Unity without singleness!

VATABEEL: [*Awed and disturbed by the rush and confusion.*] Spirits of the first order of earthly council. This mystery of living, how I have pondered it! Vast orders and powers of which I know nothing. The terror of the after life—what may it be—Death? Annihilation? No continuance?— Forever and ever? And in life itself—the mystery of the blood, of articulated bones, of organized society. Poverty, waste, hunger, pain, wealth, sickness, health—I have tried to think there was some good in what I've done. Vanity, hate, love, greed, patience, generosity. My fame is so wide, I know so little. [*He sighs deeply.*] Ah!

GAILEY: [*Noting the tendency toward greater vitality, and so toward consciousness.*] A little more gas, perhaps. This cutting is affecting him.

DRYDEN: [*Administering more.*] I think so.

BAIL: [*Gouging at a second sac.*] This is apt to shake him a little. Perhaps ether would have been better, after all. It is going to take longer than I thought. How is your oxygen? [*He is thinking of how much gas will have to be administered and how much oxygen may be required to restore the patient.*]

DRYDEN: [*Who has received his supply from the institution.*] All right, I think. [*He tries it. The examination proves that it is dangerously low. To* WILLIAMS, *his assistant.*] See if you can find another tank. [BAIL *frowns slightly, unconsciously irritated by the unpreparedness.*]

SECOND SHADOW: [*Of the second group—a stern, almost invisible figure.*] I perceive near the cardiac region a tendency to weakness which is affected by gas. His condition is serious. Powers inimical and above us are at this moment producing error. This man is a powerful thinker and original investigator. Of him much might be expected.

[*The operating table sweeps on.* THE RHYTHM OF THE UNIVERSE *asserts itself.*]

VATABEEL: [*In vast depression, lying as under an immense, suffocating weight.*] Precarious! Precarious! And I do not want to die. I have so much to live for, so much fame to seek, so much to do. [*He sighs again.*]

DEMYAPHON: [*Nitrous oxide, also with the power of generating and superimposing huge ideas without let or hindrance, the capacity of the individual permitting. They come without word or form, taking possession as a mood or as understanding without thought.*] So life is to be studied, and what for? Your little experiments! What do they teach you? You seek to find out, to know!

THE RHYTHM OF THE UNIVERSE: Om! Om! Om! Om!

ALCEPHORAN: [*At an angle to the waves of* DEMYAPHON.] Vast! Vast! Vast! Measure without time—time without measure!

DRYDEN: [*Noting* VATABEEL'S *pulse to be greatly depressed and shutting off the gas, at the same time turning on the remaining oxygen.*] My assistant is long about that oxygen. See if you can find him, Miss Karns. [*A nurse departs hurriedly.*]

BAIL: [*Realizing that he has a much more treacherous situation at hand than he had imagined and anxious for the security of his patient; to* DRYDEN.] Don't let him get too low, Doctor. It is these extra pockets. I shall be done shortly. [*He hastens his efforts.*]

DRYDEN: [*Becoming disturbed at the delay of the oxygen, and lifting an eyelid to observe the condition of the patient's eyes.*] Hm! I don't like the look of that. [*Aloud.*] Chafe his feet, Miss Hale. You had better move his arm up and down. [*The oxygen gives out.*] I don't understand this oxygen business.

MISS KARNS: [*Returning.*] They have allowed the storeroom on this floor to run out. He has gone to the basement in the next building.

DRYDEN: [*Snapping his teeth.*] Run and tell him to hurry—please. I am all out. [*She departs.*]

DEMYAPHON: [*Appearing only as thoughts placed in the dreamer's mind.*] There is a solution, but you will never be able to guess it. It is ages beyond a growth, which, when it is passed, you will be unable to remember. Aeons upon aeons, worlds upon worlds. Far and above the mysteries here and below there are other mysteries—deep, deep. You puzzle over the phenomena of man. In a vain, critical, cynical ambitious way you dream. It will all be wiped out and forgotten. To that which you seek there is no solution. A tool, a machine, you spin and spin on a given course through new worlds and old. Vain, vain! For you there is no great end. [*A sense of ruthless indifference, inutility, futility, overcomes the spirit of* VATABEEL.]

THE RHYTHM OF THE UNIVERSE: Om! Om! Om! Om!

ALCEPHORAN: Behind, before, beneath, above, presence without reality—reality without presence.

FIRST SHADOW: [*Of a third group, vague and yet clear, young, experimental, curious, indifferent, obviously operating as a surgeon in charge.*] We shall soon be done with this now. He bleeds a lot, doesn't he? A bony old duffer! A ligature, please. A hemostat. I don't see why I should have been given this to do. They say he is needed. [*He seems to bend over. Other faces are near.*]

SECOND SHADOW: [*Seemingly operating in charge of gas and nose cone.*] It looks as though this gas might prove too much, Doctor. His pulse is a little feeble.

FIRST SHADOW: [*Indifferently.*] That can't be. We are two periods this side the danger mark on this plane. We can leave him until he reaches the next one. He's safe enough.

[*The operating table, like a bier, rushes on. The shadows recede. Once more darkness and space, and a sense of rigidity and tomb-like confinement.*]

DRYDEN: [*Anxiously.*] Will you please go and see what's keeping them, Miss Hale? He can't stand this much longer. His pulse is one hundred and forty now. [MISS HALE *dashes from the room.* BAIL, *conscious of the lapse of oxygen gas, increases his efforts to clean and close the wound.*]

THE RHYTHM OF THE UNIVERSE: Om! Om! Om! Om!

DEMYAPHON: [*Continuing.*] So complicated that even the littlest things concerning man you cannot suspect. You think of forces as immense, silent, conglomerate, without thought, humor or individuality. I am a force without dimension or form, yet I am an individuality, and I smile. [*A sense of something—vast and formless—smiling cynically comes over* VATABEEL, *though he cannot conceive how. He is conscious of a desire to smile also, though in a hopelessly mechanical way.*] I am laughing gas, for one thing. You will laugh with me, because of me, shortly. You will not be able to help yourself. You are a mere machine run by forces which you cannot understand. This life that you seek—you may have it on condition, by a condition. You will find out what that is a little later, yet you will not know for certain.

THE RHYTHM OF THE UNIVERSE: Om! Om! Om! Om!

FIRST SHADOW: [*Of a fourth group—a young doctor—material, much more material than the last.*] A little Valerian, please. Some iodine. Doing very well, don't you think, Doctor?

SECOND SHADOW: [*In charge of gas and feeder cone.*] I am not so sure, Doctor. You will have to hurry. He isn't very strong. He should have been taken care of on that last plane. His eyelids—

FIRST SHADOW: [*Working briskly but indifferently.*] Nonsense! That can't be. He's one point this side the danger mark on this plane. No hurry. He'll do well enough.

THE RHYTHM OF THE UNIVERSE: Om! Om! Om! Om!

THIRD SHADOW: [*A nurse suggestive of mild materiality, bending over.*] He's sinking, Doctor, I tell you. He can't go much longer. Look at his hands! Look them! He ought to be hurried to the earth plane.

[*The bier rushes on into space. The voices fade and cease.*]

THE RHYTHM OF THE UNIVERSE: [*Resuming.*] Om! Om! Om! Om! Om! Om! Om! Om!

ALCEPHORAN: A rising, a sinking! An endless rising! An endless sinking! Outward without inward—inward without outward. . . .

DEMYAPHON: Material planes that recede—each one more material than the other, as you sink to your own. Spirits almost more material than yourself. Because of the points spoken of as in your favor, you think you will regain life. You do not know that they are standards set by you in previous experiences, aeons apart. To live you will have to attain a new one now.

VATABEEL: Ah!

DEMYAPHON: Round and round, operation upon operation, world upon world, hither and yon, so you come and go. The same difficulty, the same operation, ages and worlds apart. Your whole life repeated detail by detail except for slight changes. Now if you live you must make an effort or die. [*The gas smiles.*]

THE RHYTHM OF THE UNIVERSE: Om! Om! Om! Om!

DRYDEN: [*To* GAILEY.] He can't get back, Doctor, unless we get the oxygen here in thirty seconds. This tank is run out. His condition is desperate. [*He does the nurse's work, chafing one of* VATABEEL'S *hands. To himself.*] If he does, it will be the most wonderful case I ever heard of. A new standard, by George. [*He wipes perspiration from his brow.*]

VATABEEL: [*Struggling desperately to assist himself to live.*] A thing of the spirit, this, plainly. I suppose I am a test but how futile so to be. Round and round and round, an endless, pointless existence. Yet I cannot help myself. I must live. I must try. I do not want to die. [*He makes a great effort, concentrating his strength on the thought of life.*] Oh how ruthless and indifferent it all is. Think of our being mere machines to be used by others! [*He struggles again without physically stirring.*]

MISS KARNS AND MISS HALE: [*Hurrying in.*] Here it comes now!

THE ASSISTANT: [*In charge of tanks, following.*] I had to go to the second building for the key. The floor man was over there. [*He quickly couples the connections and the oxygen is turned on.*] Fine work, I call that!

DRYDEN: [*Bitterly.*] What a system! And half dozen important operations on today! [*He adjusts the cone and feeds the oxygen, full force.*]

VATABEEL: There is something vastly mysterious about this—horrible! In older worlds I have been, worlds like this. I have done this same thing. Society has done all the things it has done over and over. We manufacture toys—the same toys over and over. Does Life produce its worlds and evolutions the same way? Great God!

DEMYAPHON: [*Cynically.*] The resistance which you are now displaying is in part by reason of your previous efforts and previous successes. You are a victim of the experiences of which you have been made the victim. A patient, a subject, a tool, a method, round and round and round you go, a servant of higher forces, each time seemingly a step further, each time in this way, for the same purpose, the same people, to no known end, over and over.

VATABEEL: Ah!

THE RHYTHM OF THE UNIVERSE: Om! Om! Om! Om!

GAILEY: [*Disturbed by his weakened condition, and uncertain whether or not he can be revived.*] I am afraid that you will have to hurry, Doctor. He is very weak. His pulse is scarcely distinguishable.

BAIL: [*Desperately scraping the last pocket and tying the veins.*] I am not supposed to be handicapped by poor service in this institution. Try to hold him a few moments. [*To* TUFTS.] Sponge! [*To the first nurse.*] Scissors!

FIRST SHADOW: [*Of a fourth group just outside the gates of life, a very material young doctor, whose hands and white uniform are almost luminous.*] Say, there isn't so much to do here—is there? A few stitches. Those veins ought to be clamped, though. [*He works briskly, lightly, with an inconsequential air.*] He'll do all right, don't you think?

SECOND SHADOW: [*At the gas tank.*] Pretty weak, I should say. God, yes! He may hold out, though. They didn't shut off the gas at the last plane—that's a good sign. They usually do if it's serious. He's just at the turning point.

THIRD SHADOW: [*A nurse apparently impressed by the uncertainty of the occasion.*] He's very low, I tell you, Doctor. Look at his nails. You'd better shut off the gas. He's nearly all in! Look at his eyes! He's william, I tell you. He's william. He can't live thirty seconds more.

[*An intense, disturbed rate of vibration indicates crisis. The* SECOND SHADOW *shuts off the gas. The operating table rushes on into darkness.*]

VATABEEL: [*Thinking.*] On, on—and I am now to die—I am dying, unless I can help myself. An endlessly serviceable victim—an avatar! The mystery of life—its gloomy complications! But I don't want to die! I won't die. [*He concentrates vigorously on the thought of life.*]

DEMYAPHON: [*Smiling.*] The points which you established on your previous circuit of this orbit of materiality, and which have been counted in your favor, have now been exhausted. This safety mark, which you have heard frequently mentioned, you yourself established. If you live it will be by setting a new standard—rendering a new service in an old way—over and over and over. Unless you struggle to live—unless you succeed in living—

VARIOUS VOICES: Try, oh try, oh try! You, above all others!

[VATABEEL *senses some vast, generic, undecipherable human need. He wishes to weep, but cannot.*]

THE RHYTHM OF THE UNIVERSE: Om! Om! Om! Om!

[*A sense of derision, of indifference, of universal terror and futility, fills* VATABEEL. *Suffocating, he tries to move.*]

ALCEPHORAN: Deep below deep! High above high! No beginning, no end! No end—no beginning!

VATABEEL: [*Terrified and yet seemingly helpless.*] The dark! The dark! The ultimate dark! Plane upon plane! Aeon upon aeon! To do over and over! Or annihilation! Why—oh—why. But I won't die. I can't. [*He struggles again.*]

DEMYAPHON: It has no meaning! Over and over! Round and round! The orbit of which you are a part brings you back and back again and again in non-understanding. [*The thought seems to become rhythmic and painful.*]

VATABEEL: [*Struggling.*] Am I really to die! My God! What if I do go round and round! I am a man! Life is sweet, intense, perfect! If I do go round and round, what of it? Beyond this, what? Nothing! I serve! [*He stirs. His spirit struggles with materiality. The vital spark is rekindled within the inert frame. With a gigantic effort, it re-establishes itself and resumes control and respiration. The effort to inhale, feeble at the surface of materiality, is immense.*]

DRYDEN: [*Working the one free arm as vigorously as possible, while* MISS HALE *and* MISS KARNS *chafe his hands and feet.*] There, he has caught it. Chafe his arms, Miss Karns. I am not sure that we can bring him round even yet. His vitality is amazing. I don't understand it at all. His heart was all right, though—extra strong.

BAIL: I shall have to have a few more seconds. I have three stitches to take. You may let him come out if you wish. This is the last time I shall use gas—here. I have had trouble with it before. [*He tries to think where.*]

DEMYAPHON: [*To* VATABEEL.] And the humor of it is that it is without rhyme or reason. Over and over! Aeon after aeon! What you do now, you will do again. And there is no explanation. You are so eager to live—to do it again. Do you not see the humor of that?

[*With sardonic intent the rate of vibration which is laughter is set up in* VATABEEL'S *body. Even as he struggles to breathe and regain his material state, he realizes that the impulse, a part of something vast, unearthly, mechanical, wavelike, is sweeping him into its rate. Weak from loss of blood—in danger of rupturing the large artery in the centre of the wound, close to the surface, he begins to swell with pent-up laughter. A dry, hard, sardonic desire to shout overcomes him, although he is yet unable to move.*]

DRYDEN: [*To* GAILEY, *noting the customary action of nitrous oxide as the patient approaches consciousness, and uncertain what to do.*] He is coming to. I'm a little afraid to use more gas in his present condition, Doctor. If he laughs too hard—!!

BAIL: [*Irritably.*] Can you keep him under ten more seconds? I have one more stitch to take. [*He takes one.*]

DRYDEN: I think he'll last that long, Doctor, anyhow. [*Nurses and assistants seek to hold* VATABEEL *rigid in order that the operation may not be disturbed.*]

DEMYAPHON: And I told you you would laugh. You will eventually forget why, but you will shout and shout and shout and see no reason. I am the reason. I am the master of your personality. I am Demyaphon—Laughing Gas. Shout! Shout! Shout! [*It leaves him in a waking condition.*]

VATABEEL: [*As* BAIL *takes the last stitch and* GAILEY *begins the bandaging of his neck; seemingly bursting into consciousness, the wound still unbandaged, the pain of the needle still fresh.*]
        Oh, ho! ho! ho!
        Oh, ha! ha! ha!

Oh, ho! ho! ho!
Oh, ha! ha! ha!
Oh, ho! ho! ho!

GAILEY: [*Holding an arm to calm him, uncertain as to whether he is mentally clear or not—as yet.*] Something very funny, Doctor?

BAIL: [*Accustomed to the effects of laughing gas, but disturbed by his patient's condition—to* GAILEY.] Make those bandages very tight. I am afraid of that wound. It is too bad we couldn't have kept him under longer. He's very close to death even yet. I scarcely had time to take those stitches properly. And, of course, the effects of the gas have to be the very worst possible. [*He shrugs his shoulders.*]

VATABEEL: [*Still shaken by the rate of vibration set up in him, his mouth open, his face a mask of sardonic inanity.*]
Oh, ho! ho! ho!—oh, ha! ha! ha!
Oh, ho! ho! ho!—oh, ha! ha! ha!
Oh, ho! ho! ho!—oh, ha! ha! ha!
I see it all, now! Oh, what a joke! Oh, what a trick! Over and over! And I can't help myself! Oh, ho! ho! ho! Oh, ha! ha! ha! And the very laughing compulsory! vibratory! a universal scheme of laughing! Oh, ho! ho! ho! Ah, ha! ha! ha! I have the answer! I see the trick! The folly of medicine! The folly of life! Oh, ho! ho! ho! Oh, ha! ha! ha! Oh, ho! ho! ho! Oh, ha! ha! ha! What fools and tools we are! What pawns! What numbskulls! Oh, ho! ho! ho! Ah, ha! ha! ha! [*His face has a sickly flatness, the while he glares with half-glazed eyes, and shakes his head.*]

GAILEY: I never saw gas act more vigorously. Did you, Doctor?

BAIL: [*Annoyed by the incident.*] I never did. [*Taking his friend's arm.*] Come, Jason, you're all right now! Get over this! Just laughing gas, you know. It's all over. You have a serious cut in your neck. [*He presses his arm fondly.*] You're just laughing because of the gas.

VATABEEL: [*Wearily—with the sense of immense futility still holding him.*] Oh, ho! ho! ho! Oh, yes, yes, yes. Just laughing gas! And that's why I laugh! Oh, ho! ho! ho! Ah, ha! ha! ha! I don't wonder it laughs! I would too! You would if you knew! The mystery! The cruelty! The folly! Oh, ho! ho! ho! Oh, ha! ha! ha! [*He stares and glares the while his friends and hearers view him with kindly, condescending tolerance mingled with a touch of awe and amazement.*]

BAIL: [*Genially.*] Just the same, it's all over, Jason. Come on!

VATABEEL: [*Shaking himself and beginning to recover his natural poise and reserve.*] And was it only the gas, then? That is very strange: I thought—I thought—I wonder? I wonder—? [*His mouth remains open.*]

DRYDEN: [*His calmness restored.*] It seems odd to see *him* laughing like that.

GAILEY: The fumes are still in his head. He'll be all right now, though. That was a pretty close shave. I thought we had lost him. There'll be a new storekeeper here tomorrow, if I have my way.

THE SECOND ASSISTANT: I never saw Dr. Bail so irritated. He'll hold this against us.

[*The various doctors and nurses and assistants go about their duties.* BAIL *slowly leads* VATABEEL *to his automobile.* VATABEEL'S *face retains a look of deep, amazed abstraction.*]

# CURTAIN

# IN THE DARK

## CHARACTERS

JOHN REPISO, *a fruit-peddler.*
BRADY,
BOCOCK,
DINGWALTER,
TRAIN,
KELLY, } *Officers.*
SYPHAX,
EMMETT,
BONES,
JACOB WOITEZEK, *upholsterer.*
GEORGE STEPHANIK, *shoe-dealer.*
FRUIT DEALER.
OLD WOMAN.
THE GHOST WITH RED EYES.
THE WRAITH.
      *Spirits, Passers-by, Voices of Various Dogs.*

## SCENE

*Kerry Patch, adjoining the car-yards, at one in the morning. Long, dimly lighted streets, with here and there a gas lamp flaring in the wind. On the fourth floor of Kerrigan's flats—a detached, tatterdemalion row of buildings facing Eleventh Avenue—a dim light behind a tightly drawn curtain is suddenly put out.*

FIRST SPIRIT: [*Sweeping by.*] A murder! A murder!

CALLAHAN'S GRAY BULL: [*In the next block north.*] Wow! Wow! Wow! Gr-r-r—

SECOND SPIRIT: [*Sweeping by.*] A murder! A murder!

MOINYHAN'S HOUND: [*Three blocks east.*] Yow-wee! Yow-wee! Yow-wee!—ee!—ee! [*Subsiding with a whine.*]

THIRD SPIRIT: [*Sweeping by.*] A murder! A murder! A murder!

KORNBLUM'S GREAT DANE: [*From the back yard of the grocery store, three blocks south.*] Ow-wow! Ow-wow! Ow-wow! Yoof! Yoof! Yoof! Ur!

A DOZEN DOGS: [*In all directions, taking up the chorus.*] Ow-wee! Ow-wee! Yoof! Yoof! Ur! Ur! Ooo! Ooo! Ooo!

OFFICER BRADY: [*Stepping out of the family entrance of Dryheisen's Café, three blocks south, and wiping his mouth with the back of his hand.*] 'Tis a strange noise these dogs do be makin'. What's scratchin' them?

FIRST SPIRIT: [*Sweeping by.*] A murder! A murder!

OFFICER BRADY: [*Suffering an odd tremor of the flesh and adjusting his belt and revolver. He scratches his ear meditatively.*] A windy night.

JOHN REPISO: [*Coming down the back stairs of Kerrigan's flats in the dark, the wraith of a new spirit before him, a vile ghost with red eyes behind. Over his shoulder a thick, brown bundle. He opens the door carefully and peers out.*]

Alla right so far. Musta no maka da noise. [*Peers out still further, sees a home-hurrying plumber and retreats.*] Jesu! Santa Maria! San Tomo! [*He wipes his brow with one grimy finger and listens until the steps die away in the distance.*]

THE GHOST WITH RED EYES: [*From behind.*] Fine! Fine! Ah, life! Life! The smell of new blood! Fine!

THE WRAITH: [*Before.*] Ah, me! Ah, me! Am I really dead? Where am I? I do not want to die!

A SCORE OF SPIRITS: [*Rushing from street to street.*] A murder! A murder! Awake! Awake! [*The dogs begin to howl as before.*]

JACOB WOITEZEK: [*Upholsterer, a victim of insomnia and Bright's disease, opening his window on the third floor opposite and leaning out.*] Ach, I sleep so badly. I think I am going to die. What is all the noise? The dogs! They never sleep! Why do they howl?

A SPIRIT: [*Sweeping by.*] A murder! A murder! Awake! Awake!

WOITEZEK: [*A tremor passes down his spine.*] Dark! And empty! The streets are very bare. When the dogs howl they say someone is dead. I must go back or I will take more cold in my back. How they howl! [*He rubs his flabby, sickly face, looks up and down the long, dim street, and puts his hand on the window-frame to pull it down.*]

OFFICER BRADY: [*Strolling north, twirling his night-stick nonchalantly.*] 'Tis a great racket they make. Ye'd think they'ud lost their last fren'. Me gran'mother used to belave that whin dogs howled someone was dyin'. That was in the country. 'Tis different in the big cities, no doubt. [*He thumbs his belt and looks inquiringly around.*]

FIVE SPIRITS: [*Circling around him in a wreath.*] A murder! A murder! A murder! Awake! Awake! Watch! Wake!

[*He feels the same tremor as before, and peers into every entry and storefront.*]

REPISO: [*Still waiting, but hearing no sound.*] No can wait. They no can tell without the head. One, two, three block. Then cars! Then alla right! [*He steps out.*]

THE GHOST WITH RED EYES: Courage! Well done! Fine! Fine! Ah! Life is fine! [*It keeps step behind.*]

THE WRAITH: [*Drifting on before.*] Perhaps I am not dead. I must stay near. I do not want to die!

CHORUS OF SPIRITS: [*Clouding the air overhead.*] A murder! A murder! Vengeance! Come one! Come all! Vengeance!

WOITEZEK: [*At his window.*] There comes a man with a bundle at this hour in the morning. I wonder what is in it? He keeps close to that wall.

A SPIRIT: [*Sweeping by.*] A murder! A murder!

GEORGE STEPHANIK: [*A shoe-dealer, coming home from a lodge meeting.*] That was a fine business I did this afternoon. Fourteen pairs in three hours. It is because of the cold weather. If I could do as well as that every day I would open a bigger store in a little while. In a better neighborhood, too. This is nothing—very bad, trash. But why do the dogs howl so?

[*There is continued yowling in near and far places.*]

THREE SPIRITS: [*Swirling about him.*] A murder! A murder! Watch! Behold!

STEPHANIK: [*Hunching his shoulders, drawing his coat tight, and looking about him.*] I don't like these dark neighborhoods. I never did. They are dangerous. Is that a man with a bag in the next block? He is going into Santangelo's, or the next place to it. But Santangelo is asleep. No, the man is just stopping there. What can he be carrying in a bag at this hour of the night?

THE THREE SPIRITS: [*Still swirling in a circle above him.*] A murder! A murder! Awake! Watch!

STEPHANIK: [*Bustling on.*] It is half-past one. It will be hard to get up at seven in the morning. I do not like these late hours.

REPISO: [*Crowding into a dark doorway, waiting for the stranger to pass, and adjusting the bundle on his back.*] Jesu! Santa Maria! San Tomo! One—two block more. Then no can see. Railroad track. No can tell. Come back same as any man. [*He adjusts the bundle and grasps the handle of a knife in his shirt-front.*]

STEPHANIK: [*Passing by on the other side of the street and peering over.*] There he is—someone waiting there. It is too dark to see. Someone with a bundle. There ought to be an officer hereabouts. They never do their duty, these police. You never can find one when you want one.

THE CLOUD OF SPIRITS: [*Over Santangelo's door.*] A murder! A murder! Come! Come!

THE THREE SPIRITS: [*Circling over* STEPHANIK'S *head.*] A murder! A murder! Come! See!

STEPHANIK: [*Unreasonably disturbed.*] It is strange—that man! Why should he hide here? He may be trying to break into Santangelo's store! And these dogs! They make me feel creepy! If I could see an officer now! [*He hurries on, looking right and left, for he is a great coward.*]

OFFICER BRADY: [*Two blocks away, twirling his stick.*] 'Tis the divil's own night for dogs! I never heard the like! [*He peers in at other doorways.*]

STEPHANIK: [*Drawing nearer on the other side of the street, and crossing over to him.*] Officer! I saw a man in the next block, there, on this side of the street, hiding in a doorway. He had a bundle over his shoulder. It looked to me as if he had broken in somewhere or was going to. He didn't want me to see him. There are so many thieves around I thought you might want to see him. He is in Santangelo's doorway.

OFFICER BRADY: [*Stiffening with a sense of duty and adventure.*] In the next block, you say? I'll have a look at him. Come along if you like.

[*Clouds of spirits wheel overhead, crying "A murder! A murder!"*]

REPISO: [*Peering out.*] Alla gone! Two more block! No more can tell without the head! Jesu! I no meanta he die. [*He wipes his brow and starts.*]

THE GHOST WITH RED EYES: Fine! Fine! Two more blocks! The smell of new blood! Ah! Ah! [*It keeps step behind.*]

THE WRAITH: [*Going before.*] Am I alive? Am I dead? I must stay near. I do not want to die!

THE SPIRITS: [*Circling above in a great cloud.*] A murder! A murder! Come one, come all!

[*The dogs begin to howl again.*]

OFFICER BRADY: [*Sighting the figure in the distance.*] There he goes now. That's the man ye mean, no doubt. Well, we'll have a look at what he has in that bag. Come, now. [*He sharpens his pace.*]

THE GHOST WITH RED EYES: Hurry! Hurry! Ah, a good deed. Good life! Good life! Would that I were alive!

THE SPIRITS: A murder! A murder!

REPISO: [*Hearing steps and looking about.*] Ah, Jesu! Ah, San Tomo! [*He begins to run.*]

OFFICER BRADY: [*Beginning to run, also, two blocks behind.*] Come, now! None o' that! [*He raps on the sidewalk with his night-stick, then extracts his police-whistle and blows a blast.*]

[WOITEZEK, *who has only just closed his window, opens it. Other windows fly open.*]

SPIRITS: [*Sweeping before one and all.*] A murder! A murder!

REPISO: [*Turning into the car-yard.*] Ah, Jesu! Ah, Santa Maria! Gratia Dio! [*He slips between two lines of idle boxcars, dark and sombre, and hurries past ten before he deposits the bag under the trucks of one of them.*] They may not find it yet. The police! That is my terrible luck, that there should be a policeman!

[*He slips under the cars, the while spirits hover overhead, passing through the wood and steel, leaving* THE WRAITH *beside the bag. Outside the whistle of* OFFICER BRADY *is sounding, the while other police-whistles answer from a distance, drawing nearer and nearer.*]

THE WRAITH: [*Hovering over the body.*] Am I dead? Am I dead? I do not want to die!

OFFICER BRADY: [*Turning into the yard.*] We may have a job finding him in here. And the river is just beyond. [*He blows new blasts.*]

OFFICER BOCOCK: [*Running up.*] What's the trouble? What's the trouble?

OFFICER BRADY: A thief, be God! He's just turned in here with a bag. Right through here he went.

OFFICER DINGWALTER: [*Arriving breathless.*] What's the row?

OFFICER BRADY: Wait here and tell the others. A thief has just turned in here with a bag.

[*Other officers arrive. A spirited search begins. The place is surrounded.*]

THE GHOST WITH RED EYES: [*At the heels of* REPISO.] Fine! Fine! Well done! The body smells of blood! Fine!

THE SPIRITS: [*A cloud over each officer.*] A murder! A murder! This way! [*They pass to* REPISO *and then back to the officers. The air is vibrant with their motion.*]

REPISO: [*Stumbling out from the last line of cars at the water's edge, and surveying the retaining wall. The water flows silently below.*] Jesu! No can swim! [*He hears the con-*

*tinued shrieks of many whistles and at the same time discovers a sewer-vent.*] Ah! Gratia Dio! Ah, Santa Maria! Gratia! [*He seeks, via rocks and a projecting beam, to lower himself into it.*]

OFFICER BOCOCK: [*Reaching the water's edge and flashing a bull's-eye out over the wall.*] This is where he would make for first. [*He keeps a cocked revolver poised lightly in his hand.*]

OFFICER DINGWALTER: [*Revolver and bull's-eye in hand.*] I'll look after the other end, George.

OFFICER TRAIN: There's a sewer-vent here somewhere. He may make for that. [*He walks along the wall toward it. A police-boat passes. He calls.*] Shoot a light in here, captain, will you? We think a pigeon may have ducked in here. [*The boat draws near and a powerful ray is flashed.*]

SPIRITS: [*Filling the air like gulls.*] In here! In here! In here!

AN OFFICER: [*On board the boat, detecting* REPISO *crouching low.*] Come out of that. [*Revolvers are drawn. Three men are landed. They return with* REPISO.]

THE GHOST WITH RED EYES: [*Close behind.*] Ah, blood! More blood! Fine! Fine!

OFFICER BRADY: [*Forcing himself to the front.*] Now ye'll be tellin' me what ye did with that bag ye had. Where did ye put it?

ANOTHER OFFICER: [*Shaking him roughly.*] Come, now! Out with it! Where did ye put it?

REPISO: [*Cautiously.*] No spika da Anglais.

OFFICER BRADY: Ye Guinea scut! It's no English, is it? Well, we'll make ye talk somethin' before long. Bring him along, boys. The bag's here, if it ain't in the river. We'll soon be findin' it. Ye say it's not in the sewer there?

AN OFFICER: It's not in the sewer.

[*The air is full of spirits weaving between the body and the searching police. Determined effort is made by the former to transmit knowledge in terms of thought.*]

OFFICER KELLY: [*Of the fifth precinct, throwing a bull's-eye light between the trucks of each car of the second row.*] Hi, now, here's somethin'! [*He reaches under and draws forth the bag.*] This'll be it, I'm thinkin'. [*He takes out a knife, cuts the cord and reveals the wet wrappings of the body.*] Mother of Mary! [*He blows his police-whistle.*]

OFFICER BOCOCK: [*Appearing.*] You've found it, have you?

OFFICER DINGWALTER: This'll be more black-hand work, I'm thinkin'. Well, he'll talk English or somethin' like it before we get through. [*Other officers attend. Spirits, a legion, thread and weave.*]

REPISO: [*Arriving with several officers, the light of various bull's-eyes on his face. To himself, sotto voce.*] Jesu! Santa Maria! I will pretend not to know.

OFFICER BRADY: Here ye are, my fine one. So that's what ye had in the bag? Now will ye speak and tell us where ye brought it from?

OFFICER DINGWALTER: [*His hand on his collar, shaking him.*] Come, now, speak, will you?

REPISO: [*Wet and blanched.*] No spika da Anglais! No understan'!

OFFICER KELLY: [*Outraged by the horror of it.*] We'll spika da Anglais for ye, ye black scut! Ye'll swing for this.

OFFICER SYPHAX: [*Newly arrived on the scene, and edging his way through.*] A murder? Whaddye know about that! Is that the man? Say [*edging closer and peering into* REPISO'S *face*], I think I know this fellow. He used to be hangin' around Kerrigan's flats when I did the day trick there. Where'd ye see him first?

OFFICER DINGWALTER: Brady saw him here in Eleventh Avenue somewhere.

OFFICER BRADY: [*Eagerly.*] Sure, I thought that's where he might a been comin' from when I seen him with the bag. Them flats is full of Eyetalians.

OFFICER BOCOCK: We'd better take him down there then and see what we can find out.

[*The air is still thick with spirits weaving and threading;* THE GHOST WITH RED EYES *standing behind* REPISO, THE WRAITH *over the dead body repeating its vacuous plaint.*]

THE WRAITH: Am I dead? Am I dead?

THE GHOST WITH RED EYES: Blood! More blood!

OFFICER DINGWALTER: [*Officiously.*] That's the idea. Someone ring for an ambulance. Someone ought to stay here and look after this.

OFFICER KELLY: [*Too old to be eager for publicity.*] I'll be lookin' after that. [*The procession starts, with* REPISO *held by* DINGWALTER *and* BOCOCK *and followed by* THE GHOST WITH RED EYES. *In front,* SYPHAX *and* BRADY; *behind, Officers* TRAIN, BONES, EMMETT. *Over the body in the caryards,* THE WRAITH. *Overhead, a legion of spirits. The procession approaches the entrance to Kerrigan's flats.*]

OFFICERS SYPHAX AND BRADY: [*To citizens who have crowded in before.*] Out of the way there! [*They make their way up the stairs to the first landing, followed by* DINGWALTER *and* BOCOCK *with* REPISO *and the others.*]

OFFICER SYPHAX: [*Pounding vigorously on the door.*] Hello! Hello!

[*An Italian fruit dealer puts his head out of the door.*]

THE FRUIT DEALER: [*Recognizing* REPISO *in the hands of the police.*] What's da mat'! What's da mat'?

OFFICER BRADY: [*Irritably.*] Cut that, ye hoythen Guinea! Ye'll soon know what's da mat'. Did yez ever see this man before?

THE FRUIT DEALER: [*Fearing Italian retaliation.*] No un'stan'! No spika da Anglais!

OFFICER SYPHAX: [*Vigorously.*] You lie, you scut! They're all in cahoots. Somebody watch this man until we see about the others.

[OFFICER EMMETT *takes charge of* THE FRUIT DEALER. *They turn to another door.*]

OFFICER BRADY: [*Beating it.*] Hello! Hello! [*He shakes the doorknob. An old woman puts her head out of the door.*]

THE OLD WOMAN: Whatever is the matter?

OFFICER BRADY: Tell me, now, have yez ever seen this man before?

THE OLD WOMAN: [*Unconscious of* REPISO'S *strain and terror.*] Why, yes, that's Mr. Repiso. He's a nice man. Whatever are ye holding him for?

[REPISO *shivers convulsively.*]

OFFICER SYPHAX: [*Facetiously.*] A fine man! Oh, perfectly good! What floor does he live on, old lady?

THE OLD WOMAN: The fourth. I'm very sorry, I'm sure. What's he done?

[REPISO *shivers again. The eyes of the* GHOST *become vaguely luminous.*]

OFFICER BRADY: What *hasn't* he done! Be all the saints! Does he speak English?

THE OLD WOMAN: Sure he speaks English. He always speaks it to me.

REPISO: [*To himself.*] Jesu!

THE GHOST WITH RED EYES: Blood! More blood!

SPIRITS [*Sweeping in clouds through wood and stone.*] Up here! Up here!

OFFICER DINGWALTER: [*To* REPISO.] I thought so. Now maybe you'll talk, Charley. [*They mount the stairs.*]

OFFICER SYPHAX: [*Pounding on the door.*] Hello! Hello! [*No answer.*] Open the door! Hey! Open the door! [*He presses to break it in.*]

OFFICER BRADY: [*To* REPISO.] Is this where yez live? Say!

OFFICER DINGWALTER: You might as well talk. It's all up with you, anyhow. It might do you a little good to be honest.

REPISO: [*Weakly, almost in a fainting condition.*] No can spik. No un'erstan'.

SPIRITS: [*Sweeping in circles.*] In here! In here!

[*The door is broken down with a crash. They enter a tenement kitchen, oilcloth on the floor much worn, the stationary washtubs dirty and filled with junk, the walls painted a dull green and badly smeared. Beyond, a sitting-room badly arranged with cheap red-plush furniture, so worn that it looks as if it had been collected from ash-heaps. In one corner an imitation walnut table upset and the white marble top broken. A chair is piled on a black iron and wire couch. A zinc washtub holds the segments of a man's arms. In one corner of the room lies a roundish bundle. In another, on oilcloth, lies a pair of legs. In the zinc washtub on a newspaper are laid a small saw and a knife. Brooding over it all,* THE WRAITH, *unconscious of duality.*]

OFFICER SYPHAX: [*Sweeping a bull's-eye around, then striking a light.*] Well, I'll be damned! Here's a how-dy-ye-do! Whaddye know about this? He's been tryin to cut him intah bits. Say, you're a wonder, Spaghetti! They'll make a hell of a noise over this. [*He kicks the zinc tub with his foot, proud of his official association with so grim a crime.*]

OFFICER BRADY: [*Interested in the publicity he will get as the original pursuer, yet nauseated and anxious to have done.*] Mother iv Moses! And I thought he was a second-story man! [*He sees the round bundle, suspects what it contains, but refrains from approaching it.*]

THE WRAITH: Am I dead? Am I dead?

THE GHOST WITH RED EYES: Blood! Good blood!

OFFICER DINGWALTER: [*Shaking* REPISO.] Come, me fine man! What've ye got to say to this? Can't ye talk English now a little?

OFFICERS TRAIN AND BOCOCK: [*Crowding close.*] Speak up now! Whadjah kill im for? Hey?

THE GHOST WITH RED EYES: Blood! Good blood!

OFFICER SYPHAX: [*Bringing forward the round bundle.*] Here's somethin' else. [*He unties the rough twine and reveals a gory head, black-haired and curly, with a short black mustache. At sight of the face* REPISO *falls on his knees, uttering a cry and rocking emotionally to and fro.*]

REPISO: [*Frenzied and incoherent, the while the spirits sweep and swirl.*] No meana to kill. No maka da strong word, no maka da first blow! I alla time maka da safe word. He alla time follow me roun'. He my brod. Hata da job! Hata da work! No maka da mon! Alla time beg! Alla time maka da lie! Say he no can find job. Alla time maka da game. No maka da fair game. He cheata da cards. Showa da stiletto—taka da mon—Madre de Dio! No can see, no can hear. He grabba all what I got. [*He raves on incoherently as to the details of the crime, the while the spirits weave and twine.*]

OFFICER DINGWALTER: That's the stuff. Now it's comin' out. Good for you, Italy!

OFFICER BONES: Sure, that's the way. They had a card game. This fellow gets sore and cuts him up. It's always the way with these spaghetti.

OFFICER TRAIN: [*Coming back from the legs.*] Well, it's the chair for him, hey?

OFFICER SYPHAX: Sure; not a ghost of a chance.

[*They ring for an ambulance. The coroner arrives. Officer-surgeons gather up the remains. The second representation of* THE WRAITH *follows them. Spirits fill the air, thinning and disappearing as they lead* REPISO *down the stairs.*]

THE GHOST WITH RED EYES: [*Glowing with a strange lustre.*] Blood! More blood!

## CURTAIN

# THE SPRING RECITAL

## CHARACTERS

WILMUTH TABOR, *an organist.*
AN OLD DOOR-KEEPER.
MRS. PENCE.
MRS. STILLWATER.
TWO LOVERS.
A FAUN.
SIX HAMA-DRYADS.
A CAT.
A BUM.
THE MINISTER OF ST. GILES.
THREE PRIESTS OF ISIS.
A MONK OF THE THEBAID.
    *Troops of Fauns and Nymphs, clouds of Hags and Wastrels, persistences of Fish and Birds and Animals, various living and newly dead Spirits wandering in from the streets.*

## SCENE

*A prosperous First Church in the heart of a great city. Outside the city's principle avenue, along which busses and vehicles of all descriptions are rolling. An idling sense of Spring in the gait and gestures of the pedestrians. Surrounding the church a graveyard, heavily shaded with trees, the branches of which reach to the open windows exhaling soft odours. Over the graves many full blown blossoms, and in the sky a round May moon. In front of the church hangs a small lighted cross, and under it swings the sign, "Organ Recital, 8:30; Wilmuth Tabor, Organist." The doors giving into the church are open. The interior, save for the presence of a caretaker in a chair, is empty. On either side of the pulpit, below a great dark rose window, burns a partially lighted electrolier. In the organ loft, over the street doors, a single light.*

FIRST STREET BOY: [*To a companion, ambling to discover what the world contains, and glancing in as they pass.*] Gee! Who'd wanta go to church on a night like this?

SECOND STREET BOY: I should say! Didja see the old guy wit de whiskers sittin' inside?

FIRST STREET BOY: Sure. A swell job, eh? [*Their attention is attracted by an automobile spinning in the opposite direction, and they pass on.*]

AN OLD LADY: [*To her middle-aged daughter, on whose arm she is leaning . . . sympathetically and reminiscently.*] The dear old First Church! What a pity its parishioners have all moved away. I don't suppose the younger generation cares much for church going anymore. People are so irreligious these days.

THE DAUGHTER: Poor Mr. Tabor. I went to one of his concerts in the winter and there were scarcely forty people there. And he plays so heavenly, too. I don't suppose the average person cares much for organ music. [*They pass with but a glance at the interior.*]

A BELATED SHOE CLERK: [*Hurrying to reach Hagan's Olio Moving Picture & Vaudeville Theatre before the curtain rises, but conscious that he ought to pay some attention to the higher phases of culture—turning to the old door-keeper.*] When does this concert begin?

THE OLD DOOR-KEEPER: [*Heavily.*] Half past eight. [*He glances at the sign hanging over the youth's head.*]

THE BELATED SHOE CLERK: Do they have them every Wednesday night?

THE OLD DOOR-KEEPER: Every Wednesday. [*The* CLERK *departs, and the old man scratches his head.*] They often ask, but they don't come in. [*He shifts to a more comfortable position in his chair.*] I see no use to playin' to five or six people week in and week out all summer long. Still, if they want to do it they have the money. It looks like a good waste of light to me.

[*Enter* MRS. PENCE *and* MRS. STILLWATER, *two neighbors of the immediate vicinity.*]

MRS. PENCE: [*A heavy pasty-faced woman in white lawn—lowering her voice to a religious whisper as they pass through the door.*] Yes, I like to come here now and then. I don't know much about music but the organ is so soothing. We had a parlor organ when I was a little girl and I learned to play on that.

MRS. STILLWATER: [*Short, blonde, and of a romantic turn, though the mother of three grown sons.*] I just think the organ is the loveliest of all instruments. It's so rich and deep. [*They seat themselves in a pew.*] Isn't it dim here? So romantic! I love an old church. I don't suppose people want much light when they hear music. See the moonlight in that window over there. Isn't it lovely?

[*A pair of lovers enter.*]

THE BOY: I've heard of him. He's a well-known organist. I wish he would play a Chopin Nocturne or something of Grieg. I love Grieg.

THE GIRL: Oh, yes, the Solvieg's Lied. Isn't it still here! [*They seat themselves in a remote corner. She squeezes his hand and he returns the pressure.*]

THE ORGANIST: [*A pessimistic musician of fifty, entering and climbing slowly to the organ loft, surveying the empty auditorium gloomily.*] Only four people! [*He turns on the bracket lights, uncovers the keys, and adjusts the sheets of his programme before him. Surveying himself in the mirror, and then examining the opening bars of Bach's Toccata and Fugue in D, he pulls out various stops and looks into the dim, empty auditorium once more.*] What a night! And me playing in this dim, empty church. It's bad enough to be getting along in years and to have no particular following, but this church! All society and wealth away at the seashore and the mountains and me here. Ah, well. [*He sighs.*] "Worse and worse times still succeed the former." [*He sounds a faint tremulo to test the air pressure. Finding all satisfactory, and noting that the hands of his watch stand at eight-thirty, he begins the "Overture to the Magic Flute."*]

[*Enter through an open north window even with the floor of the organ loft, a horned faun, with gay white teeth, grimacing as he comes. He begins pirouetting. He carries a kex on which he attempts to imitate the lovely piping of the overture.*]

THE FAUN: [*Prancing lightly here and there.*] Tra aa ala-lala! Ah, tra-la-la, Ah, tra-la-la! Tra-la-leee! Tra-la-leee! Very excellent! Very nice! [*He grins from ear to ear and spying the church cat, a huge yellow tom who is mousing about, gives a spirited kick in its direction.*] Dancing's the thing! Life is better than death, thin shade that I am!

THE CAT: [*Arching its back and raising its fur.*] Pfhs—s—st! Pfhs—s—st!

[*The FAUN pirouettes nearer, indicating a desire to dance with it, where upon the CAT retreats into a corner under the organ.*]

THE FAUN: Ky-ey-ey! You silly dolt! [*Kicks and spins away.*]

THE ORGANIST: [*Noticing the spit-fire attitude of the* CAT.] He seems to see something. What the deuce is ailing him, now? I wonder whether cats do see anything when they act like that. [*He yields to the seduction of the frail harmony, and closes his eyes.*]

THE BOY: Wonderful! So delicately gay and sad! It's just like flowers blooming in the night, isn't it? [*His sweetheart squeezes his hand and moves closer.*]

[*Enter* SIX HAMA-DRYADS *from the trees without and circle about, wreath-wise under the groined arches of the ceiling. They are a pale, ethereal company, suiting their movements to the melody and its variations.*]

THE SIX HAMA-DRYADS:
    Arch of church or arch of trees,
      Built of stone or built of air,
    Spirits floating on a breeze,
      Dancing gayly anywhere.

    Out of lilac, out of oak,
      Hard by asphodel and rose,
    Never time when music spoke
      But a dryad fled repose.

    Weaving, turning, high and low
      Where the purpled rhythms fall,
      Where the plangent pipings call,
    Round and round and round we go.

THE FAUN: [*Dancing forward and about them.*] I can dance! Let me dance! [*He grins in the face of one.*]

THE HAMA-DRYADS: Go way! Don't bother!

THE FAUN: Oh, don't be so fussy. [*He dances away by himself.*]

THE CAT: [*Prowling under the organ.*] I saw a mouse peeping out of that hole just now. Wait! [*He crouches very low, ready to spring.*]

THE ORGANIST: [*Dreamily.*] This passage always makes me think of moonlight on open fields and the spicy damp breath of dark, dewy wood, and of lilacs blowing over a wall, too. So suitable, but I would rather live than play. [*He sighs.*]

[*A gloomy ghost with hard green eyes enters from the sacristy, and pauses in the dark angle of the wall.*]

THE BUM: [*A barrel house bum a dozen years dead, but still enamored of the earth.*] What's doing here, I wonder? [*He stares.*] A lot of fools dancing. Hm! [*Turns and departs.*]

THE GIRL: Oh, sweetheart, isn't it perfect! [*She lays her head on his shoulder.*]

THE BOY: Darling!

THE CAT: [*Springing.*] There! I almost caught him. [*Peers into the hole.*] Just the same, I know where he is now. [*He strolls off with an air of undefeated skill.*]

THE ORGANIST: [*Missing a note.*] This finale isn't so easy. And I don't like it as well, either. I always stumble in these allegro movements. [*He wipes his brow, improvises a few bars, interpolating also a small portion of the triumphal march from "Aïda."*] This is different. I can do it better.

MRS. STILLWATER: [*Shifting her arm and moving her knee.*] I never like loud music as well as the softer kind. That middle part was beautiful.

MRS. PENCE: Well, I can't say I like loud music, either, but now this—[*He begins upon the Grail motif from "Parsifal."*]

THE SIX HAMA-DRYADS: [*Still circling.*]
Rose of fancy, gold of soul,
Of all fragrance taking toll,
Of all rhythm weaving wiles,
We, the fabric of all smiles.

[*They cease dancing and drift out of the window, followed by the* FAUN. *As they do so an* ENGLISH MINISTER, *once of St. Giles, Cirencester, who died in 1631, a* MONK *of the Thebaid, A. D. 300, and three* PRIESTS OF ISIS, *B. C. 2840, enter. On detecting the odour of reverence, they materialize themselves to themselves as servitors of their respective earthly religions—the Egyptians in their winged hoods,* THE MONK *of the Thebaid in his high pointed cowl,* THE MINISTER OF ST. GILES *in his broad-brimmed hat with high conical crown, knee-length coat, and heavy, silver-buckled shoes.*]

THE MINISTER OF ST. GILES: [*To himself.*] An unhappy costume this that I wear, yet it is all that identifies me with my former earthly self, or with life. [*He notes the Egyptians and* THE MONK, *but pays no attention to them for the moment.*]

FIRST PRIEST OF ISIS: [*To his brothers.*] A house of worship, I take it. How the awe of man persists. I thought I detected exquisite and harmonious vibrations here.

SECOND PRIEST: [*Tall and severely garbed, yet in the rich colors of his order.*] And I. It is melody, I feel the waves.

THIRD PRIEST: [*Signing in the direction of the organist.*] There is the musician. How pale his emanation. He is arranging something. And here is a very present reminder of one of our earthly stupidities. We worshiped the forerunner of that in our day. [*He motions to the church* CAT *who strolls by with great dignity. They smile.*]

THE CAT: [*Surveying them with indifferent eyes.*] At least I am alive.

FIRST PRIEST: [*A master of astrology.*] Small comfort. You will be dead within the year. I see the rock that ends you. Then no more airs for you.

THE MONK OF THE THEBAID: [*To himself.*] This is a religious edifice—heavily material and of small pomp—Christian, possibly. That spirit yonder [*he surveys* THE MINISTER OF ST. GILES] was also a priest of sorts I take it, and these three Egyptians—how they strut! They give themselves airs because of the memory of them and their rites that endures in the world.

THE MINISTER OF ST. GILES: [*Surveying* THE MONK.] A sombre flagellant. I wonder has he outgrown his earthly illusion!

[*He approaches.*] Brother—do I not meet an emancipated spirit?

THE MONK: You do. Centuries of observation have taught me what earthly search could not. I smile at the folly of this. [*He waves an inclusive hand about him.*]

THE MINISTER OF ST. GILES: And I, I also—though I was of stern faith in my day, and of this very creed. Even now I suspect some discoverable power worthy of worship. My mere persistence causes me to wonder though it does not explain me to myself.

THE MONK: Nor does mine to me, nor the persistence of their seeming reality to them. [*He points through the transparent walls of the church to where outside moving streams of shadows—automobiles, belated wagons, and pedestrians are to be seen—and to the lovers.*] Yet there is no answer that I can discover—at least I drift and speculate. How much longer shall we persist? I often ask myself. They [*he waves a hand at the mass outside*] have their faith, futile as it is. A greater darkness has fallen on you and me. Endless persistence for us if we must, let us say, but merging at last into what?

THE MINISTER OF ST. GILES: Ay, what! And when I died I imagined I should meet my maker face to face.

THE MONK: [*Smiling.*] And I the same. And they—[*he nods toward the Egyptians*]—their gods were as real to them,— shadows all of the unknowable.

THE ORGANIST: [*Plunging into the minor-theme which speedily dies off into unfathomable mysteries of bud notes and flower tones.*] I wonder if I'm boring them by this heavy stuff. Still, what do I care? There are only four. [*Nevertheless he passes from the Grail motif into the dance of the flower maidens.*]

THE BOY: Isn't it lovely!

THE GIRL: Perfect!

THE ORGANIST: Lovely and very difficult. These pedals are working rather stiffly,—and that automobile has to honk just now.

[*He fingers lightly three notes of a major key indicative of woodland echoes and faint bird notes. Re-enter the barrelhouse* BUM, *who is seeking anything that will amuse him.*]

THE BUM: Still playing! Hell! And there are those two old stuffs of women. Not an idea between 'em. [*He turns to go but catches sight of* THE MONK *and the Egyptians. He pauses, and then turns back.*]

THE MONK: [*Addressing the Egyptians.*] Soothing harmonies these! Most strange combinations, the reason for which we cannot guess, the joy and beauty of which we know. I find earthly harmonies very grateful.

FIRST PRIEST: And I. But I cannot fathom the origin of them.

[*He observes the* BUM *and dematerializes to avoid him. The others follow. When they reappear in another part of the church* THE BUM *instantly pursues them.*]

THE BUM: [*Staring interrogatively and irritatingly at* THE MONK *and the Egyptians, who, however, pay not the slightest attention to him.*] You thought you knew somepin' when you were alive, didn' jah? You thought you were smart, huh? You thought you'd find out somepin' when yuh died, huh? Well, yuh got fooled, didn' jah? You're like all the other stuffs that walk about and think they know a lot. Yuh got left. Har! Har! Har! [*He chortles vibrantly.*] I know as much as you fellers, and I've only been dead a dozen years. There ain't no answer! Har! Har! Har! There ain't no answer! An' here you are floatin' aroun' in them things! [*He indicates their dress.*] Oh, ho, ho! [*He grins maliciously and executes a crude clog step.*]

THE MONK: [*Repugnantly, and pulling his cowl aside.*] Away, vile creature—unregenerate soul! Has even the nothingness of materiality taught you nothing?

THE BUM: [*Straightening up and leering.*] Who's vile? What's vile? [*He thinks to become obstreperous but, recalling his nothingness, grins contemptuously.*] You think you're still a monk, don' jah? You think you're good—better'n anybody else. What jah got to be good about, eh? Oh, ho, ho, ho, ho! Ah, har, har, har, har! He thinks he's still a monk—say, cull—!

FIRST PRIEST: [*To* THE MONK *sympathetically.*] Come away, friend. Leave him to his illusions.

SECOND PRIEST: Time alone can point out the folly of his mood. Let us vanish.

THE MINISTER OF ST. GILES: [*Drawing near and scowling at the* BUM.] Out, sot!

THE BUM: [*Defiantly and yet indifferently.*] Who's a sot? An' where's out? Oh, ho, ho, ho, ho!

THE ORGANIST: [*Passing into the finale.*] And this is even more beautiful. It suggests graves and shrines—and fauns dancing. But I don't propose to play long for four people—!!

[*A troop of* FAUNS *and* NYMPHS *dance in, pursuing and eluding each other. The* SIX HAMA-DRYADS *return weaving and turning in diaphanous line. A passing cloud of* HAGS AND WASTRELS, *the worst of the earth lovers, enticed by the gaiety of sound, enter and fill the arches and the vacant spaces for the moment, skipping about in wild hilarity.* THE BUM *joins them, dancing deliriously. Persistances of fish and birds and animals, attracted by the rhythm which is both color and harmony to them, turn and weave among the others. Ancient and new dead of every clime, enamored of the earth life and wandering idly, enter.* A TIRED PEDESTRIAN *of forty, an architect, strolling for the air and hearing the melody, enters. After him come spirits of the streets—a doctor and two artisans, newly dead, wondering at the sound.*]

THE MINISTER OF ST. GILES: [*Noting the flood of hags and wastrels.*] And these are horrible presences! Succubi! Will they never get enough of materiality?

THE MONK: In my day the Thebaid was alive with them—the scum of Rome and Alexandria, annoying us holy men at our devotions.

THE MINISTER OF ST. GILES: Do you still identify yourself with earthly beliefs?

THE MONK: A phrase! A phrase! In the presence and thought of materiality I seem to partake of it.

THE FIRST PRIEST: And I! A sound observation!

THE THIRD PRIEST: The lure of life! It has never lost its charm for me.

THE MINISTER OF ST. GILES: [*To himself.*] Nor for me.

THE FAUN: [*Cavorting near, his kex to his lips, piping vigorously.*] Heavy dolts! Little they know of joy except to stare at it.

THE MINISTER OF ST. GILES: [*Indicating the* FAUN.] And this animal—to profane a temple!

THE MONK: [*Mischievously.*] And do you still cling to earthly notions of sanctity?

THE MINISTER OF ST. GILES: I hold as I have said, that there must be some power that explains us.

THE SIX HAMA-DRYADS: [*Dancing and singing.*]
Round and round a dozen times,
   Three times up and three times down,
Catch a shadow circlewise,
   Fill it full of thistle down.

Fill it up and then away—
   How can stupid mortals know
All the gladness of our play—
   Where the dew-wet odours blow,
   Round and round and round we go!

THE BUM: [*Spinning near.*] This is glorious! Gee!

FIRST PRIEST: [*Unconscious of anything save the charm of the rhythm.*] Sweet vibrations these. But not our ancient harmonies. In our time they were different. Would that I could dance thus!

SECOND PRIEST: Our day! Our day! Endless memories of days. Oh, for an hour of sealed illusion!

THE BOY: Isn't it perfect!

THE GIRL: Divine! It's like a dream, and I want to cry.

THE THIRD PRIEST: The harmony! The harmony! [*He calls his friends and points to the* BOY *and* GIRL. *The three approach and stand before the lovers, viewing them with envious eyes.*] In ancient Egypt—on the banks of the Nile—how keen was this thrill of existence! How much greater is their reality than ours! And all because of their faith in it.

THE MINISTER OF ST. GILES: [*Heavily.*] I grieve for life, brother.

THE MONK: And I also. Would that I might return! [*They sigh.*]

THE ORGANIST: [*Finishing with a flourish.*] Well, there's the end of my work tonight.

[*He closes various stops, begins to gather up his music and turn out the lights. The* DRYADS *and* NYMPHS *flood out of the windows, followed by* FAUNS, HAGS, *and* WASTRELS. *The green-eyed* BUM *starts to go, but pauses, looking back wistfully. The Egyptians, fading from their presence as such, appear only as pale flames.*]

MRS. STILLWATER: [*Pluming herself.*] Now that was lovely, wasn't it?

MRS. PENCE: Charming, very charming!

THE BOY: Don't you love Wagner?

THE GIRL: I do! I do! [*In the shadows they embrace and kiss.*]

THE ORGANIST: [*Wearily, as he bustles down the stairs.*] Why should I play any more for four people? It is nine o'clock. A half hour is enough. At least I can find a little comfort at the Crystal Garden. [*He thinks of an immense beer place, and shrugs his shoulders the while. The old doorman, hearing him go out, prepares to put out the lights.*]

MRS. STILLWATER: [*Rising.*] I do believe it's over.

MRS. PENCE: Well, there are so few you can scarcely blame him.

THE BUM: [*Gloomily.*] Now I gotta find somepin' else.

THE CAT: [*Prowling toward the organ loft in the dark of the closed church.*] Now for one more try for that mouse.

## CURTAIN

# THE LIGHT IN THE WINDOW

## CHARACTERS

TRURO KINDELLING, *a social butterfly.*
LAURA, *his wife.*
JOHN KITTS, *a prosperous hat dealer.*
TUBBS, *officer of the beat.*
BURTON, *the butler.*
MISS MARTHA BUDD, *spinster.*
A MILLIONAIRE IRON MANUFACTURER,
A MESSENGER BOY,
A LAWYER,
A SCRUB WOMAN,
A DEPARTMENT STORE MANAGER,
A DISH WASHER, } *Passers-by.*
A YOUNG SCRIBBLER,
A SHOP GIRL,
MRS. COUPLES, *a neighbor,*
MRS. ARTHUR DEEKER,
HAND ORGAN.

# SCENE

The best residence section of an old but fashionable district in the heart of a great city. To the east and west and south large districts of trade and manufacture. Crowds of workers and organizers of all degrees of ability and prosperity pour across and through it at all hours. At the corner of two intersecting streets where the tide of traffic is heaviest a large square brick house with white marble steps and window lintels. A wide parquetry stone walk leads to the front door and about one side of the house to the rear. A low box hedge encloses uniform lawn spaces. Square French windows are decorated at the bottom by boxes containing dwarf evergreens and English ivy sufficiently hardy to survive the winter. The interior faces of the windows are fitted with thin net of delicate texture and the sides draped with warm yellow brocade, visible from the street in the daytime or when the interior is lighted at night.

On the outside, of a late December evening, heavy flakes of snow are falling and the street is already white. Interiorly the rear parlor is lighted by a tall lamp, shaded with yellow silk. Looking in through the windows a fire, judged by the flickering glow, is burning somewhere. Before it, not visible from the street, a man and woman, the former standing, the latter sitting. Outside the ruck of traffic and pedestrians, the majority of whom give the old house at least a passing glance.

A MILLIONIAIRE IRON MANUFACTURER: [*Speeding north in his brown limousine, to a wealthy customer whom he is taking home to dinner.*] One of the oldest and prettiest residences of this section. I once tried to buy it! Owned now by the Kindellings—one of the best families here. [*They speed past.*]

JOHN KITTS: [*A prosperous hat dealer, to* OFFICER TUBBS, *whom he has encountered on his way home, talking on the street corner opposite.*] Yes, old Colonel Kindelling used to be a great figure around here. I've seen him with his boy who lives over there now—a big, broad-chested, side-whiskered man. The mother's a hard, cold, clever woman, they say. I've seen her, too, but not often. I don't know much about the boy.

OFFICER TUBBS: [*With an air of knowing much more than he cares to communicate.*] Many's the time I've seen him comin' in with more than was good for him—and her, too.

MR. KITTS: [*With a thought to his own children.*] "What the father earns the children spend."

LAURA KINDELLING: [*Formerly the principal of the Lyceum Players, and the heroine of an unsanctioned society-theatrical marriage, rising and walking irritably to the mantel. She is of medium height, lithe, graceful, with a wealth of brown hair, and trailing an afternoon gown of green velvet. Her hands are unfortunately much too plump—her face the rounded oval of the petted beauty.*] You know I never said that! I never gave her the least cause to take offense. She's never forgiven you for marrying me, that's all. She resented it from the first, and she resents it now. Has she ever called on us except to suggest that you go somewhere without me? Has she ever written a letter that hasn't had a criticism or a suggestion that wasn't directed against me in it? Has she—I ask you?

A MESSENGER BOY: [*Passing and observing the glow in the window through the snow.*] Gee! I wish I could live like dat! It must be nice to be rich.

GEORGE WILSON ATTERSON: [*A sentimental lawyer, living at the Elzevir Club in the next block.*] The snow gives that doorway a very artistic look in this light. Red brick through snow is very effective. And that yellow light! If I could only find the right woman and establish a comfortable home like that. [*His footfalls sink noiselessly into the fresh fallen snow.*]

TRURO KINDELLING: [*A sleek, languid, carefully dressed individual of good height, but no great force—disturbed and bored, and finding it difficult to conceal his mood, but admitting to himself the truth of his wife's charges. One carefully poised hand is twirling first one and then the other of a handsome pair of mustaches. The other is resting on the mantel.*] But, Laura! I know you don't understand mother. I'm sure you never have. She isn't as tactful as she might be—at times—owing to her affection for me, perhaps; but as to that, if you didn't take such a savage attitude—

LAURA: [*Irritably and scornfully.*] Savage attitude! Tactless! I'd like to know who has been savage if she hasn't. She didn't try to get you to come and visit Great Oaks alone the third week we were married, did she? She didn't get you to stay there two weeks when you only went to stay a day—did she?

KINDELLING: [*Lying whole-heartedly.*] But she was sick when I got there—

LAURA: Sick! Sick! Yes, I know how sick she was. She wasn't so sick but what she could go to the Redowa's house party and the Shadow Plains Hunt, and you with her. Oh [*as KINDELLING'S eyes lift*], you needn't try to deny it. I *know!* Kitty Stapleton was there and she told me. [KINDELLING *abandons his hope of lying out of it and relaxes his eyes.*] And all the time I thought you were telling me the truth.

A SCRUB WOMAN: [*Making her way toward one of the office buildings south.*] Ah, the rich have the easy time! No worries . . . and the warm fire . . . and the good bed. . . . [*She pulls unthinkingly at her brown shawl, and trudges on.*]

KINDELLING: [*Thinking as* LAURA *talks.*] Mother really does dislike her terribly. I never imagined she could be so bitter. I'll never get a dollar of the estate as long as she can prevent it—as long as I stay with Laura. She is even going to hold up that inheritance of Uncle Will's unless I divorce her and marry some one she approves of—and on the ground of incompetence. If I sue! God! And yet she loves me. I don't know but what she's right at that. Laura isn't in our set, and I can't put her there. [*He decides what to answer.*] The fact is we went both times because she was feeling so bad that I thought the outing would do her good. She was sick all right.

LAURA: Oh, was she? Well, you forget that you told me that you hadn't gone anywhere. That your mother had been too sick to leave the house! [*Her lip curls contemptuously.*]

KINDELLING: [*Not recalling that he ever made such a statement, but judging it to be true.*] When did I say that? I don't recall making such a statement. [*To himself.*] God! She has a sharp tongue! Perhaps mother's right. I did make a miserable mistake in marrying her. She's beautiful, but she's slovenly, and she never takes the hair out of her comb. Now Althea Cameron—[*He thinks to find an opportunity to pet her and so soften her mood.*]

A BRISK DEPARTMENT STORE MANAGER: [*In charge of white goods at Swinton's—Christian, home loving, believing in all the conventions as preached.*] Now, that is what I call a lovely home. All peace and quiet and family affection. Hard-earned, no doubt. After all, prosperity depends on moral order and honesty. People get rich and stay rich because they deserve to. [*He eyes a shabby restaurant dish washer who is passing with suspicion as to his moral worth.*]

THE DISH WASHER: Gee! That light through the snow makes me think of Christmas. I wish I could buy Annie a new coat.

LAURA: Why, just after you came back. You have an awfully poor memory, Truro. You're not the one to try to lie out of things. [*She smiles superiorly.*] You're letting your mother poison your mind against me in spite of anything I can do or say. I can tell.

KINDELLING: What do you mean—poisoning my mind? I don't see that I've changed any. [*He resumes his former position before the fire.*]

LAURA: [*Bitterly, and with a touch of heart pain as she recalls the intoxication of the first six months.*] Oh, don't you! You don't recall how you laced my shoes and corsets every morning, do you! Or that you insisted on buttering my bread and sugaring my coffee, and bringing me my negligee. [*She represses a tendency to sob.*] You've done those things every day this year, haven't you? [*Her eyes harden as she thinks of his mother.*]

KINDELLING: [*Wincing at the memory of his lapsed passions, but desiring not to revive them, and yet failing to connect the change with his mother.*] Do you mean to say that I haven't done any of those things this year?

LAURA: [*Her eyes swelling confutingly.*] You know you haven't!

KINDELLING: [*Defiantly, and not wishing to put himself in a position where more billing and cooing will be necessary.*] Well, anyhow, I don't see how you can connect mother with that.

LAURA: [*Realizing that another affectional transport has eluded her, and troubled by the ominous import of his indifference.*] Mother! Mother! It's always mother, never me. How can you stand there and say that she isn't poisoning your mind when over eight months ago you were planning to sue if your inheritance wasn't released and here you are, just where you were before. First she was sure to love me and we were to live at Great Oaks; then after she refused to have anything to do with me, you were going to stay away from her and let her do as she pleased; we were going to live in Europe; then you had to go there and try to persuade her to give you what is yours, what you could get by suing. Now there isn't a week goes by without your spending at least two or three days with her, and maybe more. It's mother here and mother there, and mother this and mother that, while I sit here and get no more consideration than a housekeeper or a servant. [*Her eyes blaze.*]

KINDELLING: [*Thinking of Althea Cameron—the daughter of the millionaire bond broker—whom his mother favors and to marry whom his mother plans to have him divorce his wife. He sees her slim, aloof, not nearly so animal or tactless as* LAURA. *On marrying her his mother's fortune would come to him without question—as well as Althea.*] Well—she's my mother, isn't she? You don't expect me to ignore her entirely? Besides—she has me in her power—you know that. What can we do without money? We've talked it over lots of times. She can keep my share of father's fortune or give it away if she wants to. It was left entirely to her. [*A vision of his father's contempt for him clouds his thought for a moment.*] As for that eighty thousand Uncle Will left, I know she hasn't any right to keep it back, but she threatens to declare me incompetent if I sue her. [*He assumes as good a look of injured innocence as he may.*]

LAURA: [*Turning on him bitterly.*] Is that why you have changed toward me?

KINDELLING: [*To whom the idea comes as a blow.*] Why, no, certainly not. What makes you say that I have changed when I haven't?

LAURA: [*Heavily and sneeringly.*] No, you haven't. But you're preparing to go out for the third time this week to your mother's! That isn't any sign of change, is it? Oh, I know what she wants! You needn't try to deceive me! She thinks I can be bought off, and you can marry someone else,—that Althea Cameron she and you are always going around with. You think I don't know, don't you? You think I'm a silly fool. Well, I'll show you and her! [*She walks passionately toward one of the front windows and begins to sob.*]

BURTON: [*The butler, who has been requested to order the car, entering from the dining room.*] The car's here, sir.

KINDELLING: [*Remorseful for the moment, but noting that she is less graceful than Althea Cameron, and that her face takes on unsatisfactory lines when crying.*] Very well, Burton. [*To* LAURA.] Now, Laura—really you are impossible at times. Whatever put such an idea in your head? You know it isn't true. I promised her to go. My troubles are certainly enough without your adding to them. You must see how it is. [*He approaches to lay a consoling but indifferent hand on her.*]

A YOUNG SCRIBBLER: [*An assistant magazine editor and self-imagined poet—seeing the car in front and her in the shadow, outlined against the light.*] Ah, the lovely woman! A maiden—probably dreaming of love! And wealthy! If only some rich and beautiful girl would fall in love with me. A house like that and an automobile. [*He stiffens himself so as to present his best address and walks stiffly by. His thoughts are on how well he would look paying court to one such in an exceptional parlor.*]

MRS. COUPLES: [*A resident of one of the side streets, a simple, homely housewife, fond of her husband and her children—noting the glow of the windows in the deepening gloom.*] That house always looks so charming, so well kept. It must be a happy family that lives there. They certainly love flowers and they have everything to make them happy.

BURTON: [*Surveying Schreiber, the gardener, who is packing in a small tree for the winter in the back yard.* BURTON *is comfortably lounging in the warm dining room.*] 'E might 'a' done that a month ago, the loafer. And the 'edge not clipped this fall either. [*He sniffs.*]

A LITTLE SHOP GIRL: [*Bustling home, full of impossible romance, and surveying the windows and the car with bursting sentiment.*] Oh, to be rich! And happy! [*She pictures a society youth imploring her to be his.*]

OFFICER TUBBS: [*Beating the lamp post with his club, and still talking to* MR. KITTS.] I saw that Truro Kindelling riding with his wife here the other day. His name was in the paper not long ago. He won some coaching prize or other.

MR. KITTS: Oh, yes, he's well known for that. There's some trouble between his mother and the daughter-in-law as I understand it. Old Colonel Kindelling didn't think much of his son, I guess. He left everything to his wife to do with as she chose.

OFFICER TUBBS: These rich sons don't know what to do with their money—half of them. [*He strikes an attitude indicative of his own ability as a careful citizen.*]

LAURA: Don't touch me! Don't come near me! I know how it is. I know how you feel. If you didn't you wouldn't have neglected me the way you have. [*The thought passes through her mind that she enjoys herself elsewhere than at home on occasions, but she puts it aside.*] Anyone who can let his mother act as yours has toward me and still neglect his wife for her certainly can't care much. [*She waits for him to make some comment, but he merely stares at her.*] If there's nothing more than that left I'd better let you get a divorce, and—[*The telephone bell rings.*] There she is now! You haven't come soon enough. [*She snaps her teeth savagely.*]

BURTON: [*Appearing at the door.*] You're wanted on the phone, sir. [KINDELLING *and* BURTON *leave.*]

MRS. ARTHUR DEEKER: [*Speeding north in her machine and noting the lights.*] It looks as though the Kindellings were home tonight. He must find it dull since he can't take her out anywhere. [*She subsides into her furs.*]

MISS MARTHA BUDD: [*A spinster saleslady, occupying the front room in a boarding house opposite on the side street, preparing to go down to a lonely dinner. From her window she can survey the entire Kindelling home.*] It is so dreadful to be lonely. I haven't a single place to go. Another evening of reading. [*She notes the light opposite.*] If I only had a home! Think of all those who are rich and happy.

MR. KITTS: When I was in Havana once the Colonel came down there with his horses and autos. He had an immense sugar plantation among other things.

LAURA: [*Alone, soliloquizing.*] I know it's she, the devil. Now for one last play. If he goes tonight, after all I've said, all is lost. I might as well give up. [*She goes to the mirror and back, distrait, a kind of horror of defeat upon her, takes out her handkerchief and pretends to cry.*]

KINDELLING: [*Coming in.*] It's mother—I'm late as it is. [*Looks at his watch.*] I promised to be there at six-thirty. [*He notes her tears.*] Why will you cry, Laura? I haven't changed, really I haven't. [*To himself.*] This is a damned nuisance. [*Comes over and puts his arm about her.*] Why not let this go until tomorrow. I have to go tonight. I promised. She has guests there who are expecting to meet me. But tomorrow—[*He pauses, disturbed that he has been so foolish as to mention guests and another day.*]

LAURA: [*Taking fire at the thought of pleasant and possibly alluring company while she remains at home. She hopes he will invite her to ride with him.*] Are you really going? I suppose your dear Althea will be there, the cat! Doesn't the fact that I am here alone while you are away enjoying yourself make any difference to you at all? Don't you love me any more in any way? [*She begins sobbing dramatically.*]

KINDELLING: [*Thinking to himself as* LAURA *weeps.*] This is really too much. Mother is right. Why should I stick to some one of whom I am tired? I'm sorry—I made a mistake, that's all. Laura whines too much. She's too clinging. She's too sharp tongued. I think when I go tonight I'll stay a long time and see what she does about that. I can give her a hundred thousand eventually. It's the only way. [*He addresses her.*] Now I must go, Laura—I can't get out of it. This is nonsense. I'll come back late in the evening if you wish, but I must go now—really. You mustn't keep me. [*He begins to loose the hand which she has laid on his shoulder.*]

LAURA: [*Realizing that she is in danger of defeat and beginning to moan.*] Oh, dear! Oooh, dear!

KINDELLING: [*Irritated and therefore firm.*] Now, Laura, this is ridiculous. Here I have a dinner appointment with my own mother at six-thirty, and at seven or nearly so I am still here, arguing with you. You always begin—just at the time when I have to leave. I haven't time now, and I've got to go. What you say isn't true, and anyway I'm not going to stop and argue it now. Mother isn't as terrible as you think—and anyhow [*he loosens her hand and puts her away firmly but gently*] there's no use in our taking this particular time to settle it. [*He starts to move, but she clings to him. He forces her hands off and moving to a chaise longue puts her into it.*]

LAURA: [*Hysterically, sensing the import of his departure.*] Oh, God! Oh, God! He forsakes his own wife for his mother, and another woman, and after only two years! To think that I should come to this. To think that that cold, scheming cat should be able to separate us—and after all that has been between us! Oh, oh, oh!!!

KINDELLING: [*Seeing an excuse for anger and anxious to use it to effect a permanent separation.*] You call her a cat?

LAURA: [*Losing her self-control and her tact.*] Yes, I do. She's a vile, treacherous, cold-hearted, scheming woman, and you know it. She planned to twist you around her finger, and she's done it. You're no better than she is. You're just as anxious to break with me as she is to have you. You're both in a scheme to wreck my life. [*She pauses, realizing she has said too much.*]

KINDELLING: [*Coldly and with an air of injured innocence.*] Oh, very well—if that's the way you look at it. I don't see that we're very well mated as it is. You go your way and I'll go mine. I'll not stay to listen to your charges. This is the end so far as I'm concerned. [*He steps into the hall and takes down his hat and coat.*]

BURTON: [*Who has overheard much of the storm, appearing to assist him.*] Will you be coming back before midnight tonight, Mr. Truro?

KINDELLING: [*Irritably.*] I'll not be back at all tonight, Burton, [*to himself*] or ever, I hope.

BURTON: [*Smugly.*] Very well, sir. [*Fearing the possible approach of* MRS. KINDELLING *he discreetly retreats.*]

LAURA: [*Realizing that she has overplayed her part and that he has a seeming excuse for anger.*] Oh, Truro, I didn't mean that. I wasn't thinking what I was saying. I was just angry and hurt. [*She sees him pull on his overcoat with a jerk and imagines him temporarily outraged.*] Please don't go. Please don't say you mean to go for good. It was just a slip of the tongue—really it was. I didn't mean it. I know you love me—some, anyhow. Oh, Truro! [*He puts on his hat and pushes his way to the door.*] Oh, Truro! Truro! Please don't go! Please don't! Please tell me that you love me before you do, anyhow! [*He opens the door and pushes out into the entry way.*] Truro! For God's sake!

KINDELLING: [*Forcefully, irritably, taking full advantage of his chance.*] Let go! [*He forces her hands loose from about his neck and pushes her back.*] What do you want! All the neighbors to hear you? I'm done, I tell you; you're too much for me! [*He pushes her in, pulls the door to, runs down the steps and jumps into the car. To the chauffeur.*] Mother's.

LAURA: [*Reopening the door frantically.*] Truro! Truro! Oh, for God's sake, Truro! Don't leave me! Don't leave me, Truro! Oh, Truro, if you love me—[*She sees him disappear in the snow up the street.*]

OFFICER TUBBS: [*Not noting the exit.*] But it's a beautiful home they have, servants and autos, and all that.

MR. KITTS: And twenty millions when his mother dies.

OFFICER TUBBS: And twenty millions.

THE SPINSTER: [*In her front room, noting* KINDELLING'S *departure.*] A man to love you! To take you in his arms in front of a warm fire!

LAURA: [*Twisting her hands feverishly.*] But he must come back! He will! He can't mean that—so soon—— Oh, my God! My God! [*She runs feverishly to dress and follow him.*]

A HAND ORGAN: [*Wheeling into position in front of the house.*] Everybody's doin' it, doin't it, doin' it—
Everybody's doin' it, doin't it, doin' it—

BURTON: [*From the library window, left front.*] Hi do wish these 'ere 'and organ men would stop playing in front of hour residence. They're always a doing of it, and Hi've spoken to the hofficers 'ere-abouts more an once. Wretched beggars! [*He frowns darkly.*]

MR. KITTS: [*Realizing the flight of time.*] Well, good-night, officer.

OFFICER TUBBS: [*Staring at the hand-organ man, but, enjoying the melody, permitting him to remain.*] Good-night to you, Mr. Kitts.

## **CURTAIN**

# "OLD RAGPICKER"

## AN EPISODE

### CHARACTERS

BROGAN,  
MULLARKY, } *Officers of adjoining beats.*  
"OLD RAGPICKER."  
AN OLD WOMAN.  
A GROCER BOY.  
    *Children and Passers-by.*

## SCENE

*A street corner in the lower west side in New York City. Low red brick three and four story buildings make the prospect on either hand, corners almost invariably being made into stores. In the front of one of them and next to a store stand two garbage cans conspicuously full.*

*On the corner under the wooden awning of one of two stores diagonally opposite to each other two policeman meet. One, the officer of the beat, is an oldish man, well over forty, genial, contemptuous. He stands twirling his club and looking indifferently about him. The other, younger still, a brute of a boy, but polished as to shoes and buttons, and conspicuous for his very large hands pinched into snow white cotton gloves, is equally bored. They salute.*

## TIME

*Noon of a raw, January day.*

OFFICER BROGAN: [*Contemptuously and wearily, desiring to show off before his fellow officer.*] This is a hell of a beat, this is! This is a hell of a beat. I've chased two cats out of a garbage can since mornin' and made one drunk move on. This is a hell of a beat, this is! [*He twirls his stick.*]

OFFICER MULLARKY: [*Also contemptuously, but with a devil-may-care air, twirling his club like a baton.*] Whaddy yah want, anyhow? What're yuh lookin' for, a murder? We don't have anythin' like that down here. This is a respectable neighborhood, this is. We have nice people here. None o' your Brownsville, Tottenville, Canarsie shenanigans around here. These people go to church on Sunday. They're respectable. If yuh want any o' them other things you'd better come over to my side o' town where the real ones live.

OFFICER BROGAN: Whadda *you* know about real ones? Ever pounded the pavements in Dugan's flats yet? Ever walked Hell's Kitchen between one and six in the mornin'? When you've handled one of them beats for a year or so you can talk. I've been in riots, I have.

OFFICER MULLARKY: [*With a faint curl of the lip.*] Riots?

OFFICER BROGAN: Yes, riots. Real live riots, an' all over a can o' beer, or a stranger passin' the time o' day to a kid. None o' your jackrabbit sports in them neighborhoods, I kin tell you. Real live riots with the reserves out—an' heads broken for a block aroun'. See this arm? [*He pulls up a coat sleeve and bares his wrist.*] That's where I damned near had me left tendon cut. The nut was makin' for my neck. If he'd a caught me he'd 've opened me juggler, an' I'd a been a dead one sure. As it was I threw me hand up like this and caught it right there. Whaddy yah know!

OFFICER MULLARKY: [*Interested.*] Well, whaddyja do?

OFFICER BROGAN: Whaddid I do? Whaddid I do? Yuh better ask me! But I'm not tellin' what I did. I want to stay on the force for a while, yet, I guess. [*He smiles as who should say, "I committed endless horrors!"*] But if he'd a reached me juggler I wouldn't be here now, to be tellin' about it.

OFFICER MULLARKY: [*Condescendingly.*] Pretty tough, eh?

OFFICER BROGAN: [*Shoving his thumbs into his belt.*] But this here beat, I never saw the like o' this. I might as well be on dooty in Central Park watchin' the sparrows. There ain't nothin' goin' on here. I kin hardly keep me eyes open half the time. [*He takes out his stick again and twirls it disdainfully.*]

OFFICER MULLARKY: [*Idly, but with a resigned air.*] Well, it's kinda tough. I used to do time over here. Ever see old man Windhorst that owns the brewery? He lives up the street here. [*He jerks a thumb over his shoulder.*]

OFFICER BROGAN: Sure. I seen 'im loads of times. He always bids me the time o' day. Nice old feller, eh? They say he's wort' millions.

OFFICER MULLARKY: That ain't no merry jest, either, I guess. He give ol' Bielstock fifteen dollars when he had the beat here last Christmas! An' him ownin' six houses in Hoboken! Whaddy yuh know? But looket what's comin' up the street, will yuh? Get onto the walk—an' the pants! An' no overcoat, either. Gee! But it's tough!

OFFICER BROGAN: That? Oh, that's only "Old Ragpicker." That's what the kids call him aroun' here. He don't amount to nothin'. He's harmless. He's been aroun' here as long as I've been here, an' for four or five years before, they say. Didn'jah ever see him before?

OFFICER MULLARKY: He's a new one on me! He's nutty, ain't he?

OFFICER BROGAN: Is he nutty? His gallery's clean empty. He sleeps over on the water front, under one of them docks. He's got a hole over there that he creeps into that's somepin awful. I followed him one night before I knew who he was, thinkin' he might be a light-fingered gent, stoogin' it. But I was wrong. Say, yuh ought to see the place he lives in, though. It's a wonder! I don't see how he keeps from freezin' in this weather. Rags, an' dirt, an' wet piles! I onct thought o' takin' 'im up to be kind to 'im, but I changed muh mind. He's makin' a livin', an' he's as well off here as he would be there. [*They continue to gaze up the street.*] He picks rags and tins an' bottles out o' the ash cans. All the junk men aroun' here know him. They don't give him very much for them, I expect, but they buy from him. He never steals nothin', I guess. Once I seen him eatin' a piece o' bread outen an ash can, an' another time a potato. It's tough, but what kin yuh do? I tried t' give 'im a dime onct, but he wouldn't take it. I couldn't get nothin' outa him. He just looked at me.

OFFICER MULLARKY: He wouldn' take the dime?

OFFICER BROGAN: Naaa-a-a-a!

OFFICER MULLARKY: He's bats all right.

[*Enter* "OLD RAGPICKER." *He is a man between sixty and seventy, frowsy, lean, dirty. A mop of grayish white hair protrudes from under a battered felt hat, the brim of which sags down on all sides. His face is long and seamed and yellow. His eyes are bleary and the rims sore and red* with dust and cold. His hands are long and clawlike and dirty. His coat and trousers mere torn and fluttering rags, showing other coats and trousers underneath. His shoes are loose, mouldy and broken. He walks with a swinging limp, a great hemp bag over his shoulder in which are stuffed cans, bottles, and rags in lumpy confusion.]

"OLD RAGPICKER": [*Spying the two garbage cans beyond the officers, and pausing. He seems totally unconscious of anyone, passes, looks about, looks into the cans, then turns his back to the wall and drops his pack. He clears his throat feebly, then stirs in the cans.*] Eh hem! Eh hem!

OFFICER BROGAN: Look at that now! Will yuh? An' them clothes! Can yuh beat it?

OFFICER MULLARKY: The limit, eh?

"OLD RAGPICKER": [*As he picks over one thing and another, finally extracting a tomato can and a milk bottle.*] They always eat tomatoes. Yes. They always eat tomatoes. Yes! Lots of tomatoes! It's cold. My hands are cold, and my feet. Yes. Once they were warm. Yes. Once they were warm enough. Yes. Now they're cold. No matter. [*He reaches down and finds another bottle, this time a small cream one.*] Yes. That's a milk bottle and this is a cream bottle. Cream. It's a long time since I've had that. That'll bring me one cent. Yes. And this'll bring me a cent. [*He holds it up.*] Once I had milk and cream, and a farm, too, and horses and cows. Yes, I did. Once I had horses and cows and pigs. People worked for me in those days, men did. Yes, they did. You wouldn't believe it to see me now, would you? Well, they did. They worked for me. Yes, they did. [*He stirs about and brings up another tomato can.*] Another tomato can! So many of 'em eat tomatoes. Yes, they do. So many of 'em eat tomatoes. Yes. So many eat tomatoes. [*He stares about vacantly.*]

[*A young woman in a trim business suit goes by giving him a wide berth. An old man in a black fur-trimmed coat enters, sending him a sidelong glance, and goes on. An old woman in black enters, a market basket on her arm, passes a few steps and returns.*]

THE OLD WOMAN: You poor man! Aren't you cold? Don't you want to come to my house up here and let me give you a coat? I have an old one that would fit you I'm sure.

"OLD RAGPICKER": [*Surveying her with only slightly comprehending eyes.*] A coat? Yes. I understand. A coat. I'm cold and you want to give me a coat. I understand. Yes. Once I was warm, but now, now I'm cold. Yes. Once I lived in a cellar under a dock. Yes. Once I picked rags and bottles and tin cans, but now, now I don't do that any more. No. Not now. Now I'm a gentleman again. I'm a manufacturer, like I was. Rags and bottles and tin. Rags and bottles and tin. Then I got cold and couldn't do it any more. You understand. I picked rags and bottles and tin and then I got cold. But I'm all right now. I'm all right now. That was a long time before I got poor. That was after I got old and lost my fortune, and my wife died. Yes, yes, that's how it was. I remember now. That's how it was. That was after I got old—but now. [*He turns to look into the can again.*]

THE OLD WOMAN: Don't you want the coat, mister? Don't you want me to give it to you?

[*He pays no more attention to her and she looks about confused. Enter a* GROCER BOY *with a basket on his arm.*]

THE GROCER BOY: [*Pausing and surveying the scene.*] What're yuh tryin' to do, lady? Give 'im a coat? He don't un'erstan' yuh, lady. Yuh can't do nuttin' wit' him. He's crazy. Dat's all. His name's Old Ragpicker. Dat's what dey call 'im aroun' here. He's aroun' here all de time, more or less. I seen 'im often. Yuh can't do nuttin' wit' him, missus. He's bats. He's light in de upper story. Nobody home, missus. [*He moves on.*]

THE OLD WOMAN: The poor old thing! The poor old thing! [*She begins to move on.*] Goin' around in this January weather with no coat on. It's dreadful. I should think that some of these charity societies that are always talking so much would do something. I should think there'd be someone to do something. [*She spies the two policemen and approaches them.*] Can't you do something for that poor old man, officer? I should think that the charity societies or someone could do something. [*She sniffs righteously and defiantly.*]

OFFICER BROGAN: [*Very respectfully.*] I don't think you can do very much for him, Madame. He's not in his right mind, anyhow. He's always around like that.

THE OLD WOMAN: [*With considerable asperity.*] Well, I should think somebody might do something. He won't pay any attention to me. What are you police good for if you won't do something? I'm sure somebody ought to do something, even if I can't make him understand. The idea! Letting him pick out of a garbage can at his age and in his condition! It's a shame, that's what it is! [*She goes off heatedly.*]

OFFICER MULLARKY: Well, listen to old fuss and feathers, will you! Whaddy yuh know? Ye'd think we made 'im do it!

OFFICER BROGAN: Aw, they're all bats, these old ones, every one of them. They make me sick.

[*Enter a crowd of school children, newly excused from a nearby school. They come running and shouting. As they note "OLD RAGPICKER" some of them come running, but some of them, seeing the policemen, pass on. Others, not so easily overawed, remain longer. Finally all go out except two boys and a girl.*]

FIRST BOY: [*A lad of ten, sarcastically.*] Ragpicker! Ragpicker! Look at the ragpicker!

SECOND BOY: He's picking out bottles and cans. Here's a can for you! [*He picks up a can and throws it. It cuts "OLD RAGPICKER'S" hand. He bends over it in pain.*]

THE SCHOOL GIRL: You nasty thing! Aren't you mean! I'd think you'd be ashamed of yourself. Nasty Irish! [*She strikes at the boy.*]

OFFICER BROGAN: [*Noting the deed of the boy and starting toward him.*] Come now, get out of here, you little devil!

Beat it! If I catch you around here again I'll fix you. [*He shakes his club at him.*]

OFFICER MULLARKY: [*Slightly sympathetic.*] They're the limit, these kids. He hurt his hand, I guess.

OFFICER BROGAN: The little devil! If I could catch him I'd pan him.

"OLD RAGPICKER": [*Looking at his hand in a futile way and touching it.*] They're always hitting me, these boys. They never seem to care what they throw at me. They hurt, I tell you, those old cans! [*He puts his hand to his mouth, then turns to the garbage cans as if to continue his search. Suddenly a wild look comes into his eyes.*] Now I'll tell you something! You let me alone! I'm not crazy! You say I'm crazy but I'm not crazy! I was crazy. I did lose my mind. But I lost my money! I lost my wife! I lost my boy! I lost my friends! [*He sobs convulsively for a moment or two, then as suddenly stops.*] But I'm not crazy now. I got better, I tell you. That's why I'm out. I got better. I live by myself now. I'm all alone where I can watch the water go by and the boats and the clouds. That's why I live there. I'm not crazy. [*His voice and manner soften.*] I like the water and the boats and the clouds. I'm all right. That's why I live alone. I don't bother anybody. I don't ask for anything, do I? [*His manner becomes more intense.*] Why don't you let me alone, you little devils? Why don't you let me alone, eh? I'm not crazy. I'm just cold. That's what's the matter with me. I'm cold. I know what's the matter with me. I'm lonely. [*He returns to the ash cans.*]

OFFICER MULLARKY: [*Interested.*] He talks a lot, don't he?

OFFICER BROGAN: Sure. He always goes on like that. I've seen him do it lots of times. There's no harm in him, though. He just talks. You'd talk too if you had your hand cut.

ANOTHER STREET BOY: [*Aroused by the spectacle but withdrawing to a safe distance.*] Ragpicker! Ragpicker!

A SCHOOL GIRL: [*Equally interested and amused.*] Goodness! Look at his shoes!

"OLD RAGPICKER": [*Picking out another can.*] Ragpicker! Ragpicker! Yes. That's what they call me. Ragpicker! Yes! That's what they call me. They throw stones at me, they do. They hit me once here—[*He puts his hand to his head above his ear.*] They hurt me and I had to run. They're devils, those boys. They're devils! Yes, they are. [*He straightens up and the wild look comes into his eyes.*] Now you let me alone, I tell you. You let me be, do you hear? You cut my hand, you did. Why do you want to throw stones at me? I'm an old man, I am. Now you let me be. [*The light in his eyes subsides completely. He returns to the garbage cans.*]

OFFICER BROGAN: [*Observing him narrowly.*] Some other kids must have been throwing stones at him somewhere.

OFFICER MULLARKY: Sure, he seems to be goin' on a good deal to me.

"OLD RAGPICKER": [*Ruefully.*] But that was a long time ago before I was old and cold, before I got bad again, I remember. The devils! They cut me. [*He pulls up a small brass measuring cup, broken and dented, and a whiskey flask with a metal top to it. Pausing and examining the flask.*] Yes, some of them drink. That's the way. When you're old it doesn't matter what you do. It doesn't count. Nothing matters. You can drink if you want to when you're old. It may keep you warm. It would me if I could get it. [*He rummages again.*] But I'm old now, and I don't mind. No, I don't mind. [*He finds a small brass rod in the second can.*] Here's a few cents, now. Brass is worth fifteen cents a pound and copper twenty. This metal cap, now— [*he unscrews it from the whiskey bottle and puts it in his bag with the cup*]—is worth a cent anyhow. I found a pair of rubber shoes yesterday. Two of them. Rubber is worth eight cents a pound. Small bottles are worth four cents a dozen if they're the same size. [*He pauses and his mood changes.*] Oh yes, once I was young. Yes. I was young and used to sing, too. Yes, I remember. [*He begins singing in a cracked falsetto with no melody at all.*]
  Oh heigh ho!
  It's marching we go.
  It's marching, it's marching, the boys you know,

> Oh ho ho! Oh ho ho!
> Marching so the boys do go.

[*He ceases and begins mumbling again.*]

OFFICER MULLARKY: [*Nonchalantly.*] Wouldn't yuh think now that there'd be someone related to an old screw like that that'd look after him? Here he is a roamin' around without even a friend and there ain't any one that knows his name. I'll bet he don't know it himself, if you get right down to it. It's funny, a nut like that without anybody to look after him.

OFFICER BROGAN: Well, if he's bats maybe they don't know where he is. I never thought of that. [*They contemplate him speculatively.*]

OFFICER MULLARKY: There's a lot of cases like that in the papers. How would it do if we ragged him a little, eh? He might come across with his real name. We might find out somepin about him. Whaddy yuh say, huh?

OFFICER BROGAN: Oh, all right. I'm game. Sure. It can't do no harm. We better scare the kids away first though, an' then go after him. [*They make a demonstration in force. To the children.*] Come on now, git out o' here. All of you! Beat it! Git, now! Quick! Get along or we'll run you all in. [*They shoo them away.*]

CHORUS OF CHILDREN: [*Defiantly.*] Oh wow wow wow! Ragpicker! Ragpicker! Wow! Wow! Wow! Wooooooooow!

OFFICER MULLARKY: [*Coming forward and touching "*OLD RAGPICKER*" on the arm.*] Here, old sport. Stop a minute. Hold on, now. What's your name? Who are yuh? Whaddy yuh got in that bag, eh? What's your name, an' what're yuh doin'? [*He attempts to look wise and serious.*]

"OLD RAGPICKER": [*Straightening up and seeming to recognize them for a moment. As he does so he quails and a troubled light comes into his eyes, but this passes after a few moments and he is as he was before.*] I—I—was picking bottles out of the garbage can here, sir. That was all I was doing, sir. Nothing more, sir, no sir, nothing more. Just bottles and cans and old rags, if there are any. Nothing more, sir. That's all, sir. [*He stares uncertainly before him.*]

OFFICER MULLARKY: [*Gaily and with condescension.*] Sure, that's all right, old sport. We know all about that. It don't make no difference about the bottles. What we want to know is—who are yuh, anyway? What's your name? Where'd yuh come from, eh? Kin yuh tell us that now? Where'd yuh come from and what's your name, eh? [*He lays an encouraging hand on his shoulder.*]

OFFICER BROGAN: Your name, sure, that's what we want. What's your name, now? Come!

"OLD RAGPICKER": Name? Name? Yes, my name! What is my name? Let me see. [*He fingers his coatsleeve aimlessly and picks at his buttons.*] I had a name, let me see now. [*He puts his hands to his brow and kinks his forehead while the officers contemplate him silently.*] My name? My name? What was my name? I had a name. It just slips me now for the moment but it will come back to me. I'm sure of that. It'll come back to me. My name. My name. What is my name? [*He stares vacantly.*]

OFFICER BROGAN: [*Heavily.*] Well, can't you remember it, sport? Sure you got a name. Don't yuh know what people called yuh before yuh came down here? Can't you remember? Where were yuh before yuh came down here? Come on now, think! Where were yuh before yuh came down here? Come on, now? What was your name? [*He beams on him encouragingly.*]

"OLD RAGPICKER": [*Apparently straining to think.*] I can't seem to remember where I was. No, sir, not just at the moment, sir, I can't. It'll all come back to me though if you'll just give me a little time. It always does. My name! My name! [*He snaps his fingers helplessly.*]

OFFICER MULLARKY: [*Gallantly and tolerantly.*] Come on now and try, old Skeezicks. That's a good old sport. Try hard.

"OLD RAGPICKER": I'll tell you how it is. When you get old it don't seem to make so much difference any more, don't you see? Nothing really matters. You don't have to eat so much and it don't seem to make so much difference whether you're warm or not. I never seem to care now. No sir, really, I never think of it, you know. Once I had a factory, yes I did. I had three hundred people working for me. That was in eighty-six, before the panic. Oh those were great times. I made woollen blankets in those days—and jeans—and I made a lot of money. Yes, I was very successful. I had my horses and carriages, and my children went to school—all my children—and some of the neighbors'. There was a big demand for those things then. You can't imagine. Then I had two fires, and the trusts came along, and my wife died, and my boy, and I got—I got—I got—[*He begins to sob again.*] You can't imagine what a difference it made, all those things going so fast. Oh, a great difference, yes, sir. But it's all the same now. I'm just as happy.

OFFICER MULLARKY: [*Still very gaily.*] Oh, yuh're happy, are yuh? Well, that's good. But how about your name now? Can't yuh remember that?

"OLD RAGPICKER": Name? Name? [*He looks about vaguely.*] My name? That's funny. It's gone completely again. [*He beats his head foolishly.*] I can't seem to think. [*Half sobbing.*] I—can't seem to think. I—I—have a name, but what is it? [*He stops crying and stands opening and shutting his hand.*]

OFFICER MULLARKY: [*With a faint trace of sympathy.*] Sure, it's funny yuh can't remember that, old sport. Yuh can remember about your factory all right. What was the name on the factory? Can't yuh remember that?

"OLD RAGPICKER": Factory? Factory? What factory was it? I don't remember any factory.

OFFICER BROGAN: Will yuh listen to that, now! One minute he remembers a factory an' the next minute he don't. Yuh don't suppose he kin be stringin' us, do yuh?

OFFICER MULLARKY: [*Sternly.*] Look here, ol' feller, none o' yer con, now. Cut out the bull, dyah hear? None o' yer slick tricks. Out wi' yer name. Who are yuh? Where dyah come from? Gimme yer name damn quick now, or we'll lock yuh up. Yuh don't want tuh go to jail, do yuh? Dyuh want to go to jail? [*He leans toward him threateningly.*]

"OLD RAGPICKER": [*At first frightened by his manner but subsiding into a dreamy state.*] Jail? Jail? Is it warm there? [*He begins to look around him.*] Name? Name? It's funny, though, I can never think of it, or of hers, or of his, or of anybody's. They're all gone. Well, it doesn't matter. When yer old it doesn't really matter, does it? [*He smiles benignly.*]

OFFICER BROGAN: [*Quietly taken aback by the smile.*] Whaddy yah know about that? Kin yuh beat it? If I thought he was stringin' us I'd beat him up, but I don't. He's clean dips, nutty, empty. [*He lifts his finger to his forehead suggestively.*] All gone. Empty as a can.

OFFICER MULLARKY: [*To* BROGAN, *but looking at* "OLD RAGPICKER" *suspiciously.*] I don't know about that. I don't know whether he is or not. He might be foolin' us at that. Yuh never kin tell about these old nuts. [*Aloud.*] Do yuh think it would do any good if we took him to the station and locked him up for a while? Maybe he'd git his name back sittin' in a cell, eh? Whaddy yah say, Brogan? Dyah think that 'ud brighten him up any? [*He looks at* "OLD RAGPICKER" *to see if his remarks have had any effect, but they have not.*] Come along then. [*He takes him by the arm.*] We'll see what a few days in jail'll do. [*He starts to pull him.*]

"OLD RAGPICKER": [*Sweetly.*] Is it warm there?

OFFICER BROGAN: [*Who has seen* "OLD RAGPICKER" *about too long.*] Cut it, Bill, it won't do no good. Can't yah see he's nuts? Yuh can't scare him. He ain't right. Besides, the sergeant won't stand for it. He knows him. We'd better let him go. He's light in the upper story. That's all. There's no use runnin' him in.

OFFICER MULLARKY: [*Irritably, but mock pleasantly.*] All right then, old Skeezicks, I'm goin' to let yuh go, but beat it now! Git yer bag up and dust along. Yuh kin un'erstan' that all right, can't yuh? Yuh don't need to be told that twice, I'll bet. Well, git yer bag an' mosey, now. Mosey! Yuh've got all yuh kin git out of this can, anyway. [*He smiles broadly and gives him a hearty shove.*]

"OLD RAGPICKER": [*Fumbling at his bag and looking around.*] Yes, I must be going now, that's so. I must be going. Yes. [*He begins to gather the neck of his bag into his hands.*] If I just had a few more cans. It's cold, I tell you.

A PASSING STREET BOY: [*Seeing the conference over.*] Ragpicker! Ragpicker! Look at the ragpicker!

OFFICER MULLARKY: [*To* OFFICER BROGAN, *strolling away.*] He is nutty for fair, I guess, eh!

OFFICER BROGAN: [*As they exit.*] Sure he's nutty. I told you that.

THE PASSING STREET BOY: [*Repeating.*] Ragpicker! Ragpicker! Look at the ragpicker!

"OLD RAGPICKER": [*Still struggling to place his bag on his back and listening to the cry of the street boy as it dies away.*] Ragpicker! Ragpicker! Yes, that's it. Now I remember. That's my name. Ragpicker! Ragpicker! Yes, that's what they call me. Ragpicker! Ragpicker! That's my name. That's what they wanted to know. Why wouldn't I think of it when they wanted to know it? It was on my card case. Three thousand pounds of wool. Ragpicker! Yes! Ragpicker. Yes. Ragpicker. Now I remember. Ragpicker. Yes. Why couldn't I remember that when they wanted to know? Ragpicker! Yes. Old Ragpicker. Yes. Old Ragpicker. Yes. [*As he mumbles he slowly gets his bag placed on his back and trudges off.*]

# **CURTAIN**

# THE DREAM

## CHARACTERS

GEORGE PAUL SYPHERS, *Professor of Chemistry.*
FORBES MITCHELL, *Professor of Philosophy.*
ABNER BARRETT, *Professor of Physics.*
PATSY LAFERTY, *a messenger boy.*
    *A Telegraph Instrument, Dream Soldiers, Cannon, Lightning, Thunder.*

## SCENE

*The vicinity of 115th Street and Broadway, New York City, on a warm, lowery May night. Time, 11:15.*

*Approach along Broadway from 116th Street* GEORGE PAUL SYPHERS, *Professor of Chemistry;* FORBES MITCHELL, *Professor of Philosophy;* ABNER BARRETT, *Professor of Physics.* SYPHERS *is medium in height, slim, fiery, black-whiskered, barbered to perfection. He is loquacious and demonstrative.* MITCHELL *is attenuated, humped, gray. He is quite old.* BARRETT *is fifty, blonde, bald, heavy, silent.*

SYPHERS: [*As they reach the corner.*] Well, I turn off here. That was an interesting discussion we had, eh? The fact is, Mitchell, as I told you the other day, I have passed out of my old materialistic point of view to a certain extent—not entirely—but now I see more order in things than I once did—a necessary if mechanistic order. It seems more or less inescapable to me, doesn't it to you?

MITCHELL: [*Doubtfully.*] Well, yes, I might say—only—of course—

BARRETT: [*Dogmatically.*] I do not see how any one can doubt law. Everything obeys law of one kind and another.

SYPHERS: Quite so! Quite so! Law, of course. Everything obeys a law or laws of one kind and another. Nevertheless, there are so many confusing contradictions. Laws seem to conflict at times, don't you think, even in chemical and sidereal space. You don't deny that, do you?

BARRETT: Still, more knowledge might prove them to be anything but contradictory.

SYPHERS: Well, I admit that, too. Only I was merely suggesting that I see more definite order than I once did. A few years ago I could see nothing but disorder, chaos, the inexplicable clashing of forces. Of late I am not so sure. This matter of orthogenesis now; it appeals to me very much as demonstrating an intellectual if not a spiritual order, some great controlling force somewhere. I seem to see a definite tendency to order in things. Life has certainly built itself up through the ages in a very intelligent way indeed, don't you think?

BARRETT: [*Loftily.*] Yes, of course, only there have been many errors and conflicts there too—sudden stoppage of plans in various directions.

MITCHELL: True, as I was about to point out.

SYPHERS: [*Almost unconscious of interruption.*] I admit that. I admit that. What I am getting at is this: all life, as we know it, is based on the cell—cell origination, cell multiplication, cell arrangement. That is an old story. Now here is something which is my own idea—it's a mere theory, of course—that the whole thing may have been originated, somehow, somewhere else, worked out beforehand, as it were, in the brain of something or somebody and is now being orthogenetically or chemically directed from somewhere, being thrown on a screen, as it were, like a moving-picture, and we mere dot pictures, mere cell-built-up pictures, like the movies, only we are telegraphed or telautographed from somewhere else, like those dot pictures that are now made electrically, built up dot by dot, millions of them coming rapidly by wireless or wire and being thrown on a screen of some kind—ether, the elements—you know what I mean. You have seen the telautograph pictures I mean, of course?

BARRETT: Yes, of course. Very ingenious. Very ingenious. But how do you prove the origination of the cell in the fashion that you want?

MITCHELL: [*Aside.*] A rather slow movie, I should say, considering the length of time it has taken to build it up.

SYPHERS: Well, in this way—it has its drawbacks, of course; you remember the experiments of that Irish scientist Burke, don't you? He generated what he called a radiobe—a single cell in a plasm culture which he had hermetically sealed and which he kept under the influence of radium. I do not recall the exact facts of the case at the moment, and I do not believe that his deductions have since been accepted, but that is neither here nor there. That idea of his illustrates mine very well. If we could prove that one cell, one radiobe, had been or could be originated or generated by an outside influence of this kind—radium, if you wish, in a plasm of that kind—we would have to admit that the whole thing might be built up in some such fashion. Why, you could base a new philosophy on that, Mitchell. One radiobe generated in a plasm culture under radium or something else, some autogenetic force manifesting itself through a thing like radium, and there you are. After that you would have to grant the possibility of millions and billions of cells coming in that fashion, whole nations constructed of cells, as they have been.

MITCHELL: My dear Syphers!

BARRETT: There was some hitch in that experiment, however. The chain wasn't quite complete.

SYPHERS: I know—I know. I grant you that. All I'm insisting on is that if one cell, one radiobe, say, can be generated by a synthesis of energy, why not millions? And if millions, why not billions, the whole human family, in short, since we are a synthesis of cells—this whole visible scene in all its details? I know it sounds wild, but [*to* MITCHELL] I have heard you yourself say that you thought it might be possible that we were all a part of some invisible psychic body, force body, in the mechanism of which we function in some way, just as the cells do in ours.

MITCHELL: [*Much flattered.*] Yes, I have said as much.

SYPHERS: Well, then, why may not my theory be true?

BARRETT: May? May? Of course it may. But how are you going to prove it? I myself have suggested that Mitchell's larger psychic body, as he calls it, may be nothing more than a fetus, a secondary creature being built in the womb of a still larger organism, but what of it? All of us, everything that we see here, may be nothing more than parts of organs that are being constructed in some huge womb. This so-called higher psychic body may not even be complete yet, not ready to be born in its realm. But how do we know? There's nothing to prove it.

SYPHERS: Just the same, if I had a few hundred thousand dollars I would enlarge my laboratory and pursue this subject. I believe that something may be discovered. I believe that I could prove it in the course of time. Why, snow crystals, tree and flower forms, everything, gives us a hint, sometimes instantaneously. Why do snow crystals assume almost instantaneously and out of nothing their beautiful forms? The controlling impulse is certainly artistic, isn't it, and outside of anything we know? [*He notes that he is pressing the matter too far and boring his two friends.*] Well, good night. Glad to see you two at the meeting tonight. It was interesting, wasn't it?

BARRETT: Very. [*To himself.*] He's a terrible bore.

MITCHELL: Delightful. [*To himself.*] I'm glad he's done. [*They bow and depart.*]

SYPHERS: Dolts! Fogies! That's always the way, dull and cautious.

BARRETT: [*As they walk up the street.*] An ingenious theory, but dangerously speculative. He ought to read Stromeyer on "Impulse."

MITCHELL: I often wonder about his work and just how sound he is.

[SYPHERS *reaches his own door and goes up the steps, unlocks it and mounts the inside stairs to his room. He lights the gas in a chamber which is half library and half bedroom.*]

SYPHERS: [*Seating himself and gazing about dreamily.*] A great idea. I'm sure of it. Along this line is coming a scientific revolution. If I had enough radium and stromium, why—but they cost so much. [*He yawns.*] Life is really a dream. We are all an emanation, a shadow, a moving picture cast on a screen of ether. I'm sure of it. [*He gazes about, yawns again, and begins to undress.*]

A TELEGRAPH INSTRUMENT: [*At 110th Street Station.*] Tick—tick-tick—tick-tick-tick—tick-tick—tick—tick-tick-tick-tick-tick—

TELEGRAPH OPERATOR: There goes that blamed machine again. [*Begins to write.*] "Professor George Paul Syphers, 621 West 115th Street, New York City. Your uncle, Edward Fillmore, died at eleven tonight. By the terms of his will you are the sole heir to the bulk of his fortune, three hundred thousand dollars. Come at once. A. J. Larywind, Counsellor." [*Aside.*] I wish someone would leave me three thousand cents. [*To a waiting messenger.*] Here, Patsy. Take this up to 115th Street.

PATSY LAFERTY: [*Cock-eyed, overgrown, contentious.*] Sure, it's just de night to keep busy. It's goin' to rain, an' it's me late watch. Oh, well, dere's nuttin' like bein' poor an' honest. [*He seizes a black cotton umbrella almost as large as himself and goes out.*]

SYPHERS: [*Crawling into his bed.*] The curious thing is: why should any dominant force outside this seeming life wish to create it—the smallness, the pettiness, the suffering? I must write a book about that. Here I am—[*He suddenly bethinks him of opening a window and gets out. Looking out.*] It's going to rain, I do believe. [*He returns and stretches himself to rest.*] There, it's thundering already.

PATSY LAFERTY: [*Trudging solemnly up Broadway.*] It's funny, dese mokes wot git messages at one in de mornin'. I'll lay a even bet I don't git nuttin', neider. If you'd come wit a million dollars after twelve o'clock dere's guys wot'd git sore.

SYPHERS: [*Dozing, but still continuing his speculations hazily.*] I must try to find the psychic impulse which originates and directs the cell. That is the great thing. We're all shadows, I say, shadows—adumbrations—impalpable nothings—rumors—dreams. [*He turns on his side.*] If our ills become too great we might be able to wake up or drive them away by thinking of this. It may be that that's what we do when we die—wake up. But that's Christian Science, isn't it? Bah! [*He snores slightly.*]

PATSY LAFERTY: [*Arriving at the door and closing his umbrella.*] A fine night, dis. An' he won't be in. Dat's my luck. [*He rings the bell.*]

SYPHERS: [*Beginning to dream.*] Radiobes! Radiobes! Flying radiobes as big as houses—monsters—

[*He stirs. As he does so the ringing of the bell, the rising wind and the thunder and lightning, which rapidly become violent, identify themselves in some weird way with his thoughts. He is on a large plain now over which a battle is being fought. The flashes of lightning and bellows of thunder gradually identify themselves in his mind with some impending disaster, vague and yet oppressive. He begins to cerebrate in an imaginative, illogical way. A sense of something ominous pervades him, a feeling of great change. Then the rat-a-tat-tat of machine guns begins and armed figures running and fighting appear in the distance.*]

SYPHERS: [*Who once saw military service.*] War! And fighting men! [*It begins to rain.*] That is a machine gun. Now I am in real danger. How did I come here, anyhow? [*He moves a hand, thinking he is hurrying to cover.*]

PATSY LAFERTY: [*Standing at the door, ringing the bell and shifting from one foot to the other.*] Wot a swell night! Wot a swell night! Now it's startin' to pour an' I'll have to stand here aw'ile, I guess. Holy Cripes, dem drops is as big as marbles! [*He pushes the bell again.*]

SYPHERS: [*Hearing the whirr of the buzzer in his dreams and taking it for the rush of artillery and men.*] Ah, the horror of war! What was I thinking?—ah, yes! If one had some method of waking up. [*He mingles the dream notions of his waking philosophy with the figures of his dream.*] Then there would be no more war, no horrors. It is entirely possible, now that we know this existence of ours is a dream. I may be dreaming now—who knows? If so, I could wake up and all my ills would vanish—or would they? [*As the thunder and lightning increase.*] How horrible this is! [*The dream sky lights up as if with red fire.*]

PATSY LAFERTY: T-r-r-r! T-r-r-r! T-r-r-r-r-r! Wot's de matter wit dis bell? W'y don't de guy answer?

SYPHERS: [*Dreaming and looking about him in apprehension.*] War! War! How terrible! How did I come here? How does there happen to be war? Those are fighting men over there! They are killing each other! Horrors! But the great thing is to escape. That fire is dreadful. It means death. [*He struggles to put himself in motion and grunts in his sleep.*]

PATSY LAFERTY: [*Ringing again.*] Well, dis is some sleeper, all right. Or else dere ain't nobody home. I'll kick, I will. [*He kicks.*] Come to! I ain't supposed to stand here all night. [*Kicks and knocks are without result.*]

SYPHERS: [*Still dreaming heavily.*] And here comes a file of soldiers—I hear them tramping—a great company. Merciful heavens, they see me! [*He begins to run. As he does so* THE FILE OF DREAM SOLDIERS *begin to run also.*]

THE FILE OF DREAM SOLDIERS: Halt!

SYPHERS: [*Breaking into a heavy sweat.*] Great God! I haven't a place to hide! Oh, Lord, what shall I do? [*He turns, and in his dream he imagines a deserted stone hut set in a grove of thick tall trees, which seems to offer shelter. He runs towards the hut.*] As I live, here is a stone hut among thick trees! I'll hide in it. Perhaps they won't see me. [*He dashes wildly in, slamming a heavy door behind him.*]

A SCORE OF DREAM SOLDIERS: [*Hurrying after him and knocking with their musket butts on the door.*] Knock! Knock! Knock!

PATSY LAFERTY: [*At the door.*] Knock! Knock! Knock! Gee, wot a night! Dese raindrops look like spits. An' dat lightning! Dat last one looked like a telegraph pole standin' straight in de air!

SYPHERS: [*Cowering in a corner.*] Oh, Lord! My life is worth nothing! Here I lie hiding in an empty stone hut, and those men at the door want my life. What is life? A dream! A dream!—but, oh, such a precious dream! I would not want to disappear—not yet! No, no! I would not want to wake up. I don't want to die—not yet. Not yet!

[*As he lies there cowering, all the coruscations and thunder of a great battle afflict him: cannon, machine guns, human cries, commands. He cowers lower, and yet in spite of the thickness of the walls which seem to protect him he can see through them to the surrounding trees to where the dream soldiers await him—tall men in red coats and towering shakos—and beyond them again to the battlefield, red with flame and gore. As he stares, the men in the shakos glare at him.*]

FIRST DREAM SOLDIER: [*Pointing at him and speaking to another.*] We'll easily get him out of there. Can't you see him lying there, close by the wall? [*To the other soldiers.*] Bring a battering ram. [*A soldier starts off.*] No, bring a cannon. We'll blow him out. [*A second soldier goes.*] He thinks we can't get him, but we can.

[*Other soldiers draw near. They move in the curious, indefinite way common to figures in dreams. Nothing is clear, and yet there is a sense of impending disaster.* SYPHERS *studies the nature of his predicament with a sense of horror.*]

SYPHERS: [*Lying on the floor, close to the wall.*] Ah, if I could only escape! I was thinking a while ago that life was a shadow of something else, an adumbration, a thing built up point by point like the dots of a telautographed picture. Now if that were so I could get out of here. It would be a dream. I could wake. I could cry "Avaunt!" I could stir and it would all disappear and become as nothing. But here! Here—[*He pauses and stares. A company of dream soldiers on horseback gallop up and swing a cannon into position.*]

THE CAPTAIN OF THE DREAM SOLDIERS: [*Dramatically.*] Position! [*They unhook the horses and man the guns.*] Load! [*A shell is put in.*] Fire! [*It belches flame and smoke. A great hole is torn in the wall of the hut.*]

PATSY LAFERTY: [*At the door.*] Gee, dat las' crack was a boid! If he kin sleep troo dat he soitenly won't hear me—or maybe he ain't home. Well, I might as well stand here. I can't go back in dis. [*He decides to make himself comfortable in the doorway.*]

SYPHERS: [*Imagining he is crying.*] Help! Help! Oh, save me! Save me! [*He realizes that he emits no sound, and groans.*]

FIRST DREAM OFFICER: Once more, men! Another shell here! [*Another is put in.*] Fire!

THE CANNON: Poof! Boom! [*Another great hole is torn in the wall.*]

PATSY LAFERTY: [*As a second electric crash occurs.*] I don't know wedder I'd better stay here. I don't wanna get killed. [*He walks about uneasily.*]

SYPHERS: [*Heavily and desperately.*] I am lost! I know it. Oh, if my idea were only true! What if all this turmoil and agony were a figment of the mind merely, a cell or dot picture? Here I am in this hut; these soldiers are about to destroy me. If I could just cry "Avaunt!" "Disappear!"—or if I could know that I am not real, and disappear myself. I wonder if I might not try it? [*He jumps to his feet.*]

A FLASH OF LIGHTNING: Click—Ssssssss!

A CLAP OF REAL THUNDER: Boom———!

SYPHERS: [*To the dream soldiers, defiantly.*] I defy you! Do your worst! You're not real! I'm not real! This whole thing is a dream! I'm a dream, or I'm dreaming! I defy you!

FIRST DREAM SOLDIER: [*Drawing near with a rifle.*] Is that so? You defy me, do you? I'll show you whether I'm real or not. [*He takes deliberate aim.*]

SECOND DREAM SOLDIER: Yes, kill him. That's the way!

SYPHERS: [*Lifting his hand.*] Wait a moment! Don't! I—I'm not sure!

FIRST DREAM SOLDIER: But I will, just the same. You say I'm not real? I'll show you whether I am or not! [*He fires.*] How does that feel?

SYPHERS: [*Who has twisted himself about until he has one hand under him in a most painful position.*] Oh, God, I'm shot! And now I'll die! This whole scene, real or not real, will pass away and I will never know—or will I? And yet once I was a man, and it was good to be alive. Oh! Oh! Oh! [*He weeps and sinks down. A powerful clap of thunder half arouses him. The knocking of* PATSY LAFERTY *becomes dimly audible, a cross between the clatter of musketry and a knock. He stares at the soldiers, some of whom seem already to be growing thin and wavering.*] Dying! Alas! I'm dying! Never will I see this wonderful world any more! [*He partially wakes.*] Or will I? What's this—I'm not dying, after all! They're not real! I'm only dreaming. How astonishing! [*To the dream soldiers, defiantly.*] You're not real, after all. You're mere shadows, thin air. I'm dying, but you're not real. This house isn't real. It couldn't have holes in it if it were, or at least I couldn't have seen through it in the first place if it hadn't. You're shadows, tissues of nothing, a mere fancy of the brain. Oh, wonderful!

FIRST DREAM OFFICER: [*Standing by the cannon.*] Are we? Well, you're a fool! Wait! You may be waking into another state, but you'll be dead to this one. But we won't. Ha! Ha! We'll still be here, alive. [*To the* SECOND DREAM SOLDIER.] He thinks he's not real. He thinks we're not real. He thinks he's not going to die, but wake up into something else! Ha! Ha! [*They look at each other in a strange, fading, unreal way.*] When he passes out of this won't he be dead to this, though?

SYPHERS: [*Amazedly.*] What is this? Am I dying, or waking up? Which is it? Are there various worlds, one within another? Are those soldiers really real? Great heavens! How strange! I am waking up, and yet this world in which I am is real enough. I died there. I certainly did, or I am dying there! [*The house begins to dissolve like smoke; the trees can be seen through the bodies of the soldiers.*]

PATSY LAFERTY: [*At the door.*] I'll give dis guy one more spin an' den I'll quit. I ain't gonna stand here all night, rain or no rain. Clump! Clump! Clump! [*He kicks with his heel at the same time that he rings.*]

SYPHERS: [*Bounding out of bed.*] Oh, blessed heaven! What is that? I'm not dead, after all! I am really alive! It was a dream, all of it. How glad I am to be awake! [*He reaches for his trousers.*] But those soldiers! They argued with me about it! They did! They made fun of me! Isn't that amazing! This dream is a call to me to seek out this mystery. If ever I get money enough to do it that is certainly what I will do. I shall devote all my life to solving this mystery. If only I could find somebody who would endow a laboratory for this purpose. [*He pauses and stares, as the bell whirrs.*] Yes, yes! I'm coming! [*He bustles downstairs, turning up the light as he goes.*]

PATSY LAFERTY: [*Irritably, as the door is opened.*] Syphers!

SYPHERS: Yes.

PATSY LAFERTY: Tellygram. Sign here. [*He produces about a half inch of pencil and holds up a signature blank.* SYPHERS *signs. Absentmindedly he tears open the message, but while doing so turns and closes the door.* PATSY LAFERTY *stares at it disconsolately.*]

SYPHERS: [*Reading.*] A miracle! $300,000! Just what I need for the laboratory! It's a sign! The dream is a portent, a call! My poor dear, good uncle! What moved him to leave me that? Now I know the dream was an omen. And yet— [*thinking of a certain maiden he has been courting*] — should I really do this? Three hundred thousand are three hundred thousand, and where would I ever get that much again? [*He hesitates mentally.*] We could live beautifully on that. I'm not so sure. Perhaps I could get some one else to furnish that money. [*He starts upstairs.*] But that poor boy! I forgot to give him a penny, and it's storming. [*Returns and reopens the door, looks up and down the street, and comes back.*] Dear, dear, dear! I should have given him a dime, anyhow—bringing such a fortunate message. But I must think about this laboratory, though, and this money. I must not act too hastily or inadvisedly. Three hundred thousand are three hundred thousand, and—[*He goes upstairs again solemnly.*]

PATSY LAFERTY: [*One block south, staring at the sidewalk.*] Wot did I say? Wot did I say? Dey never comes across wit nuttin' after twelve—nuttin'. Not if you handed dem a million.

## CURTAIN

# PHANTASMAGORIA

## CHARACTERS

THE LORD OF THE UNIVERSE
BEAUTY
AMBITION
PITY
LOVE
HATE
DESPAIR
REASON
HOPE
FEAR
GREED
    FIRST
    SECOND
    THIRD
    FOURTH    POWERS OF DARKNESS
    FIFTH
    SIXTH
SERAPHIM
CHERUBIM

*Clouds upon clouds of birds, snakes, fish, animals, men, flowers, trees, planets, suns.*
        SCENE I—*The House of Birth*
        SCENE II—*The House of Life*
        SCENE III—*The House of Death*

## SCENE I: THE HOUSE OF BIRTH

### SCENE

*Darkness and illimitable space. Aeons of time, as measured by the illusion of time, elapse.* THE LORD OF THE UNIVERSE, *as force—inert, yet all-in-all—rests quiescent. A faint pulsing begins. Without thought or reason, restless, chaotic, the idea of separateness and individuality generates—an insane dream. The cloudy lengths of a giant outline itself, reclining in endless space. It appears, disappears, now a thigh, now an arm, only to fade again. The vague outlines of a brow and cheek appear, only to fade again. Aeons of time elapse. The illusion reasserts itself. Cloudy fire mists pour from his reasserted nostrils. Poles of light erect themselves from materialized temples. Blazing suns and meteors burst forth and swirl about his head. Strange and multitudinous forms manifest themselves—animals, birds, fishes, horned and winged things. They appear and disappear, as his thoughts form and fade. He is blind, aged, insane. He erects imaginary titanic arms, and rubs his changing, stupendous face with his changing hands.*

THE LORD OF THE UNIVERSE: Oh, ho, ho, ho! Oh, ho, ho, ho! [*He sinks back wearily, all but the outlines of his head disappearing.*]

BEAUTY: [*A thought, leaping, pink-limbed and perfect, from his brain, a figure of delight.*] Lord, thou hast created me! I am thy perfect thought, thy happiest illusion! I will be worshipped! I will be worshipped! [*She springs sinuously among the spinning, changing spheres, a radiant smile upon her face, her arms tossed upward in delight.*]

THE LORD OF THE UNIVERSE: [*Materializing himself fully, a paretic smile upon his lips. He rubs his face and imagines eyes, giving himself sight, and surveys her broodingly.*] Have I created thee? Oh, ho, ho, ho! [*He rubs his flaming hair.*] I must not forget thee! I must not forget thee! Oh, ho, ho, ho! Thou art beauty! Thou art beauty! [*His expression changes. An unimaginable weariness settles upon his face, aged, aeonic. He frowns and leers and partly fades, re-establishing himself after a time. As he does so,* AMBITION, *a sinister thought, club in hand and darkling and scowling, a figure of terror, leaps from his eyes.*]

AMBITION: [*Brandishing his weapon and flourishing.*] I will be obeyed! I will be obeyed! Out of thy terror, God, thou hast created me! War and strife will I have! War! War! [*He struts and stares.*]

THE LORD OF THE UNIVERSE: [*The darkling mood passing, a light of momentary peace settling on his face. He gazes at the figure tolerantly.*] Have I created thee? Weary! Weary! I am weary! [*He stretches his arms.*] But stay! I am lonely. Be thou what thou art. [*He draws himself to a sitting position, all the height and depth of space.*]

BEAUTY: [*Threading a necklace of suns.*] I will be worshipped! I will be worshipped! [*She croons joyously.*]

THE LORD OF THE UNIVERSE: [*His mood changing, a giant despair creeping into his eyes.*] Forever and ever! Oh, ho, ho, ho! Forever and ever! It is a dream! [*He staggers to his feet, the great, shadowy arms flailing wildly. As he does so, he imagines space and time, and begins to wander down their lengths, staggering as he goes. From his brow leap* HATE, DESPAIR, LOVE, PITY, HOPE, FEAR—*thoughts, all—the last two with great round eyes and open mouths. At the same time, clouds upon clouds, unimaginable multitudes of forms and characters previously non-existent, come into being, the product of his fancy. Suns, worlds, fire mists, swarms of birds, snakes, fishes, animals and men are born—strange wraiths that float in wreaths about him and traverse all immensity. They circle, murmur, mutter, cry. The avatars of men come forth, huge forms of gas. They are preceded and followed by vast clouds of thoughts of their own—ravening, embodied fancies that bicker and contest. These, immense companies and semblances, appear and disappear, as the primary figure thinks or loses memory of what he has thought. He alternately laughs and groans, maundering.*]

BEAUTY: [*Dancing on before.*] I will be worshipped! I will be worshipped!

AMBITION: [*Gathering at his back vast clouds of restless, threatening figures like himself.*] I am his thought of strength! I am his thought of power! I am his thought of rage! I am his thought of contest! Oh, ho, ho, ho! Follow me! Follow me! See, we will sow destruction! We will spread despair! We will slay! We will burn! Oh, ho, ho, ho!

THE LORD OF THE UNIVERSE: [*Wildly, his fancy flaming furiously.*] Oh, ho, ho, ho! I am God! I am that I am—all in all! I am my dream of myself! I will dream me dreams, visions. These are my creations, all! [*He turns and surveys his endless fancies of horror and delight.*] Oh, ho, ho, ho! Come, Art! Come, Love! Come, Hope! Come, Death! Dream as I dream! Create, destroy, suffer! I am God! I cannot die! Insane! Insane! Insane! Oh, ho, ho, ho! [*He shouts in agony, then joy, then sobs, staggering as he does so, ending in a gale of wild lunatic laughter.*]

PITY: [*To* LOVE, *hovering near.*] We are his children; can we do nothing?

LOVE: Nothing, save he think on us.

PITY: [*To* HOPE.] Canst thou do nothing?

HOPE: Nothing, save he think on me and thee.

HATE: [*Clasping the hand of* DESPAIR.] Come aside. Are not we his thought also? And what have we in common with them?

DESPAIR: [*Darkly.*] Nothing! Nothing! Yet are we his thought also, but not of them. No, no, no! He should sleep again! He should sleep!

THE LORD OF THE UNIVERSE: [*Staggering and writhing.*] Oh, ho, ho, ho! Oh, ho, ho, ho! I am God! I dream me dreams! I will build me endless wonders, endless pleasures, endless horrors! Oh, ho, ho, ho! [*He staggers madly on.*]

BEAUTY: Build thou me vast temples of beauty, Lord! I will be worshipped! I will be worshipped!

AMBITION: Make thou me worlds and legions! Worlds! Worlds! I would rule! I would slay! I would burn!

LOVE: Oh, but wilt thou make flowers and vast realms of quiet places, Lord? Or but little valleys, if thou wilt? Make streams and pretty shelters! Give not all to Ambition, Lord! Give not all to war!

HATE: [*Springing before his face.*] Make thou me implements of terror! Create thou me forms of horror, of evil! Spin thou me dark chains and darker places! Make thou tortures of failure and regret, Lord—tortures! Tortures! [*He glowers about him.*]

PITY: Nay, Lord, let not all be of horror and hate! Think, thou, on me, Lord, of sweet pity and tender things! Or if thou canst not, think thou but of ways that I may heal what Hate destroy—what Ambition would crush. Think thou thus, Lord! I am a thought of thine also!

THE LORD OF THE UNIVERSE: [*Wearily.*] Oh, ho, ho, ho! [*He staggers on.*]

FEAR: Lord, do thou protect me! Do thou conceal me! Forget me not, Lord! Forget me not! I fear! I fear!

DESPAIR: Why dost thou not sleep, Lord? Of what avail are we, thy fancies? Oh, why dost thou not sleep? Sleep! Sleep! Sleep!

THE LORD OF THE UNIVERSE: [*Staggering on.*] Oh, ho, ho, ho! Oh, ho, ho, ho! Space, Time—I have made me these! Suns, Planets—I have made me these! Love, Hate—I have made me these! Hope, Fear—I have made me these! Beauty—I have made me this! Oh, ho, ho, ho! Oh, ho, ho, ho! [*He staggers on, gesticulating and laughing stupendously.*]

BEAUTY: [*Wildly.*] I will be worshipped! I will be worshipped!

## SCENE II: THE HOUSE OF LIFE

### SCENE

*The cloudy realms of space. At a point, halls of illimitable and indescribable splendor, the colorings of the dawn. Beyond, a swirling belt of suns and satellites glittering thinly against the dark. Beyond this, in measureless nothingness, the suggestion of other clouds of suns and planets, spinning. At the centre, the Presence, couched upon gold and porphyry, high-piled, cloud on cloud. Poles of flame, outpouring thoughts, radiate from his brows; about him, a nimbus of fire. He is now fully self-materialized and concentrated, but sits quiescent, weary, lonely, a compendium of vagrom, changeful, insane emotions and ideas. Immediately before him, BEAUTY, LOVE, PITY, HOPE, REASON— colorful shadows of all forms, dignified and fair—as well as beasts, birds, fishes, reptiles, flowers, trees, men and women in cloudy, wraith-like masses. Above him, immense legions of CHERUBIM and SERAPHIM, figures of translucent light, radiant, choral. In the background, AMBITION, about whom swirl, darkling, HATE, FEAR, GREED, DESPAIR, and behind them, cloud upon cloud of sinister figures, emissaries, dreams, the darker products of the Lord's fancy.*

SERAPHIM AND CHERUBIM: [*Fanning with glittering wings.*] Hail, our Creator! Hail, Lord! Do thou remain for ever in thought, our Creator, our Thinker! Blessed be thy reality! Hail! Hail!

BEAUTY: [*Surveying from a glistering footstool, nearest of all the swarming universe.*] Am I not beautiful, Lord? Am I not thy thought of Beauty? Art thou not content to think on me, thy first thought? And shall I not be thy last? Thou hast not commanded, and they worship me! Thou but thinkest, and I am supernal in beauty! [*She smiles.*] They worship me! They worship me!

THE LORD OF THE UNIVERSE: [*Broodingly.*] Sweet thought—my dearest thought!

AMBITION: [*Clanking ponderous armour—a cloudy giant in moody meditation, gloomily.*] So! He thinks not on us! We wait! We wait! He thinks not on us! Now are his thoughts of drooling pleasure—of Beauty, of Hope, Peace, pale nothings, all—Seraphim and Cherubim—mere fluttering figures of light! Beauty reigns! Hope and Reason and Pity are at her feet! See how the universe peoples itself with these, his fancies! He dreams but fair dreams!

THE LORD OF THE UNIVERSE: [*To* BEAUTY, *turning slowly and viewing contentedly the immensity and beauty of his fancy.*] Art thou pleased then with what I have made for thee? See, see—dreams—dreams—sweet dreams, all—mad fancies, all—Mad! Mad! That which I make is madness, all—disordered dreams! I am mad, mad!

BEAUTY: Wondrous, Lord, of whom I am the first! Great Creator! Wondrous! Thou art wonder and beauty, all. Sweet are thy dreams! Sweet thy madness! Sweet am I! But sleep no more, Lord! Dream on. It is sweet to be worshipped so! I would be worshipped! I would be worshipped!

THE LORD OF THE UNIVERSE: Sayest thou so, perfect thought? It is sweet madness? Oh, ho, ho, ho! A thing of now, and then no longer! Thou art a fair dream, a dear one, but nothing—nothing! Is not that transcendent sorrow—madness?

BEAUTY: [*Caressingly.*] Oh, think not so, Lord! Think not so! A dear dream! A wondrous dream!

THE LORD OF THE UNIVERSE: [*Darkly and broodingly.*] What am I? What art thou? What are these? [*He waves a vast hand.*] What it all is, I cannot think—or why—or whence—or where. I dream and sleep—I sleep and dream! Oh, ho, ho, ho! Oh, ho, ho, ho! A dream! A dream! Thou callest it sweet—sayest thou so? A sweet dream! Oh, ho, ho, ho! I have lost the key! I have lost the key! [*He laughs loudly, sadly.*]

AMBITION: [*In the background rumbling.*] He has lost the key! He has lost the key!

BEAUTY: A sweet dream, Lord! A sweet dream! Sleep no more, Lord! Sleep no more! It is all too sweet! Sleep no more! [*She smiles.*]

AMBITION: [*Restlessly.*] He dreams but useless things! We grow to thin nothings! [*He clanks his armour weakly.*]

PITY: Think kindly, Lord! Kind and tender thoughts! It is best ever!

THE POWERS OF DARKNESS: [*Rumbling.*] Hail! Let Hope be forgotten! And Love! And Pity! Hail!

BEAUTY: [*Rising and laying a hand upon his brow.*] Lord, I am thy first-born. After me came all these. [*She motions to* HOPE, PITY, REASON.] I am thy first thought, thy thought of Beauty! Say it. Remember me! Forget me not! All else avails so little! And think thou not on Ambition or Hate. They would destroy—even me! Even me! [*She smiles.*]

THE POWERS OF DARKNESS: [*Thundering.*] Yea, even Beauty, Lord! What is Beauty to thee?

THE LORD OF THE UNIVERSE: [*Gazing dully.*] Beauty! Beauty! Can I remember thee always, even though I would? Thine eyes! What is it I meant by thine eyes? [*He gazes into them.*] Mad! Mad! Mad!

AMBITION: [*Angrily, clanking his armour.*] He drools and dreams! Me, his best thought—his greatest—he forgets! I am his horror, his strength, his despair, his power—yet he thinks not on me! Beauty! Beauty! And I wait in shadow! I, his rage—yet he sleeps in vagrom thoughts of beauty! Awake, Lord! Forget these pale shadows! Are not thy darker thoughts better? Think thou on me! On Power! Come, Hate! Come, Anger! Come, Despair! Come, Fear! Sit ye all with me!

FEAR: Only let me return unto thee, Lord! I fear! I fear!

BEAUTY: [*To* AMBITION, *angrily.*] And if he thought on thee, what then? Storms, horrors, all blackness and rage! Thou art such! Is not Beauty better? This light? This song?

These Cherubim and Seraphim? Wilt thou have naught but shadow? Avaunt! To think on thee is death, destruction, the end of all! Oh no, Lord! Oh, no, no, no! Put them all hence! Think thou on me! Are not all thy fair dreams, in which suns cluster and lovely forms bud forth, more to thee than these, thy darker? [*She smiles winningly.*]

THE LORD OF THE UNIVERSE: [*Heavily.*] I am that I am!

AMBITION: [*Fiercely glowering and sulking.*] Yea, Terror, Might, Strength, Death, thou art! Think thou on me!

BEAUTY: Nay—Love, Beauty, All Perfectness, Light, Joy, Song— so art thou, and so only! Think thou on me, Lord! Think thou on me! [*She smoothes his hands.*]

HATE, FEAR, GREED, DESPAIR: [*In chorus.*] Nay, think thou on us! Are not we of thee?

LOVE, PITY, HOPE, REASON: [*In chorus.*] Think thou on us! Are not we of thee?

CHERUBIM AND SERAPHIM: Thou everlasting glory—Hail! Hail!

AMBITION: [*Angrily.*] Vanish, vain things! Dream, Lord, no more! [*He glowers and sulks.*]

THE LORD OF THE UNIVERSE: [*To* BEAUTY *sadly.*] I know not whether thou art best or worst. But stay, stay! Stay thou with me but yet a while! Let me not forget this thing that thou art—wonder, light, a glorious dream! Oh, ho, ho, ho! [*He sighs.*] Let me think no more of horrors! Of that I am a-weary! Mad! Mad! Mad! Yet now have I thee— thou art a pleasant thought, thou joyous dream of fair things! Beauty! Beauty! Oh, lovely Beauty! [*He smoothes her face with his hands.*]

A CLOUD OF SERAPHIM: [*Fluttering nigh.*] He dreams of Beauty! We will not die! Hail! Hail!

A CLOUD OF CHERUBIM: He smiles on Beauty! We will not die! Hail! Hail!

AMBITION: [*A hovering, terrible figure in the gloom.*] He rests and drools! All is light and song! He thinks not on death!

[*The shadows recede into the darkness, all but nothingness; the endless legions of suns twinkle; the clouds of* CHERUBIM *and* SERAPHIM *swirl and turn.*]

## SCENE III: THE HOUSE OF DEATH

### SCENE

*A chamber of unimaginable horrors, vast, murky, involute, in which serpents twist and writhe; tortured figures crawl and groan; beasts of many heads and paws prowl to and fro, and all slimy odourous forms interlace in welters and sloughs and draperies and festoons. At the centre, the Throne of the Lord, a mound of unclean beasts and serpents, hung over by clouds of evil spirits—his present embodied thoughts. At his side, huddled in despair, faint, pale shadows of their former selves, the thinnest of dreams—*BEAUTY, REASON, PITY, HOPE, LOVE. *Before him in glowering fullness, grown to vast proportions,* AMBITION, *and behind him the legions of his fancy, black and fulgurous, drawn close about. Insane, fevered, maundering, the* LORD OF THE UNIVERSE *bellows of destruction.*

THE LORD OF THE UNIVERSE: Oh, ho, ho, ho! Oh, ho, ho, ho! Death! Death! Death! Thou dearest death! Bring thou me heaps of dead—the endless slain! Breed winged and forked things, horrors all! Bring thou me shames, despairs, disasters, to torture with and slay! Go forth! Go forth! Sweep thou with Hate, with Rage, with Despair, with Fear! Breed me vast powers of evil, and still vaster! Rank thou me them rank on rank—file by file! [*He thinks on tortured forms.*] Make me armies of horrors, of woes, of immedicable griefs! [*As he thinks, from his brain leap forth, many-headed, forked, winged, the first six Powers of Darkness, and after them, clawed and winged forces of ravening aspect and disaster.]*

BEAUTY: [*Sadly, in a thin voice.*] Lord, am I forgotten? [*He makes no answer.*]

LOVE: [*In a thin voice.*] Lord, canst thou no longer think on me? [*He makes no answer.*]

HOPE: [*Weakly.*] Lord, am I no more to thee? [*No answer.*]

PITY: Canst thou not remember me, Lord? [*No answer.*]

REASON: Lord, am I as nothing to thee now? [*No answer.*]

AMBITION: [*To the clouds of darkness behind him as the first of the six great Powers leap forth.*] Join thou them! Forth!

FIRST POWER OF DARKNESS: [*Hundred-headed, winged and fanged, leaping from the brain of the Creator at illimitable speed.*] Hail! I go to harry! To slay!

SECOND POWER OF DARKNESS: [*Hundred-headed, winged and fanged, rushing forth at illimitable speed.*] Hail! I go to rack, to torture!

THIRD POWER OF DARKNESS: [*Hundred-headed, winged and fanged, rushing forth at illimitable speed.*] Hail! I go to ravage! To gall! To flay!

FOURTH POWER OF DARKNESS: [*Hundred-headed, winged and fanged, rushing forth at illimitable speed.*] Hail! Where Sorrow is not, I carry it!

FIFTH POWER OF DARKNESS: [*Hundred-headed, winged and fanged, rushing forth at illimitable speed.*] Hail! Where Happiness is, I destroy it!

SIXTH POWER OF DARKNESS: [*Hundred-headed, seven-horned, winged and fanged, rushing forth at illimitable speed.*] Hail! Where Peace is, and Love, I make them as not! [*They speed to his right hand and to his left, above him and beneath him, before him and behind him.*]

THE LORD OF THE UNIVERSE: Forth! Forth! Fury upon fury! Bring me masses of destruction! Undo! Undo! Undo! I would have change! Death! Woe! Tears—bring me tears, tears, tears! Wipe out all my dreams! Make ashes all my fancies! Destroy! Destroy! Destroy! Let all be of horror, of death, of sorrow, of pain! Make of life an ending in misery! Mad! Mad!—I am mad! Oh, ho, ho, ho! [*He bellows in insane anger, rage and pain.*]

AMBITION: [*Raveningly, to the clouds of Darkness behind.*] Join thou these! Forth! Forth! Out upon his glistering thoughts! Undo! Undo! He is sick of pity, of peace! Harry, thou, with these! Destroy! Make dust of suns! Breed distempers in all flesh! Reduce, level, macerate, decay! Make of everything nothing! Forth! Forth!

THE LEGIONS OF DARKNESS: [*Rumbling in anticipation, and moving.*] Hail! [*They speed outward.*]

THE LORD OF THE UNIVERSE: [*Rocking to and fro in insane pain.*] To my right hand and to my left! Above me, and beneath! Before me, and behind! Out—on! Harry, destroy! Cease, Time! Be nothing, Space! Oh, ho, ho, ho! Oh, ho, ho, ho! End thou me the weariness of this! [*He weeps in frenetic misery.*]

A CLOUD OF SERAPHIM: [*Faded to but pale rays.*] Oh, Measureless Wonder of all Wonders! Oh, Creator of all Things! Canst thou not think on us? We die! We die! [*They begin to fade.*]

A CLOUD OF CHERUBIM: [*Shrunken to a thin line.*] Nor on us—on us? We die! We die! [*They slowly fade also.*]

BEAUTY: [*Rising and viewing all with weary eyes.*] He dreams on me no more, on Beauty no more! Oh, mad, mad, Lord! Oh fevered, useless dreams! Gone all the sweet Seraphim and Cherubim! The halls of light and wonder—his suns and jewel-stars! His dreams have changed. These, his horrors, are now his mood. And death—and nothingness—for all of us, his mood! [*To* DESPAIR.] Hail! Hail, thou unutterable one! [*To* AMBITION—*glowering near.*] And thou, great evil one, his torturous swelling thought! Now is thy dark hour! But sleep and nothingness is the end of this for thee and all! Thou wouldst destroy even me, oh evil thing! Yet if he but thought on me, how different! His singing world again! But wait, wait! If he but think on thee for long, comes death and the end of all this—of thee, as of me! By death, sleep! And by sleep, if he sleep—where then is his thought of thee, or me? Pray that he change!

AMBITION: [*Arrogantly.*] Avaunt, thin thing! Now is my Lord awake—he thinks on me, not thee! To harry, burn, slay! To his right hand and his left! Above him, beneath! Before him and behind! He is for strife, strength, conflict! To harry, slay, lay waste! It is as it is! He knows thee not! [*The destroying legions rumble.*]

PITY: [*Drawing near to* BEAUTY.] He thinks not on me again! I am grown so thin! Is there no change? Is peace worth nothing—the tender heart—the end of agonies and storms?

AMBITION: Avaunt! He knows thee not! [PITY *shrinks exceeding small.*]

LOVE: [*Drawing near, a pale shadow.*] Or all the lovely thoughts that fluttered into happiness? Are they worth nothing?

AMBITION: Avaunt! He knows thee not, thin wraith! [LOVE *fades to a point.*]

REASON: Nor me? Not even order?

AMBITION: Hence! [REASON steps aside.]

HOPE: Nor yet the thought he had in me? Can he not remember me?

AMBITION: Vanish! Our Lord is for destruction! He thinks not on thee—but on me! Hence! [HOPE *pales to a thin flame.*]

BEAUTY: [*Proudly.*] Yet am I Beauty—his first thought. Rage on, thou evil one! Of what avail, since thou endest also? Destroy as thou wilt, he will not forget me! I am that which he is—Beauty! His first thought! Think madly as he may, yet will his last thought, as his first, be of me. I am in him, and he in me. From him, when he wakes, if ever, will I come! I will be worshipped! I will be worshipped!

THE LORD OF THE UNIVERSE: [*Writhing in a last insane agony.*] Oh, ho, ho, ho! Oh, ho, ho, ho! Let me have done with Life! Let me have done with Thought—Pain—with Order, Beauty, Hope! Let me have done with all things! Oh, ho, ho, ho! Sick, sick! Death! Death! Burn! Harry! Slay! Oh, ho, ho, ho! I will have done with it all! [*He tears at his snaky locks.*]

REASON: [*Sadly.*] Great Master of us all. So this then is the end! I, who was thy thought of order, am disordered! I, who was thy strength, am thy weakness! So sink I back to nothingness! [*He re-enters the brow of the Lord.*]

LOVE: And I, who was his thought of happiness! So come I to nothingness again! [*She re-enters the forehead of the Lord.*]

PITY: And I, who was his thought of tenderness! [*She fades into his brain.*]

HOPE: And I, who was his thought of love and peace! [*She disappears also.*]

BEAUTY: [*Paling.*] Yet is he not done with me! Mad though he be, even though he sleep, even now I feel his thought! He is in me as I in him! I will be worshipped! I will be worshipped! [*She re-enters his brow undiminished.*]

FIRST POWER OF DARKNESS: [*Returning and entering in.*] All that was to his left hand is not!

AMBITION: 'Tis well!

SECOND POWER OF DARKNESS: [*Returning and entering in.*] All that was to his right hand is not!

AMBITION: 'Tis well!

THIRD POWER OF DARKNESS: [*Returning and entering in.*] All that was before him is not.

AMBITION: 'Tis well!

FOURTH POWER OF DARKNESS: [*Returning and entering in.*] All that was behind him is not!

AMBITION: 'Tis well!

FIFTH POWER OF DARKNESS: [*Returning and entering in.*] All that was above him is not!

AMBITION: 'Tis well!

SIXTH POWER OF DARKNESS: [*Returning and entering in.*] All that was beneath him is not!

AMBITION: 'Tis well! Hail, Lord! As thou wouldst, I have ended thy dreams! Canst thou not rest?

THE LORD OF THE UNIVERSE: [*Writhing.*] Oh, ho, ho, ho! Oh, ho, ho, ho! I dream! I dream! It is too much! Destroy! Destroy! I will have peace! I will have peace! [*He turns and writhes, sinking in weariness as he does so, and partially disappearing. Aeons pass.*]

FIRST POWER OF DARKNESS: [*Beginning to fade in the brain of the Lord.*] It is of me that he ceases to think! I fail! [*He disappears.*]

AMBITION: [*Sadly.*] It is the end!

SECOND POWER OF DARKNESS: [*Beginning to fade in the brain of the Lord.*] It is of me he ceases to think. Oh, ho, ho, ho! I fail! [*He disappears.*]

AMBITION: [*Sadly.*] It is the end!

THIRD POWER OF DARKNESS: [*Writhing and fading in the brain of the Lord.*] It is of me he ceases to think! I fail! Oh, ho, ho, ho! [*He disappears.*]

AMBITION: It is the end!

FOURTH POWER OF DARKNESS: It is of me he ceases to think! I fail! [*He groans and disappears.*]

AMBITION: It is the end!

FIFTH POWER OF DARKNESS: It is of me he ceases to think! I fail! [*He disappears.*]

AMBITION: It is the end!

SIXTH POWER OF DARKNESS: It is of me he ceases to think! I fail! [*He disappears.*]

AMBITION: It is the end!

THE LORD OF THE UNIVERSE: [*Stretching prone in space and all but vanishing. Only faint outlines of his former self are visible here and there, the brow and face intact.*] Peace! Peace! It is enough! It is enough! I have done! I have done! Let it be as it ever was from everlasting to everlasting—a dream—a dream! Oh, ho, ho, ho! [*He sighs heavily. Darkness prevails. The last writhing beasts thin and are gone.* AMBITION, *paling and thinning, stands wide-eyed, agape, before the fading brow of the Lord.*]

AMBITION: At last! And I—it is of me he ceases to think—even me! I have done! I have done! [*He vanishes.*]

BEAUTY: [*A thin star in the brow of the Lord, glistering and yet paling.*] It is even of me he ceases to think! Lord, hast thou forgotten thy first-born?

THE LORD OF THE UNIVERSE: Peace! Peace! Enter thou into me! [*He sighs and begins to vanish completely.*]

BEAUTY: [*Fading into his sleep.*] I will be worshipped! I will be worshipped! [*She smiles.*]

*The illusion of reality ceases. Suns and planets are gone. Time and Space are not. That which was is as that which was not.*

# CURTAIN

# THE COURT OF PROGRESS

EDITORIAL NOTE: The following manuscript, recovered from one of the twenty-seven tombs of Federated Chairmen of the Post Federated Period of World Republics, A. D. 2760-3923, recently discovered in the debris centres of Exomia, Domas and Polos (Central Asia), plainly refers to some annual festival or period of congratulation which, according to the historian, Ruffstuff, who seems to have flourished toward the close of that period when the great Asiatic and American world floods (the shifting of the boundaries of the Pacific) ended the old order, was apparently held, first, at some point in Central South Africa; later in Middle Western North America, as the then continents were called. The author or dramatist, Theobromo, plainly of some period later than that of the Post Federated, when literature of all sorts, owing to the religious viewpoint of the Federation, was nonexistent, was plainly familiar with records of this great court or festival, now non-existent. (See mention in closing paragraph of Moline-Emporia-Sedalia sittings, points or places which have not as yet been identified.) The translator, Can. Theodore Dreiser, of Cambo, North Dromio, begs to explain that owing to the peculiar difficulties of the language then used the exact rendition of certain phrases and passages is not guaranteed.

## CHARACTERS

NOXUS PODUNKUS, *Grand Referendunce Chairman of the Federated Musnud of the World.*
SHISHMASH HASH HASH, *Master of Ceremonies to the Court of Progress.*

Of
{
  Savants..............
  Moonshees..............
  Roctor-Proctors..............
  Pundits..............
  Theorists..............
  Seers..............
} One hundred

Of
{
  Zadkiels..............
  Oracles..............
  Solons..............
  Nestors..............
  Gamaliels..............
  Daniels..............
} One hundred

Of
{
  Dizzards.............. 50
  Zanys.............. 100
  Fuddys.............. 100
  Hoddy-Doddys.............. 100
  Loobies.............. 1000
  Gaberlunzies.............. 1000
  Nizys..............50000
}

Of Descendent Sons and Daughters of Ancient and Honorable
{
  Anti-Vivisectionists..............
  Anti-Vaccinationists..............
  Anti-Contraceptionists..............
  Anti-Saloon Leaguers..............
  Anti-Vice Crusaders..............
  Anti-Lewd Book Examiners..............
  Eugenic Sires..............
  Free and Accepted Boy Scouts..............
  Professors of Christian Economy..............
  Feminists..............
} 50,000

{ Moral Prophylaxers ..........................
Non-Smokers' Social Unionists.......
Seventh Day Adventists....................
Sabbath Day Exclusivists....................
Holy Rollers .......................................
Evangelists .......................................
King's Daughters...............................
Women Magazine Editors................
Library Protection Association
   Guards...........................................
Watch and Ward Society Guards.....
Prohibitionists...................................
Federated Philosophers....................
Union Astronomers............................
Socialists............................................ }

Of Plaster or Ossi-
fied Specimens of
Ancient and De-
graded
{ Gamblers............................................
Saloon-Keepers..................................
Bartenders..........................................
Financiers..........................................
Thieves................................................
Vivisectionists...................................
Vaccinationists.................................
Philosophers......................................
Politicians..........................................
Astronomers......................................
Magdalens..........................................
Madams...............................................
Novelists.............................................
Playwrights........................................
Scenario Writers...............................
Musicians............................................
Painters..............................................
Poets....................................................
Cigarette Fiends................................
Dope Fiends.......................................
Sabbath Day Breakers......................
Pragmatists........................................
Predatory Rich..................................
Anarchists..........................................
White Slavers...................................
Nietzscheans..................................... } One Each

# The Court of Progress

> Scientists..............................................
> Chemists..............................................
> Physicists.............................................
> Stoics..................................................
> Liars...................................................
> Dogs...................................................
> Scoundrels...........................................

## SCENE

*A great plain, filled with a vast multitude of people. Tents, pagodas, pavilions, booths, kiosks, scattered over a wide area and alive with a swarming mass. Overhead innumerable flags, banners, shields, emblems and insignia of all kinds, as well as a welter of decoration and bunting, all symbolic of peace, prosperity and progress. Innumerable alleyways and passages suggest a maze. In the centre, behind a great open square or drill-ground, an enormous pink-and-green pavilion of silk, fluttering innumerable pinions and streamers of the most variegated hues. In the extreme west of this (centre) and facing east (to suggest open-mindedness and a spirit of receptivity and progress) a giant Musnud or throne of dried mush, straw and the polished grains of the oyster plant, each with its spiritual, ethical and social significance. This same is richly carved and tinted to represent the dawn, while at the top, by a process of higher coloring, the floridity, variety and fecundity of tropic life, signifying fullness of development, is suggested. Over this, a canopy of dried morning-glory vines stained to represent the pink glow of dawn and strung with innumerable papier-mâché flowers representative of the bursting blooms of perfection. Beneath, a large assortment of pillows, rugs, bed-ticks, mats, cushions, hassocks and the like, tinted to suggest the variety, fecundity, beneficence and generosity of Nature. On these rest the one hundred Moonshees, Savants, Pundits, Roctor-Proctors, Theorists, Seers, Zadkiels, Oracles, Solons, Nestors and profound Daniels and Gamaliels, members of the High Court of Progress of the Federated Republics of the World for the years 3913-3923, and representing in themselves the world's farthest intellectual reaches as well as its peace, progress, perfection and plenty.*

*On their heads tall cornucopias of green-and-yellow tin-*

*foil, fluttering with ribbons. On their bodies flowing silk robes of green decorated with red, yellow and blue astrologic designs, each of special ethical, social and spiritual significance. In the centre of this company, his body clad in yellow, green and blue cheesecloth, his head surmounted by a tall blue cornucopia (signifying peace and plenty), and resting on an immense stack of eiderdown pillows,* NOXUS PODUNKUS, *Grand Referendunce Chairman of the Federated Republics of the World and President pro tem of the Court of Progress of the same. He is very fat and restful. Behind and among them, fifty Dizzards in sky-blue fleshings, jackets of yellow, and pink coal-scuttle helmets, who keep watch and ward by whistling between their teeth and laying about them with feather-stuffed clubs whenever the attention of the Moonshees is desired. Among the audience, one hundred thousand already admitted and in their seats, five thousand Nizys in pink flashings and striped blue-and-green shawls, each carrying a tin wash-boiler full of orange and lemon soufflé and doling out the same in ice cream cones to all who signal. The latter are hung around their waists in long strings.*

*Before the Musnud one hundred Hoddy-Doddys, Ticklers Extraordinary to the Savants, Zadkiels, etc. These are arrayed in green fleshings and yellow silk overcoats, and carry yellow feather-dusters attached to long blue bamboo stalks. They assist the Dizzards in keeping the Moonshees awake. About the Hoddy-Doddys, ranged in a semi-circle, one hundred Zanys, Official Wind-Bag Rattlers to the Musnud. These same wear orange-and-green sweaters and running pants of black and orange, plus long-visored caps of green, and carry pear-shaped wind-bags containing dried watermelon seeds, the ethical symbol of receptivity, which they rattle whenever the attention of the audience is desired. Between the Hoddy-Doddys and the Musnud, and at the immediate base of the same, one hundred Fuddys, Wireless Telegraph Operators Extraordinary to the Court, in green silk uniforms and plug hats, who are busy sending out preliminary notices to the world of the assembling of the Court of Progress. Beyond the Zanys in the aisles and semi-circular passages between the seats, one thousand Loobies and one thousand Gaberlunzies, Official First and Second Readers to the Court, the First arrayed in blue-and-white, the Second in green-and-white polka-dot gowns and mortar-boards, and each carrying about his waist a chain to which is attached all the then permitted classics of the pre-Federated Period (A. D. 1897-1927)—Hamilton Wright*

Mabie, Orrison Swett Marden, Harold Bell Wright, Gene Stratton Porter, Ralph Waldo Trine and others—from which at all moments of undue excitement it is their duty to read soothing passages in unison.

Outside the principal entrance to the pavilion, on the Grand Concourse, separate companies or regiments of Descendant Sons and Daughters of Ancient and Honorable Anti-Vivisectionists, Anti-Vaccinationists, Anti-Contraceptionists, Anti-Vice Crusaders, Eugenic Sires, Feminists, Non-Smokers' Social Unionists, Anti-Saloon Leaguers, Free and Accepted Boy Scouts, Professors of Christian Economy, Seventh Day Adventists, Sabbath Day Exclusivists, Holy Rollers, King's Daughters, Watch and Ward Guards, Library Protection Association Guards, Union Astronomers, Federated College Philosophers, Evangelists, etc., each practicing their separate evolutions and class yells. A giant procession, fifty thousand in number, soon to start and file before the assembled Pundits and Zadkiels of the Court sitting on the Musnud within, is intended to demonstrate to it and to the Universe at large, via the assembled audience, the happy presence and persistence and strength of the forces of light and order and truth, as opposed to the quondam and now all but vanished remnants of darkness prevailing in the world before the Federation of the Commission-Governed Republics of the World. As the principal function of the Court is to catechize its adherents and delegates as to the reason for the faith that is in them, and to learn as to the present progress of truth, mercy, justice, etc., via a series of shrewd and now sacred questions (the Post Federated Tablets of the Law) especially calculated to bring forth the facts and shame the forces of darkness into silence, these same stand ready to answer all such questions as to the certainty of the final perfection of life and so to receive the approval of the Musnud and the assembled populace.

Some companies of these same are at present busy executing their preliminary maneuvers, walking on their hands, turning hand-springs and cart-wheels, whirling as dervishes and whistling and cat-calling. Others ask and answer each other the sacred questions of the Tablets; still others leap, run around in a ring, roll in the dust and kick. Still others meditate head in hand or stare in fixed absorption at Philosophers' targets fixed on posts at different points in the grounds. A general air of hope, sequacity, peace, content, well-being, ease, and other forms of human satisfaction, pervades each and every section of the field.

*Hauled about by varying groups of Descendant Sons and Daughters of Free and Accepted Boy Scouts, Anti-Vivisectionists, Anti-Vaccinationists, etc., all in attractive and unforgettable raiment of cerise, purple, yellow and nile green, are the only remaining specimens or images of now all but extinct Gamblers, Saloon-Keepers, Financiers, Thieves, Vivisectionists, Vaccinationists, Philosophers, Politicians, Magdalens and Predatory Rich still in captivity or existence. It should be stated in passing that all Liars, Thieves, Scoundrels, Lechers, Anarchists and the like were finally exterminated during the all-memorable Federated Presidency of Bonehead X, A. D. 3409-3427, just five hundred years before. Saloons and all forms of illegal as well as commercialized vice departed this earth some seven hundred years before. The ladies of the Inner High Council of Descendant Sons and Daughters of Ancient Thirty-second Degree Anti-Vivisectionists have here (muzzled and chained) the only extant examples of a Vivisectionist surgeon of the former cult of inhuman experimentalists, captured in Greenland. The Federated Union of Descendant Sons and Daughters of Ancient and Honorable Vice-Crusaders of the World present in a drop-forged steel cage, painted yellow, blue and green, the only living specimen of a simon-pure Madam, recently captured in the outlying regions of Borneo. In other portions of the field, caged and dressed to represent now extinct types of Materialists, Scientists, Philosophers, Chemists, Nietzscheans, Pragmatists, Stoics and so forth, are one hundred volunteers of the East South African School of Christian Histrionic Culture, freely giving their services for this great occasion.*

SHISHMASH HASH HASH: [*Grand Secretary-Treasurer of the Indo-African group of Commission-Governed Republics, now in federation with the rest of the world, and Master of Ceremonies to the Court of Progress. He is a tall man, in a suit of red-and-green pajamas, slightly rubberized and inflated. His ears are pierced and hung with blue earrings and his cheeks are adorned with yellow lambrequins three feet long. Temporarily he is entertaining himself just outside the stage entrance to the main tent by doing back somersaults, but at the sight of five thousand Descendant Sons and Daughters of Free and Accepted Boy Scouts, Watch and Ward, and Library Protection Guards in marching order approaching the main or stage entrance, he executes nine hand-springs, three bounds and one back somersault, landing in front of the Musnud. At sight of him the assembled multitude stirs and quivers and he-haws with delight. The associated Moonshees, Pundits, Roctor-Proctors and others stir slightly but continue to snore.* SHISHMASH HASH HASH, *executing a jig-step and tying his whiskers in a bow-knot.*] Your Referendunces! [*At this the fifty Dizzards directly in attendance on the assembled Moonshees of the Musnud, each over six feet tall and weighing exactly one hundred and twenty-seven pounds, stir the latter to wakefulness by whistling between their fingers and beating them with their feather-stuffed clubs.*]

THE FIFTY DIZZARDS: Pfs-s-t!——Pfs-s-t!——Pfs-s-t! [*They lay about them mightily with their clubs.*]

THE FIVE THOUSAND NIZYS: [*Bearers of orange and lemon soufflé to the Court. Becoming greatly excited at sight of the platform Dizzards belaboring the Moonshees and beginning to jump up and down, at the same time ladling out cones of green and pink soufflé.*] Refresh yourselves, good people! Refresh yourselves! Ssh!——Ssssh!——Sssssssh!

THE ONE HUNDRED HODDY-DODDYS: [*Shaking their long-handled feather-dusters and whirling about in a ring.*] Awake, your Referendunces! Awake! Awake! [*They tickle the noses, ears, chins and necks of the Moonshees, Zadkiels, etc., who stir feebly but continue to snore.*]

THE ONE HUNDRED ZANYS: [*Rattling their wind-bags and jigging in unison.*] Attention! Attention, good audience! Attention! Their Grand Referendunces of the Federated Musnud of the World are about to be awakened! Attention! Attention! [*They rattle their wind-bags vigorously and roll their eyes from left to right and back nine times.*]

THE TWO THOUSAND LOOBIES AND GABERLUNZIES: [*Roaming nervously to and fro, reading.*] "At this moment, the sun sinking low in the West, the faint West wind stirring in the leaves, the pellucid rill tinkling gently—so, for a heart-beat, he saw her." [*Each holds up a restful hand.*]

SHISHMASH HASH HASH: [*Executing three steps to the left and four to the right and spinning on his right toe.*] Your Referendunces! Most Worthy and Grand Referendunces! Is the High Court of Progress of the Federated Republics of the World now ready to receive the reports of the various battalions of Law, Order, Peace, Justice, Truth, etc., accredited to this Court? They await your Referendunces' pleasure without. [*At this another herculean attempt is made to arouse the assembled judges of the Musnud. The fifty Dizzards who are in direct attendance on the Moonshees begin whistling between their teeth and striking them with their feather-clubs. The one hundred Hoddy-Doddys stir up the multitude in the front rows by dusting off their ears and noses with their long-poled feather-dusters. The one hundred Zanys rattle their wind-bags, and the two thousand Loobies and Gaberlunzies read intently and with vigor, each holding up a hand. The five thousand Nizys hurry here and there offering soufflé to all.*]

THE ONE HUNDRED MOONSHEES, ROCTOR-PROCTORS, ZADKIELS, ETC.: [*Stirring slightly and opening their eyes.*] Soufflé! Soufflé! [*Great panniers of soufflé are fed to them, and they relapse into slumber.*]

THE FIFTY DIZZARDS: [*Seeing they have the Moonshees partially awake.*] Your Referendunces! Most worthy Referendunces! The Secretary of the Honorable Court desires to know is it ready to receive the first division of the assembled Battalions of Knowledge now about to report as to the present state and progress of the world? [*A vast murmur of "Hee-haw!"—the 30th century expression of approval—passes over the assemblage.* SHISHMASH HASH HASH *executes four more hand-springs, lights gracefully on his back and slowly draws his toes up to his fingers, thus gradually assuming a standing position, and bows. The fifty Dizzards whistle between their teeth and beat the Moonshees vigorously with their feather-clubs. The Zanys rattle their wind-bags lustily. Fifty of the one hundred Moonshees awake and call for more soufflé. Five hundred tons are at once distributed to the audience, and quiet is restored.*]

THE MOONSHEES, ROCTOR-PROCTORS, ZADKIELS, ETC.: [*Stirring feebly and pushing the feather-dusters out of their eyes. In chorus.*] What is the question? What is the question? [*They sink back heavily on their pillows.* SHISHMASH HASH HASH *throws four fits and attempts to insert his left foot in his mouth, then stands at attention while four Dizzards, lifting aloft silk banners on which are pictures of keys of knowledge and open books, fall to the ground and get up again. The one hundred Hoddy-Doddys tickle the noses of the Moonshees frantically. The five thousand Nizys throw handfuls of soufflé in the faces of the audience and spin on one foot. The two thousand Loobies and Gaberlunzies rear and plunge, murmuring "Shush! Shush!" then read.*]

NOXUS PODUNKUS: [*Chief Presiding Referendunce of the Federated Court of Progress of the World. Sitting up, opening one eye and gazing about.*] Indeed! You say, do you? Well, let them enter! [*He collapses again.*]

SHISHMASH HASH HASH: [*Spinning away to the stage entrance, at which the representatives of the various forces of Progress are waiting in parade array.*] Are you ready? Are you ready? [*A shout goes up. He lifts both hands, and pirouetting gracefully backward toward the Musnud is followed by the 1st, 316th, 3727th, 4728th, 6914th and 7178th Divisions of Descendant Sons and Daughters of Ancient and Honorable Free and Accepted Boy Scouts, Watch and Ward and Library Protection Association Guards, King's Daughters, Sabbath Day Exclusivists, Seventh Day Adventists, and Holy Rollers in close formation. They are all in Empire Nicollet silk, striped with blue bombazine, ruched at neck and feet, and carry immense banners of green and yellow on which are pictured barred library doors, sealed books, bon-fires of questionable or lewd books, and padlocked library safes. They are preceded by and interlarded with silver and gold harp bands in great numbers, as well as a small exhibition corps of Anti-Lewd Book Examiners, carefully examining lewd books after the manner of the years A. D. 1885-1921. These last carry large red, yellow and green-blue pencils and wear horn glasses the size of saucers. They read, blush, and blue-pencil as they come.*

*They are preceded by cage-cars containing (one each) Ossified Specimens of Ancient Lewd Novelist, Playwright and Poet. They pause and stand at attention before the Musnud, giving first an exhibition of lewd-book editing, then the Free and Accepted and Descendant yell, "Anti-Vice! Anti-Vice! Boy Scouts Forever!" after which they clog and whistle.*]

NOXUS PODUNKUS: [*Scratching one ear and blinking his one open eye, the while the five thousand Nizys distribute soufflé and the audience cheers vociferously.*] Descendant Sons and Daughters of Ancient and Honorable Free and Accepted Boy Scouts, Watch and Ward Guards, King's Daughters, Sabbath Day Adventists, Holy Rollers [*whispers to a Dizzard, "Did I get them all right?"*]—we have, as you know, as President and Referendunces of this great Court, founded so long ago by our worthy predecessor, Mush Mush I, a certain duty to perform, and that is the asking of our regular prepared and revered and revised Sacred Questions, the answers to which, given as we all know you will give them, constitute in themselves at once a record and a testimony to the wisdom, perfection, peace and plenty to which our vast Federated Republics and Peoples the world over have at last arrived. [*Great applause lasting one hour, during which transcripts of the proceedings and speech thus far are wirelessed by the Fuddys to all parts of the world.*] Once, as you well know and as we are sorry to remember, there existed a certain amount of vice and crime in the world [*vast and prolonged boo-ing and cat-calling*]—less and less we will admit, as the forces of righteousness and order such as we represent here today gained momentum [*a second burst of applause lasting one hour, during which this portion of the speech is wirelessed. The Zadkiels breathe heavily*], but plentiful enough—plentiful enough, I am glad to say—Soufflé! Soufflé! [*he sighs and is fed*]—as well as a tendency, disobedient in the extreme, to investigate and study and doubt everything, from stars to ant-hills, and even to make light of the revealed and divine facts of Nature, which as we all know are irrefutable and not to be questioned and to which our hearts are always and only our best guides. [*Enormous applause, lasting thirty min-*

*utes.*] Fortunately for us now, however, and happily, and owing, as I may say, to the benign activities of those noble workers in the cause of righteousness, Mush Mush I, Bonehead V, and Dish Rag III, who flourished A. D. 1970-2061 in America and elsewhere, the virtues of sobriety, justice, truth, mercy, industry and the like were, as we all well know, firmly and finally established. [*Tremendous applause, lasting one hundred and eight minutes, during which seven hundred wash-boilers of soufflé are consumed. Wireless messages are sent to all parts.*] Thanks to them and their beneficent efforts, we do not attempt to investigate any more. [*Prolonged cheering.*] We do not seek to reason any more. [*Immense cheering, lasting two hours.*] Man, as you all well know, has seen the line of his duty and has followed it closely. [*More cat-calling.*] With the greatest care we have been able to eliminate not only those besetting vices which scarred the face of man with their hideous thoughts, but also those equally great vices of curiosity and speculation in regard to chemistry, philosophy, physics, astronomy, sociology, political economy, those low and evil so-called sciences which once so disturbed and irritated and afflicted the human mind. [*A burst of applause, lasting forty-three minutes.*] They have been done for, and instead we have strictly and sensibly confined ourselves, I am happy to state, to those more acceptable evidences of our place in Nature and our duties as revealed by those renowned and profound teachers and thinkers, our noble and revered ancestors, Billy Sunday the Great, he of blessed memory [*applause, lasting one hour*]—Ralph Waldensicuss Trinecuss of Boston [*applause, lasting fifty minutes*]—Arise-and-Sweat Marden [applause, lasting forty minutes]—Erbert Goughman [*applause, lasting thirty minutes*]—Philip Dugmore Potts [*applause, lasting twenty minutes*]—and Edith Whiller Nox Nox [*applause, lasting ten minutes*]—revealers and thinkers all, the true forerunners and prophets of our present peaceful and happy state.

[*Prolonged applause, enduring over seven-hundred minutes, during which* NOXUS PODUNKUS *and the Moonshees snore and the two thousand Loobies and Gaberlunzies read long and refreshing passages from the works of the individuals mentioned. The Fuddys sizz at their task.*]

THE ONE HUNDRED HODDY-DODDYS: [*As the applause subsides, feathering the face of the Moonshees.*] Awake, your Referendunces, awake! [*They pole-vault in front of the Musnud.*]

THE FIFTY DIZZARDS: [*Whistling between their teeth and striking with their feather clubs.*] Oh, your Very Great Referendunces! Oh! Come to! Come to! [*They chatter and clog.*]

NOXUS PODUNKUS: [*Batting an eye and being lifted to a sitting position.*] Ah, yes! Ah, yes! Let me see . . . where was I? [*A Dizzard, prompted by a Fuddy, repeats his last sentence.*] Ah, yes! As I was saying, these our revered leaders, taught us. It is to them, their patient and enduring labors, their deep, even profound, cogitations as to life, that we all owe all that we enjoy and revere so deeply today—our peace, our Freedom from disturbing thought, from the besetting vice of questioning or investigating. All we have to do now is ask and re-ask and affirm and re-affirm our Sacred Questions, so ably asked and answered so many centuries since by our noble forerunners, Bonehead V and Dish Rag III. [*Separate and prolonged applause at each name, during which* NOXUS PODUNKUS *again slumbers, is feathered and clubbed and lifted to a sitting position.*] Ah, yes! Ah, yes! The Questions—the Questions. [*He fumbles weakly about, while seven Dizzards hand him seven engrossed and gold-plated copies of the regulation Sacred Questions as made and provided for all such occasions. He stares at one feebly and continues.*] Ah yes! Now I have them! The Questions—the Questions, on which, as I was saying, are based, as on a rock, all our peace, security, freedom from thought; the very, indeed, pillows—I mean pillars—of our ease and comfort. The Sacred Questions! To be sure! Question One—let me see—Question One—Question One—[*Aside:* "Where is it?" *A Dizzard points to it.*]—Question One is most important, the very corner-stone, I might say, of our undisturbed security and ease in thoughtlessness. [*Examines it closely.*] It reads—it reads—Ah yes!—Now I have it!— "Have you kept the faith?" That's it. "Have you kept the faith?" To be sure! Have *we* kept it, I might say? Almost the most sacred of all our Questions! Have *we* kept the faith? [*He mumbles feebly on.*] That's it! Have *we* kept the faith?

THE 1ST, 316TH, 3727TH, 4728TH, 6914TH, AND 7178TH: [*Standing at attention and in unison.*]
We have, we have!
We have, have, have!

[*They clog. Immense applause from the audience, lasting thirty minutes. The First and Second Readers read soothing passages.*]

THE MOONSHEES, ROCTOR-PROCTORS, GAMALIELS, ZADKIELS: [*Turning on the other side and imbibing soufflé.*] Excellent! Excellent! Couldn't be better! They have kept the faith! Most comforting. Ah!

NOXUS PODUNKUS: [*Reclining and imbibing soufflé.*] Charming! Charming! Most sweet of them. The dear, dear things! They would keep anything we asked them to! It is really too wonderful! [*He sighs.*]

THE FEDERATED SPECTATORS: [*One hundred thousand strong.*] Hey! Hey! Hey! Rah! Rah! Rah! Federated Republics forever! Long live the Court of Progress! [*The cheering continues for fifteen minutes.*]

NOXUS PODUNKUS: [*When comparative silence is restored, and blinking his open eye.*] Beautiful! Beautiful! It is as I thought! A wondrous scene! Now for Question Number—let me see [*eleven Dizzards point to the place*]—Ah, yes! To be sure! [*Reads.*] Question Number Two—a wonderful question—a deep and subtly devised question—a question which, as I may say, has done as much as any of the others to persuade us to and keep us all in that happy and unquestioning frame of mind which, as we all know, we now so wisely seek to maintain—Soufflé! Soufflé! [*he imbibes*]—a question the like of which is not to be found in any other sacred code the world has ever known—and here, my dear fellow-Federationists [*he raises a hand*], and here is it: Question Two—Ah, yes!

[*Reads.*] "Is it not true that all men are now honest, kind, true, moral, virtuous and wise?" [*He pauses for breath and looks benignly about.*]

THE 1ST, 316TH, 3727TH, 4728TH, 6914TH, AND 7178TH: [*Jigging vigorously.*]
   They are! They are!
   They rarr! rarr! rarr!

[*They walk on their hands.*]

NOXUS PODUNKUS: Beautiful! Beautiful! Never have I heard such perfect teamwork! It is wonderful! Not so, my fellow Moonshees? [*He turns.*]

THE MOONSHEES, PUNDITS, ZADKIELS, ETC.: [*Turning over and snoring*] Excellent! Couldn't be better! They do perfect work! [*They each catch a wink of sleep.*]

NOXUS PODUNKUS: [*Aroused and scratching the back of his neck, the while he eyes them feelingly.*] It is too delightful! That I should have lived to have the exalted honor of presiding on so wonderful an occasion! But now for Question Three, my dears—Question Three—another beautiful question. [*He fumbles foolishly about seeking the tablet. Seventeen Dizzards point to it.*]—Ah, yes! Ah, yes! Very difficult to manage all of these questions! But here it is!—And now for Question Three—a lovely question! A question lovely! I almost hate to read it and have it all over with! [*Reads.*] "And that all women are as pure as driven snow?" [*Pauses and gazes about ecstatically, one hand up.*]

THE 1ST, 316TH, 3727TH, 4728TH, 6914TH, AND 7178TH: [*Executing cart-wheels in circles.*]
   Aye! Aye! Aye! Aye! Aye! Aye!
   'Tis as easy to say as Pie! Pie! Pie!

[*They end by waving with their feet.*]

THE FEDERATED SPECTATORS:
   Hey! Hey! Hey! Hey! Hey! Hey!
   The world's now safe for ever and a day!

*The Court of Progress* 153

[*An hour of unbroken applause follows.*]

NOXUS PODUNKUS: [*As quiet is once more restored and he is dusted into semi-consciousness.*] Quite so! Quite so! Forever and a day! Ah! And—and [*he looks about for his tablet and twenty-seven Dizzards each hand him a sacred plate*]—and that—let me see—Ah, yes!—Question Four! Question Four! Here it is! [*Reads.*] "And that God is always on His Throne?" [*He collapses from exhaustion.*]

THE 1ST, 316TH, 3727TH, 4728TH, 6914TH, AND 7178TH: [*Falling flat on their backs.*]
He is! He is! It is so plain
Upon His Throne He doth remain!
By day or night, in dark or light,
We feel His presence shining bright!
All's well with the world!

[*They roll to and fro in rows of one hundred each.*]

THE ONE HUNDRED THOUSAND SPECTATORS: [*Uproariously.*]
Hey! Hey! What a glorious day!
Hey! Hey! What a glorious day!

[*The cheering is resumed for fifteen minutes more, during which ten vanloads of soufflé are distributed.*]

NOXUS PODUNKUS: [*After order has been restored and surveying his associates of the Musnud sleepily.*] Perfect! Perfect!—or nearly so! Beautiful! I never saw anything so well done! Never! Such order! Such union!! But—let me see—I believe these are all the questions to be asked of these divisions, are they not? [*Looks about him helplessly and yet benignly. The fifty Dizzards all rush together and confer. The Hoddy-Doddys ditto. The Zanys ditto. The Loobies and Gaberlunzies bite their nails, then rush together and mumble. The Moonshees sit up and confer with* NOXUS PODUNKUS. *He proceeds.*] Ah yes! As I was saying! Quite so! Quite so! Quite so! Since, then, it is the opinion of the Associated Members of the Musnud that the report of the Descendant Sons and Daughters of Ancient and Honorable Free and Accepted Boy Scouts and Anti- [*he reads the entire roster*] seems to accord with the progress of the year as reported to us from all outlying sections of the Federation, and it is their wish that it be accepted and offered and engrossed in the records of the Musnud as a true picture of the state and progress of the world for this year of our Lord A. D. 3913, they will signify as much by saying "Aye," contrary, "Nay." The "Ayes" have it. The report of these excelling representatives is accepted and they are excused. [*He falls back and into a deep sleep. The Moonshees do likewise.*]

THE ONE HUNDRED MOONSHEES: [*Weakly, in their sleep*]. Soufflé! Soufflé!

THE ONE HUNDRED THOUSAND SPECTATORS:
Hey! Hey! Hey! 'Tis a perfect day!
'Tis a perfect day! 'Tis a perfect day!
Hey! Hey! Hey! 'Tis a perfect day!

[*They cheer for one solid hour.*]

THE 1ST, 316TH, 3727TH, 4728TH, 6914TH, AND 7178TH: [*Ricocheting and executing triple hand-springs, the while* SHISHMASH HASH HASH *sidesteps and returns to the main stage entrance, left.*]
What pleasure, oh! What pleasure, oh!
To know the world is perfect, so
That never now by day or night
Need any one feel fear or fright.

[*They zigzag gaily in ranks of one thousand and exit.*]

SHISHMASH HASH HASH: [*At the stage entrance, surveying one hundred and fifty divisions of Descendant Sons and Daughters of Ancient and Honorable Moving Picture Censors, Sabbath Day Observance Leaguers, Baptist and Methodist Evangelists, and Non-Smokers' Social Unionists, now ready and in marching order just outside the tent entrance. These have arranged themselves in battalions of two thousand each and are arrayed in snow-white frock coats, bright red silk hats, lavender pants or skirts, as the case may be, and carry bright brass drum-major batons. Numerous bands of Descendant and Amalgamated Sons and Daughters of Ancient and Honorable Anti-Saloon*

*Leaguers and Billysundays are arrayed in pink-flowered business suits and silver-green capes, carrying hatchets and bearing aloft the portrait of their patron saint, Mrs. Carrie Nation, who flourished A. D. 1884-1913, playing on silver and tin horns, wind instruments, hewgags and jew's harps. These are preceded by cage-cars containing one each of Ossified Specimens of Ancient Cigarette Fiend, Simon-pure American Bartender, Lewd Scenario Writer, Sabbath Day Breaker. The bands begin playing "All Hail the Peace Which Now Prevails!" As they enter, preceded by* SHISHMASH HASH HASH *with his head between his legs and walking on his hands to the Musnud, forty thousand members of the audience rise and stand on their heads. Another forty thousand sink to the floor between their seats and gasp. The five thousand Nizys pass swiftly among them administering soufflé. The first and second readers read rapidly.* SHISHMASH HASH HASH, *landing on his feet as he reaches the Musnud and beginning to jig.*] Will the High and Mighty Referendunces of the Federated Musnud of the World deign to notice these humble instruments of moral intercession here gathered from all parts of the world to testify at this great review to the blessings of peace, morality, fecundity and other social virtues? [*As he says this he executes nine flip-flops, whereat the great assemblage bursts into thunderous applause. The fifty Dizzards on the Musnud leap on each other's necks as they whistle between their teeth. The one hundred Zanys rattle their wind-bags furiously.* NOXUS PODUNKUS, *being simultaneously beaten by four stuffed clubs and tickled by four feather-dusters, while two Dizzards whistle in his ears, opens both eyes and looks blandly around.*]

NOXUS PODUNKUS: [*With a fat, ingratiating smile, as the uproar continues.*] Are we now beholding more divisions of the unconquerable forces of Truth, Virtue, Justice, Sobriety and Righteousness? Good! Good! [*He opens his mouth, which is immediately filled with soufflé.*]

THE ONE HUNDRED AND FIFTY DIVISIONS: [*Cakewalking, shamble-shuffling and tossing their hatchets, batons, musical instruments, etc., aloft.*] Hail! Hail! The end of shame!

[*They sing.*]
'Tis now that we with joy behold
The earth of virtue yield fourfold
Of truth and right the crop is great—
Indeed, enough the world to sate!

[*Melody the same as "Behold the Power." To be sung without lining.*]

NOXUS PODUNKUS: [*Scratching one ear and making a supreme effort to think.*] A charming sight! A charming sight! The world is indeed progressing! Allow us to congratulate you, my dears and dearesses! Allow us! Allow us! Perfection is at hand! It has been long in coming, but now, as I might say, it has reached its destination. Soufflé! Soufflé! [*A pannier is brought and fed him.*] As I was saying to those last dear battalions who so gracefully testified to our Peace and Progress, Security and the like, it now becomes my duty to read from our revered and Sacred Questions—the compendium, as you know, of all our Knowledge, Law, Intelligence—Questions Five, Six, Seven and Eight—I believe that is the allotted number, is it not? [*Thirty-one Dizzards nod.*]—and as I do so will you please answer in unison so that all may know—the world—the universe indeed—how well we understand, how firmly we know, believe, that which has brought us to our present state of peace and comfort, our ease of mind and body. [*Reads.*] Question Five—Question Five—ah yes! Just as I thought! [*Reads, one hand up.*] "There is a God, is there not? We know that, do we not?"

THE ONE HUNDRED AND FIFTY DIVISIONS: [*Jabbing their batons into the ground, tossing them in the air and then catching them again.*]
There is! There is! We do! We do!
What joy to know 'tis true, true, true!

[*At this ninety-nine Moonshees, who have risen to a sitting position, fall back, murmuring "Splendid! Splendid! Wonderful!" The Hoddy-Doddys exclaim the same thing and practice at sword-play with their featherdusters, while the Dizzards play at leap-frog and the Zanys beat each other with their empty wind-bags. The five thousand Nizys plunge their heads into the soufflé but withdraw them quickly and ladle out cones to the mass. The two thousand Loobies and Gaberlunzies read many enchanting passages as the audience applauds, after which the Dizzards resume normal positions and lay about them with their stuffed clubs.*]

NOXUS PODUNKUS: [*Scratching his nose and making another great effort to think, the while he beats the railing before him.*] Ah, yes! That is it! "There is! We do!" It is on our knowledge of that that we rest so peacefully, all else being of no importance. [*Reads.*] Question Six—[*pauses*]—"He is on His Throne, is He not? We know that, do we not?"

THE ONE HUNDRED AND FIFTY DIVISIONS: [*Jigging.*]
He is! He is! We do! We do!
This truth is ever new and true!

NOXUS PODUNKUS: [*Sinking into his pillows and peacefully closing his eyes.*] Quite so! Quite so! We need that knowledge to sustain us in our present ease. It is so comforting! As I often say, what would we do without our dear Questions? [*He falls asleep. Seven Dizzards and seven Hoddy-Doddys club and feather him. He resumes.*] And now for—ah yes!—let me see—Question—Question [*various Dizzards gather about him and point*]—Ah, yes! Seven—Question Seven! [*Ecstatically.*] Let me read this to you, this beautiful Question, the answer to which, as I so often say, reassures us all so much, keeps us all so sweet and content, always. [*Raises one hand.*] "All is well with the world, is it not? We know that, do we not? It is, is it not?" Come now, all together—One, Two, Three—

THE ONE HUNDRED AND FIFTY DIVISIONS:
Yea, ho! Yea, ho! Yea, Bo! Yea, Bo!
A truer thing we do not know!

[*They fall to the ground and roll rapturously to and fro.*]

NOXUS PODUNKUS: [*As wave on wave of applause sweeps over the pavilion and bags out the sides and top, leaning forward and opening one eye.*] 'Tis beautifully said! Beautifully said! A perfect answer to a perfect Question! A wonderful testimony to the ever upwardness and onwardness of things! It is almost more than one could hope for—than any one *can* hope for! And now, my dears and dearesses, comes Question—[*looks at the tablet while all the Dizzards lean and point*]—Question Eight, a very, very great Question, a Question which, as I always say, has undoubtedly more than any other Question brought us at last to this very perfect and peaceful state, in which we rest as, I might say, a babe in its cradle, as a—a—Soufflé! [*He is fed.*] Here it is: "How is it that we know that God is on His Throne and all is well with the world? How is it?" Can't you see how important that is, how wonderful? Come now! We must have a perfect and compelling answer to this! All together—One, Two, Three! [*Leans forward expectantly, intently.*]

THE ONE HUNDRED AND FIFTY DIVISIONS:
Our hearts, our hearts, they tell us so—
What is it that our hearts don't know!

[*Each places a hand over his heart.*]

NOXUS PODUNKUS: [*Falling back on seven pillows and taking a deep breath.*] Beautiful! Beautiful! Even so! And given as it should be! Let me hear you say that again, my dears and dearesses! Let me hear it again! [*They repeat it, waving pink handkerchiefs. The audience bursts into deafening applause lasting seventy-eight minutes. The Loobies and Gaberlunzies leap in the air, turn three somersaults before landing, and fall on their feet. Five thousand wirelesses are sent.* NOXUS PODUNKUS, *falling back and strangling with joy.*] This is too much! Too much! Who can say now that the world has not progressed! [*He is lifted up, feathered and doused with soufflé.*] With the consent of my fellow Moonshees [*looks about him affably at the sleeping Moonshees*], I will now excuse these very good people. [*Feeble calls of "Beautiful! Beautiful!" and "Let them be excused!" from the Moonshees.*] You may go, my dears and dearesses! You may go! [*He collapses.*]

THE ONE HUNDRED AND FIFTY DIVISIONS: [*Executing a flank movement and assuming an open formation five hundred abreast and marching briskly away, twirling their ba-*

*tons and wagging their heads.*] All hail the power of Podunks' name! [*They exit. Enter seven thousand Union Astronomers and four thousand Federated College Philosophers in close formation, all in green knee pants, white spike tailcoats and blue silk hats. The Astronomers carry green telescopes instead of canes. The Philosophers are all chewing tutti-frutti. They are preceded by cage-cars containing each one Specimen of Ossified and Ancient and Unmoral Stoic, Nietzschean, Pragmatist, Anti-Christ, Chemist and Physicist.*]

SHISHMASH HASH HASH: [*Preceding them and climbing up the feather pole of a Hoddy-Doddy he has seized.*] The Union Astronomers, your Referendunces! The Federated College Philosophers, your Referendunces! [*He leaps and tumbles three times around the arena, holding his toes with his hands.*]

THE ONE HUNDRED HODDY-DODDYS: [*Pole-vaulting over the procession as it approaches.*] The Union Astronomers, your Referendunces! The Federated Moral College Philosophers! [*The Dizzards give an exhibition of feather-club swallowing. The five thousand Nizys each juggle nine ice cream cones in the air.*]

THE SEVEN THOUSAND UNION ASTRONOMERS: [*Marching to "Oh, Believe Me If All Those Endearing Young Charms," and doing a hop, skip and jump as they near the Musnud.*]
 The universe is moral! The universe is moral!
 'Tis as true—'tis as true—
 As that a green horse isn't sorrel!

[*One-half the division stand on their heads, the others on their feet.*]

THE FIFTY DIZZARDS: [*Receiving soufflé handed up by the Nizys below. In chorus.*]
 "The universe is moral! The universe is moral!
 'Tis as true—'tis as true—
 As that a green horse isn't sorrel!"

THE ELEVEN THOUSAND PHILOSOPHERS AND ASTRONOMERS: [*In chorus.*]
>Hail! Hail! The Comet's Tail!
>All is well! All is swell!
>Never was there an age like this!

[*They wave their feet or hands, as the case may be.*]

NOXUS PODUNKUS: [*Rising on one elbow and rubbing his eyes.*] What! What! More? What have we here? The Union Astronomers, you say? The Federated College Philosophers? Excellent! A fine body of men, indeed! And, as you say, the universe *is* moral. Very, very, very moral. One of the most moral universes I have ever known. [*Scratches an ear and sinks into his cushions, but the nearest Dizzards lift him up.*]

SHISHMASH HASH HASH: [*Excitedly touching his toes with his hands nine times.*] The questions, your Noble Referendunce! The Sacred Questions!

NOXUS PODUNKUS: [*Heavily and benignly.*] Ah, yes! Ah, yes! The Sacred Questions! It is not intention, but memory, that seems to fail me. Quite so—the Sacred Questions! [*He takes one of fifty plates offered him and examines it closely.*] Ah yes! Here it is! One of the most significant and wonderful questions that has ever been planned, I think, to ease our minds and comfort us. [*Reads.*] Question Nine: "Is it not true that the universe is ordained for Truth, Justice, Virtue, Mercy, Tenderness, Purity?" [*His voice trails off in utter exhaustion.*]

THE SEVEN THOUSAND UNION ASTRONOMERS: [*Doing a light come-all-ye and waving red bandana handkerchiefs.*]
>It is! It is! We know! We know!
>The stars we see, they tell us so!

THE FOUR THOUSAND COLLEGE PHILOSOPHERS: [*Masticating their gum vigorously.*]
>It is! It is! Hail, loud and long!
>Our works, they sing the same sweet song!

[*Loud and prolonged cheering by the audience. Wirelesses are sent to the waiting world. The Dizzards gnaw excitedly at their feather-clubs, then do a double-quick clog. The two thousand Loobies and Gaberlunzies read many, many soothing passages. The Nizys dole out soufflé.*]

NOXUS PODUNKUS: [*Biting his nails and crossing his legs.*] So! Quite so! The stars tell us! It couldn't be different! And now, my dears [*sighs from weariness*], for the Tenth Great Question—one of those beautiful things that I always love to read and re-read. The most important one, I always think, in so far as astronomy is concerned, that has ever been devised. A Question so perfect that, when we pause to consider its absolute truthfulness and perfection, answers fully—oh, so fully!—all our astronomical needs. [*Reads.*] "Are not the stars maintained in their courses in order that man may progress and be moral?" [*He contemplates a fly which has lit on the end of his nose.*]

THE UNION ASTRONOMERS: [*Juggling their telescopes after the manner of a shillalah and doing a come-all-ye.*]
  They are! They are! The stars, they say
  That man to truth is on his way!

THE COLLEGE PHILOSOPHERS: [*Catching hands and dancing around in a circle.*]
  The Universe was made for man—
  And man for good, by God's dear plan!

[*They slap each other on the back.*]

NOXUS PODUNKUS: [*Rolling back in ecstasy and smearing his face with soufflé.*] Lovely! Lovely! "The stars they say!" This certainly is the most inspiring session we have ever had! Such trinity of feeling! Such innate wisdom! Surely the waiting world must realize now how completely we have progressed—how absolutely—[*He sinks to his pillows and is lifted to a sitting position by the Dizzards, who place the tablet in his hand, while the Moonshees turn over and murmur "Excellent! Excellent!" The wireless operators send out five thousand messages.* NOXUS PODUNKUS *pulls himself together and continues.*] And now, my dear children—and now comes one of the keenest, the most searching really, of all the Great and Sacred Questions made and provided for these immortal occasions and handed down to us by our renowned and dear bygone leaders and saints, Bonehead V and Dish Rag III. Really, when I stop to think of their great work for mankind, when—[*he sinks back and the Hoddy-Doddys proceed to dust him off*]—Ah yes! Ah, yes! Question Eleven—almost the most wonderful, the most important of all—[*reads*]—"How—how," so it reads, "do we know that, me good men? How?" [*He smiles and waits expectantly, one finger up.*] How do we know? That is the famous, the keenest and most searching of all the Twelve Sacred Questions. How?

THE SEVEN THOUSAND UNION ASTRONOMERS: [*Telescope to eye and weaving in and out in a wild dance.*]
Our hearts, they tell us! We can hear
This truth they whisper, year by year!

[*They kiss each other on each cheek.*]

THE FOUR THOUSAND COLLEGE PHILOSOPHERS: [*In chorus, and doing a hop, skip and jump.*]
Our hearts do tell us! We do know—
Besides, our Astronomers do say so!

[*They swallow their gum. The multitude breaks into tumultuous applause, which lasts for one hour, during which one thousand messages are sent out and five thousand more wash-boilers of soufflé are consumed.*]

NOXUS PODUNKUS: [*Aiming at the fly and missing it.*] Ah! Ah! Could the world wish for anything more—more enlightening? Our hearts tell us! Oh, dear! Our dear Astronomers and College Philosophers stand in absolute accord as to this! Wonderful! Wonderful! [*Turning to the Musnud.*] I am sure that you, my dear fellow Moonshees and Savants, must be greatly impressed and inspired by this! It is what we all so much wish to hear, always! [NOXUS PODUNKUS *rolls over on his side, while the Moonshees turn over and murmur "Excellent! Exquisitely put! Couldn't be better!" The Union As-*

tronomers and College Philosophers now march off singing, "Hail! Hail! The Gang's all here!" the Philosophers weeping on each other's necks for joy while the Astronomers wig-wag the song with their telescopes. The Moonshees, Zadkiels, etc., squeak feebly for soufflé.]

[Enter forty-eight divisions of five hundred each of Descendant Sons and Daughters of Ancient and Honorable Anti-Vice Crusaders, Prison Visitation Leaguers, Moral Prophylaxers, Anti-Contraceptionists, Eugenic Sires and Women Magazine Editors, in green, yellow and blue burnouses and pink papier-mâché casques, fox-trotting as they come. An immense banner of Chinese silk and Australian wool mixed (symbolic of the general sequacity, tranquillity, plasticity, yet not to say florescence or flaccidity which now hovers over all the world) is carried before. This same contains a pale representation of a jail, such as existed in former centuries when the world was evil, but now (in the picture), in order to symbolize the present peace and progress of the world, crumbled and covered with vines and spiderwebs, while four angels of peace, one at each corner, hold up palms of victory. They are preceded by cage-cars containing each one Specimen of Ossified and Ancient White-Slaver, Gambler, Thief and Predatory Rich. As they approach, the Loobies, Gaberlunzies, Nizys and Zanys bustle hither and thither among the audience, the former reading, the latter calling for silence and explaining the exact significance of the symbol while they ladle out soufflé. On and before the Musnud the Hoddy-Doddys and Dizzards hover over NOXUS PODUNKUS and the Moonshees, who have fallen into a sound sleep. Two thousand members of the Inter-Federated Association of Inter-Asiatic Descendant Sons and Daughters of Ancient and Honorable Eugenic Sires approach first, the men wearing green Zouave trousers, white silk overcoats and blue shakos. They carry lilies. The ladies are wrapped in nine layers of pink asbestos each one inch thick and carry poisoned hatpins. After charging and counter-charging they form a square in front of the Musnud, the ladies stacking hatpins, the men presenting lilies.]

SHISHMASH HASH HASH: [*Tumbling back from the entryway where he has been supervising the general formation of the new division.*] Your Referendunces! Your Referendunces! Look, oh look! The Inter-Federated Association of Inter-Asiatic Descendant Sons and Daughters of Eugenic Sires crave the honor of approaching and testifying before this great Court as to what Progress has done for them! Your Referendunces!

THE ONE HUNDRED HODDY-DODDYS: [*Ranging in a line and presenting arms with their feather-dusters.*]
    Oh, never, never has there been
    A sight to equal this, we ween!
        Glorious!

[*They clog, and chatter their teeth.*]

THE MEMBERS OF THE INTER-FEDERATED ASSOCIATION OF INTER-ASIATIC DESCENDENT SONS AND DAUGHTERS: [*Pirouetting and bowing to each other.*]
    'Tis six full centuries at least
    Since un-Eugenic weddings ceased;
    And now each youth and maid you see
    Is married full Eugenic-ly.
    In us behold the perfect fruitage
    That followed on the former brute-age!

[*They ring-around-the-rosy.*]

NOXUS PODUNKUS: [*Lifted to a sitting position by the Dizzards, tickled with feather-dusters, beaten with wind-bags and doused with ice-water until he opens his eyes.*] What a sight!—A beautiful sight, I mean! My word! O never, my celebrated and associated Referendunces [*he turns to them*] have I seen so much beauty and virtue! Never! So much modesty! So much—much—everything! Really this is the worst—I mean best—I ever saw! This in itself is a complete refutation of that foul charge, once so common, that the world was in danger of not progressing. Look! Behold! O Progress, where is thy sting? [*He collapses, calling for soufflé, but is bolstered up and ice-water poured over him.*]

ONE HUNDRED EUGENIC MAIDS: [*In pink Mother Hubbards and green Quaker bonnets. Stepping forward and sinking on one knee, hands on their chins. They sing.*]
It is our duty to attest
How by Eugenics we are blest!
O 'tis a wondrous art divine,
Which causes all the world to shine!

NOXUS PODUNKUS: [*Leaning over the railing and eying them closely.*] Really! This is the limit—I mean almost too much—too much! Sweet maids! Dear sweet maids! This spectacle of the perfect fruitage of Progress under the great moral care of our forefathers—blessed be the name of the ever-to-be-remembered Anthony!—[*he bows, and the audience with him*]—is all but too much! Progress can do no more! I would, if any service which the mere sight of you does not render—could render—ask you the Twelfth and final Question, but what would be the use? How well we know the import of your message, even before you speak! How well we know the import of you yourselves—wonderful creatures that you are! [*They bow their heads.*] This vast assemblage, which in itself is a testimony to the value of Eugenics, understands full well that by the practice of Eugenics alone all weakness, vice, crime, art, philosophy [*except that which our dear Union Astronomers and Federated Philosophers instinctively know and proclaim*], the need of white-slave laws, saloons, the theatre—all, all have long since been done away with, so that we have now—the most of us, I am glad to say—not even so much as an historic memory of them. Indeed, as we all know, on this once most unsafe but now safest of planets [*applause lasting seventeen minutes*], men and women are now as safe and perfect and pure as ever our worthy forefathers could have dreamed of or desired. Why, to look at you alone is enough! [*He sighs and rests.*]

Dear Eugenic citizens and citizenesses, without taxing you further with these deep and brain-racking questions, so sacred to us all of course, the one message of this great Court to you is to go and do as you have always done: think no more than is absolutely necessary. Don't tax your brains. This, our great Federation of Commission-Ruled Republics, is here to do all that for you. [*The Moonshees stir.*] The less we know the better, as we all know. [*Long and loud applause lasting eighteen minutes.*] In former and darker, and therefore sadder, times, there were many who thought differently. But they and all those who were a part of them have long since been disposed of. [*Long and uproarious applause.*] And is not, I now ask you, the world happier, fairer, sweeter to the eye and the mind? [*Cries of "Hear! Hear!" and "Yea! Yea!" lasting two hours.*] Now, dear Eugenic citizens, you need only consider how thoughtless you are and therefore how happy in these sweet exercises and games such as we see here today which contribute only to the sustenance, docility and fertility of man, to know how true all this is. Be thoughtless. Be happy. And by so being, as I always think, you contribute and testify to the efficiency of Truth, Virtue, Justice, Mercy, Sobriety, Love, Beauty, Simplicity, Peace—[*he collapses from sheer exhaustion*]— Soufflé! Soufflé! [*A bucket of soufflé is brought and administered.*]

THE ONE HUNDRED MAIDS: [*Wishing not to tire their noble Referendunces, singing in chorus.*]
 O, sweet Eugenic thought—to know
 That our dear Noxus loves us so!

[*They fall back in the ranks.*]

[*Enter fifteen thousand Descendant Sons and Daughters of Ancient and Honorable Anti-White-Slavers of the pre-Federated Period (A. D. 1870-1927), in green-and-white kilts and galligaskins, with perukes and billy-cocks on their heads. They march swiftly forward, an expression of grim determination—historically correct—on their faces, and pause before the Musnud. Over their left arms, after the fashion of the world's great Anti-White-Slave Leaders and in accordance with historical descriptions of the same, hang immense mantles of dark green bed-ticking intended to shield naked fleeing white slaves. Over their shoulders are carried papier-mâché broadaxes of the kind known to have been used by all Anti-White-Slavers, male and female, in felling the enemy. These they occasionally*] *brandish as they walk. At their belts hang lanterns, files, skeleton keys, medicine kits containing concentrated food pills, digitalis and the like, all intended for the rescue and resuscitation of overcome white slaves. Their eyelids and mouths are painted a bright cerise to give a look of extra vigor and force, and as they walk, one hundred abreast, they peer to right and left in the most searching and secretive and yet detecting way from beneath their hands, and occasionally flash their dark lanterns on the surrounding spectators.]*

SHISHMASH HASH HASH: [*Leaping up and cracking his heels nine times before descending.*] Your Referendunces! Your Referendunces! We have here the only living Descendant Sons and Daughters of Ancient and Honorable American Anti-White-Slavers—the organization which in its day gave rise—laid the foundation, as it were, of our present great and perfect World Federation, over which at present your Referendunces are so ably presiding. It claims to be the only existing organization that preserves in all their purity the customs, manners and instincts of the original pre-Federated Anti-White-Slavers of seven and eight centuries since. I beg of your Referendunces—I beg of you!—on this very special occasion—I know you are tired—Will your Referendunces be pleased to receive them? [*He runs swiftly around in a ring and falls over three extended feather-dusters. NOXUS PODUNKUS groans. The Moonshees moan.*]

THE ONE HUNDRED ZANYS: [*Dancing on before them and rattling their wind-bags.*] The Anti-White-Slavers! The Anti-White-Slavers! Look! Behold!

THE FIFTY DIZZARDS: [*Beating the Moonshees with feather-clubs and whistling between their teeth.*] Awake! Awake! [*The Moonshees stir feebly and call for soufflé. By the aid of a dozen gallons of ice-water NOXUS PODUNKUS is once more aroused and now surveys the approaching procession, which marches about the arena and back to the Musnud.*]

NOXUS PODUNKUS: [*Scratching his left ear and surveying the assembled throng.*] What—more? Oh! Well, welcome, noble citizens! Welcome! I see by your brows that you possess the unconquerable love of Liberty, Virtue, Truth, Justice, Beauty, etc., so necessary to the happy maintenance of our present Federated condition. [*He collapses and more soufflé is administered. Recovering.*] Stick to it! What supreme comfort it must be to you and your exceedingly courageous ancestors to know that our very happy present condition is almost entirely due to them—their noble deeds of valor performed in order that we might become so—so—[*he coughs*]. What supreme deeds would not you now, I am sure [*they brandish their battleaxes*] gladly perform were it not that fortunately all provocation had long since been done away with. [*Loud cheering. All the Nizys, Zanys, Hoddy-Doddys, etc., walk on their hands.*] Night after night in the wilds of the great cities of those far-off centuries, now so happily past, did your forefathers fearlessly and tirelessly seek out the enslavers of resisting and lovely womanhood and battle to the death with those who would have corrupted our worthy sires—I mean siresses—Soufflé!—[*he imbibes*]—performing astounding and now almost unbelievable feats of valor, felling the vile and rapacious enslaver to the plain and chopping him to bits, leaving us, their humble descendants, little if anything to do save revere and historically represent the marvels which they then performed. [*Immense and prolonged cheering. Eight thousand wireless messages are sent forth.*] Literature, by their aid, as we all well know, has at last been completely done away with. [*Riotous applause.*] Profane art in all its forms and all its seductive wiles has long since ceased. [*The audience shouts for one hour.*] The vile newspapers of ancient days [*innumerable swells of booing and cat-calling*], wont to chronicle only the private and social vices of unregenerate man, now, thanks to the unremitting toil of those who had only the moral regeneration of the world in view, its true spiritual progress [*prolonged and enduring applause*], chronicle only the sweet messages of hope and cheer by which we sustain each other in our happy state—Soufflé! Soufflé! [*He dips his head in a pannier. The audience cheers for one hour.*] Now we are not troubled with politics, armies, or any vile evidences of commercial strife and contest. [*More applause.*] Nothing disturbs us in any way! Could we ask more? [*Cries of "Hear! Hear!"*] As I was saying to those dear creatures who just left, our beloved Eugenic citizens and citizenesses, we need now only concern ourselves with the simple arts of peace and pleasure as we here see manifest in this great assemblage. On you, therefore, more than on any other group which at this time could come before this august Court to testify to the Truth, Peace, Virtue, Sequacity and Docility of our present world-realm, devolves, as lineal descendants of these our great sires, the sweet task of keeping bright the memory of their great deeds. I am sure that you, my dears and dearesses, by maintaining so earnest a stand against all thought of any kind, by persisting in your aversion to moral heresies of all sorts and indeed learning and science in every form, and by your persistent and industrious mutilation and destruction of all profane facts, so long the curse of society [*loud cries of "Down with all facts"*], will succeed—I know you will!—in keeping the world as fresh and pure and innocent as on the day it was made. [*Cries of "Yes, yes," and "we will, we will." Applause for one hour.*] Soufflé! Soufflé! [*He is fed.*]—Cruel, disturbing thought, that one great curse of humanity in its earlier ages must never be allowed to trouble us again. [*Immense applause.*] And since, by what processes of hardy non-thinking only our revered ancestors know, profound peace has at last been reached, I caution you, O my fellow-citizens, let not a single irritating disturbing fact ever again impinge upon the sweet idealism and mental slumber which now reigns. Behold our happy Dizzards! [*They wiggle their stuffed clubs.*] Could any of the so-called and boasted mental processes of former ages have produced them? [*They walk on their hands.*] And our dear Zanys! [*They rattle their wind-bags.*] What would our great peaceful Federation be without them? [*They beat each other over the head.*] Or our graceful Nizys! [*They take up wash-boilers of soufflé and ladle it right and left solemnly.*] The gentility and wholeheartedness of their service! [*They playfully pelt each other with cones filled with soufflé.*] Or our kindly Hoddy-Doddys! [*They vault.*] What more could humanity desire in the shape of perfect and helpful men? [*They leap on each other's backs and fall gracefully to the floor.*] When I contemplate these, and this great audience [*profound applause lasting seventeen minutes*], and these our assembled cohorts of Virtue, Truth, Justice, Mercy [*more applause, lasting one hour*], come here from all parts of the known world to testify to the great fundamental truths which have made them so, I—[*At this point the great audience rises en masse and cheers for one hour, seventeen and one-half minutes and thirteen seconds. Rival groups of Descendant Sons and Daughters of Ancient and Honorable Anti-White-Slavers, Anti-Vivisectionists, Anti-Contraceptionists, Billysundays, Eugenic Sires, Anti-Saloon Leaguers, Watch and Ward Guards, King's Daughters, Free and Accepted Boy Scouts, etc., rush forward and seize upon the cages containing the only remaining specimens of Gambler, Saloon-keeper, Predatory Financier, Philosopher, Magdalen, Vivisectionist, Madam, Nietzschean and other early examples of now nearly or quite extinct miscreants or papier-mâché representations of the same, and haul them before the Musmud amid the cheering, hee-hawing, cat-calling of the audience. The Zanys, Nizys, Dizzards, Loobies, Hoddy-Doddys, Gaberlunzies and Fuddys, forgetting their regular duties, spin, squeal, play at leap-frog, beat each other with feather-dusters and wind-bags. Various regiments of Descendant Sons and Daughters of Ancient and Honorable Feminists, Professors of Christian Economy, Prohibitionists, Socialists, etc., who have not yet had the privilege of parading and testifying before the Musmud, crowd the entryways, swarm the aisles and so obstruct the peaceful and orderly development of the proceedings of the Court that, in view of this and because ordinarily the proceedings consume from twenty to thirty days anyhow, so great is the anxiety of all to testify to the magnificent progress of the world since vice and crime have been done away with,* NOXUS PODUNKUS, *now thoroughly awake and after due counsel with the ninety-nine other Moonshees, Savants, Roctor-Proctors, Pundits, Theorists, Zadkiels, Seers, Oracles, Solons, Nestors, Gamaliels, Daniels, etc., also disturbed in their slumbers, decides that, all things considered, and notwithstanding, it were as well if the taking of testimony were to be discontinued for this day, and to this end, after various signs, grunts, squeals, motions to the Zanys, Dizzards, Nizys, Loobies, Hoddy-Doddys, Gaberlunzies,*

Fuddys, etc., the latter are brought to their senses and through them the audience calmed.]

[It was then that NOXUS PODUNKUS, speaking for the Musnud, announced that the proceedings for this day were hereby ended and that the Court stood adjourned until the following morning at ten o'clock; after which SHISHMASH HASH HASH, as Master of Ceremonies, Chairmaster, etc., led the outgoing throng with a magnificent example of rotary hand-spring motion. At this point, also, owing to lack of space and by reason of the fact that enough is as good as a feast, the humble recording Dramatist quits and the curtain is hereby drawn on this historic scene. For those, however, who desire a fuller report of the same, it may be found in Volumes MMCCCIII, MMMMMMMMCCCLLVI, Proceedings of the Federated Court of Progress (Moline-Emporia-Sedalia Sittings) for the years 3913-'14-'15, NOXUS PODUNKUS presiding; SHISHMASH HASH HASH, Secretary and Master of Ceremonies.]

**CURTAIN**

# THE VOICE

## CHARACTERS

THE WOMAN, *Edith.*
THE MAN, *Harold.*
THE VOICE, *Edith's dead lover.*

# SCENE

*A simple room with a round reading table in the centre, an open fire, right, and at the back two French windows, the one giving into a bedroom, the other out upon a balcony. Left, a baby grande piano.*

THE VOICE: Tof! Tof! Tof! You see I make the same sound as of old.

THE WOMAN: [*At the table.*] I hear you. Oh, I hear you. [*She stops her sewing, leans her elbows on her knees, her face in her hands, and stares into the fire.*]

THE VOICE: Thus up the balcony in that other place I climbed, while your parents slept, and held you in my arms. Do you remember how I held you? Do you remember how I looked?

THE WOMAN: Yes, yes. I remember. I can see you now.

THE VOICE: And the loveliest thing about you to me was your throat. Oh, how I loved it! It was like a white pillar, full and round. You wore your dress cut low in front with quantities of soft lace billowing up at the back of your neck and falling forward over your shoulders. An amethyst heart hung on a slender chain—so hung that it rested in the tiny hollow at the base of your throat. Do you remember? You are dressed that way tonight for him.

THE WOMAN: [*Stirring and putting a hand over her eyes.*] Oh, I remember. I was so young and dreamful—so altogether lovely,—and you too.

THE VOICE: And now he has come and he is neither young nor lovely. He is coarse, Edith, gross. And so, in a way, are you. I loved you for that too in that day, the hard richness of your beautiful body, the blazing fire in your eyes. Your arms—I love them even now. [*She holds one out.*] Your neck! Your neck! Do you remember?

THE WOMAN: I remember.

THE VOICE: But now!—but now!—Soon he will be coming and then I will be forgotten once more. You live in a hard world of reality. I live in dreams. That is why I am forgotten.

THE WOMAN: Oh, not forgotten. I think of you always, always!—your hair and eyes. So great a love one never can forget. It never comes a second time. [*She sighs.*]

THE VOICE: Ah, but where I lie the grass is long and brown—the wind is stern.

THE WOMAN: I know, I know. [*The door bell rings. She goes and pushes a button. Enter a man. He is solid, phlegmatic, of much force but soft to her.*]

THE WOMAN: Oh, Harold. Home so soon? [*She kisses him.*]

THE MAN: Glad to see me, sweetheart? Still sewing? What are you making? [*They return to the fire.*]

THE WOMAN: A service cloth for the wicker table. We need something prettier than we used last summer.

THE MAN: Why so solemn?

THE WOMAN: Am I solemn? I didn't notice. Just absorbed in my work, I presume.

THE MAN: Did you phone the Lamberts to come? [*He stands behind her and strokes her neck.*]

THE VOICE: You see! He loves your neck too.

THE WOMAN: [*Stirring slightly.*] Yes. Does it feel cold in here, to you?

THE MAN: No, but then I've been walking. I'll bring a shawl for you and stir up the fire. Did they say they'd come? [*He goes into the back room.*]

THE WOMAN: Yes.

THE VOICE: Did I not say he was strong and gross—very—you love him for that.

THE WOMAN: No, no. I do not. I do not really love him. I do not know what to do. I cannot love anyone—anymore. I tell you I can only think of how I loved. [*She sighs.*]

THE MAN: [*Annoyed.*] Why do you sigh?

THE WOMAN: Did I sigh? I didn't notice. I must be just a little tired, I presume—sitting here so. We will go somewhere presently. Or, I will brighten up and play. Did you have a good day?

THE MAN: Very. I've turned the best trick I've turned yet in many a year, sweet. I've made a deal with the Winchell-Foster Company. That means a hundred thousand of our wire nibs to be used by them every year. Do you know what that means, sweetheart? It means a country house for Edith, and a much bigger auto and all the pretty dresses that she wants—more than I have ever been able to give her yet. Doesn't that make a little difference to my Billykins girl? [*He bends down and kisses her cheek and neck.*]

THE VOICE: See how he loves your cheek and neck. [*She sits meditative—still.*]

THE WOMAN: [*Recovering herself of a sudden.*] Yes, it is lovely, isn't it? Beautiful! We will both be so much happier.

THE VOICE: Will you, Edith? Will you truly?

THE MAN: But what about Margaret Grimes? Will she come?

THE WOMAN: [*Resuming her sewing.*] Yes, and the Walt Crosses and Daisy Lumiphere, and Eddie Pond, and the Gordons.

THE MAN: [*Darkening.*] Why the Gordons? You know I don't like Walt Gordon. And he doesn't like me very well, either, I fancy.

THE WOMAN: Because of Mrs. Walt, Harold. You know she had been so good to me.

THE MAN: Because her brother was your lover, and because you can't forget him, that's why. I forgave you all that and decided to let bygones be bygones. But you can't, or won't. You have to invite her here because she looks like him. I know. You can't forget and you don't want to.

THE WOMAN: Harold! Harold! You don't know. What makes you so sensitive! Why will you be? She is such a charming woman, and so generous. She was so good to me, years ago. Must I not see her any more at all?

THE VOICE: You see, he would rub out even the picture of me in your mind. I with the pale face and black hair.

THE MAN: Well, why bring her here? There are other places to see her. Why not let bygones be bygones? Why brood over him? You've married me now. Either you love me or you don't. If you don't why don't you leave me? I can get along. This constant dreaming of somebody else. Oh, I know what you're thinking about. [*His eyes darken.*]

THE VOICE: You see! You see! Not even my memory.

THE WOMAN: [*Irritably.*] I'm not thinking and I wish you wouldn't thrum on that one subject. It is of the past, and why not let it lie? What do you want me to do? I will leave you, if you say. [*She rises.*]

THE MAN: Edith! Edith! I'm sorry. Damn but I love you.— You're so beautiful. I'm even jealous of the dead! Don't cry. Your lashes are all wet. Sweetheart! You beautiful thing! Oh, hell. I'm a brute and a fool.

THE VOICE: And now you will love him because he is repentant and an animal.

THE WOMAN: Harold—I am sorry. To think we should quarrel so. You're such a big bear and such a big baby. It was just a mood, wasn't it? You don't really mean to be so hard.

THE MAN: No, sweetheart, no. Pretty thing. You lovely, lovely thing, with your beautiful neck and your smooth arms. It was just a mood and I am a jealous fool. But you know it is because I love you so, don't you? I get wild at the thought of even a memory. Was he so wonderful as you once told me?

THE VOICE: And now, what will you say?

THE WOMAN: Dearest, don't speak of him. Let bygones be bygones. It was sad—his death. But that was a long while ago. Can't we let it rest? I wish to.

THE MAN: Yes—only I love you so much. [*She leans forward and rests her chin on her hand. He takes her throat in his.*] There. I love your neck. It is so white—so beautiful. It is almost hypnotic to me. It has always been so.

THE VOICE: My very words.

THE WOMAN: You're always telling me how beautiful I am. You know you see dozens of prettier women every time you leave the house!

THE MAN: Dozens? None. Not one! Not one! I have the loveliest girl in the world—she has the loveliest eyes, the loveliest neck, the loveliest cheeks. [*He smoothes her neck.*] Only once in a score of years perhaps would one see a neck like yours.

THE WOMAN: Oh, Harold!

THE VOICE: So goes what was mine,—youth, love, beauty. It is sad to die.

THE WOMAN: [*Darkling.*] Oh!

THE MAN: Now what is the matter?

THE WOMAN: [*Turning.*] I thought I heard some one on the balcony.

THE MAN: You sighed.

THE WOMAN: No, I didn't.

THE MAN: Yes, you did. And besides, you didn't hear anyone on the balcony. There isn't anyone there—there couldn't be—five stories up. [*He gets up, opens the windows and looks out. Then he comes back and seats himself in silence.*]

THE VOICE: Edith! Edith!

THE WOMAN: Please don't brood. You are making yourself mad over me. It is useless. It is without grounds. We will never get on in this way. Can't you see? [*She looks wearily down on him.*]

THE MAN: I see but I cannot help myself exactly. I do not see what to do. I have this feeling that I should leave you, that I will never get rid of this thing that is between us.

THE WOMAN: [*Kneeling and catching his hand.*] No! No! Don't talk so, Harold. Don't think such things. It is a fancy of yours. You are brooding upon it. You are becoming mad upon the subject. Come, sit here as we were before. Sit here at the table. Hold my neck in your hand. It will reassure me so much. Do you know I am becoming absolutely dependent on the feel of your hand on my neck? It is so warm, so comforting. I must have your love. It is what keeps me content with life. The sun dawning in the jungle must feel to the chilly savage as your hand does to me. You used to say it was the first thing you fell in love with.

THE VOICE: It was I that said that.

THE WOMAN: [*To herself.*] Oh, pardon. But me, too. Oh, the curse of loneliness.

THE MAN: [*Holding her throat.*] It is odd but you saying that leaves me cold. It is as though you were talking to some one who is not here at all. It is true that you say it but I feel as though it would make no difference to you if you never saw me again—

THE WOMAN: Oh, Harold!

THE VOICE: If it were but true.

THE MAN: —That you would leave me for a cleverer man.

THE WOMAN: How terribly you talk—how groundlessly! How foolishly! What have I said! What have I done!

THE MAN: It is not what you say or what you do exactly. It is what you make me feel—all the time and all the time what I feel.

THE VOICE: The long ago! The long ago! Then you do love me, after all.

[*A telephone bell rings.* THE MAN *rises.*]

THE MAN: That is for me, I think. I am expecting a final conference in the lobby here tonight. If it is for me, I will not be long. [*He goes.*]

THE VOICE: Then you do love me—you do?

THE WOMAN: Yes, yes—and always.

THE MAN: [*Returning.*] It is for me. But I'll be back shortly. Don't grieve, sweet. [*He smoothes her neck.*]

THE VOICE: Oh, let him go, forever and ever.

THE WOMAN: He is a good man, loving and kind, for all his rages. [*She turns facing the fire and takes up her sewing.*]

THE VOICE: And now we are alone again, you and I. We are happiest when we are alone. Isn't that true?

THE WOMAN: It is true. It is a pity, but it is true. Why do you come! Why haunt me?

THE VOICE: "Do you deny me, then"? Do you truly love him?

THE WOMAN: No, no. But you are dead and I am a woman. I have lips and eyelids made for kisses. My arms hunger for love and you are no longer here. Why do you come in this thin form?

THE VOICE: Because I cannot stay away and because you will not let me. I lie still at times but you call and call. Then I come tapping to hear your reproaches and self-reproaches and doubts.

THE WOMAN: But I am only a woman. I do not understand. I have this body—this beautiful, craving body—and you are gone.

THE VOICE: But only a little way—such a little way. I am a pale flame, it is true, but with you as one we could still dance together. Over hill and hollow—you and I. You cannot really know, but side by side with you the past would come back all its lovely self. We could be many things, two birds, two snakes, two minds, two dreams, one flame. Side by side we can run or blend our flames in a delicious glow.

THE WOMAN: [*Recovering herself.*] Oh, but this is not sane. It is unreal. It is making me unreal and very unhappy. [*She rises.*]

THE VOICE: Edith! Edith! My Edith!

THE WOMAN: Your voice! Your voice! I hear it always.

[*Re-enter* THE MAN.]

THE MAN: Well, it's really done. I thought they'd never go. But it's through with now. All that I said is true. We'll be richer than ever from now on.

THE WOMAN: And happier.

THE MAN: Yes, and happier—I truly hope—indeed I know. Now sing for me.

THE WOMAN: Very well. [*She goes to the piano.*] What shall I sing?

THE MAN: "Still as the night, deep as the sea."

THE WOMAN: Oh, no. Not that.

THE MAN: Why not?

THE VOICE: That is our song.

THE WOMAN: I am not in accord with it, tonight. I will not do it very well.

THE MAN: You are never in accord with it, and you will never sing it. I know why. Damn him and damn you.

THE WOMAN: Oh, Harold.

THE MAN: Don't "Harold" me. This is lunacy on my part and on yours. I have stood it long enough. Either you are in love with me or you are not, and I know now that you are not. You are never really happy. [*He turns.*] To be in love with a woman who is in love with a shadow—a man who died five years ago. Ye Gods. I wonder that I ever married. I wonder that I can be such a fool. Well, this ought to cure me. It will. [*He goes to get his coat but comes back and sits down.*]

THE WOMAN: Harold! Harold! I think I am mad at times myself. I do not know what ails me. Dearest! Dearest!

THE VOICE: Dearest! Dearest! Don't you see? It is all for the best.

THE MAN: [*Thinking her truly repentant.*] Why, Edith, how white you are. Do you really care for me?

THE WOMAN: Oh, yes, yes. Can't you see?

THE VOICE: She cares for me. Alas! Alas!

THE WOMAN: [*Trying to slide out of his arms.*] Now, now. I am all right. Perfectly all right. Let me play for you.

THE MAN: I'd rather you didn't. I want to look at you.

THE WOMAN: But I don't want to be looked at. Please, Harold, let me go.

THE VOICE: If that were but the most . . .

THE MAN: [*Releasing her.*] Very well. [*He gets up and goes to the balcony. She follows him, putting her hands on his shoulders. He turns.*] Well?

THE WOMAN: Oh, nothing.

THE MAN: You are hiding something from me.

THE WOMAN: What could I hide? I living alone with you and for you?

THE VOICE: A dead man.

THE MAN: Your dead love.

THE WOMAN: My dead love? Oh, no. You know all of him. I have told you all.

THE MAN: But not given me all, that is sure. I have the fated feeling of unhappiness now. It cannot go on.

THE WOMAN: Oh, yes it can, Harold. I have changed so. Can't you see?

THE VOICE: Have you changed?

THE MAN: That you have changed? No—except for the worse. It is I who am changing. Just now I asked you to play a song for me—the song you two were fond of—and you grow as white as wax.

THE WOMAN: Oh, but I do not care for that any more. It was not that. I am weary of it and really tired of music. Let us read something together. Let me read to you. Please.

THE MAN: Very well, read then. [*He looks after her as she turns. The spell of her beauty is in his eyes. He clenches his hands.*]

THE WOMAN: [*Fingering a volume on the table.*] Here is *Abelard and Heloise*.

THE MAN: No.

THE WOMAN: [*Aimlessly.*] *The Story of a Lie.*

THE MAN: No.

THE WOMAN: Would you like poetry?

THE MAN: Rather.

THE WOMAN: [*Fingering Keats.*] How about—

THE MAN: Read from Swinburne. I like so much of him. [*He opens a book and pushes it toward her. They settle themselves in their chairs.*]

THE WOMAN: Here is one—"Ave Atque Vale." Shall I read?

THE MAN: Yes. I like it as I remember it.

THE WOMAN: [*Reading.*]
Shall I strew on thee rose or rue or laurel,
    Brother, on this that was the veil of thee?
    Or quiet sea-flower, molded by the sea,
Or simplest growth of meadow sweet or sorrel,
    Such as the summer-sleepy Dryads weave,
    Waked up by snow soft sudden rains at eve?
Or wilt thou rather, as on earth before,
    Half—

THE MAN: Stop! What makes you read that?

THE WOMAN: [*Paling.*] I don't know. You opened the book there. I never read it before. Shall I stop?

THE MAN: No more of that for heaven's sake. [*He gets up.*]

THE WOMAN: Is there anything the matter?

THE MAN: No! No! Nothing!

THE WOMAN: [*Approaching him with outstretched hands.*] Sweetheart?

THE MAN: [*Pushing past her.*] I'd rather you'd let me alone just now.

THE WOMAN: Have I done anything, dear?

THE MAN: Nothing! Nothing whatever!

THE WOMAN: [*On the verge of tears.*] But Harold! [*He answers with a deprecating gesture. She commences to weep violently.*]

THE MAN: [*Irritably.*] Edith—I beg of you!

THE WOMAN: Oh never mind! I'm sick of it, sick of it, sick of it! You are always venting these dreadful moods on me. Why can't you be human and not try to make every one else suffer with you? Oh I—I know I've done something!

THE MAN: Well, have you?

THE WOMAN: Do you really think I have?

THE MAN: I'm merely asking you.

THE WOMAN: [*Weeping harder than ever.*] Well, I haven't, I haven't! Oh, dearest, why can't you cease being so suspicious of me?

THE MAN: I don't mean to be. You act so strangely suggestive of hidden things at times.

THE WOMAN: But I don't hide things, sweetheart, truly I don't.

THE MAN: All right, then. Forget about my mood. Everything will be all right in a little while.

THE WOMAN: And you do love me, don't you?

THE MAN: I do, of course I do.

THE WOMAN: [*Sinking into her chair and drying her eyes.*] Harold, you frighten me to death at times you become so savage. I cannot understand how you can love me and be so cruel.

THE MAN: [*Coming back to his chair.*] I don't mean to be cruel, Edith. It's only—

THE WOMAN: [*Apprehensively.*] Only what?

THE MAN: Oh—nothing!

THE WOMAN: Now you're off again!

THE MAN: My God, Edith! [*She cries miserably in her chair and he pretends to read. Finding it quite impossible to concentrate against the noise of her sobbing he first throws away the paper and then slowly begins to soften. Finally he turns around.*]

THE MAN: [*Holding out his hand.*] Dearest?

THE WOMAN: [*Throwing herself across the table to grasp it.*] Oh, my darling! [*She lays her head on their clasped hands and sobs while he strokes her hair with his free hand.*]

THE MAN: Don't cry, sweet. Don't cry! It'll come out all right. We love each other, and that's what really counts.

THE WOMAN: [*Looking up.*] I know—I know. Only it hurts so dreadfully.

THE MAN: Yes, dear, but we're really very happy. Come here. [*He holds out his hand for her to rest her throat in it, which she does, smiling.*]

THE WOMAN: Oh, you make me so happy.

THE MAN: Do you know this terrible jealousy that comes on me at times is dreadful?

THE WOMAN: You don't realize that any more strongly than I do, especially when I am so innocent. [*He looks at her searchingly.*] Don't you believe it?

THE MAN: Really, I don't know.

THE WOMAN: Why, I never heard of such a thing!

THE MAN: Edith! You're too frightened! Look at me! Look me square in the eye!

THE WOMAN: [*With a wavering gaze.*] Well?

THE MAN: [*Clutching her throat.*] God damn it all anyway. I don't believe you're telling me the truth! You don't really love me at all. You're dreaming, dreaming. You're loving a dead man. [*He tightens his fingers.*]

THE VOICE: Tighter! Tighter!

THE WOMAN: Harold! Don't hold me so tight. You hurt. You don't understand. Oh.

THE MAN: Why do you always grieve? If you want to die, die. I'll help you. [*He holds her firmly—brutally.*] Your beautiful neck. How I have fallen for it—your smooth, white face. [*He pulls her farther across the table toward him.*]

THE WOMAN: Oh! Oh!

THE VOICE: Tighter! Tighter!

THE MAN: I'm killing you! I'm killing you! But then I can't, I can't. Your white body. Your white face and neck. I love them! I love them so! I can't do without them. [*He gathers her up in his arms. She lies limp.*]

THE VOICE: And so you are not coming, after all.

THE MAN: [*Smothering her with kisses.*] Oh, Edith, Edith! Edith!

THE WOMAN: [*Breathing after a time.*] I do not want to live! I do not want to live! [*She weeps.*]

THE MAN: [*Angrily.*] Then die for all I care! But not by me. I've had enough. [*He pushes her to the floor and rises.*] From this time on you will not see me any more. Damn your white neck anyhow. [*He goes.*]

THE WOMAN: Oh! Oh! Oh! I do not want to live.

THE VOICE: Will you not come to me? I love you so much. I love your white neck. Two minds, two dreams, one flame.

THE WOMAN: Yes, yes. Wait. [*She rises and hurries feverishly to a chest of drawers, hunting nervously for something. Suddenly she lifts up a small bottle and puts it to her lips.*]

THE VOICE: Now.

THE WOMAN: Yes, Richard, yes. At last. [*The door bell begins to ring. She turns, surveying the bell with her eyes.*]

## **CURTAIN**

# THE HAND OF THE POTTER

## CHARACTERS

AARON BERCHANSKY, *the father, an old Jewish thread peddler.*
REBECCA, *his wife.*
ISADORE—21
JOSEPH—17 } *their sons.*
MASHA, *lame, an embroideress by trade*
RAE, *a manicuress* } *their daughters.*
ESTHER (MRS. GREENBAUM), *an elder sister*
GEORGE GREENBAUM, *Esther's husband.*
TILLIE, *the Greenbaum's daughter.*
KITTY NEAFIE, *aged eleven, daughter of an Irish neighbor.*
MARY NEAFIE, *her mother.*
MRS. LERSCH, *a neighbor.*
RUTGER B. MILLER, *Assistant District Attorney.*
THE CLERK OF THE GRAND JURY.
FOREMAN OF THE GRAND JURY.
A DOORKEEPER.
EMIL DAUBENSPECK, *a German cabinet-maker.*
RUFUS BUSH, *an expressman.*
SAMUEL ELKAS, *keeper of a furnished-room house.*
HAGAR ELKAS, *his daughter.*
THOMAS MCKAGG, *policeman.*
ED ARMSBY, *of the Herald*
STEPHEN LEACH, *of the Times* } *reporters.*
DENNIS QUINN, *of the Sun*
MCGRANAHAN
HARSH } *detectives.*
SKUMM
AN INSPECTOR OF POLICE.
NEIGHBORS.
JURORS.
VOICES.

# THE HAND OF THE POTTER

## ACT I

### SCENE

The top floor flat of AARON BERCHANSKY in the crowded Jewish section of the Upper East Side of New York City. In this instance the dining and living rooms are one. Forward of left centre a door, giving out into the general hall, where occasionally noises of tenants going to and fro on the stairs below can be heard. Back of this door a little way, and against the wall, a cheap yellow bookcase filled with more or less shabby books, old magazines and papers. On the top of this bookcase, centre, an old-fashioned wooden clock which ticks noisily whenever other sounds cease; to its right, facing it, a five-branch candlestick of brass containing half-burned candles. Right centre, a window with a fire-escape giving into a court, and beyond this court the whitewashed wall and window of another apartment, obviously vacant. In the centre of the room a general dining and work table of the same quality as the bookcase, and on it a red cotton tablecloth, a basket filled with sewing (socks, underwear, buttons), and to one side an inkstand and pen. A few chairs of poor design are scattered about. Right centre, against the wall, an old sewing machine, severely battered, with a cheap velour cover on it. On it a samovar of brass. Forward of left centre, a door giving into a bathroom. Rear of left centre, two doors, one giving into a small bedroom or alcove, the other, beyond it, into the kitchen. The doors into the bedroom and kitchen are curtained with faded half-cotton, half-silk portières. On the inside of the door which gives into the hall, a mezuze, the Jewish luck-piece.

### TIME

About two-thirty of a hot Saturday afternoon in July. As the curtain rises, the father, mother, and lame daughter MASHA are disclosed. Owing to the fact that Saturday is the Jewish Sabbath, no work is being done, though the Saturday afternoon gayety and activity of the city are plainly in the air. AARON BERCHANSKY is sitting at the table reading. The lame girl is also reading, between the table and the window. MRS. BERCHANSKY, *who has been in the kitchen, is seen entering. She is wearing a worn black silk shawl, and is obviously prepared to go somewhere. She is of that order of poor Jewess who has suffered much, whose face is sad and careworn, and who, at her time of life, goes uncorseted.*

MRS. BERCHANSKY: [*Speaking with the Yiddish accent and in the vernacular of her class.*] You hear me! Are you ready to come? Oi, it's hot!

MASHA: [*A dark, pale, thin-faced girl, with delicate, bloodless hands. She pauses from her reading and looks up.*] Oh, yes; come. Let's go to the park. The sun on this tin roof is terrible. It makes me sick. No wonder the Hirshes moved out. [*She looks across the court to the empty apartment.*] They couldn't stand that top floor.

BERCHANSKY: [*Looking up and over also, and closing his book. He is a kind-faced, slightly stooped and grizzled man of fifty-five, with sunken bloodless cheeks, a very spare frame, and deep-set, heavily eye-browed eyes. His partially bald head is surmounted by the customary Jewish black cotton skull-cap. Tufts of hair protrude from over his ears. He has a weary, indefinite and yet meditative air.*] So! Dey vent! Yes, but Masha, my dear, it takes money to move. I vould never live under a tin roof if I could afford somet'ing better. [*Rises and walks over to her and takes her hand and pats it.*] Come, now. You read later. Mamma, leben, ve vill go, den. Yes. [*Returning to the table.*] But dis book—it interests me. Here is a writer—oi! But he knows! If t'ings should be so as he makes dem, den ve vould not live under tin roofs in hot vedder—de rich so rich, de poor so poor. Ach! [*Picks up the book.*] Masha, my dear, come here. Look. Oi, it's fine leather! In a second-hand store I got it. Twenty-five cents! [*With a movement of his hands.*] But I should care! New, it vould be vorth five dollars. Ach, I take it along. Under de trees I can read.

MRS. BERCHANSKY: [*Bringing the lame girl her hat and cane.*] Stop talking books. Vot you read, it don't help. Ve verk just de same. [*Aside, nudging her daughter.*] Tell him he should hurry.

MASHA: [*Cheerfully, taking her hat and cane.*] We're ready, papa. [*Steps are heard on the stair; the door opens.*] That's Rae, I guess.

BERCHANSKY: [*With a desire to be cheerful.*] So, you're home, den.

RAE: [*Entering.*] Hello, everybody! Gee, it's hot! I'm all in. I've done seven heads this mornin' without a break, not a minute between. Maybe ya think that ain't work. Say! Wotcha doin', everybody? Where ya goin'? [*Takes off her hat and coat, and begins to undo her waist. She is of that vulgar-smart class of young Jewess that affects the latest and most gaudy of everything. Her hat is of varnished black straw with a white band, giving her face a mannish look. Her suit of linen is of a black-and-white check. White silk stockings, high-heeled slippers, a plain lawn shirtwaist decorated with a large pink cameo, complete her costume. As she unloosens her waist she starts to walk to the bedroom.*]

MASHA: [*Limping to the window and looking out.*] To the park. Do you want to come?

RAE: [*From the bedroom.*] Park? Quitcha kiddin'. Think that's all I gotta do—sit on a bench in a park? Good night! I've got something better'n that. [*By this time she has partially disrobed, and returns in skirt and kimono.* BERCHANSKY, *by a motion of the hands and a lift of the eyebrows, has signified plainly that he does not approve of this modern looseness of tongue and manners.*] Say, whaddya think I heard t'day? Who d'ya think saw Isadore, an' where? At a prize fight! Two weeks ago. An' whaddya think he was doin'? Carryin' a bucket an' a sponge to rub off one o' the men! A prize fight rubber! An' him only out o' the penitentiary three months, an' on probation!

[*At the mention of this, a visible pain passes over the faces of the others.* MRS. BERCHANSKY *looks at her husband. He stiffens and looks into space, avoiding their glances.*

MASHA *looks from mother to father, helplessly and in pity.*]

BERCHANSKY: Rae! Dat you should say such t'ings!

RAE: [*Hurriedly, and without appearing to notice the effect, the while taking the pins out of her hair.*] Well, it's so, ain't it? A swell job, eh? Abe Gruber had a box seat an' saw him. Gee, I thought I'd drop when he told me! I thought my ears 'ud fry an' fall off! First it's two years in the penitentiary for assaultin' a little girl, an' now he's gotta come an' hang around here an' sponge at prize fights! A swell chance we've got tryin' to do anything or be anybody. We'll never get away from that. Why don't he get out o' New York if he can't do any better than that?

BERCHANSKY: Rae! I forbid you! Your own brother!

MASHA: [*Appealingly.*] You know he isn't quite right. Why do you talk so? Why don't you give him a chance? Think of his spells.

MRS. BERCHANSKY: Ach, Rae! [*Putting her hands to her face and sighing.*] Ach, mein Gott! Mein Gott! Trouble, trouble, trouble!

RAE: [*Defiantly.*] A chance! Fine use he's made of his chances! What use could he make of it if he had it? [*She stares.*] Why don't you put him away before he does any more damage? You say he ain't right; sure, he ain't. Then what's he doin' outside Bloomingdale?

MRS. BERCHANSKY: [*Lifting her hands.*] Bloomingdale!

BERCHANSKY: [*Horrified at the mention of an asylum.*] An asylum! Ach, dat's horrible!

RAE: Oh, well! Have it your way. You'll probably find out when it's too late. [*She walks off into the bedroom, shrugging her shoulders.*]

MRS. BERCHANSKY: [*Coming over to her husband and patting him on the shoulder.*] Ach, Aaron. Let's go. It vill be nicer in de park.

MASHA: Yes, let's. [*She picks up her book, which she has put down, and the three prepare to leave. As they approach the door to open it, other footsteps are heard. Pleasantly.*] It's Joe.

[*Enter* JOSEPH, *a clean, spruce, brisk-looking boy of seventeen. He is neatly, but somewhat extremely, dressed in a light tan suit and straw hat, and has an air of gayety and playfulness about him. As he enters, he takes off his coat.*]

JOE: [*Looking lightly from one to the other.*] Cold, ain't it? What's the row? [*He goes toward the bedroom.*]

BERCHANSKY: [*Wearily and gloomily.*] Plenty! Plenty! It is vith love for one anudder dat I vould hev my children grow up, but instead, vot do I hear? Nutting but quarreling an' hard t'ings! Oi! Oi! Such a business! Such a business! [*He shakes his head.*]

MRS. BERCHANSKY: [*Sadly.*] Alvays dis fighting, dis fighting!

RAE: [*Coming to the bedroom door.*] Who's fightin'? Who said anything? I'm sure I didn't.

JOE: What's the row? What's the trouble?

MASHA: [*Soothingly.*] Oh, nothing. It's about Isadore, but let's not talk any more. We were just going out in the park.

JOE: Well, what about him? Where is he?

MASHA: Oh, some one saw him at a prize fight, and told Rae.

JOE: What fight? Well, what of it? What's he doin'? Has he got a job? [*He walks into the bathroom, takes off his tie, and returns.*]

MASHA: Oh, we don't know. Rae's mad because he was helping sponge one of the men.

JOE: [*Interestedly.*] Him! With his game arm? What fight was it—the Neil-Kerens bout?

MASHA: [*Sadly.*] Oh, I don't know. One of Rae's friends saw him.

RAE: [*Appearing at the bedroom door.*] Yes, an' you know as well as I do he oughtn't to be there. He oughtn't to be out at all. He ain't right, an' you know it. [*Returns.*]

BERCHANSKY: [*Excitedly.*] Are ve goin' to begin again? Are ve goin' to begin again?

JOE: Well, what's so bad about that? I don't see. He hasn't done anything very wrong, has he? Plenty of fellows help at prize fights. [RAE *clicks her tongue disdainfully.*] He hasn't been around here, has he?

MASHA: No. Rae wants us to put him away.

JOE: Where?

MASHA: Bloomingdale.

JOE: [*Thoughtfully.*] Oh, I don't know. He ain't so bad. There are plenty of fellows worse'n him walkin' around. [*Pauses.*] Of course, with that arm—[*Pauses again.*] If he'd only get a job an' stick to it, he'd be all right. [*He disappears into the bathroom again.*]

MRS. BERCHANSKY: [*Heavily.*] Ach, my poor boy! My poor boy! Vot vill become of him? Vot vill be de end?

[*She,* BERCHANSKY, *and* MASHA *move toward the door, when other steps are heard, and* ISADORE *enters. He is a tall, lithe, broad-shouldered young man of twenty or twenty-one, so strangely composed mentally and physically that he is bizarre. He is so badly compounded chemically that he seems never to be of one mood, and has a restless, jerky, fidgety gait and manner. From moment to moment his facial expression changes. Also, he has an affliction of the left arm and shoulder, which causes it to twitch or jerk involuntarily. He has an odd, receding forehead, black hair, large brown eyes, and a pale yet healthy skin. A huge seal ring of a cheap quality is on one finger, a glass garnet of great size in his tie, which is of a flaring yellow. His hat is a small, round, saw-edge straw, with a bright striped band. His collar is very high, of the turn-down order, and slightly soiled. His shoes are yellow and patched, his socks white. Under his arm are a number of newspapers rolled up.*]

ISADORE: [*Mock cheerfully. Surveying the family with an air of general well being.*] Well, here I am.

[*At the sight of him* MR. *and* MRS. BERCHANSKY *and* MASHA *fall back.* BERCHANSKY *opens his mouth slightly,* MRS. BERCHANSKY *squeezes her daughter's arm,* MASHA *stiffens and stands up very straight.*]

BERCHANSKY  
MRS. BERCHANSKY } Isadore!  
MASHA

RAE: [*Looking out of the bedroom.*] Well, of all things! So you're back, are you?

MASHA: [*Gently and calmly.*] We're glad you've come, Isadore. [MRS. BERCHANSKY *crosses over to where he is.*] How are you?

ISADORE: [*With a slight touch of irritation at their surprise.*] Oh, I'm all right. What's the matter with you all? Whaddy ya all want to stare at me for?

MRS. BERCHANSKY: [*Pleadingly.*] Isadore! Ve're not staring. Ve're glad. [*She smoothes his hand.*]

MASHA: You know we're always glad to see you, Isadore. Why shouldn't we be?

JOE: [*Appearing at the bathroom door.*] Hello, Is! Where do you come from?

ISADORE: Well, where do you think? New York, of course. But I'm not goin' to use that name Isadore any more. It's a kike name. People laugh at it. I'm Irving from now on. You get me?

JOE: [*Lightly.*] Oh, all right. You can't get me mad. [*He smiles.*]

BERCHANSKY: For vy you change your name? Ain't Isadore good enough?

ISADORE: Didn't I just tell you? It's a joke. Whoever picked that out must 'a' wanted to hoodoo me.

MRS. BERCHANSKY: [*Tenderly.*] Isadore, vy should you say dat?

ISADORE: [*Softening and turning to her.*] That's all right, mom. I don't mean nothin'. You know me. [*Smoothes her arm.*]

MRS. BERCHANSKY: [*Solicitously, to* MASHA *and* BERCHANSKY.] You go, an' I'll stay here an' talk to Isadore. [*She takes his hand.*]

ISADORE: [*Loftily.*] No, you all go. I don't need anybody here while I work. I want to answer these ads. [*He goes to the table, takes off his coat, and unfolds the papers.*] I'll be all right. You don't mind me stayin' here, do you? I'll come an' meet you later. Where'll you be? [*His shoulder jerks.*]

JOE: [*Coming out of the bathroom and passing into the bedroom, accidentally kicking over a box in the bedroom, en route.*] What's this box doin' in here?

RAE: [*Coming out to make room for him.*] It's mamma's rags. I'll put 'em away after a bit.

BERCHANSKY: [*Coming over to* ISADORE, *who has sat down at the table and is spreading out his newspapers—nervously, and with a rising inflection.*] You lost your last place? Den dey found out?

ISADORE: Sure, they did. A detective snitched on me. But I'll fix 'em this time. I'm goin' to get out o' New York soon. I'm goin' to get a job an' earn a little money an' then I'm goin' to go.

BERCHANSKY: [*Shaking his head and wringing his hands.*] More trouble. Oi! Oi!

ISADORE: [*Lightly and with a careless bravado and half-charm, the while his shoulder jerks occasionally.*] Don't worry any more about me, pop. I'm all right. Can't you see? [*Takes hold of his hand in an affectionate way.* MRS. BERCHANSKY *comes over and stands by him.*] I'm goin' to get a good job soon, mom. You know me. I like to work. I just got some newspapers, an' I'm goin' to answer the ads. [*To* MASHA.] You haven't got any paper an' envelopes, have you?

MASHA: [*Going to a drawer in the machine.*] How many do you want? Will six do?

ISADORE: [*Judicially.*] Better give me a dozen. [*He turns to his father.* MASHA *brings them over and puts them down. His shoulder jerks, and* MRS. BERCHANSKY, *who is behind him and out of his view, shakes her head sadly.*] How's the needle an' thread business, pop? Not much in it, eh? An' hard work, too. Well, never mind; I'll get a job now, an' everything's goin' to be all right. I'm not goin' to hang around here any more. *He scratches his ear meditatively. Seeing* RAE, *who has come out of the bathroom, looking at him.*] You needn't be afraid of me, Rae. I'm not goin' to stay in New York much longer to disgrace you. I wanted to see the folks an' get these ads answered. That's why I'm here. Gee, it's hot out. Terrible. Where were you folks goin'?

MASHA: Out to the park.

JOE: [*Bustling out fully dressed.*] Well, so long, everybody. I've gotta go. [*He goes out.*]

MASHA: [*Nudging her father.*] You better come with us and leave him alone for a while. Don't ask him too many questions now.

BERCHANSKY: [*Heavily.*] Yes. Yes. Vell, you'll come, den? Ve'll be near de statue out here under de trees.

MRS. BERCHANSKY: You'll come, Isadore, yes? Ve'll vait for you. Everyt'ing vill be all right. You'll stay for dinner, yes?

ISADORE: Well, maybe. [*He nods condescendingly. They all go—all but* RAE. *As they disappear, he turns to his papers.*

*To himself.*] But how am I goin' to do it—that's what I'd like to know? What kind o' references can *I* give? Say, every time a detective sees me now he wants to know what I'm doin'. [*The clock strikes three.*] An' I can't seem to keep one when I get it. [*His shoulder jerks.*] An' I've gotta report to that probation officer every month like a schoolboy. Say! [*He pauses and stares at the paper.*] But it ain't that. It ain't that. It's their faces an' their nice make-ups an' the way they do their hair. That's what's the matter with me. It's their stockin's an' their open shirtwaists an' their shoulders an' arms. I can't stand it no more. I can't seem to think of nothin' else. It's the way they walk an' talk an' laugh—their teeth always showin', an' their red mouths. It's gettin' worse all the time. [*He gets up, stiffens. A strange, fierce, animal light comes into his eyes. He breathes heavily and clenches his hands.*]

RAE: [*Entering from the bedroom and noting him standing. She is powdered and painted—a picture of gauche tenement-house finery. She is trifling with an imitation gold chain purse.*] Wotcha doin'?

ISADORE: [*Startled, and sinking back into his chair and his normal mood.*] Answerin' some ads. Didn't I tell you? Whaddy ya think I'm doin'? Whaddy ya wanta look at me that way for? [*Surveys her, and as he does so his mood changes. He softens and becomes objectionably mushy.*] Gee, but you look good, kid. [*Beckons.*] Come over here. Give us a kiss, will you?

RAE: [*Savagely.*] Say, what the devil's the matter with you, anyhow? Cut the comedy! Whaddy ya think I am? Another ten-year-old? [*She sniffs and switches toward the door.*]

ISADORE: [*Jumping after her and reaching the door first. He seizes her by the arm, the while his face becomes livid and his shoulder jerks.*] What's the matter with you, anyhow, Rae? Whaddy ya think I am? Whaddy ya wanta throw up my past to me for? You ain't like a sister to me, anyhow. You never was. [*He attempts to pull her to him. She strikes him in the face.*]

RAE: Let go! What's the matter with you, anyhow? Whaddy ya think I am? Don't try to pull that stuff on me. You nut! [*She pushes him back.*] Want me to call the police or the neighbors? A fine brother you are! [*She pulls loose and opens the door.*] You must be crazy—your own sister! [*She steps into the hall.*] I should think you'd be ashamed of yourself. Wait'll the family hears o' this!

ISADORE: [*Weakening as she mentions the police and the family.*] Gee, I must be crazy. I don't seem to be able to stand anything no more, You look so nice,—that's the trouble. Don't say anything to the folks, will you, Rae? I ain't quite right, I guess. Ain't I suffered enough? Don't you know what I'm up against, havin' the feelin's I do? I ain't so bad. I just can't stand things, that's all. [*His shoulder jerks; his face contorts.*] It's just their pretty faces, an' their mouths, an' their shoulders, an' the way they fix their hair. [*He becomes incoherent. Steps are heard outside. He turns, relaxes his expression, and straightens up.*]

[*Enter* MRS. GREENBAUM, *with her six-year-old daughter. She is tall, statuesque, neatly dressed. From the quality of her apparel it is very plain that she is in considerably better circumstances than her parents. A tan silk foulard dress, white hat, and black-and-white striped parasol are the chief outstanding features of her garb. Her daughter is neatly dressed in a starched, stiff white dress and a green straw hat.*]

TILLIE: [*Running forward.*] Hello, Aunty Rae! [*Kisses her.*]

RAE: Hello, Tillie! How are you?

MRS. GREENBAUM: [*Observing only* RAE *at first, and her expression.*] Hello, Rae! What's the matter? [*Seeing* ISADORE, *and being plainly astonished.*] Why, hello, Isadore! Home again? Where'd you come from?

ISADORE: Oh, around town. Where'd you think I come from? But my name's not Isadore any more from now on. It's Irving. I'm changin' it. I'm tired of that kike name. Don't forget that, will you?

RAE: [*Looking up semi-sarcastically at her sister and smiling, as if to say:* "Something new." *She twitches her head indicatively in* ISADORE'S *direction. Sotto voce.*] Look out for him. He's off today. Crazy about girls again. [*Aloud.*] But I've gotta go right away. The folks are all out in the park near the gate. [*Lowering her voice.*] Don't stay here long alone, will you? Get him to go out in the park, if you can. So long! [*Goes out.*]

MRS. GREENBAUM: [*Placatively, but unafraid, crossing to the bedroom and looking in.*] So you're changing your name, are you?

ISADORE: [*Pleasantly.*] Sure. I can't land a job with this one. It's a kike name, anyhow. Whaddy they wanta give me that kike name for, huh? [*His shoulder jerks. He returns to the table and takes up his papers.* TILLIE *runs to him and grabs him by the knees. He looks down at her, picks her up and kisses her.*] You're a pretty kid, eh?

MRS. GREENBAUM: [*Walking into the bedroom and stumbling over the box.*] Goodness! What's this?

ISADORE: [*Looking around.*] Mom's rags, I guess. She always keeps 'em there.

MRS. GREENBAUM: [*Coming out.*] Where'd all the folks go, anyhow?

ISADORE: [*Pinching* TILLIE'S *cheek.*] They're all out in the park. Mom an' pop an' Masha. Out near the gate, they said. [*He fingers* TILLIE'S *hair.*]

MRS. GREENBAUM: [*Going to the rear window and looking out.*] The Hirshes have moved, haven't they? [ISADORE *turns and looks through the window.*] My, but it's hot up here! I don't wonder they went. I wonder papa and mamma don't move. They could get some other place than this, just as cheap. It's dreadful! What are you doing?

ISADORE: Oh, I'm answerin' some ads for a job.

MRS. GREENBAUM: I thought you just had one.

ISADORE: I did, but I lost it. These damned detectives keep followin' me around. Gee, but I don't seem to be able to keep anything no more. [*He scratches his head. His shoulder jerks. He ignores* TILLIE *for the moment.*] Everybody seems to know me. [*His shoulder jerks, and he looks up, unhappy.*]

MRS. GREENBAUM: [*Coming over, leaning down and patting his shoulder, the while she experiences a wave of sympathy.*] Now listen, Isadore [*he looks up*]—Irving, I mean—you're not so badly off. Your life's all before you, really. You've still time to make good, Brace up. You should do it for mamma's and papa's sakes. You've had a hard time but you can get something. You know how they worry. People aren't going to always remember. They forget soon enough when you make good. You know how they forget. Look at Harold Greenberg. See what he did! And now he's made good no one questions about his past. We're all willing to forget. Why keep reminding us? George is always willing to help you. He can give you a job, if you want it. Why don't you ask him?

ISADORE: [*Irritably.*] Yes, he would! Like hell! Didn't I ask him three months ago? An' did he give me anything? He did not! [*His shoulder jerks.*] I've been walkin' around tryin' to get sompin steady ever since. I know the folks don't want me here, an' I can't blame 'em, either. It's all my fault, of course, but—[*His shoulder jerks and his face contorts.* MRS. GREENBAUM, *who is only partially interested, makes a gesture as much as to say, "Oh, what's the use?" and walks toward the bookcase.* ISADORE *surveys* TILLIE, *playing with her hair and turning her face so as to look into her eyes. Finally he observes.*] How old are you now, kid?

TILLIE: Six. I'll be seven next June. Then I'll be goin' to college.

ISADORE: [*Gaily.*] You don't say! Quick work, eh? Some scholar! [*He turns up her chin. His shoulder jerks.*]

TILLIE: Yes, an' I got a box of paints, an' cards that I can sew on, an' a sewing machine, an' now I'm goin' to get roller skates. An' next summer I'm goin' to learn to swim.

[*He continues to stare at her, the while* MRS. GREENBAUM *picks up a magazine and examines it, and the child babbles on. That same look of uncontrolled and unnatural sex-interest begins to show in his eyes. He pushes the child out at arm's length and begins to stare fixedly. His shoulder jerks.*]

MRS. GREENBAUM: [*Turning and observing the look. She starts and frowns, then comes over, takes the child by the hand and helps her down.*] Come, now. Say goodbye to Uncle Irving. We're going down into the park to see grandma. You'll be here for dinner, won't you?

ISADORE: [*Recovering, and rising.*] Sure. Sure. You're goin', are you? See you later, eh? [*He follows them to the door as they go out. After they have gone he returns to the table, apparently quite unconscious of what has just happened, and sits down. Continuing, as he takes up a newspaper, his shoulder jerking.*] Gee! At last! I gotta do this now. [*He stretches his arms, and reads.*]
"WANTED, ACTOR, experienced stock man, to assist producing, on part or full time; write particulars and lowest figure considering permanent city engagement. CARO, 92 Steuben St., Brooklyn."
[*Aside.*] Well, I ain't an actor. I wish I was. But half the time they're out of a job, too. [*Meditates.*] I might act, though. Gee, that's the life! All them pretty girls! I might answer that. [*Marks it. Begins to read again.*] "Automobile mechanic, automobile mechanic, automobile mechanic, automobile mechanic" [*aside*]—say, look at all the automobile mechanics! Well, I ain't an automobile mechanic. I wish I was. I'd get a job now, maybe out o' one o' these. [*Meditates.*] But this bum arm o' mine—that's the trouble. I can't really do nothin' steady with that. People don't like it. [*His shoulder jerks. Reads.*] "Boy, boy, boy, boy"—look at all the boys, will yuh? There's a whole procession of 'em. [*Smiles.*] "Chauffeur, chauffeur, chauffeur, chauffeur." That's a good job, too, ridin' around in a good car. I wish I'd get a chance to learn that. I could pick up a nice girl if I had a car like that. [*Meditates.*] But where'd I find out how to run one, with this arm o' mine? [*His shoulder jerks. He*

*reads.*] "Collector, collector, collector"—
"COLLECTOR, Young man; reference. 11 Murray Street, 7th floor."
I wonder how much money they make. I oughta be able to do a thing like that, if I could behave myself and give any references. Greenbaum oughta help me to get that. [*He marks it. Silence. The clock ticks. He begins to hum a portion of a popular song. Reads. A knock is heard at the door—very soft.*]

ISADORE: [*Pausing in his work and soliloquizing.*] But look at me, anyhow! I ain't no good, much. I don't amount to nothin'. Here I am of a Saturday afternoon when everybody else is off sportin' around, an' I ain't got no place to go, an' no work, an' no money. [*He looks at his patched shoes, feels one, then feels in his pockets and produces a few cents.*] An' look at my shoes! I'm a bum, that's what I am. I ain't no good, an' I never will be. I ain't had a job in two months—not a good one. An' nobody cares for me now no more, nobody but mom an' pop an' Masha, really. They got their own lives, an' they go on an' do things, an' they don't count me in on 'em, not one of 'em. They can't, really. [*He stares at the floor. His shoulder jerks. The clock ticks. The slight tap at the door is renewed but he pays no heed.*] Mom an' pop! [*He shakes his head.*] But they ain't got anything, either. They're as bad off as I am. Poor mom. I'm sorry for her. She tries so hard—all the work she's had. [*His shoulder jerks.*] An' pop—he's all right, too, only he's almost as bad off as I am, peddlin' needles an' thread. Think o' that. [*He meditates.*] An' Masha, with her game leg! An' me! I'm not right. I know that. I ought never 'a' been brought in the world. They ought never to 'a' had so many children. Not me, anyhow. [*He gets up.*] I know I'll do sompin wrong pretty soon. I feel it. I can't help it. I ought to kill myself, but I ain't got the nerve, that's what's the matter! [*He half sobs.*] I'd be better off. Think of ten children, an' one crazy, an' one lame, an' four dead. Well, *they're* better off, anyhow. [*The knock sounds again, lightly. He does not hear.*] I had a good job with that dentist, if I'd only 'a' done right, but I couldn't help myself. I just couldn't. I ain't right, that's what's the matter with me. [*Meditates.*]

Gee! It's a wonder I didn't kill her, feelin' the way I did. I suppose I would, too, if they hadn't caught me. An' the way she screamed! An' the way they beat me up! Gee! An' that Island! I don't want to go back there no more. [*He turns and walks about, his hands in his pockets, his eyes staring.*]

[*As he does so the door opens, and* KITTY NEAFIE *puts her head in. She is a plump, blonde, almost red-headed child of eleven, with blue eyes and a pink skin. She has on a light brown linen dress and straw hat, with brown slippers and stockings.*]

KITTY: [*Timidly, because of the absence of the accustomed faces.*] Nobody home? Didn't Tillie come over today?

ISADORE: [*Aroused by the fact that the child is pretty and alone. His expression changes instantly, and he becomes soft and ingratiating.*] Hello! Who are you? [*She pauses uncertainly.*] Come on in, kid. They'll be back in a minute. I'm just Uncle Irving, that's all. You don't know me, but I belong here. Wanta see sompin? [*He looks around to find something to show her. Observes a pair of opera glasses on the top of the bookcase and takes them down. The child, smiling and interested by his manner, comes in.*]

KITTY: [*Diffidently.*] I can't stay very long. I thought sure I'd fine Tillie here. Ain't you Uncle Isadore?

ISADORE: Yes, that's what they used to call me, Isadore—that was my name, but I'm changin' it to Irving. I like that better—don't you? [KITTY *nods her head.*] What's yours?

KITTY: My name's Kitty Neafie. I live just downstairs here, below you, on that side. [*She points.*]

ISADORE: Well, that's a nice name, too. But who told you about me? [*His shoulder jerks.*]

KITTY: Oh, Masha. She said I hadn't seen you yet, but that you might come some day. Haven't you ever been here before? [*She takes the glasses held out to her, and examines them. Tries to see through them.*]

ISADORE: Yes, I been here once before, since we moved. Ain't they nice? [*He smiles on her winningly.*]

KITTY: Yes, but I can't see anything!

ISADORE: [*Taking the glasses and adjusting them.*] Let me show you. [*His shoulder jerks.*] See here. Now look. See how far away everything looks.

KITTY: [*Eagerly.*] Oh, lemme see! Ain't it funny! Oh, how funny everything looks! [*She looks out of the window.*]

ISADORE: [*Surveying her avidly, but with caution.*] Now wait. Let me show you. Through this end everything looks near. [*He adjusts them and gives them to her again.*] Now look.

[*She takes them, puts them to her eyes and then begins slowly to move toward the wall, looking through them at the table.*]

KITTY: Oh, how funny! Ain't it nice? I can see the table! An' your papers, an' the inkstand! [*Walks forward again curiously and bumps into him.*] Oh! [*Laughs.*]

ISADORE: [*Excitedly, with trembling hands.*] Now turn 'em the other way again. [*She does so.*] See how different it is. [*His shoulder jerks. As she looks, he stands and stares at her in a greedy, savage, half-insane way, his face coloring.*]

KITTY: Oh, it's so different, ain't it? Everything looks so funny! [*She laughs.*]

ISADORE: [*Walking to other side of table.*] Yes, but now look at me over here. Now watch me as I move.

[*He returns, slowly, coming up close to her. She puts out her hand and touches him. As she does so, his expression flares to one of fierce, demoniac hunger. He snatches the glasses away, puts them behind his back, and laughs a playful, semi-idiotic laugh.*]

KITTY: [*Half-scared, half-laughing. Her expression changes as she looks.*] Why—why—you look so funny—I—[*She laughs hysterically, but with dread in her voice.*]

ISADORE: [*Half-wild and half-intelligent.*] Oh, I was just foolin'. Can't you see? I just wanted to see if I could scare you.

KITTY: Why—why—was you? I thought—[*the clock ticks loudly*]—I better go home now. I guess—I think—my—mother—wants—me—[*She begins to back away.*]

ISADORE: [*Approaching and staring at her.*] Oh, no, she don't. You don't want to go yet. Don't be afraid. Didn't you just come from home? [*He tries to look sweet, and instead achieves weirdness. His face is slightly contorted, his smile ridiculous.*]

KITTY: [*Breathlessly.*] No, I just went to church this afternoon to confession. I was just goin' home now. I thought I'd stop in an' see Tillie if she was here—but—I—[*Pauses.*]

ISADORE: But you're a good little girl, ain't you? You ain't got nothin' to confess.

KITTY: No, no—but I have to go now. I know my mother wants me. [*She moves again.*] If Tillie comes, tell her I'll come up after while. [*She backs away and reaches the door, still staring.*]

ISADORE: [*Following, his shoulder jerking. He has a hungry, seeking look.*] Oh, no, don't go. Stay. Why don't you stay? She'll be back in a minute. I've got lots of nice things to show you. [*He looks about the room seeking something, then takes her arm.*]

KITTY: [*Fearfully.*] No—no—I mustn't. I have to go. Really, I must. I gotta go now. Please, I do. My mother wants me. I know she does. [*She begins to pull and whimper, reaching for the door.*]

ISADORE: [*Seizing her and lifting her up in his arms.*] No! No! You don't wanta go! You wanta stay, don't you? [*She begins to scream. He puts his hand over her mouth and half smothers her cries.*] Stay with me! Stay with me!

[*He lifts and carries her, struggling, into the bedroom, from which for a few seconds emerge sounds of contest, half smothered cries, words of appeal or command. Silence ensues, save for the ticking of the clock. After a time* ISADORE *emerges, the child limp in his arms. One slipper has fallen off. He is hot, disheveled, plainly insane, and yet with a shrewd, canny, cautious look in his eyes. Between his hand and the child's mouth is a handkerchief. He looks about as if uncertain what to do, comes over to the door, cautiously locks it, and returns to centre of the room. He then goes to the bedroom again, comes out, the child still in his arms, and goes to the window and stares across at the vacant apartment. Standing so, he seems to be struck with an idea, returns to the bedroom, puts the child down, comes out again, opens the door, listens, then looks up the stairway. He then goes out and disappears. In a few moments he returns in the same way, enters the bedroom, returns with the child in his arms, and disappears through the door.*]

# CURTAIN

## ACT II

### SCENE 1

*Same as Act I. When the curtain goes up, the stage is empty. It is now about six-thirty, and the sense of a hot summer evening is suggested by the light. A few pieces of colored cloth—green, blue, red—are lying about the floor between the table and the bedroom door and at the foot of the machine. On the table are* ISADORE'S *papers, undisturbed. A sound of steps is heard on the stair. Enter in this order:* MRS. BERCHANSKY, MRS. GREENBAUM, TILLIE, MASHA, *and* BERCHANSKY.

MRS. BERCHANSKY: [*Looking around and seeing the pieces of cloth, and beginning to pick them up.*] Isadore! [*Pauses.*] Isadore! [*She looks into the bedroom and kitchen.*] Gone again! It's too bed! Vell, now maybe ve von't see him again. I t'ought he vould stay. [*Looks into the bedroom again.*] Vot's diss! Somebody's been at my rags! Such upset! Such upset! Vere's de box? [*She re-enters the room, stooping and picking.*]

MRS. GREENBAUM: [*Walking about in a stately way.*] Tck! Tck! Tck!—but it's hot! Isadore's gone, has he? I thought maybe he wouldn't stay. I'll open the window in the bathroom here. Perhaps we can get a breeze. [*She goes into the bathroom and returns.*]

BERCHANSKY: Yes, it is hot, but *I* tell you how to keep cool [*gesticulating with his finger*]—a little hot tea. Dat's it! Ice cream! Ice cream soda! Who drinks dat? Poison, I tell you, poison—cornstarch. Young people, dey must alvays be in de kendy-store, nowadays, spendin' dere five-cent pieces. If dey put dere five cents in dere pockets an' hot tea in dere stomachs, believe me, it's better. [*He illustrates their disposition with his hands, puts down his book, goes into the bathroom and lights the gas.*]

MASHA: Oh, papa, that's an old-fashioned idea. Everybody likes ice cream soda.

TILLIE: [*Patting her stomach.*] Umm—m—wish I had some.

MASHA: [*To* TILLIE, *genially.*] Supper'll be ready soon. [*Bends over and whispers in her ear.*] Then if you're good, I'll give you five cents, and you can go down and have an ice cream soda after supper. Ssh!

[*Pats her cheek and points her finger, as much as to say, "Don't tell the others!" She then goes into the kitchen and begins to bring out things for the table. As she starts about her work,* MRS. GREENBAUM *clears* ISADORE'S *papers off the table, including the paper and envelopes which* MASHA *had brought him. These last she holds in her hands for a moment, then places them on top of the newspapers on a chair.* TILLIE *comes toward them.*]

MRS. GREENBAUM: Now, Tillie, let them alone!

MASHA: [*Returning from kitchen.*] This place looks upset. Where's the oilcloth from the kitchen table, mamma?—Mamma!

MRS. BERCHANSKY: [*From the bedroom.*] Yes?

MASHA: [*With a puzzled look on her face.*] Come here. [MRS. BERCHANSKY *appears at the door. She has a child's slipper in her hand, at which she is looking in a disturbed and secretive way. Before* MASHA *speaks,* MRS. BERCHANSKY *indicates it with her right hand.* MASHA *sees, starts, pales slightly, then says in a low voice.*] The oilcloth on the kitchen table—do you know where it is?

MRS. BERCHANSKY: Vere could it be? Dat's funny! An' dis! [*She holds out the slipper, which is concealed from the others by* MASHA'S *body, then slips it under her shawl.*] It's not Tillie's. [*She looks at* TILLIE, *who is standing near.*] Rae has no slippers like dis! [*They come out together, looking at each other oddly.*]

BERCHANSKY: [*Stepping out of the bathroom and listening a moment.*] Vot's funny, Masha? [MRS. BERCHANSKY *and* MASHA *exchange warning glances.*]

MASHA: Nothing . . . nothing. It's only a broken glass. Isadore didn't wait? [*She and* MRS. BERCHANSKY *go into the kitchen.*]

BERCHANSKY: [*Following them to the kitchen door.*] Vot iss it?

MRS. BERCHANSKY: [*Nervously, from the kitchen.*] Nothing . . . nothing. A little dish broke.

[*He returns to the table.*]

BERCHANSKY: [*Seating himself.*] Now, I can eat. I'm hungry. It's after seven. [*He lights the gas over the table.*]

TILLIE: [*Pulling up a chair.*] Come on, everybody! [*Fixes herself at the table.*]

MRS. GREENBAUM: [*Rising from her chair where she has been examining one of* ISADORE'S *papers.*] Aren't you going to wait for Isadore and Rae?

BERCHANSKY: For Isadore? For him you could vait a long time! He comes vunce today, den he is gone again. Last time it vuz a month. Rae, she comes an' goes ven she pleases. Coney Island, Rockaway, Beach Long—I should know vere she is! [*He lifts his hands, then subsides and strikes his chest gently.*] But, Esther, it hurts me plenty. Here it hurts me. Vunce you're old, den dey don't listen no more. [*He sighs.*] Dey t'ink dey know everyt'ing. [*With a rising inflection.*] I should advise! Yes! Remember, Esther, my child, vit' you it vuz different. You vuz de first, an' ve hed time for you. But ven the ot'ers come an' dere vuz vork—fourteen, sixteen hours a day—den I had no time no more to vatch, to find out, vere dey vuz going, vot dey vuz doing. I hed plenty troubles, plenty troubles. [*He shakes his head and reaches for the radishes. Turns again.*] Dey try an' teach us. Dey say ve are old fashion'—vot dey call "not up to date." But, Esther, dere ain't no fashions for de heart. No! [*He shakes his head.*] Only feelings. [*Puts his hand to his heart.*] An' sometimes it gets so full of feelings dat dere ain't no more room, an' I t'ink it's going to break—better dat it should. But it don't! It only goes on hurting. Nu—vot can I say? [*He shakes his head.*] But, Esther, you know I don't care how much I verk. I'd verk twenty hours, maybe twenty-two, so long as I see everyt'ing goes nice, an' ve hev enough to eat, an' my children are happy an' do vell. Some of dem—vell, it vuz to be—[*He shakes his head again.*]

MRS. GREENBAUM: [*Consolingly.*] Well, the girls are all right. They haven't done anything wrong. And the boys'll take care of themselves. I wouldn't worry about any of them.

BERCHANSKY: Yes. All except Isadore. I don't know about him. He vuz here today, an' now he's gone again! Vere? Ach! It's too bed!

[*He shakes his head.* MASHA *and* MRS. BERCHANSKY *come forward.* MRS. BERCHANSKY *goes to the machine drawer, opens it, and slips the shoe into it. They seat themselves at the table. Their faces are a study in wonder and distress. At the remark concerning* ISADORE *they exchange glances. Steps are heard on the stairs. A knock follows.*]

MRS. BERCHANSKY: Come!

[*The door opens, and a rather attractive Irish woman of perhaps thirty-seven or eight puts her head in at the door. She has a thin, intelligent face, silvery gray hair, a neat, cleanly appearance.*]

MRS. NEAFIE: Good evenin'! Oh, you're just afther sittin' down to your supper? Mine's waitin' for John. I'm sorry to be interruptin' you, but you haven't seen anything of my Kitty, have you? She went out early this efternoon to go to the church to confession, and she hasn't come back yet. [*At the mention of* KITTY'S *name,* MASHA *and* MRS. BERCHANSKY *exchange glances.*] I'm that worried! I can't understand what's keepin' her. [*Her face shows anxiety.*]

BERCHANSKY: [*Pausing, his knife and fork in the air, and looking at her.*] Kitty—

MRS. BERCHANSKY: [*Solicitously and nervously, glancing at* MASHA.] No, Mrs. Neafie. Ve hev been out in de park all efternoon. She vuzn't here up to de time ve left—vuz she? [*She looks at* MASHA *for confirmation, then at her guest.* MRS. NEAFIE *turns to go.*] Von't you sit down?

BERCHANSKY: [*Idly.*] Maybe, now—

MASHA: [*Interrupting him.*] Tea, papa? [*To* MRS. NEAFIE.] Perhaps she's just stopped somewhere to play.

MRS. NEAFIE: [*Not listening to the others.*] No, Mrs. Berchansky. No, thank you. I'm expectin' John home any minute now, an' he'll be afther wantin' his supper. I was thinkin' maybe she had come up here. Good night! [*She goes out.*]

BERCHANSKY: [*To* MASHA.] For vy you push my arm?

MASHA: [*Heavily.*] Did I? I didn't mean to. I just wanted to give you your tea.

TILLIE: [*Who all this while has been eating industriously and unobserved.*] I want some tea, too!

MRS. GREENBAUM: Hush! Don't ask. You'll get some.

MRS. BERCHANSKY: [*Pleadingly, but in an intense way.*] Esther, take some cheese. I vonder vere Kitty could hev gone to, now?

MRS. GREENBAUM: [*Indifferently.*] Oh, she'll come back. She's just out playing somewhere. Tillie, don't reach! How many times have I told you?

TILLIE: Well, then, please can I have some cheese?

MRS. GREENBAUM: And how many times have I told you not to ask? If you want anything, whisper to me. You've had enough already. You'll make yourself sick.

BERCHANSKY: [*By whom* TILLIE *sits, gently.*] Never mind, Tillie. You is a good little girl. [*He helps her to some more cheese. To* MRS. GREENBAUM.] Let de child eat. She must grow. Vot, Tillie? [*He chucks her under the chin.* TILLIE *looks up at him affectionately and smiles.*]

MRS. GREENBAUM: That's the way you always spoil them, papa. You always did.

BERCHANSKY: Ach, dey're babies only vunce. Dat time comes no more. [*He looks benignly at the child.*]

MRS. GREENBAUM: But, papa, you know how it is with children. I have a hard time enough with her, as it is.

MRS. BERCHANSKY: [*Wearily.*] Ach, Esther, children is children.

MASHA: [*Leaning her head on the table and shaking it slightly.*] It's terrible!

MRS. GREENBAUM: [*Addressing* MASHA.] What's the matter?

MASHA: [*Softly.*] The heat. [*She shakes her head again.*]

BERCHANSKY: Ven it's hot, it's hot. Inside, outside. Vot's de difference? [*The clock strikes eight.*]

MRS. GREENBAUM: Goodness, it's eight. I'll have to go. [*She rises.*] George will be home soon. I promised him I'd be home by eight. Come, Tillie. You've had enough. You've had too much. You'll be sick tomorrow. [*She goes to the corner and secures her parasol.*]

BERCHANSKY: [*Patting* TILLIE *on the back and kissing her.*] Nu, dis little von't hurt, vill it? [*Helps* TILLIE *down.*] Nu! [*Kisses her.* TILLIE *kisses her grandmother.*]

TILLIE: Goodbye, grandma.

MRS. BERCHANSKY: [*Patting her.*] So! Dat's a nice girl.

MASHA: [*As* TILLIE *approaches and puts up her mouth.*] Goodbye! [*She rises, preparatory to going into the kitchen.* TILLIE *runs to the door, then comes running back, and putting up her arms, pulls* MASHA'S *head down and whispers something in her ear.* MASHA *nods.*] Oh, yes. [*She limps to the machine drawer and takes something out.*]

MRS. GREENBAUM: Tillie! Now, Masha, I won't have that! [*To* TILLIE.] You just give that back. [*As the child pouts.*] No, no, no! Now, I'll get you some ice cream soda myself. Masha, take that. I won't have her asking for pennies. [*The child gives up the coin.* MRS. GREENBAUM *approaches the door.*] Come on, now! [*Takes* TILLIE'S *hand.*] Will you all come over tomorrow? George's mother is coming.

MASHA: [*Contemplating her mother in a distressed way.*] Yes, we'll come.

MRS. GREENBAUM: [*Going out.*] Goodbye!

TILLIE: Bye-bye! [*Exit.*]

BERCHANSKY: [*Rising and brushing off his waistcoat.*] Vell, it's nice. Esther, she gets along so vell. She has a nice home, a nice husband. He didn't hev much ven day got married, but dey verked an' saved. Now, Tillie she ken hev piano lessons, an' dey ken live in a nice place. It's good. [*He goes over to the bookcase and begins to examine some half-smoked cigars he is keeping there in an old cigar box. He picks up one and another, examining them critically.*]

MRS. BERCHANSKY: [*Softly.*] Unberufen! Unberufen!

BERCHANSKY: [*Sniffing at one fairly long butt doubtfully.*] Vell, dis vill smoke me till I go to bed. Maybe my oder two girls dey marry good, too. Ach, I vish I could play pinochle tonight! Pinochle I can play alvays, even ven it's hot.

MRS. BERCHANSKY: [*Heavily.*] Papa! [*She hesitates and says no more.*]

BERCHANSKY: Vell, vot is it? Vot is it?

MRS. BERCHANSKY: Papa, you know it's funny. I don't say it's anyt'ing . . . he vouldn't do anyt'ing now. [*She pauses.*]

BERCHANSKY: [*Coming to attention.*] Who? Vot? Vot are you talking about?

MASHA: Oh, it may be nothing, mamma. She may not have been up here. It may not be her shoe. [*She places her fingers to her lips.*] Maybe he's just gone to mail his letters.

MRS. BERCHANSKY: But de box! De oilcloth! Who vould take dem? An' my rags all over de floor! [*She stares at* MASHA.] But vy didn't I stay? [*She shakes her head.*] Vy didn't I stay?

BERCHANSKY: [*In a troubled voice.*] Box? Oilclawt? Shoe? Vot box? Vot is it you talk? [*They do not reply at once.*] Box? Oilclawt? Shoe? Vot's dat?

MRS. BERCHANSKY: You know. De box vere I keep my rags. Dat big one in de bedroom. It's gone. [*She rises and goes to the machine drawer, takes out the shoe and returns with it.*] Ven I come in I found dis in dere. [*She indicates the bedroom.*] Now Kitty Neafie is not home. An' de oilcloth from de kitchen table is gone. [*She wrings her hands.*] An' here's de rags, but vere is de box?

BERCHANSKY: [*Getting up and taking the shoe and examining it, a strained, puzzled look on his face.*] Nu! [*He beats the table with his fingers.*] It's not Tillie's? Nu?

MASHA: No, it doesn't belong to her, nor to Rae, either.

MRS. BERCHANSKY: [*Uncertainly.*] An' Kitty not home! She may hev been up here.

MASHA: [*Consolingly.*] Oh, I wouldn't be so nervous, mamma. She may not have been here. Why worry so?

BERCHANSKY: [*Folding his hands and swaying to and fro slightly. His face is a study in fear, puzzle, wonder.*] Nu? You t'ink—[*His face blanches.*]

MASHA: Oh!!

MRS. BERCHANSKY: [*Leading the way to the kitchen door.*] An' de oilcloth out here . . . it's gone!

BERCHANSKY: Oilclawt'! Ach, Gott, vot could anybody vant vit' oilclawt'? [*He pauses.*] De box—it's gone, is it?

MRS. BERCHANSKY: [*Returning.*] Yes. Here are de rags, but I can't find de box. [*They look into the bedroom.*]

BERCHANSKY: Nu!—you think—[*He throws up his hands. They return to the centre of the room.*]

MRS. BERCHANSKY: Oi—I don't understend! I don't know. Maybe he did somet'ing?

BERCHANSKY: Yes, vot? Vot could he do vit' a box? [*Pauses.*] But vy vorry before ve know? It's maybe nutting. [*He looks distressed himself.*] Don't vorry so much. [*He begins to walk up and down the floor.*]

MASHA: [*By the chair on which* MRS. GREENBAUM *has laid* ISADORE'S *papers.*] Yes. . . . And here are his envelopes. I guess he didn't write, after all. [*She looks at her mother.*]

MRS. BERCHANSKY: Ach, weh-is-mer! Weh-is-mer! [*She wrings her hands.*] I vish I know vot is is!

BERCHANSKY: [*Pausing and staring at the floor.*] Maybe's more trouble. Sometimes I don't know vot to t'ink. [*A noise is heard on the stairs. The door is thrown open.*]

[*Enter* ISADORE. *He stands in the entry way, surprised and irritated. His eyes are strained and restless, his hair disheveled, his face scratched, the marks of dust on one arm. One trouser leg is partially covered with burrs, the other has a tear. He looks irritable, somewhat savage.* BERCHANSKY *hides the shoe behind him.*]

ISADORE: [*Sharply.*] Oh, you're back, are you? [*He crosses and enters the kitchen.*]

MRS. BERCHANSKY: [*Following and looking after him.*] You vant supper, Isadore? [*She stands, awe-struck.*]

ISADORE: [*Calling back.*] Supper, no! I gotta go right away again, anyhow. [*He returns, stuffing something into his pocket.*]

BERCHANSKY: [*Nervously, a quality of fear and insufficiency in his voice, approaching and standing before him.*] Vot is dis hurry? Look at your face! Vere hev you been? Your suit—[*Leans down and picks a burr.*] Vot's dis?

ISADORE: Oh, nothing. I've been playin' ball. [*His shoulder jerks.*]

BERCHANSKY: Ball? You play ball ven it's dark? [*Touching his elbow.*] Look at your sleeve! [*Points to his left trouser leg.*] Here it's torn. Vot iss dis? [*He stares at* ISADORE'S *face.*]

ISADORE: [*Irritably.*] Nothing. Nothing, I tell you. What should it be? Leave me alone. I've been in a fight. [*His shoulder jerks.*]

BERCHANSKY: A fight? On Shabbas! Mit who? First you're playin' ball, den it's a fight. Now vich is it?

ISADORE: Oh, don't bother! I tell you I was in a fight! I'm all right, though. I've gotta go. [*He starts.*]

BERCHANSKY: [*Uncertainly, because of his lesser strength, but placing himself in* ISADORE'S *path.*] Vy you run avay? Go vash your face! Clean your suit! It's a shame! It's a shame!

MRS. BERCHANSKY: [*Gently.*] Take off your coat, Isadore. I fix it. Maybe you'll eat somet'ing?

ISADORE: [*Irritably.*] No, no, no! Don't bother! I've gotta go, I tell you. [*Starts again. His shoulder jerks.*]

BERCHANSKY: [*With a slight show of anger.*] No, no, no! I don't believe dis! You tell me first, vot is dis? [*He produces the shoe.*] Whose is dis? [ISADORE *stares at it.*] Vere did it come from?

ISADORE: [*Savagely and with a touch of wildness in his manner.*] What, that? I don't know where it come from. What're you talkin' about? [*His shoulder jerks.*]

BERCHANSKY: An' de box? An' de oilclawt'? Vot iss it about dem? Vot did you do vit' dem? Did you take dem? Vot becomes of de oilclawt' here? [*He motions toward the kitchen.*]

ISADORE: [*Savagely.*] What box? What oilcloth? I didn't see no box, nor no oilcloth! What are you people talkin' about—

what are you lookin' at me for? What do I know? What
are you tryin' to find out? [*His shoulder jerks.*]

BERCHANSKY: Vell, it vuz on de kitchen table. Now it's gone.
An' de box! An' dis! [*He holds up the slipper.*] Vot is it
about dis? Vot I vant to know is, how did dis come here?
Vuz Kitty Neafie up here today? Did you see her?

ISADORE: [*Nervously.*] I tell you I don't know! She wasn't here
when I was here. What do I know about any box or oilcloth? I haven't seen them, I tell you. [*He starts to go.*]

MRS. BERCHANSKY: [*Nervously.*] De box in de bedroom, Isadore.
It's gone, too. You didn't take it, maybe? [*She looks at
him appealingly.*]

ISADORE: Me? No, no, no! What do I want with a box? I tell
you I don't know anything about it! I haven't seen no box
nor no oilcloth. I don't know what you're talkin' about.
[*He starts again.*]

BERCHANSKY: [*Laying a hand on him.*] Ach, I don't understend!
I don't understend! Vait! I vant to know about dese
t'ings. First it's ball, den it's a fight. Your coat torn, your
face scratched! Here is a shoe! De oilclawt' is gone, an' de
box. An' dese things [*pointing to the burrs*]—I don't know
vot dey are. But I know, I feel, it's somet'ing else. You
ken't tell me it ain't, Isadore. An' I shell know now, vot
is it? Vot hev you done? Vere is Kitty Neafie? Vuz she
here today? [*He becomes very intense.*]

MRS. BERCHANSKY: [*Appealingly.*] Isadore, if it's somet'ing, vy
don't you tell? You know it's better. Ve are your parents.
Maybe ve can help you. [*She plucks at his sleeve.*]

ISADORE: [*Swinging about irritably.*] Oh, you're all crazy! [*His
shoulder jerks.*] I don't know what you're talkin' about! I
don't know anything about Kitty Neafie! I gotta go!
[*Starts. As he does so, his father seizes him vigorously by
the arm.*]

BERCHANSKY: No! Here you stay! You liar! You loafer! You
good-for-nutting! You run de streets an' get in jail, an'

den you come here an' you von't tell me vot you do! Now, you shell tell me! I vant to know! I vill know! [ISADORE'S *shoulder jerks.*] Vot hev you done? You shell tell me now before you leave dis house! [*He reaches a great height of fury.*]

ISADORE: [*Savagely, a little wildly.*] Let go! I don't know what you're talkin' about! You're all crazy. [*He jerks himself loose. A fierce angry light blazes in his eyes. He moves about the table trying to pull away from his father, who hangs on. In the struggle, his right hand, which is in his right pocket, is withdrawn, and with it a tangle of cord. His shoulder jerks.*]

BERCHANSKY: [*Shouting.*] An' dis! Vot's dis now! Ach, mein Gott! Vot for is it? [*He grabs the string.*]

ISADORE: [*Tearing it away and yet struggling with him.*] Let go! Let go! [*He throws his father about. The table is struck, the chairs upset.* BERCHANSKY *is thrown to his knees.* ISADORE'S *shoulder jerks.*]

BERCHANSKY: [*Still shouting.*] Isadore! You hear me! Ach, mein Gott! I'll know before you go from dis house. Know, I vill! You shell tell me! [*His coat is torn, his skull-cap falls off. He gets to his feet.*]

MRS. BERCHANSKY: [*To one side with* MASHA.] Don't, papa! Don't! Oh, Isadore! Don't! Ach!

MASHA: [*Limping to and fro.*] Oh, this is terrible! I can't stand it! [*Approaches her father and begins to cry.*] Let him alone, papa. Please let him alone! Don't, Isadore! For shame!

BERCHANSKY: [*Shouting to her out of the contest.*] Go 'vay! Go 'vay! Dis time I know vot I do. Tell me, he must! He vill tell me before he goes from here. [*To* ISADORE.] Before you leave dis house, you vill tell me. I am your fader. Dis time you *vill* obey me. You hear me?

ISADORE: [*Throwing him off and down. His shoulder jerks.*] Let go!

[BERCHANSKY *falls to the floor.* ISADORE *dashes to the door, pulls it open and runs down the stairs, slamming it after him.* BERCHANSKY, *getting to his feet, seizes a chair, runs after him, and, aiming it, runs as far as the door, then stops and puts it down, opens the door and shouts.*]

BERCHANSKY: Isadore! [*A pause.*] Isadore! [*The sound of* ISADORE'S *clattering feet is heard on the stairs. The hall door below is heard to slam. As it does so,* BERCHANSKY *ceases to call, drops his hands, then his head, and repeats softly.*] Isadore!

[*There is a silence in which* MASHA *goes to the window and looks out. The clock is heard to tick.* MRS. BERCHANSKY, *nonplussed and frightened, crosses over to her husband and lays a hand on his arm.*]

MRS. BERCHANSKY: Tck! Tck! Tck! Dis should heppen in our old days! Vot comes now?

[BERCHANSKY *strikes his hands and shakes his head, but says nothing. As he stands there, the curtain descends for a few moments. The theatre remains dark.*]

# CURTAIN

## SCENE 2

*Same as Scene One. Two hours are supposed to elapse. As the curtain rises the clock is striking ten.* BERCHANSKY, MRS. BERCHANSKY, MASHA, JOE, *and* MR. *and* MRS. GREENBAUM *are disclosed, scattered about the room and around the table.* JOE *is leaning against a side of the bathroom door, one foot crossed over the other.* MASHA, MRS. BERCHANSKY *and* MRS. GREENBAUM *are seated at the table.* BERCHANSKY *is standing behind* MASHA, *near the table, very pale and distressed.* GEORGE GREENBAUM *is seated on the window sill. He is a simple, unpretentious, American-looking business man—very neat and silent. The shoe is on the table.*

GREENBAUM: Well, you don't really know that he's done anything, yet. What's the use getting so worked up about it? The slipper may not belong to her, after all.

BERCHANSKY: [*Argumentatively, and with a considerable amount of emotion.*] Yes, but who else should it belong to? It's not Tillie's, an' who else vuz here? No vun! Unless Kitty, maybe, or some vun else. He hes done somet'ing, dat much I know. An' de box an' de oilclawt', de scratches on his face, de string. Vy did he run avay? He didn't look right to me—he didn't act right. [*He rubs his chin.*]

GREENBAUM: Yes, that's all true enough, but we really don't know that Kitty was up here. She isn't home yet, but that doesn't prove that he saw her.

MRS. BERCHANSKY: Oi! Oi! Oi!

MRS. GREENBAUM: Yes, and the way he looked at Tillie this afternoon frightened me. When Rae went out she said he wasn't acting right. If that little girl came in here—[*She pauses.*]

GREENBAUM: How not acting right? [*He shifts his position as though he has been talking for some time.*] What did she say?

MRS. GREENBAUM: Well, I didn't have a chance to talk to her. She had to go. But she said he was off again today, and that I was to look out for him. He didn't seem so bad, outside of the way he looked at Tillie.

MASHA: Well, I don't know that I'd listen to what Rae says, anyhow. You know how she is. He doesn't like her and she doesn't like him, and she might have excited him.

JOE: Yes, but that shoe and the box and oilcloth? What about them? It looks pretty tough to me.

MRS. BERCHANSKY: Ach, if ve could only keep him at home an' take care of him! If only I hed stayed here!

MRS. GREENBAUM: Yes, if you could afford it.

GREENBAUM: [*Thoughtfully.*] I can't see that there is any sense in getting so excited until we know something positively. It's true, things do look bad. Still, there may be nothing. You haven't heard whether she's come home yet, have you?

MASHA: No.

GREENBAUM: Well, I wouldn't inquire, if I were you. If anything is wrong it would look bad afterwards. What I don't see is why you take any more chances with him. He's not right, really—that's plain now, isn't it? I hate to say it, but it's true. I've tried to help him several times, but I'm afraid to recommend him to anybody any more, and we can't use him in our business. He hasn't any sense for that work. He doesn't look right. The best thing to do would be to put him in a home somewhere, I think, where he'd be looked after, and yet where he'd have plenty to do and not feel shut up. He's not a bad boy, actually. He likes to work. He's good-hearted, too. I know that. [MRS. BERCHANSKY *nods.*] But he can't help himself. He's too restless and excitable, and he's crazy about girls. If you let him run around much longer by himself these days, he's sure to come to some harm. He can't help it—the way the girls dress now, with their short skirts and open shirtwaists. It seems to have a bad effect on him. He may not have done anything wrong today, but he will some time. He can't help it, and it won't be his fault. [*He sits down.*]

MRS. GREENBAUM: After that look I saw him give Tillie today, I'd be afraid to have him around. Really, I would. I think something had better be done.

MRS. BERCHANSKY: Oi! Oi! Oi! Trouble, trouble, trouble!

JOE: Well, why don't we send him away, then? There's no use waitin' any longer, is there?

BERCHANSKY: An asylum! An asylum! Ach! Vell, maybe it is best. After tonight, I know it is. [*He rubs his chin. Steps are heard on the stairs. Enter* RAE, *decked out in all her finery.*]

RAE: Hello, everybody! Wotcha doin'? Wotcha talkin' about?

MRS. BERCHANSKY: Oi! Oi! Oi! Trouble, trouble, trouble!

BERCHANSKY: [*Folding and unfolding his hands on his breast.*] Plenty to vorry about. Plenty! [*He shakes his head.*]

JOE: It's Isadore again.

RAE: [*Eagerly.*] Well, what about him? What's he been doin' now?

MRS. GREENBAUM: Oh, nothing that we know of. He was in here a while ago all scratched up. With some burrs on him, and his coat torn, and he wouldn't tell where he'd been, or what he had been doing, or where he was going, and they're afraid he's done something. They found a little girl's shoe in the bedroom, and Kitty Neafie hadn't come home by seven o'clock, and her mother was up here looking for her. Mother's big rag box and the oilcloth from the kitchen table are gone.

RAE: Kitty Neafie! You found a shoe? Let's see it. [*They show it to her. She exclaims.*] An' that big piece of yellow oilcloth out in the kitchen—you say it's gone?

MRS. GREENBAUM: Yes, and papa thinks he came back for some twine. [*She gets up.*]

JOE: He come in an' went into the kitchen an' grabbed a whole handful of cord out of the cupboard, an' run out again. Pop tried to stop him, but Isadore threw him all around the place.

MRS. BERCHANSKY: Oi! Oi! Weh-is-mer!

BERCHANSKY: It is somet'ing! I know! Ach, if I only knew! He's not right. I know now!

MRS. GREENBAUM: Oh, dear, I wonder what he could have wanted with that?

RAE: Tck! Tck! Tck! This is terrible! Kitty Neafie! Goodness, if he's done anything to her—[*She stares.*] Well, I warned ja all. You knew he wasn't right, an' he oughtn't to be out an' around loose. Still you wouldn't listen. Only today he tried to stop me in here when I was goin' out—wanted me to kiss him—said I didn't seem like a sister to him. I had to slap his face before he'd let me alone. [*She takes a defiant pose.*] I was almost afraid to leave Esther, only I know he's afraid of her. [*She walks into the bedroom, taking off her hat.*] Well, I s'pose you'll agree, now, that he oughta be put away.

BERCHANSKY: [*His head down.*] Tck! Tck! Tck!

MRS. GREENBAUM: [*Softly.*] After Rae left I watched him, and it was then I saw him look at Tillie so. It frightened me so I took her and went out in the park. I didn't want to say anything because I thought he would be here when we got back, and I didn't want to make mamma and papa feel bad again.

RAE: [*From the bedroom.*] Did he finish the letters he was writin'?

MASHA: No, the envelopes are here.

GREENBAUM: [*Getting up and walking about.*] Well, as I say, we don't know anything yet, positively. He may not have done anything, even though a slipper was here and the child's missing. It does look pretty bad, I'll admit, but I can't see that there's anything to do about it except wait until he comes back, or until we hear something else, then see if we can keep him around here, or get hold of him. You'll have to be careful, though, if he does come back, and not say or do anything to let him know, otherwise he won't go. We'll have to fool him into it. [*He subsides.*]

BERCHANSKY: Rae, how long vuz you here mit Isadore? Ven did you leave?

RAE: About four. Why?

BERCHANSKY: Vell, vot vuz he doing? Vot vuz it he said to you? Did he look queer to you?

RAE: He acted crazy, like he always does, I tell ya! He tried to kiss me. He wouldn't let me alone till I gave him a good slap in the face.

MRS. BERCHANSKY: Ach, Rae! Vy did you do dat? He iss your brother. Maybe he vanted to be nice mit you again.

RAE: Say! Him? Cut that! He's dips, I tell ya. Look at what may have happened today. [*The others wince.*] It wasn't because I'm his sister that he wanted to kiss me. He's crazy about girls, I tell ya. He can't let 'em alone. He can't help it. He can't let me alone, if ya wanta know. Don't take no chances with *that* hangin' around the house. He's dips, I tell ya. Put 'im away, an' then you can breathe easy. [*She begins to take off her shoes.*] Afterwards we can move away from here, an' nobody'll know where we've gone. We can move up to the Bronx.

MRS. BERCHANSKY: Oi! Oi! Oi!

BERCHANSKY: Rae, you should not talk foolish. Ve vant to find out, don't you understend?

GREENBAUM: [*Seating himself again.*] Was there anybody else here when you left? I mean before Esther and Tillie came?

RAE: No. Joe had just gone, an' Esther came in afterwards. I thought once I better speak to her before I went. I was on the edge of comin' back after I got downstairs, but I didn't have time. I knew he wouldn't do anything to any grown-up person, though. He's too big a coward. He always is till you're alone and till it's some one he thinks he can handle. But if Kitty came in here—[*She shakes her head.*] I know him of old. He knows he can't put it over me, an' so he don't try. That's why he quit. Believe me, I'd never trust a kid with him, though, anywhere.

BERCHANSKY: [*Excitedly, and touching his heart.*] Rae! Rae!! Stop! Ve know! It's bed enough! I ken't stend it! [*He moves uneasily.*]

RAE: Well, when you all come to your senses an' put him away, I'll stop, an' not before. If you'd listened to me this wouldn't 'a' happened today—if anything has happened. For a cent, I'd have him put away myself. You'd thank me for it in the long run. You're just afraid of what people'll say, that's all. Believe me, you'd better act before sompin worse happens.

GREENBAUM: [*Amicably.*] But we've agreed to do that now, Rae.

RAE: Well, it's time, that's all I've gotta say.

BERCHANSKY: [*Shaking his head.*] Yes. Yes. It's better.

GREENBAUM: [*Getting up.*] Well, then, tomorrow I'll see if I can find some place, if you want me to. If he comes back, you'd better try and keep him here. Don't irritate him, and don't say anything. Just ask him to stay, and persuade him to, if you can. I'll talk to my lawyer, and let you know. [*He takes out his watch and begins to look around for his hat, as if he were ready to depart.*] We'd better be going, Esther. It's after eleven.

[MRS. GREENBAUM *rises. As she does this, a noise is heard on the stair. It begins as a soft murmur, and increases in volume until it is more or less of an uproar. The shuffling of many feet is heard. As the noise begins and continues, the family stop all conversation, and listen.* JOE, *who is nearest the door, crosses and opens it.*]

A VOICE: Yes, this is where they live.

ANOTHER VOICE: Neafie! They live in here. [*A knocking is heard.*]

A THIRD VOICE: Mr. Neafie! Mr. Neafie!

SEVERAL VOICES: [*In concert.*]
It's terrible, ain't it?
To think it should be their little girl!
Poor Kitty!
Do they know who done it?
No. [*A silence.*]

[*Suddenly the piercing scream of a woman is heard. As all this proceeds, the facial expression of the various members of the family changes. They become concerned, strained.*]

BERCHANSKY: [*In a low voice and with a frightened air, coming near the door.*] Vot's dat?

JOE: [*Softly, in a troubled voice.*] It sounds as if something has happened to Kitty Neafie. [*He half closes the door.*]

RAE: [*Who is standing near the bedroom door, speaking out loud.*] Gee! I wonder what's that, now? [*Crosses to* JOE.]

BERCHANSKY: [*With great intensity, clenching and unclenching his hands.*] If it should be Isadore!

MRS. BERCHANSKY: [*Crossing to her husband and shaking his arm.*] Ssh! [*Shakes her head.*]

GREENBAUM: [*Stepping to the table.*] Listen to me. If it should be anything, no one of you must say anything. You hear? You haven't seen him. You don't know where he is. Put that shoe away! Burn it! [MRS. BERCHANSKY *takes the shoe into the kitchen and returns.*] He hasn't been here, do you see! [*They all look at him without a word.*] For goodness' sake, don't all look as if something had happened! That's a dead give-away.

MRS. BERCHANSKY: Oi! Oi! Vot ken ve do? Vot ken ve do? [*She begins to cry.*]

MASHA: [*Sternly.*] Mamma! Don't cry! You mustn't!

[*More steps are heard on the stairs, as if they were coming up and to the Berchansky flat. At the sound of them,* JOE *closes the door.*]

BERCHANSKY: [*Walking the floor and twisting his hands.*] Ach, Gott! Vot comes now?

[*A brisk knock is heard. No one offers to go to the door.*]

GREENBAUM: [*Commandingly, to* JOE.] Open it!

[JOE *opens the door. Enter in a crush four neighbors, tenants of the building—an elderly red-faced woman, greasy, unkempt, fat; a younger, cleaner, but more vacuous and curious woman of thirty-three or four; a young boy of seventeen; a small girl of eleven.*]

THE ELDERLY FAT WOMAN: [*Pushing before the others.*] Oh, Mrs. Berchansky! Have you heard what's happened to Kitty Neafie? They've just took her away in the ambulance! She's all cut up! They just found her in the lot back here, right back of the house, an' she can't live. The policeman said so. Oh, it's terrible! Poor Mrs. Neafie, she's just fainted an' they can't bring her to an'—[*She pauses for want of breath.*]

BERCHANSKY: [*Striking his hands.*] Ach, Gott! Ach, Gott!

MRS. BERCHANSKY: Oi! Oi! Oi!

MASHA: [*Heavily.*] Poor little Kitty!

RAE: [*With great presence of mind, coming forward and staring at the four.*] Gee, that's terrible! How long ago did it happen?

THE YOUNGER WOMAN: Just now they found her. Nobody knows who done it. She was in a box, an' there was a piece o' oilcloth over her. [BERCHANSKY *strikes his hands together.*] A man was comin' through the lot an' heard a noise. He went past, an' then he went back. She wasn't dead, but she was almost. She couldn't talk no more. He hurry up an' got the police. Gee, it's awful! The crowd was sompin terrible! Mr. Melka, on the ground floor, was out there, an' he told who she was. He knowed her. They told Mrs. Neafie just now, an' she's almost crazy—she fainted, but she's come to, an' she's gone to the 'ospital, her an' Mr. Neafie.

BERCHANSKY: Don't talk no more! [*He strikes his head with his hands.*]

MRS. BERCHANSKY: Ach, Mrs. Neafie! [*She strikes her breast.*]

THE LITTLE GIRL: [*Her head between the elder and younger women.*] Yes, an' o-o-h, she looked terrible! She was all marked up an' bloody. I saw her just when they was takin' her away.

THE YOUNG BOY: Gee, it's fierce! She'll never get well. If dey ever get d' fellow dat did dat, he'll get d' chair. The police're all around here now. They're lookin' everywhere.

BERCHANSKY: Don't talk! Don't talk!

MRS. BERCHANSKY: Nu, dat's enough! Don't say no more, please. Ve must go down—

MRS. GREENBAUM: Tck! Tck! Tck! That poor little girl!

THE ELDER WOMAN: Yes, it's awful! The whole neighborhood's out. [*More noises and voices are heard below. They turn and listen.*] Maybe they've found sompin else.

[*The four depart.* JOE, *nearest the door, half closes it after them.*]

JOE: God!

BERCHANSKY: [*Sinking into a chair.*] Now, it's over. Vot could be vorse? Now, it vill all come out. Dis is de end!

MRS. BERCHANSKY: Oh, if it only vuzn't him! Poor Isadore! Poor Kitty!

GREENBAUM: [*In a low, concerned, earnest voice.*] Listen to me, all of you! It's pretty bad, but it's best not to say anything—not yet, anyhow. We really don't know that he did it—not yet, anyhow. It looks that way, but don't talk! Don't let on that you know anything! [*To* MASHA.] You've burned the shoe? [*She nods her head.*] Don't ever say anything about it!

MRS. BERCHANSKY: [*Agonizedly.*] Yes! Yes!

GREENBAUM: It may not come out—not yet, anyhow. We can have him put away right off. If he's crazy, they can't do anything to him. They can't blame us, anyhow. Some of you had better go down to see Mrs. Neafie when she comes back. Cover that table out there with something, and don't mention the box! As soon as you can, you'd better move away from here—but not too soon. You see— [*As he talks, the curtain descends.*]

## CURTAIN

# ACT III

## SCENE 1

*The grand jury room of New York County in the Criminal Courts Building, New York City, adjoining the offices of the district attorney and his assistants. The right and rear walls of the stage contain each three and two large windows respectively, reaching nearly to the ceiling. Through them pours a flood of morning light, a pattern of which from the windows, right, marks the floor. The tops of other buildings in the vicinity are to be seen. The space between the two windows at the rear of the stage is broken by a large, circular gilt clock, the hands of which stand at ten-forty-five.*

*The left wall of the stage contains a door of good size which is standing open, showing an exterior office or ante-room of some sort and some desks protected by a wire cage in which clerks are working. In the centre of the room, and facing the door, a semi-circular desk of great size, to the rear of which are twenty-two chairs of exactly the same pattern, with the exception that the chair in the centre is larger, each occupied by a grand juror. Between this desk and the door, a table at which is sitting the grand jury clerk, his back to the jury. A few feet from him, and facing the jury, another chair, in which is sitting a short, stout, very phlegmatic-looking German, of about fifty-five, plainly under a strain and nervous. To the right, but between him and the jury, a chair on which has been laid a child's light brown linen dress, soiled and torn, a light green straw hat, a pair of tan stockings, also soiled and torn, a child's slipper, and a suit of light reddish-brown hair, soft and silky, and tied about with a string. Behind the seated jurors, an Assistant District Attorney, standing and facing the witness over their heads. The room is very still. A juror or two coughs and stirs. The woodwork is yellow oak; the walls a pale cream. No pictures or ornamentation of any kind is visible. As the curtain rises, the Assistant District Attorney is just about to address a remark to the witness. In this act a pair of light curtains, the color of the walls of the juryroom, close or open on the remarks of the various witnesses, the while the regular stage curtain remains up.*

MILLER: [*With the air of one who has been talking for some little time.*] Now, Mr. Daubenspeck, if you please, will you kindly tell the grand jury just what occurred on the night of July 17th last? I mean in connection with what you found in the lot back of 1727 First Avenue, this city. Tell it as simply and briefly as you can.

DAUBENSPECK: [*Heavily, and arranging himself slowly.*] Ya, I do. Ess I say, ich bin, now, ein cabinet-maker by trait und als ich by Sixty-nint' Sthreet near Fairst Affenoo, vuss coming about zehn uhr, ich vuss by a liddle chob in Sixty-fift' Sthreet, und vuss going down troo der lot py Fairst Affenoo back of mein house da, I hert a kynt of noiss or groan, als if some vun might haf site a liddle—oder groant, und daraan I sthobbed und kynta looged arount me, so. [*He illustrates.*] Ich couldn't see nudding. Id vuss ganz dunkle. Darauf ich stharted to go on again, but yust as ich dat done ich heered vunce more anudder noiss, und darauf ich vunce more sthobbed again. Der vuss someding—ach, ich weiss nicht ve mann sagt "verloren" [*he moves his hands to illustrate the sound*] in der sount, und darauf ich loogt all arount vunce more und vent back, so ve dreissig oder vierzig fuess—(ich hab ess later gemeasured)—und daraan, because der vuss a liddle light in a vintow ubstairs in von off der flats, ich saw a kiste—how you say?—box—oder someding, mit a piece off oil clawd offer it, yust as if it hat been cuffered py some vun, und from unten vuss stickin' aus dass kind's het und her hants und arms—so [*he illustrates*], und she vuss lying on her site, so [*he illustrates*].

MILLER: Yes.

[*Several of the jurors place their elbows on their knees and their chins in their hands and contemplate him fixedly.*]

DAUBENSPECK: Her face vuss very weiss, und der sleef off her tress vuss torn open at der haltz [*he illustrates*], und her neck vuss cut a liddle right here [*he indicates the place*]. At fairst I toud she vuss todt, but I listened, und den I saw dat she vuss still breading. I took der cuffer off, und den ich see dat she vuss in a box, yust als she hat herself darein gesezt, und ess hat uber gefallen. It vuss offer on vun site, so [*he illustrates*]. She vuss so weiss ich hab gedacht she mide be todt, und I vuss so schkairt—ich vuss almosd afrait to pull at her, but ich did, but she couldn't speag no more—she vuss nearly todt. So ich hab am strasse—on der sthreet—py 1727 gerunt, und als ich ans eck da kaam dair vair sthanding sechs oder seben manner. Ich hab—I tolt dem dere vuss a liddle girl pack in der lot der gekilt, und dey stharted to run down dere. Daan hab ich nach einer politzei gerufen—ein policeman—und ich vuss say some vun shoudt on der telefone go. Ich couldn't einer find aber, so ich hab nach meiner frau gerufet (she vuss py der vintow ubstairs dere), und she vuss unten gekommen—down—und uns beiden haben zurick gegangen. Ven ve vuss pack gekommen, der vuss olretty dreisig oder vierzig people da und some vun hat olretty einer policeman geholt. Dey vuss telefoning noch der ambulance, und der vuss nudding more zu tuhen.

MILLER: Yes. [*To the jury.*] You understood most of what Mr. Daubenspeck said, didn't you, gentlemen? [*The jurors nod their heads.*] Anything more, Mr. Daubenspeck?

DAUBENSPECK: [*Slowly.*] No. I didn't see nudding more. Der vair seferal mens benting offer her, und my vife tolt me afterwards das she hat gesagt das einer mann hat ihr uberbekommen. Den ich vent mit der police to der station.

MILLER: [*Addressing the jury.*] He says that his wife told him that Kitty Neafie had said to some one that a man had stabbed her. [*The jurors nod their heads.*] That's all you know, is it, Mr. Daubenspeck?

DAUBENSPECK: Ya, dass ist alles.

MILLER: Gentlemen, do any of you wish to question this witness further? We have a great many to hear. I'll have the clerk write out this testimony so that any of you can examine it at your leisure if you wish. The less time we take in the beginning, the better. You may not need all the testimony that will be offered. [*He looks around inquiringly.*]

THE FOREMAN OF THE JURY: [*Tentatively.*] Perhaps we'd better let him go for the present.

JUROR SIXTEEN: [*A somber, heavy, taciturn-looking man.*] Did he say who it was stabbed her, or did she say?

MILLER: Did she say, Mr. Daubenspeck, who killed her?

DAUBENSPECK: Ich hab nicht—I didn't hear. My vife she tolt me afterwards dass she hat gevispered "a man, a man." Den she dies.

JUROR THREE: Was she lying on her face or on her back, did he say, when he first came up?

DAUBENSPECK: On her site, so [*he illustrates*].

JUROR NINE: [*Addressing* MILLER.] Did he notice or could he tell in that light what the color or pattern of that oilcloth was?

[*As he speaks the inner stage curtains close, then immediately open. As they do so, the clock stands at twelve-fifteen. The sun pattern on the floor has moved. In the witness chair, in the place of* MRS. DAUBENSPECK, *sits the elderly fat woman who appeared in the doorway of the* BERCHANSKY *apartment on the night of the murder. She is speaking.*]

MRS. LERSCH: An' as we went in they was all standin' up around the table, an' I says, "Oh, Mr. Berchantsky, did you hear the news? Little Kitty Neafie's been killed!" And at that he throws up his hands like this, an' he says, "My God, it's my son Isadore!" An' at that I didn't know wot to say. I felt sorry for 'im, an' I didn't say nothin'.

MILLER: But, Mrs. Lersch! Mrs. Lersch! One moment, please, one moment! This won't do. You're not telling the same story you told me yesterday afternoon at all. I thought you told me that there were three others present beside yourself, and that Mr. Berchansky only exclaimed, "My God!" Isn't that what you told me?

MRS. LERSCH: [*Pausing abstractedly.*] Did I say that? Well, maybe it was that-a-way, but it seems to me he did say something about his son Isadore. Leastways, it seems so to me. "He done it," or "Oh, my God, I'm sure he done it!" or something like that.

[*The jurors stir impatiently, as though they had been annoyed by previous exaggerations.* THE FOREMAN OF THE JURY *looks as though he would interject a question.*]

MILLER: But, Mrs. Lersch! Mrs. Lersch! One moment, please! This won't do at all! You forget that you are on the witness stand and under oath. You have sworn on the Bible to tell the truth, the whole truth, and nothing but the truth. A man's life is in jeopardy here. If you do not tell the truth, the exact facts only—just what you know to be so, not what you think somebody said or what somebody told you afterwards or what you read somewhere—you may send an innocent man to the electric chair, to death, do you understand? An innocent man!

THE FOREMAN OF THE JURY: [*Sternly.*] Tell only what you know, madam. [*He stirs and whispers to a neighbor.*]

MRS. LERSCH: [*With some show of uncertainty and distress, rolling her hands.*] Well, of course, I didn't understand that. I wouldn't want to do anybody any harm, leastways not the Berchantskys. I ain't got a thing against Mr. Berchantsky. I wouldn't lay a straw in his way. He's a good man, so far as I know. Course, you gotta remember I was very much excited myself at the time, after hearin' the terrible news of poor little Kitty's death, an' I hardly knew what I was doin'. But you better not take my word for it alone. You better let me go, an' ask somebody else. I don't want to do nobody any harm. [*She half rises.*] When I think of poor Kitty, though—[*She begins to weep.*]

THE FOREMAN OF THE JURY: One moment, please, madam, one moment! Just sit down, please.

MILLER: [*Gently.*] One moment, Mrs. Lersch. Keep your seat, please. Now, just calm yourself and try to recollect what it was you did hear and see. You needn't be afraid of these gentlemen. They are not here to prosecute you. Now, you have stated that you and several other people left the crowd that was knocking at the door of Mrs. Neafie on the fourth floor, and climbed to the fifth, where Mr. and Mrs. Berchansky lived, and that then you or some one knocked and that some one opened the door. And then what happened? Remember, you're not here to say what you think happened, or what you imagined you saw or heard, or what some one told you they saw or heard, or what you read, or what somebody else read in the paper, but just what you yourself saw with your own eyes, and heard with your own ears. Now what was it that you saw or heard?

MRS. LERSCH: [*Subdued, in a low voice.*] Well, as I say, we all went in, an' there was Mr. Berchantsky, an' Mrs. Berchantsky, an' Miss Rae Berchantsky, an' Joe, an' several other people standin' around, an' they all looked kind o' queer to me, as though they might be excited about something. An' I says to Mrs. Berchantsky, "Oh, Mrs. Berchantsky, have you heard the terrible news about Kitty Neafie? She's been murdered—stabbed fifty times—an' there's a young man they think done it." [*The jury gives evidence of new astonishment.*] At that they all gathered around, an' Mr. Berchantsky throws up his hands, or that's the way it seemed to me, an' says sompin—"Oh, my God!" or sompin like that, an' Mrs. Berchantsky, if I remember right—I'm not sure about Mrs. Berchantsky, I was that excited myself. I begun to cry, an' then they all wanted to know who done it, an' how it all happened, an' between explainin' an' other people talkin', I forget, kinda, just what did happen, but I know we went downstairs, an' Mrs. Droney, she says to me—now, I don't just remember whether it was that night or the next day—but anyhow, she says—

MILLER: [*Wearily, with the air of one desirous of ending this particular examination.*] Well, now, Mrs. Lersch, we're not interested in what Mrs. Droney or anybody else said to you at this or any other time. As a matter of fact, you didn't know then whether there had been one or fifty stab wounds found on the body, did you?

MRS. LERSCH: Well, now, Mrs. Droney was sayin' last Wednesday—

MILLER: [*With a show of irritation, in a loud voice.*] You didn't know at that time whether there was one or seventy wounds on the body, did you?

MRS. LERSCH: [*Humbly.*] No, sir.

MILLER: So you couldn't have told the Berchansky family of those?

MRS. LERSCH: Well, Mrs. Droney—

MILLER: [*Sonorously.*] Never mind Mrs. Droney. Could you?

MRS. LERSCH: No, sir.

MILLER: And as for a young man having been suspected, you really never thought of that at that time, did you?

MRS. LERSCH: Well, Mrs. Droney—

MILLER: [*Angrily.*] Never mind Mrs. Droney. Forget her. Just stick to what you saw and heard in the Berchansky flat at the time you were in it. Did you, or did you not, see or hear anything which caused you to think that anyone connected with that particular family was in any way connected with this crime?

[*As he talks the inner curtains close, and immediately open again. This time they disclose* MRS. BERCHANSKY *seated in the witness chair. She is very pale, her hands and face exceedingly thin. She is dressed in a black skirt, small bonnet, and black shawl. She sits with drooped head, staring at the floor. The hands of the clock now stand at twelve-forty-five, and the sunlight has left the room. The gaze of the Assistant District Attorney, and that of all the jurors, is fixed intently on her.*]

MILLER: Tell us, Mrs. Berchansky, why it was you made up your mind to move so quickly after this happened? [MRS. BERCHANSKY *does not answer.*] Why did you move two days after the crime?

MRS. BERCHANSKY: [*After a long pause, and twisting her fingers.*] My family vunted it.

MILLER: Yes. Why?

MRS. BERCHANSKY: It vuz too hot. Ve didn't like de place. [*She lifts her hands slightly.*]

MILLER: Yes. Well, how long before this was it that you or your family made up your minds that it was too hot?

MRS. BERCHANSKY: [*Slowly.*] Maybe's a month—maybe's two.

MILLER: Then it was some time in May or June that you did this?

MRS. BERCHANSKY: Yes.

MILLER: Can't you remember which month exactly?

MRS. BERCHANSKY: No.

MILLER: Well, now, it wasn't so very warm in May, was it?

MRS. BERCHANSKY: [*After a long pause.*] It vuz vorm, yes.

MILLER: [*Restlessly, as though he had been examining a long time.*] Mrs. Berchansky, how long before the night of the murder was it that you last saw your son Isadore at your apartment, or anywhere—how long?

MRS. BERCHANSKY: [*Turning and entwining her fingers. She does not look up.*] Maybe's von month—maybe's two or three.

MILLER: [*Sternly.*] Look at me, Mrs. Berchansky. Look at the jury. Lift your head. [*Slowly the witness elevates a wan and haggard face—then lowers it again.*] Are you telling the truth?

MRS. BERCHANSKY: Yes.

MILLER: Well, Mrs. Berchansky, there was a newspaper reporter in that chair not more than a half hour ago who testified that when he called on you at the apartment of your daughter, Mrs. Greenbaum, on the upper west side, ten days after you had moved from 1727 First Avenue, you told him that you had not seen your son Isadore in two weeks. That would have been two days before the murder. Now, what did you mean by that? [*She does not answer.*] Mrs. Berchansky, answer me! What did you mean by that?

MRS. BERCHANSKY: Maybe's von month—maybe's two.

MILLER: Listen to me, Mrs. Berchansky. Don't answer in a routine way, without thinking. You are now in the witness chair, before this grand jury, under oath. The newspaper man said that at that time you said to him that you had seen your son two days before the murder. Now, whom are we to believe—you, or this reporter? [*He pauses and waits.*]

MRS. BERCHANSKY: [*Without looking up.*] Maybe's von month—maybe's two.

MILLER: [*Irritably.*] Don't make that stereotyped reply always! Did some one tell you to say that?

MRS. BERCHANSKY: [*After a time, folding and unfolding her hands.*] No.

MILLER: Mrs. Berchansky, you swore just now to tell the truth, the whole truth, and nothing but the truth. Is this the truth you are telling now?

MRS. BERCHANSKY [*Without looking up.*] Yes.

MILLER: You swear to that, do you—by all that you hold sacred?

MRS. BERCHANSKY: [*After a pause.*] Yes.

MILLER: Now, Mrs. Berchansky, isn't it true that your son was at your home the very day and evening that the crime was committed—that you and your husband had a quarrel with him, and that he ran out of the house, and that you or your husband called after him down the stairs?

MRS. BERCHANSKY: [*Stirring, and then subsiding after a pause.*] No.

MILLER: You deny that he was in your house the day or evening of the crime?

MRS. BERCHANSKY: Yes.

MILLER: Or a day or two before?

MRS. BERCHANSKY: Yes.

MILLER: Or a day or two after?

MRS. BERCHANSKY: Yes.

MILLER: You swear on your sacred honor—by the life of your husband and your children, that this is true?

MRS. BERCHANSKY: [*Tightening her fingers for the least fraction of a second.*] Yes.

[*The inner curtains close. As they open again the clock stands at two-ten. The clerk is completing the roll call of the afternoon session. All but three jurors are in their seats.*]

MILLER: [*To* THE CLERK.] Call Miss Rae Berchansky.

[THE CLERK *goes to the door, whispers the call to the doorkeeper, who in turn calls it outside. In a moment or two* RAE BERCHANSKY *appears, dressed in white linen skirt—pearl buttons down the front—a white starched shirtwaist, black tie, black sailor hat with a white band, black slippers, white stockings, and carries a black bag in her hand. She seats herself in the witness chair, rises, then sinks back again—very brisk and self-sufficient.*]

THE CLERK: Name, please?

RAE: Rae Berchansky.

THE CLERK: Address?

RAE: 2221 Portchester Avenue, Bronx.

THE CLERK: Business?

RAE: Manicuress.

MILLER: [*As the clerk writes.*] Now, Miss Berchansky, the grand jury, through me, would like to ask you a few questions in regard to the death of Kitty Neafie on July 17th last. Will you kindly tell me, in your own way, what, if anything, you know about this case?

RAE: [*Briskly.*] I don't know anything!

MILLER: [*Archly.*] Not anything?

RAE: Nothing except what I've seen in the papers—mostly lies.

MILLER: Now, Miss Berchansky, will you kindly tell the jury where you were on the afternoon and evening of July 17th last?

RAE: I was at Coney Island.

MILLER: When did you leave your home to go to Coney Island?

RAE: Oh, about two in the afternoon.

MILLER: And when did you return home again?

RAE: About eleven or twelve at night.

MILLER: Can't you remember exactly at what hour?

RAE: No, sir. It was between eleven and twelve, I think.

MILLER: [*Suavely.*] Now, Miss Berchansky, this is a very trying case, and we're only anxious to find the perpetrator of this very heinous crime—not to throw unnecessary suspicion on anyone, your family in particular—so will you be kind enough to tell this jury how long before the day or hour of this crime, or after, was it that you last saw your brother Isadore?

RAE: [*Coolly.*] It's been a little over two months now, I think.

MILLER: You haven't seen him in all that time?

RAE: No, sir.

MILLER: Nor heard from him?

RAE: No, sir.

MILLER: Has any member of your family, in so far as you know?

RAE: Not that I know of.

MILLER: Well, now, he usually came around the house once a week or so, didn't he, up to that time?

RAE: Up to what time?

MILLER: Up to the time you last saw him. Up to the night of the murder.

RAE: I just told you I didn't see him on the night of the murder, or the day, either.

MILLER: Yes. . . . I remember now. Up to the time you last saw him, I mean—two months ago.

RAE: Oh, he came home whenever he felt like it—once in two or three weeks, I should say.

MILLER: And then suddenly he stopped coming?

RAE: Oh, I wouldn't call it sudden. We never knew when he was comin', or when he was goin' again.

MILLER: Quite so! Quite so! Now, Miss Berchansky, it has been suggested here by one witness and another that your brother was not exactly right in his mind, that he had an aberration or delusion—an abnormal interest in little girls. Is that true?

RAE: He's always been all right, so far as I know.

MILLER: You're positive as to that?

RAE: Yes, sir.

MILLER: Nothing wrong with him, whatsoever, in so far as you know?

RAE: So far as I know, no.

MILLER: In so far as you can remember, you have never seen the least little thing wrong with him mentally?

RAE: No, sir. Not that I recall.

MILLER: Well, then, how do you explain that on March 15, 1914, he was sentenced to two years in a State penitentiary of this State for attempted—for assaulting—[*he pauses*]—a little girl? You knew of that, didn't you?

RAE: [*Eyeing him fixedly.*] Yes, sir.

MILLER: Well, would you consider that the deed of an absolutely normal person, assuming, of course, that the jury did not err in its judgment?

RAE: Well, *he* never admitted that he did it, did he? A jury might be wrong once in a while, mightn't it?

MILLER: [*With the shadow of a condescending smile, and rubbing his chin.*] Yes, a jury might he wrong once in a while. But, tell us, Miss Berchansky, your brother did suffer from a nervous affliction of the left arm, didn't he—a jerking like this? [*He illustrates.*]

RAE: [*With some hesitation and show of anger.*] Yes, sir.

MILLER: Ever since he was born—is that not true?

RAE: [*Snappishly.*] Yes!

MILLER: Still you are convinced that there was absolutely nothing wrong with him mentally in any way?

RAE: [*Defiantly.*] Yes, I am!

MILLER: And also you are absolutely sure that he wasn't at home the afternoon or evening or night of the crime?

RAE: Not that I know of.

MILLER: Nor at any time within forty-eight hours before or after the news of Kitty Neafie's death?

RAE: Not that I know of.

MILLER: Is this the absolute truth? Remember, you are under oath here.

RAE: Yes, sir.

MILLER: Do you know for certain that he was not there?

RAE: No one told me that he was. No, sir.

MILLER: But you're not positive that he was not there?

RAE: Well, if he had been, it seems to me I would have heard about it.

MILLER: But you're not positive?

RAE: No, sir.

MILLER: Miss Berchansky, do you know a Mrs. Margaret Lindstrom?

RAE: Yes, sir.

MILLER: Where does she live?

RAE: I don't know where she lives now, but I know where she did live.

MILLER: Where was that?

RAE: On the floor below us at 1727 First Avenue.

MILLER: You know her personally?

RAE: I've seen her.

MILLER: You don't know her to talk to?

RAE: Oh. I've said "Good morning," or nodded to her in the hall.

MILLER: Miss Berchansky, if there was a loud noise in the Lindstrom apartment, an angry argument of some kind, do you suppose you could hear it in your apartment upstairs?

RAE: I don't know whether I could or not. I never heard a loud argument down there.

MILLER: So you couldn't say, supposing there was a loud argument or quarrel of some kind in your apartment, whether the Lindstroms or any other family immediately around you could hear it or not?

RAE: No. I don't think they could.

MILLER: You mean they couldn't hear such a noise?

RAE: Yes.

MILLER: Why not?

RAE: Because of the noise in the street up there.

MILLER: It's pretty bad, is it?

RAE: It was. It was sompin fierce!

MILLER: Now, Miss Berchansky, isn't it a fact that your brother Isadore was home the very day of the death of Kitty Neafie, and that your father and mother had a quarrel with him, and that he ran downstairs about eight-thirty of the night of the crime, and that your father shouted his name after him? Isn't that true?

RAE: I don't know anything about it. I was at Coney Island.

MILLER: Well, you would have heard of it if he had been there, wouldn't you?

RAE: [*Calmly.*] Yes, I think so.

MILLER: But you never heard anything about it?

RAE: No, I didn't.

MILLER: [*Suavely.*] Well, now, Miss Berchansky, will you explain to this jury why it was that on the evening of July 21st last, or thereabouts, about five days after this crime had been committed, and about two days after your family had moved from 1727 First Avenue, that you returned to the house of your friend, Miss Bertha Solomon, at 1711 First Avenue, and secured a picture of yourself, and one of your brother Joe which contained a portrait of your brother Isadore?

RAE: [*With considerable surprise and hesitation.*] Well, I wanted them, that's why. [*She stirs uneasily.*]

MILLER: Yes.... Why?

RAE: Oh, I didn't want any old cheap pictures of mine floatin' around back there in that neighborhood, that's all.

MILLER: Yes—but why not in *that* neighborhood? Wasn't it good enough for you?

RAE: [*Hesitatingly.*] Well, it's a cheap neighborhood, that's all. I never liked it, and so long as we were goin' away, I thought I'd not leave anything of mine by which people could follow us up.

MILLER: That was the only reason, was it?

RAE: Yes.

MILLER: You hadn't committed any crime, had you?

RAE: No, of course not.

MILLER: Nor any member of your family, let us say?

RAE: I said I didn't know anything about that.

MILLER: [*Sweetly.*] To be sure! To be sure! You just didn't think the neighborhood was good enough for you? Was that it?

RAE: Well, something like that.

MILLER: Miss Berchansky, do you know a girl by the name of Peterson—Zella Peterson?

RAE: Yes, sir.

MILLER: Where does she work?

RAE: At the same place I do.

MILLER: Where is that?

RAE: At the Marie Manicure Parlors, in Sixth Avenue.

MILLER: She is a manicuress, is she not?

RAE: Yes, sir.

MILLER: She's a rather good friend of yours, isn't she?

RAE: Well, we've been friends, yes.

MILLER: Isn't she, any longer?

RAE: Well, I suppose so. I haven't seen her recently.

MILLER: Do you remember asking her, on the morning of the 22nd of July last, what she thought of the Neafie case?

RAE: [*With some hesitation.*] No, sir.

MILLER: You don't recall asking her if she thought in case the murderer of Kitty Neafie were found, and he had brothers and sisters, and a father and mother, whether his whole family, in her judgment, would be disgraced on account of it?

RAE: I saw she said I did, in the papers, but I didn't. No, sir.

MILLER: You didn't?

RAE: No, I didn't!

MILLER: Did you ask her anything at all about the case? What she thought of it, or anything like that?

RAE: No, sir.

MILLER: Not a word? Never even referred to it?

RAE: No, sir.

MILLER: Well, it was a very startling case to you, wasn't it?

RAE: [*Hesitatingly.*] Yes.

MILLER: It must have shocked you a great deal at the time, being in your neighborhood—next door to you?

RAE: It certainly did.

MILLER: And it was on your mind a great deal at the time, wasn't it?

RAE: Well, not any more than on anybody else's, I guess, but it was, yes.

MILLER: Yet you didn't even mention it to Miss Peterson?

RAE: Not that I recall, no.

MILLER: Her manicure table is right next to yours, isn't it?

RAE: Yes.

MILLER: And you used to walk home with her occasionally across Forty-second Street?

RAE: Yes.

MILLER: Frequently, since July 17th, haven't you?

RAE: I don't remember exactly whether I did or not.

MILLER: Oh, come now. You can remember that, I'm sure.

RAE: [*Stiffly.*] I say I don't remember exactly whether I did or not.

MILLER: Yet you never mentioned this case to her—not once?

RAE: Well, I may have. I don't remember. Not that I recall.

MILLER: And yet it was in all the papers at the time?

RAE: Yes.

MILLER: And it occurred right next door to your home?

RAE: Yes.

MILLER: And it has in your mind—some?

RAE: Yes.

MILLER: But yet you can't remember that you ever mentioned it to your friend, the girl you used to walk home with—whose table was right next to yours in the manicure parlor?

RAE: No, sir.

MILLER: [*With considerable emphasis.*] Not even if I tell you that your friend Miss Peterson was in here not more than an hour ago, and, sitting in that chair, testified under oath that you did ask her, and that you looked worried? Now, is that true, or isn't it?

RAE: It's not true.

MILLER: She lied, did she?

RAE: If she said that, she did. Yes, sir.

MILLER: Miss Berchansky, you say you have lived at home with your family right along, all your life?

RAE: Yes, sir.

MILLER: Well, now, tell the grand jury why it was that your family decided to move all of a sudden, on July 19th last.

RAE: We didn't decide to move all of a sudden. We'd been talkin' of it for months.

MILLER: Why?

RAE: Well, it was too hot up there under the roof, and too high up.

MILLER: You wanted a cooler apartment, did you, and one lower down?

RAE: The family did, yes, sir, and so did I.

MILLER: Well, can you tell the grand jury why it was that your father and mother, or whoever it was decided on this, chose to move in the middle rather than at the end of the month? People generally choose to move at the end of the month, don't they?

RAE: Oh, I don't know. We didn't.

MILLER: [*Gently.*] Well, I know, but people generally do, don't they?

RAE: Well, I don't know about other people. I only know about us. We moved in the middle of the month, the time before that.

MILLER: When was that?

RAE: February 19, 1916.

MILLER: Five months before this crime was committed?

RAE: Yes.

MILLER: And you're sure this short stay of only five months had nothing to do with anything your brother Isadore did at this time?

RAE: No,—I mean yes.

MILLER: [*Coming around in front, between the witness and the jury.*] If the jury pleases, I would like to excuse Miss Berchansky for the moment. We can recall her in a little while, if we choose. I have another witness I would like to present at this time. I believe it will throw a little extra light on this case, and may save your time and mine. [*The jurymen nod their heads. To* RAE.] You are excused for the present, Miss Berchansky. Please don't leave the building. I may want you again. [RAE *goes out. To* THE CLERK.] Call Rufus Bush.

THE CLERK: [*Going to the door and speaking to the attendant.*] Rufus Bush!

THE ATTENDANT: [*Outside.*] Rufus Bush! Rufus Bush!

[*The door opens, and a lank, slithery, badly-washed man of about forty-three, in obviously his best Sunday store clothes, enters. He has large red hands, large feet, a leathery, weather-tanned face, and a long strong nose and jaw. He walks briskly forward and starts to take the chair indicated, but is interrupted by the clerk, who holds out a Bible to him.*]

THE FOREMAN OF THE JURY: Do you solemnly swear to tell the truth, the whole truth, and nothing but the truth, so help you God?

BUSH: I do. [*He sits down, sees the little dress, hat and shoe on the chair, and stares.*]

MILLER: [*From his position behind* THE FOREMAN OF THE JURY *once more.*] Now, Mr. Bush, you moved the furniture and belongings of one Aaron Berchansky from his apartment or flat at 1727 First Avenue some time during the latter part of July, didn't you?

BUSH: Yes, sir.

MILLER: Just when was that? Do you recall?

BUSH: [*With a great show of importance.*] It was the mornin' of July 19th, 1916.

MILLER: Well, now, Mr. Bush, where did you take that furniture?

BUSH: To the Central Union Storage house at Avenue A and East Twenty-third Street, New York City.

MILLER: Now, Mr. Bush, please tell the grand jury just as briefly as you can what were the circumstances under which you came to move this furniture—who came to see you about it, what they said, what you did, what you saw, how whoever you saw acted, and so on. Be as brief and direct as you can, now, please.

BUSH: [*Straightening himself in his chair, smoothing his hair, and wetting his lips.*] Well, as I was sayin' to you yesterday, Mr. Miller, I was standin' at the corner of First Avenue and Sixty-seventh Street—I keep my wagon standin' there when I ain't got nothin' else to do—when who should come up to me but this here, now, Mis' Berchantsky. She's a little woman, kinda thin-like, with one of them black wigs the Jewish women wears, an' a white band or sompin around her head kinda tied over her ears like [*several members of the jury stir impatiently*], an' she says to me—I can't give you her exack langwidge—but she says to me, "Could you come right over with me now to 1727 First Avenue an' git a load o' furniture out o' there for me, right away quick?" an' I says, "Sure, I could. Where is it you want it moved to, madam?" an' she says, "I don't want it moved to no house—just to a storage warehouse, only will you come right away, if you're comin', because I gotta git out o' there before three o'clock today," she says. An' I says to myself, "That's funny! She must be tryin' to make a get-a-way from 'er husband or the landlord, or sompin like that," an' bein' she was kinda nervous an' a-fidgitin' with 'er hands this-a-way [*he illustrates*], I felt sorry for 'er, so I jumps on my wagon an' drives right over there. I was thinkin' that maybe, since it was a hurry-up case, I might git a good tip extra, but I didn't. [*The jury laughs.*]

MILLER: Yes—go on.

BUSH: Well, when I seen the place, I wuz a little su'prised again, because most people when they send for a movin' man only have part of their stuff ready to be took out, an' the rest we gotta git together ourselves, but she had everything done up as neat as a pin—you oughta seen it—an' there was an old man with one o' them there little kike caps on 'is head, an' he wuz a-bustlin' around an' a-tyin' up things, an' sayin' "Ga swind! Ga swind!"—or sompin like that. There was a girl there, too, a cripple-like, hobblin' around on a cane an' helpin' in one way an' another.

MILLER: Yes?

BUSH: Well, the old lady kep' sayin' "Hurry, hurry, please!" so much that I was sure there must be sompin up. I got the furniture out as quick as I could, an' got it down there to Twenty-third Street an' Avenue A, an' there she was, a-waitin' for me on the corner, an' she paid me, an' I give 'er the receipt, an' that's all I know.

MILLER: And you didn't get any tip?

BUSH: No, sir.

MILLER: Well, gentlemen, unless you can think of something more to ask this witness, I should like to excuse him also, and call some one else that we have waiting. We can recall him at any time, you know. [*A silence follows this.*] We have quite a number of witnesses still, and it may be that we shall not need all their testimony. [*The jury nod their heads in acquiescence.*] You're excused, Mr. Bush. Please don't leave the building at present.

BUSH: No, sir. [*Goes out.*]

MILLER: [*To* THE CLERK.] Call Mr. Berchansky.

[THE CLERK *goes to the door.*]

THE DOORMAN: [*Outside.*] Aaron Berchansky! Aaron Berchansky!

[*Enter* AARON BERCHANSKY. *He is very pale and nervous and careworn, and is dressed in a plain, threadbare black suit, the sleeves and trouser legs of which are too long and worn at elbows and knees, a black ready-made bow tie, black derby hat, rather loose shoes. As he enters he observes the chair with the child's clothes on it, stops, puts his hands before his eyes, falters, then walks lamely on to the witness chair. His manner is that of one who is en-*

*during intense suffering and strain.* THE CLERK *rises and holds out the Bible.*]

THE FOREMAN OF THE JURY: [*Rising.*] Do you solemnly affirm that you will tell the truth, the whole truth, and nothing but the truth, so help you God?

[BERCHANSKY *nods, looks at the chair, then looks away again.*]

THE CLERK: Name, please?

BERCHANSKY: Aaron Berchansky.

THE CLERK: Address?

BERCHANSKY: 2221 Portchester Avenue.

THE CLERK: Business?

BERCHANSKY: [*With some hesitation.*] Thread and needles.

MILLER: You have a store where you sell thread and needles, have you, Mr. Berchansky?

BERCHANSKY: No. [*He looks at the chair again.*]

MILLER: Well, what kind of a business is it then, Mr. Berchansky? Will you kindly explain?

BERCHANSKY: [*Very softly.*] I sell to my customers. I carry my goods in a bag.

MILLER: Yes. Who are your customers, Mr. Berchansky?

BERCHANSKY: Some shops, some that make shirts, cloaks, pants. [*He glances at the chair.*] I hev customers.

MILLER: [*Overawed by his sad presence and speaking in a soothing voice.*] Mr. Berchansky, we are engaged in the very unpleasant task of unraveling, or attempting to do so, the details of a terrible crime, with some of the details of which you are already familiar. I shall have to ask you some very personal questions, Mr. Berchansky, some very trying ones, I am sorry to say, but it will not be with any intention of injuring your feelings. I hope you will understand this, that it is a duty on my—on our—part—on the part of the law and the state which makes the law—not mere inquisitiveness. [*As he speaks,* BERCHANSKY *continues to stare at the chair.*] Now, Mr. Berchansky, will you kindly tell the jury how many children you have?

BERCHANSKY: [*Heavily.*] Two boys an' three girls living. The rest are dead. [*He picks at his coat lapel.*]

MILLER: And how old is your oldest boy—Isadore is his name, is it not?

BERCHANSKY: [*Starting, and with an effort.*] Yes. Twenty-one.

MILLER: And the youngest?

BERCHANSKY: Seventeen.

MILLER: Were all your children born in this country?

BERCHANSKY: All but my oldest. She is dead now. [*He clenches and unclenches his fingers.*]

MILLER: And where were you born?

BERCHANSKY: In Odessa.

MILLER: Russia?

BERCHANSKY: Yes.

MILLER: And your wife?

BERCHANSKY: The same place. [*As he talks, his glance constantly strays to the chair. He folds and unfolds his hands.*]

MILLER: [*Coming out from behind the foreman, picking up* KITTY NEAFIE'S *dress, hair and stockings, and placing himself squarely in front of the witness. He half holds the articles before him, as if exhibiting them. As he does so,*

BERCHANSKY *shrinks back slightly.*] Mr. Berchansky, you knew little Kitty Neafie, didn't you?

BERCHANSKY: [*His voice rising to a thin, half-vibrant, half-smothered cry.*] Yes.

MILLER: She came to your house fairly often, did she not?

BERCHANSKY: [*In the same high, suppressed key.*] Vunce in a vile. Yes. [*He picks at his coat.*]

MILLER: Now, Mr. Berchansky, this grand jury is greatly concerned to know who, if anyone, connected with your family knows anything about the murder of this little girl, whose hair and torn clothes you see here. It has been alleged by one person and another—newspaper reporters, the police and detectives, your neighbors—that your oldest boy is of such a disposition and character as to warrant the fear and the suspicion that he may have had something to do with it. He is not exactly of sound mind, is he?

BERCHANSKY: [*Staring before him, as if meditating something.*] Nu . . . yes. He is all right.

MILLER: He is absolutely of sound mind—you are sure of that?

BERCHANSKY: Yes.

MILLER: But he did serve two years in a penitentiary, did he not, for an assault on a little girl?

BERCHANSKY: [*Half-rising, then sinking back again.*] Yes.

MILLER: [*Somewhat sympathetically.*] And it is equally true, is it not, that he is, or was, still interested in little girls up to a very little while ago—in some of them, anyhow? Is not that true?

BERCHANSKY: [*Stirring, with an effort to speak, but unable to do so.*] Nu. [*He shakes his head negatively.*]

MILLER: Mr. Berchansky, I do not want to make this examination too difficult for you. We all realize how trying your position must be. We know you are a father. We know that you are fond of your boy and would like to protect him, but the law is the law, Mr. Berchansky, and the law compels us to seek out the slayer of this harmless little girl, whosoever he may be, and bring him before the bar of justice in order that he may be dealt with according to the law. It is only right—it is our duty to ourselves, to our fellow-men, to humanity, to the stricken parents of this poor little dead girl whose clothes you see here—[*He moves the dress from one arm to the other.*] Now, I shall have to ask you to tell me, on your sacred honor: Do you, or do you not, know whether your oldest boy Isadore had anything to do with the taking of this little girl's life? [*He pauses, looking earnestly at the witness.*]

BERCHANSKY: [*Staring at the dress, then suddenly rising. As he does so, he sways to and fro as if ill, moves his hands to his face, then beats them together.*] Nu! Nu! Take dem avay! Take dem avay! I kent stend it! I kent stend it! It is too much! I hev lied! My vife, she hes lied! My daughter Rae, she hes lied! My son Joseph, he hes lied! Ve all hev lied! It is true. My son did it. He killed her! He is not right! Since he vuz so small [*he indicates with a gesture*], he vuz not right. I know it all de time! It vuz killing me! Here it hurts me, here, here! [*He strikes his heart.*] I hev vatched, I hev prayed. Ach, Gott! Since two veeks now already, I know. But he is my boy! I could not speak. [*He chokes.*]

MILLER: Mr. Berchansky—

BERCHANSKY: Vait! Vait! You shell hear me! Now I shell tell all! All! I told him vot to do! He should kill himself, I told him! He wrote vun day I should meet him in Grend Street. I go to Grend Street. He vuz dere on de street. Even den he vuz not right, but he knew. He told me how it vuz—she come in vile ve vuz in de park, he choked an' smodered her, he carried her up de stairs an' over de roof to de next house. I told him I could not forgive him, his mudder an' sisters an' brudder could not forgive him—de best t'ing vuz for him to jump in de river an' drown himself. Den he lef' me, an' I hevn't seen him since. [*He pauses, shaking.*] He is gone now. Maybe he is dead. So, it is better. I pray he is. [*He sobs.*] I hev vatched, I hev verked, I hev tried to be a good fader—no vun knows how hard I hev tried. Ach! Ve hev verked, all of us, ve hev saved. De ot'ers are all good. Vy he should be so, I don't know. Since he vuz twelve he hes not been right, but he hes not alvays been bed. He hes been a good boy, too. He hes a good heart. He hes verked. He vuz not quite right here. [*He points to his forehead.*] Maybe it vuz not all his fault. [*He breaks down completely and sobs. His voice sinks to a low murmur.*] Maybe I hev not done all dat I should. It is so hard. [*He ceases talking and sobs between his hands. Some of the jury take out their handkerchiefs, others lower their heads.*] Dat dis should heppen to me, now dat I am old. [*He shakes his head in silence.*]

MILLER: Calm yourself, Mr. Berchansky. Calm yourself. This jury understands. It sympathizes with you completely. Most of the gentlemen here have children of their own. [*He lays a hand on* BERCHANSKY'S *arm.*] *Sit* down. You can tell us the rest of this when you are calmer. [*He forces* BERCHANSKY *back into his seat.*]

BERCHANSKY: [*Weeping, and yet speaking through his fingers.*] No. He could not help it! He is not right. He is not a bed boy. He hes a good heart. If I hed been a better fader maybe dis vould not heppen. Maybe ve did not understend him. [*He weeps in silence.*]

MILLER: [*After a pause, to the jury.*] Gentlemen, I am sure that you will agree with me that the rest of Mr. Berchansky's testimony can be taken later. He is too much overcome to continue. There is no need, I think, for our examining any further into this case.

[*As* MILLER *speaks, the outer curtain is slowly descending.* THE FOREMAN OF THE JURY *nods his head.*]

# CURTAIN

# ACT IV

## SCENE 1

*A stuffy, wretchedly furnished hall bedroom on the top floor of a five-story tenement, the very appearance and atmosphere of which suggest heat, odours, poverty. Time, about four-thirty of a late August afternoon. A door, left, gives onto a stair landing, the squeaky boards of which can be heard. A small window, back centre, shows chimneys, roof copings—a red, dry, colorless prospect. The windows are broken, patched and dirty. The wall-paper is a faded yellowish-gray, showing patches of paper of another color underneath. The bedstead of white iron enamel is slimsy, has peeled, and is creaky. It is unmade and tousled, with soiled sheets, a dirty pillow-case, and a soiled and torn bedspread. A more or less dilapidated chair stands at the foot of it. On the floor, a scrap of ragged carpet. Against the right wall, centre, a cheap bureau or chest of drawers, above which hangs a small oblong mirror, the upper corners of which are curved, and the glass of which is cracked. A soiled and torn cover of some kind graces this bureau. From the ceiling in the centre of the room descends a one-burner gas pipe. On the wall, over the bed, an old, fly-specked poster of a girl in red advertises a face cream.*

*When the curtain rises the stage is empty. Enter* ISADORE. *He closes the door quickly, stands with his hand on the knob, one ear to the crack above. Several copies of different evening papers are in his hands. He is haggard, shabby, a full week's growth of beard on his face. His suit is worn and soiled, his shoes dusty, and his hair, which is partially concealed by a broken straw hat, is tousled and frowsy. He looks pale, hungry, half-wild. As he stands there his left shoulder jerks.*

ISADORE: [*Looking straight before him with a stiff, expectant stare.*] I thought he was followin' me. [*Pauses and listens a while longer, tries the key to be sure it is turned, listens once more, then locks it again. His shoulder jerks.*] They ain't got me yet! It's the red ones, that's it. [*He listens once more, then goes over to the window and unfolds one of the papers, which reveals his picture nearly quarter-page size. Type five inches high, and plainly visible to the audience, reads:* "FIND ISADORE BERCHANSKY!" *He stares at it, then speaks in a low voice.*] They're after me, all right, for fair. I ought to 'a' gone away in the first place. [*He strikes at something.*] G'wan away! Well, I don't look like that now. [*He holds up the paper and examines his picture with care, then drops it and opens a second and a third, each one revealing a large picture and blazing with type. As he does so his shoulder jerks. He studies the headlines. After each one he exclaims:* "Gee!" *then drops it. Wearily.*] I guess it ain't no use. They'll sure get me. It's the red ones. That's it. That's the trouble. They won't let me alone. [*He strikes at something.*] G'wan! This shoulder an' arm'll give me away, if nothin' else does. [*His shoulder jerks.*] It's the red ones, that's the trouble. If they'd let me alone I'd be all right, but I can't work. They won't let me. [*Stares and strikes at something.*] G'wan! It's that two thousand dollar reward makes everybody so anxious. [*His shoulder jerks.*] But I'm sick now, an' dirty, an' they don't know me. [*Pauses and reflects.*] Poor mom! How she must 'a' suffered! An' pop! [*His shoulder jerks.*] He couldn't stand it, he said. Well, I don't blame him. I can't, either, much longer. G'wan! [*Strikes at something.*] I'm crazy, all right, an' I'm afraid to die. [*Pauses.*] Sneakin' around this way! [*He wipes his eyes on his sleeve. His shoulder jerks.*] If I had the nerve, I'd kill myself. I oughta. Pop said I should. I've been tryin' to do it for three days, now. G'wan! [*Strikes at something.*] I ain't right, I tell you! An' I never was! [*His shoulder jerks.*] It's the red ones, that's it. They won't let me alone. These spells keep comin' quicker an' quicker. [*His shoulder jerks and his face contorts slightly. He goes before the mirror, stares at himself, then darkens savagely. A weird expression passes over his face. He strikes at something.*] G'wan! [*He takes off his hat and coat and hangs them on a nail, then goes over to the window, picks up a paper and looks at it.*] Gee, what liars newspapers are! G'wan! [*Strikes at something.*] Here it says I tried to lure little girls to my room four years ago, an' I never even thought of it then. [*Strikes at something.*] I didn't have the nerve, an' I wasn't as crazy then as I am now. [*Strikes at something.*] An' this arrestin' men all over the country for me—they make me sick. [*He stirs irritably. His shoulder jerks.*]

G'wan! [*Strikes at something.*] Nineteen they've arrested so far, an' they ain't got me yet. [*He smiles and examines a small item closely.*] If they don't get me pretty soon they'll hang some other fellow for me. That's the way they do! These fly cops! [*His lip curls, his shoulder jerks. He strikes at something. He tears off a small corner of a newspaper and writes on it, then pins it on the wall above his bed. Talks as he does it.*] G'wan! [*Strikes at something.*] An' that parole officer! [*Indignantly.*] What a liar! He says I broke my parole. I never did! G'wan! [*Strikes at something.*] He said not to come no more unless he sent for me—the damned faker. [*He pauses again, looks out the window, stares at some imaginary thing in the corner, goes over to the door and listens, then comes back to the bureau and looks at himself. His shoulder jerks. As he does so, his expression changes, he loses control of his normal self and makes queer faces at his likeness in the mirror. Suddenly he crumples up the newspapers in his hand, hurls them at his image, then jumps back and seizes the one chair. As he does so he imagines he hears a noise, pauses, puts down the chair, goes over to the door and listens. There is no sound. He half-strikes at something, then straightens up. Once more his mood appears to change. He goes over to the bed and lifts one corner of the mattress, extracting from under it a considerable length of rubber gas tubing. Surveying it, and looking at the gas jet.*] It's the red ones, that's the trouble—the blacks ain't so bad. They wouldn't hurt me, nohow. What's the use, though? I'm crazy, an' they're sure to get me. I can't beat 'em. G'wan! [*Strikes at something.*] I might as well quit now. [*His shoulder jerks. He measures the distance from the gas jet to the bed to see if he has enough.*] It's no use. [*His shoulder jerks.*] I'm hungry! An' I'm gettin' thinner an' thinner all the time. [*He goes to the mirror once more and examines himself, then looks about and strikes at something.*] An' the red ones won't let me alone. G'wan! [*He stares at an invisible something.*] Why won't you let me alone? Say? G'wan! [*He strikes at something, turns and sits down on the bed. Meditatively.*] An' I wanted to live just like other people, an' be happy. I wanted a girl an' a home too, an' now look at me! [*He pauses, then wipes his eyes with the back of his hand.*]

I'm not all bad. I've worked an' I've tried to be all right, too. [*Strikes.*] But they won't let me alone! They won't ever do it. G'wan! Get away, I tell you! [*Strikes.*] I ain't right. Look at 'em! Look at 'em! [*He gets up, moves away as if from pursuers; his shoulder jerks. Stiffening, his expression changing.*] But it's their pretty mouths an' their hair—that's it! It's the way they wear their shirtwaists an' paint their faces! I can't stand it! It's the red ones. It ain't my fault—it's theirs! I can't help myself no more. They make me do it. [*He grows savage, vigorous. His shoulder jerks.*] Well, I won't die, either. [*Throws down the tubing.*] Why should I? It ain't my fault. I ain't done nothin' much, have I? I couldn't help it, could I? I didn't make myself, did I? [*He stares sternly before him. His shoulder jerks.*] I'll tell 'em that, I will! I'll write it. [*He picks up one of the newspapers, tears off a small corner, fishes about in his coat for a lead pencil, and finding a small bit goes to the dresser and scribbles on the paper, pausing once as he does so to strike. Quotes.*] "I didn't make myself, did I? G'wan!" [*Reaches up and fastens it against the wall alongside the mirror. His shoulder jerks.*] Well, I won't quit yet, either. I'm not all in. G'wan! G'wan! [*Strikes at something.*] They ain't got me.

[*He goes to the nail, takes down his hat and coat, and puts them on. As he does so, he hears a noise. He thinks some one is coming up the stairs, goes over and listens. A period of silence follows in which no noise is heard. His shoulder jerks. A newsboy's voice is heard crying.*]

THE NEWSBOY: Extro! Extro! All about Isadore Berchansky! Extro! Extro! [*The voice fades.*]

ISADORE: [*Listening.*] Huh! I wonder who it is now. I bet they've found somebody else. I better not go out, though. They might know me. [*His shoulder jerks. He goes back to the bed.*] G'wan! [*Strikes at something.*] It's the red ones all the time, not the blacks. They won't let me alone—always followin' me around. G'wan! [*Strikes.*] I gotta eat, though. I can't go on this way. I gotta eat or die. [*His shoulder jerks. He moves toward the door.*] I gotta get out o' New York an' get sompin to do, or I gotta quit. It ain't no use. [*Pauses.*] It's the red ones. That's it. They won't let me alone. G'wan! [*Strikes at something.*] Nothin' but a cup o' coffee an' a sandwich since Wednesday! [*He sniffs, reaches in his pocket and pulls out some change. His shoulder jerks.*] Eighteen cents! An' I ain't got the strength to earn any more. Look at me! [*He surveys himself in the mirror. His shoulder jerks.*] It's all up with me, I guess. G'wan! [*He strikes at something.*] These papers'll fix me. They're all talkin' about my arm. [*Pauses.*] I wonder why Joe ain't answered my letter, an' Greenbaum, the stiff! [*He gulps.*] G'wan! [*He draws back his arm threateningly.*] I guess he's afraid. Well, that's the way—when you ain't got nothin'. [*He stiffens and strikes at something. His shoulder jerks.*] Gee, but it's tough, though! All the world goin' on an' happy, an' me—

[*He half sobs, then starts to pick up the gas tube. The sound of steps is heard on the stairs. Hastily he puts away the tube and papers, and straightens up, listening intently. His shoulder jerks. A knock sounds, then another.*]

A VOICE: [*Outside.*] Mr. Abrams! Mr. Abrams! [ISADORE *does not answer. The door rattles.*] You are in there. I know you're in there! Vy don't you open the door?

ISADORE: [*Stirring.*] Wait a minute! [*He goes to the door and opens it slightly. His shoulder jerks.*]

SAMUEL ELKAS: [*A small, dark, restless, inquisitive, ferret-like Jew, clothed in a dirty shirt, open at the neck and rolled up at the sleeves, a pair of baggy, messy trousers, the suspenders of which are hanging down, and the leg-ends of which gather in folds above his instep. He wears slippers. His hair is tousled, his face and hands are damp and dirty.*] Good efternoon, Mr. Abrams. So, you are not verking yet? Hev you my rent for me?

ISADORE: [*Taking off his hat and rubbing his stomach and hair.*] I've been sick today. I couldn't look very well. But I've got a job, now, for tomorrow. [*His shoulder jerks. He turns it away from* ELKAS.] A friend o' mine is goin' to give it to me. By tomorrow night I'll have your rent for you. [*He starts to strike at something, but pauses.*]

ELKAS: [*With a gesture.*] Tomorrow! Tomorrow! Alvays tomorrow! Vell, if I don't get it by den, you vill haf to get out. You t'ink ve verk to give rooms free to people? [ISADORE'S *shoulder jerks.*]. Vot is it vith your arm? Is it hurt?

ISADORE: [*Savagely.*] No, no, no! Nothin'! [*He starts to close the door.*] I'll get it for you tomorrow, sure. [*His shoulder jerks.*] Can't you trust me till then? I'll pay you, sure. [*His shoulder jerks. He pushes the door nearly to.*] I can get a dollar an' a half. It's only a week yesterday.

[*As the two stand there speaking, a little girl of nine or ten, dark, elfish, pretty, appears and stands behind* ELKAS, *who is evidently unaware of her presence. She peeps around as if anxious to be neither heard nor seen. She has on a worn blue gingham dress, sleeveless and cut low at the neck, which is very soiled and torn. Her legs as well as her arms are bare and dirty, and her hair is disheveled and not very clean, but she has the charm of sprightliness and curiosity.*]

ELKAS: [*Lifting his hands.*] Vell, vy dontcha, den? I ken't, an' I need it bed enough. Ve haf to verk, too. [*He gesticulates antagonistically.*]

ISADORE: [*Crossly.*] Well, I'll have it for you by tomorrow, I tell you—by six o'clock. [*His shoulder jerks. He looks to one side as if to strike at something.*] Don't bother me no more today, will you! I'll pay you then, sure. [*He pushes at the door as if to close it.*]

ELKAS: [*Pushing at his side of the door to hold it open.*] By six o'clock! By six o'clock! Den, if you don't pay, I lose Sunday, too! Vy not by noon?

ISADORE: All right, by noon. I'll get it to you as soon as I get it—by noon I'll send it over. [*His shoulder jerks.*] You'll get it, all right. Please don't worry me now. [*Aside.*] G'wan!

ELKAS: [*Doubtfully, moving back. The child disappears.*] Vell, if it vuz some von else, I vouldn't do it. Since you're sick, I'll let it go today as a favor to you.

[*He goes out.* ISADORE *closes the door, listens, then after a time looks up.*]

ISADORE: [*His shoulder jerks.*] Yes, the pig! Tomorrow I'll pay him—tomorrow—huh!—I won't be alive tomorrow! G'wan! [*Strikes at something.*] It's the red ones, that's it. They won't let me alone. A lot of difference it'll make by tomorrow! I might as well quit now. I gotta. It's the red ones. I can't get away. He saw my arm. [*Goes over to the bed.*] Gee, it's a wonder he didn't connect me! G'wan away! [*Strikes at something. With a frown.*] Maybe he did! [*Takes out the rubber tube, fastens one end of it over the gas jet and carries the other end to the head of the bed and rests it there. His shoulder jerks. He takes off his hat and coat, then gets out the pencil and begins feverishly to scribble on the wall at the head of the bed. As he writes he talks.*] "Parole—officer—Gavan—is—a—damned—liar." G'wan! [*Strikes.*] "He—told—me—not—to—call—" G'wan! [*Strikes.*] "—any—more. He—never—told—me—to—sign—any—papers—" [*Stops, frowns, and stares at something.*] G'wan! [*Strikes. Writes.*] "It's—the—red—ones—not—the—blacks. He—told—me—he'd—send—" [*Stops and frowns.*] G'wan! "—them—to—me—in—a—blank—envelope—" [*Pauses and thinks. Frowns, then writes.*] "Seven—is—right. Don't—cry—" [*Strikes.*] G'wan!

[*A tap is heard at the door. Instantly he stiffens, removes the tube from the gas jet, tiptoes to the bed and puts it under, then draws a small knife from his pocket and listens. The tap is repeated. He does not answer.*]

A SOFT, LOW VOICE: Mr. Ab'ams! Mr. Ab'ams!

ISADORE: [*Relaxing, and putting back the knife.*] Yes?

THE VOICE: [*Softly.*] Oh, Mr. Ab'ams! It's Hagar!

ISADORE: [*Gruffly.*] Yes? Whaddy ya want? [*His shoulder jerks.*]

THE VOICE: [*Sweetly.*] I've got sompin for you, Mr. Ab'ams. [*He opens the door and looks out. The little girl is there. She has an apple and is holding it out to him.*] Want this?

ISADORE: [*Starting. His shoulder jerks.*] Oh, it's you, is it? What made you wanta bring it to me? [*His expression changes from one of fear and doubt to one of smiling sympathy. He forgets to strike. A weird smile passes over his face.*] Come on in. [*Takes her by the arm and pulls her in.*]

HAGAR: [*Uncertainly.*] I don't think I'd better. He'll scold if he ketches me up here. I'm not allowed. [*Looks about as if to see if any one is coming. She laughs.*]

ISADORE: [*Warmly.*] Aw, come on. [*His shoulder jerks. His face grimaces oddly. Over his shoulder.*] G'wan!

HAGAR: [*Looking at him and smiling.*] I heard what you said. You said you ain't got no money, an' I felt sorry, so I thought I'd bring you this. [*She holds up the apple.*] Didn't you see me? I was behind papa. [*She laughs.* ISADORE *shakes his head. He looks at her greedily, staring at her arms and bare feet. His expression changes. He leers and smoothes her arms and neck. His shoulder jerks. He shivers.*] Don't you know me?

ISADORE: [*Darkly.*] Sure. You're Hagar Elkas, ain't you? [*She nods.*] You like me, Hagar, don't you? Somebody likes me, anyhow. [*To one side.*] G'wan!

HAGAR: [*Nodding her head and smiling.*] Uh-huh! Who you talkin' to? [*She looks around behind him.*]

ISADORE: Nobody! Nobody! [*He controls an inclination to strike.*]

HAGAR: I seen you goin' out this mornin'. [*Looking at the papers on the floor.*] Wotcha doin' with all them papers—lookin' for a job?

ISADORE: [*Looking about apprehensively, then stooping to gather up the papers from the floor and stuff them in a bureau drawer. He smiles wanly.*] That's right! You've got it! I'm lookin' for a job. [*His shoulder jerks.*] Come on up here. [*He picks her up and seats her on the bureau and begins to trifle with her hair and feel her knees. His shoulder jerks. Again his expression changes to a leer.*

*His face contorts. He glances over her, then looks up, sees himself in the mirror. Pauses. Puts his hand to his head and begins to back away. As he does so, a noise is heard in the hall below, a voice calling "*HAGAR! HAGAR!*" A door slams. Voices sound, then die away. The voice of a newsboy in the street is heard—"*Extro! Extro! Isadore Berchansky!*—" Silence.* ISADORE *stares at* HAGAR, *who stares back at him in astonishment.*] Naw! Naw! That's right! I'd better not do that any more! I won't! I can't! It's the red ones, that's it! They won't let me alone. [*His shoulder jerks.*] I'd better quit now before I do, though. I'm crazy, all right. [*He goes to the door and listens, then returns and lifts* HAGAR *down and pushes her toward the door, his shoulder jerking. Roughly.*] Get out, kid! Quick! Quick! Get out, I tell you, before I do sompin! Get out! You don't know me! Can't you see? Quick! Quick! Hurry! [*His manner is very rough. He pushes her out, and as she gives him a frightened glance, slams the door, locks it, and then stands with his back to it, and stares.*] Naw! Naw! I'd better not do that no more! I better go, though, before I kill somebody else! I'm sure to! Poor little kid! [*His shoulder jerks. He goes to the bed, pulls off the coverlet and lays it along the crack at the bottom of the door, the while his shoulder jerks. He takes the newspapers out of the drawer and making twists of them, begins stuffing them into the cracks along the sides and between the windows and in the keyhole. As he works he talks.*] Mom, you'll understand this. You know me. It's for the best. I couldn't help it. You'll understand. They won't let me alone. G'wan! [*Strikes at something.*] Don't cry! I'm no good, anyhow. I never was. [*His shoulder jerks.*] You know that. [*He wipes his eyes.*] Be good to Masha. Tell her I always thought she was the best of 'em all. [*He pauses and stares at something, moves as if to strike, but subsides without doing it.*] She knows I like her. [*His shoulder jerks,*] An' pop! Poor old pop! [*He stops, picks up another bit of newspaper, writes on it and looks about for a suitable place to fasten it, finally sticking it in the mirror frame. His shoulder jerks. He stares curiously at something. Heavily.*] I guess they'll see that, all right. [*His shoulder jerks.*] G'wan! [*Strikes at something, goes over to the bed, takes out the gas tube, fastens one end* *over the gas jet and taking out his handkerchief, stretches it by the corners and ties the tube to it. Looking over his shoulder.]* G'wan! *[Then he gets his coat, spreads it over the window with pins and goes back to the bed, picks up the other end of the tube and stands there, his shoulder jerking from time to time. The curtain begins to descend.]* Well, I guess it's all day for me, all right. They won't let me be. G'wan! *[Strikes at something.]* I ain't all bad, an' I don't wanta die, but—oh—*[He sits down.]*

## CURTAIN

### SCENE 2

*The same as Scene One, except that it is now about eleven in the morning of the next day. Everything is as before, except that the window and door are open, the gas tube hanging straight from the jet to the floor.* ISADORE'S *hat and coat are lying on one corner of the bed. On the floor in different places are the twists of paper used in stuffing the window and keyhole. Plainly outlined on the bed under a sheet is a body. A stout Irish policeman is standing in the doorway. Another is outside. Three reporters are grouped together near the window, examining a bit of paper.*

FIRST POLICEMAN: Ye'll be tellin' thim to bring his father or some one, eh?

SECOND POLICEMAN: That's right.

[*Exit. The* FIRST POLICEMAN *strolls over to where the three reporters stand, and looks over their shoulders.*]

ARMSBY: [*Reporter for the Herald. He is short and stout and florid, with hair growing over his coat collar. In one pocket are various newspapers.*] Say, this'll create a real row, this will! It's Berchansky, all right—no doubt of it.

Look at what he says here [*reads, the other two looking over his shoulder*]—"I'm guilty, and I'm insane, caused by the beautiful make-ups of girls that has set me very passionate. Don't cry." [*He looks up with a quizzical light in his eyes.*] Whaddy ya know about that! [*Smiles.*] No one gets the two thousand reward, do they? That was for catching him alive, wasn't it?

LEACH: [*Reporter for the Times. Young—about twenty-two—tall, slender, cynical, very neat, a pair of large gold-rimmed glasses on his nose.*] Yes, that was it. No one gets the two thousand now. Who found him? [*He stares about the room and at the bed.*]

FIRST POLICEMAN: Sure, the landlord here. Elkas is his name. He's gone to the station now. But he don't know it's Berchansky yet. No more did I till that young felly from the *American* come in. He took some of these papers away with him, I'm thinkin'. I was standin' downstairs waitin' fer me partner to come up, when who should come runnin' out but the landlord here, a-yellin' at the top of his voice. Sure, I thot he was killed himself, I did. "What's ailin' ye?" I says. "A man's moirdered in me house," he says; "he's killed himself," he says. So I blows me whistle an' beats me sthick, an' at that I runs up here, an' here he was, a-lyin' there with that tube in 'is mouth, an' that pilly over 'is head. "Come, now," I says, shakin' 'im, "come out o' that!" but he was dead, aal right.

QUINN: [*Reporter for the Sun. Irish, short, slender, red-headed, quick, almost waspish in his speech, about thirty-five years of age, and with a slight brogue.*] He didn't know it was Berchansky, ye say?

FIRST POLICEMAN: Divil a bit. It was the little felly from the *American* that was in here just ahead o' ye b'ys that told me that. He told me naht to say naathin', but since ye've found out fer yerselves, sure, there's no haarm in tellin' ye. [*Grins.*] Sure, ye'll be after sayin' that Aafficer McKagg was called in, an' that I was here dooin' me dooty? [*He pokes* QUINN *on the elbow.*] Sure, ye'll be afther knowin' how to fix it up.

QUINN: Sure! Sure! That's all right! What's the full name? [*He begins to write it.*] If that landlord had only known yesterday, he might have had that two thousand. Say!

MCKAGG: [*Solemnly.*] By God, you're right! Think ave him losin' that! [*He looks over their shoulders as they write.*] Aafficer Thomas McKagg, twelfth precinct.

LEACH and ARMSBY: [*Together, as they show their papers to* MCKAGG.] That's right, isn't it—M-c-K-a-g-g?

MCKAGG: Yes, that's it. [*He smiles gratefully.*]

QUINN: I suppose the father'll be down here pretty soon, now. Have any detectives been here yet?

MCKAGG: Divil a waan. I'm doubtin' if they know it yet. This'll be afther makin' thim sorer still.

QUINN: [*Jubilantly.*] A foine lot of detectives they have in this town! Say! Two hundred of 'em on the job, and they haven't turned up a thing—not waan. We've turned up everything that's been turned up so far—the mother, the sister, and now this poor divil. [*He waves a hand toward the bed.*]

LEACH: [*Briskly.*] Whaddy ya know! Isn't that a scream—the whole force looking for him—and we newspaper men find him! [*He laughs.*]

ARMSBY: [*Who is going about looking for other evidence—softly to* LEACH.] Sure, they're all no good, a lot of hoboes. [*He sees something on the floor and picks it up. Starts to conceal it, but sees* QUINN *and the officer looking at him, and opens it.*] Here's some writing. [*He reads. As he does so, the other two come to his side.*] "Tell—mother—I—should—have—died—two—years—ago. So—let—her—forget—as—though—it's—two—years—already." [*He takes out his notebook and begins to jot it down.*]

QUINN: [*Approaching with his pencil and paper.*] Not bad, that! Not bad! A nice bit o' sentiment. [*He begins to write.*] The poor divil was crazy, aal right. Sure enough! I begin to feel sorry for him. He couldn't help it, I suppose.

LEACH: You think not? Oh, I don't know. Let me have that first paper, Armsby, will you? I want to copy it. [ARMSBY *gives it to him.*]

ARMSBY: [*Going to the bed, picks up a paper containing* ISADORE'S *picture, turns back the sheet and compares the two.* LEACH *follows.*] It's him, all right. I see it now. The very fellow!

LEACH: [*Excitedly, looking at the wall above* ISADORE'S *head.*] Say, here's something else! He's written all over the place! [ARMSBY *looks up.*] He must have been clean crazy! [*Reads slowly.*] "Parole—officer—Gavan—is—a—damned—liar. Go—'way! He—told—me—not—to—call—any—more. He—never—told—me—to—sign—any—papers. It's—the—reds—not—the—blacks. He—told—me—he'd—send—'em—to—me—in—a—blank—envelope. Seven—is—right. Don't—cry. It's—no—use—much! Ha! Ha! Yes. I'm—a—prize-fighter!"

[*Takes out his pencil and paper, as does* ARMSBY. *They begin to write.* QUINN *comes over.*]

QUINN: What's this, now? Let me see! [*Reads the writing over their shoulders.*] What d'ye think of that? What d'ye s'pose he means by those things, anyhow—the reds and the blacks? [*He writes also.*] He must have been crazy, sure enough. That's quairer than the last, that. We aaht to get his faather down here to identify him. The papers are interested in him.

LEACH: That's right. Only, the officer says he thinks some one from the *American* has gone for him.

MCKAGG: [*Leaning against the door, his hands behind him.*] Make yerselves aisy on that score. That little felly from the *American* has gaan, aal right. He told me naht to let any waan else in till he come back with him, if I could help it. Of course, he's a nice little felly, but I couldn't do that. Aal the papers have a right here. [*He smiles.*] Vallally, that's me partner, has just been afther tellin' headquarters, an' they'll be gettin' him here in no time, too. They're sure to bring 'im, even if the little felly don't. [*He straightens up and puts his thumbs in his belt.*]

ARMSBY: We'd better not be too sure of that. He might not bring him back until we're out of here. One of us ought to go, I'm thinking. [*Then, as* LEACH *picks up another bit of paper from the floor and unfolds it, and then attempts to slip it into his pocket.*] What's that? [*He comes over.*]

LEACH: [*A little shame-facedly.*] Nothing much, I guess. [*Takes it out and unfolds it.*]

ARMSBY: Let's see it. [QUINN *comes over.*] It's fifty-fifty on all this, isn't it?

QUINN: Sure! You're not goin' to hold anything out, are you?

LEACH: [*Irritably.*] Not at all! Not at all! Who's holding anything out? Can't I see it first if I find it? [*Opens it.*] Look at this! [*Reads.*] "This is to my dear mother who I am always homesick for, and same to rest and pop, whose word I am taking by doing this. Go 'way! Maybe you think it's easy. Well, maybe it is. I don't know. It's the reds, not the blacks. Mostly red. They won't let me alone. I figure easiest of my own. I want to say if I don't die this way I'll take my medicine just the same. Fields, carriages, four trees. Don't cry. My last job was in pants manufactor at 61 Norfolk. He owes me two days' work. I ain't et in three. Please secure pay and give to my dear mother who is very poor and for truth my mind ain't right. Go 'way! My oldest sister has lots of money and Greenbaum and don't help as she should, or Rae either. Eleven buttons—four seams—and the bottoms turned up. I'm sorry to cause all this trouble to my neighbor in particular, but all he's gotta do is call a cop! Go 'way! Go 'way! Gavan is a liar! Tell mother I'm really guilty and she'll not cry her eyes out— heart. Poor mom! You think I'm innocent, even yet, don't you? Mothers is wonders! Great! I am, too, only I ain't made right. Red, not black. We ain't made right— not all of us—all wrong. It's their pretty mouths an' hair an' the way they walk an' them shirtwaists so fine—that's it! Sorry. I got crazy like I often do, an' you can't blame me or nobody else. It don't do things right always. Can you blame a man when he ain't right?

Isadore Berchansky."

ARMSBY: [*Looking up.*] Tough, eh?

QUINN: You're right, it's tough. Ye never can tell about these poor divils, as [*he points to the letter*] ye can see by that. Here's the whole city runnin' him down an' he may not have been as bad as the people have been thinkin'. Life's a pretty stiff thing at times.

LEACH: [*Going to the bureau and smoothing out the paper he has found, preparatory to copying it.*] Oh, I don't know about that. I wonder sometimes just how crazy some of them are. I know a doctor who has made a study of these cases at Johns Hopkins, and he isn't so sure that they deserve so much sympathy. I can't understand it myself, wanting to attack a little girl like that, especially when he might interest a grown girl. The public wouldn't feel one-fiftieth as terrible if he had tried to attack a grown one instead of this little kid. But a little girl! And to torture her! Hell, you might as well talk about having sympathy for a mad dog. What I can't understand, though, is how it comes that a man like that should be allowed to walk about the streets here in New York free—not a person to touch him. And he had tried to attack another little girl two years ago. Why shouldn't his parents have done something about him then? He himself says he should have been dead two years ago. Well, why didn't they lock him up then? What's the big idea, letting a fellow like that run at large?

ARMSBY: [*Thoughtfully and apologetically.*] Oh, I know, but then you can't always tell, either. Everything isn't on the surface in this world. His parents might not have thought him as bad as he was, or they might have been sorry for him. Supposing you had a brother like that—then what? Would you want him locked up right away? People don't like to break up their own homes, especially parents. They feel too bad about it. At the same time, they're likely to think he'll get better. A single offense don't always prove a man's crazy, especially in a case like this. He might change.

QUINN: You're right there. The public doesn't understand them yet. I've been readin' up on these cases for some time, an' from what I can make out they're no more guilty than any other person with a disease. Did ye know, ayther ave ye, that there's something they've called *harmones* which the body manufactures an' which is poured into the blood streams of every waan ave us which excites us to the m'aning ave beauty an' thim things—"sensitizes" is the word they use. Now if a felly is so constituted that he has more ave that an' less ave somethin' else—somethin' which balances him a little an' makes him less sensitive to the beauty of women or girls—he's likely to be like that. He can't help it. There's something in him that pushes him on in spite of himself. This felly's letter says so. I believe if the public knew more about these cases it might be able to catch some of these fellies earlier an' begin to treat 'em or put 'em away somewhere where they'd come out aal right. They're naht aal bad—that's one thing sure, as ye can see by this. [*He points to the letter* LEACH *has been reading and is still holding.*]

LEACH: [*Superiorily.*] Oh, all right. Just the same, this business of sympathizing with people can be carried too far, I tell you. When I was at Cornell we made a study of some of these fellows. They have a pretty fine psychiatric laboratory there. We studied dozens of such cases. In every one we found that however feeble-minded a fellow like that might actually be, or queer, still, ordinarily you couldn't tell it, you know, and often he was able to do better if he wanted to. They look just like other people.

QUINN [*Irritably, and yet lightly.*] Ave course! Ave course! What taalk have ye? Man, ye don't mane to say ye went to Cornell to find that out, do ye? It's in a hundred books. Haven't ye ever read Havelock Ellis or Kraft-Ebbing? They give thousands ave cases—thousands. [*He takes the letter from* ARMSBY *and begins to write.*]

LEACH: [*Testily.*] Sure I've read 'em. Of course. What do you think? What makes me so tired, though, is your taking up for those fellows as though they were deserving of nothing but sympathy. I don't see that so much sympathy is to be wasted on 'em, really. How about the little girl he killed? Her life was as good to her as his was to him. And I notice that fellows like that are nearly always shrewd enough to take care of themselves and get what they want. Take this Berchansky, there, now. [*He nods toward the bed.*] He was clever enough to lure that little girl to that empty apartment in some way. You can't say that that was so very fine. You can't have too much sympathy for them, I tell you. They ought to be watched, and at the first sign, shut up for good—that's what I say. It's just as well that they are hounded in this way. It has to be so. [*As he talks,* ARMSBY, *who has been prowling about looking for other things but now scenting an argument, draws near.*]

QUINN: [*Stopping his writing and coming directly under* LEACH'S *chin, staring up at him, argumentatively.*] Who's denyin' it, I'd like to know? Me? What ye say is aal true enough, and I'm naht sayin' that he shouldn't have been locked up long ago if they could have caught him—I think he should have—but what makes me tired in you an' others an' the papers is aal this shoutin' about human tigers lurkin' on the East Side an' everywhere else, men without a spark ave anything but evil in 'em—plain murderers—an' doin' naathin' aal day long but lie in wait for little girls, to kill 'em. Ye'd think there was only waan side to the story. Ye'd think from the papers ave the past six weeks that this felly was aal wolf—naathin' but murder an' rape in his mind, a sane, calculatin' villain turned to this sort of thing for the fun of it only—naht a poor, crazy wastrel like this, without a place to go an' no way ave gettin' himself anything ave any kind. If he was such a divil, what was he doin' workin' for a dollar a day—an' naht gettin' his pay, at that? Now, for aal ye've been to Cornell—an' I don't doubt ye learned a lot there—there's another side to this, an' ye're just the waan to know it if ye've been there. People judge these fellies solely by their acts, when as a matter ave fact they aaht to take into account the things which make up their natures an' dispositions. This felly could no more help bein' what he was than a fly can help bein' a fly an' naht an elephant, an' that's naht at aal. Nature is deeper an' stronger than anything we know. An' by that I'm naht sayin' that the human race hasn't the right to defend itself from this sort ave felly. It has, an' does. What I'm taalkin' about is aal this palaver in the papers about wolves an' divils. Why, man, by the papers ave the last six weeks ye'd think the streets were full ave demons in the shape ave men. Ye've seen 'em arrest at least a hundred men for even smilin' at a child or ahfferin' it a stick ave candy. And now look at 'im. There he is—hungry an' dirty an' thin an' hidden away in this pe-latial room, an' there's that letter to his mother tellin' her not to cry an' that he aaht to have been dead two years ago, an' that he's naht right. Ave course he wasn't right, the poor divil, an' perhaps no waan knew it better than his mother, ayther, an' that's why he writes to her. [LEACH *shakes his head argumentatively.*] An', me boy, while we're on this subject, let me tell ye just waan thing more; I'm an older man than ye by fourteen years an' I've seen a little somethin' ave life that maybe ye haven't seen yet, anyhow. Don't be so cocksure in your judgments of who are the good an' who are the bad in this world. Facts an' proofs are naht aal on the surface, by any means, as Armsby here was aafter sayin'. Ye were sayin' a while ago that he aaht to have taken a grown woman or girl. How do ye know whether any girl or woman would give him a single look or no, let alone a second waan? But supposin' ye were like him—hungry an' tortured by their pretty mouths an' their hair an' the way they walk an' their shirtwaists so fine—I believe that's what he says here [*he looks at the letter*]—then what? Are ye sure ye'd do so very different from what he did, driven by the things that were drivin' him?

LEACH: Oh, I don't know. I might not, of course.

QUINN: Ye're tootin', ye might naht, nor any other man in the same state an' place. Now, I wouldn't have a single word to say ave this case if it weren't for all the noble palaverin' that's been goin' on in an' out ave the papers, in the churches an' everywhere else. Everybody seems to know exactly just what a low, horrible scoundrel he was without a spark ave decency in him. Well, it just so happens that I've been studyin' these very kinds ave cases for years, an' I know what I'm taalkin' about. Aal men are naht balanced or normal be their own free will an' say-so, any more than they're free an' equal in life, an' that's naht at aal. They're naht aal endowed with the power or the will to do an' select, aal the rules of the copybooks to the contrary nahtwithstandin'. Some are so constituted mentally an' physically that they can't do otherwise than as they do, an' that's what ye never can get through the average felly's brain, nor through the average newspaper's, ayther. Most people have a few rules, a pattern, an' everybody's supposed to be like that. Well, they're naht. An' naathin' will ever make 'em exactly alike, ayther—ayther aal good or aal bad, or a little ave waan or the other, accordin' to anybody's theory. Nature don't work that way. An' nature makes people, me young friend, me an' you [*he taps him on the chest*], an' every waan else, an' she don't aalways make us right ayther, by a damned sight. Some people don't aalways have aal they waant mentally or physically—if they did I'd be a millionaire today—nayther can they aalways do as they'd like to, or aaht to, aal theories to the contrary nahtwithstandin'. Sometimes they're made to do things—lots ave thim—by forces over which they have no control. [LEACH *stirs argumentatively.*] Man, ye're naht goin' to deny that? Sometimes I think we're naht unlike those formulae they give ye in a chemical laboratory—if ye're made up right, ye work right. If ye're naht, ye don't, an' that's aal there is to it—laa or no laa. An' another thing I'm tellin' ye, me young friend, an' I'd like ye to think it over from time to time, whether ye like it or naht—that Dennis Quinn said it—an' that is that laa is merely somethin' that forces people to do what they don't waant to do whether they will or no, naht somethin' that aalways shows 'em how to do it—ye get me? Remember that, me young friend. I'm tellin' ye. If ye waant to come out exactly right in this world, which nobody does, ye waant to be pairfectly balanced, or nearly that—an' damn few are that. It's more luck than anythin' else, an' that's true, too. Now ye were sayin' a while ago that ye can't understand why a man like that should be attackin' a little girl, unless he were a low, vile creature, even if he wasn't balanced quite right—but I can. If ye'd ever made a study ave the passion ave love in the sense that Freud an' some others have ye'd understand it well enough. It's a great force about which we know naathing as yet an' which we're just beginnin' to look into—what it manes, how it affects people.

LEACH: Oh, I'm ready to admit all that. Let's cut this, anyhow. We haven't got time.

[*The voice of a newsboy sounds:* "*Extro! Extro! All about Isadore Berchansky!*"]

ARMSBY: [*Energetically.*] Yes, fellows, you'd better cut the argument and make copies of this. Look around! Look around! The bulls'll soon be here! Then they'll be wanting to shut everything off.

[*He opens all the drawers and looks under the bureau.* QUINN *goes over to the body and feels in the pockets. He looks under the bed and picks up a collar, and starts to conceal it.* LEACH *examines more of the walls. A step is heard on the stairs.* MCKAGG *looks down.*]

MCKAGG: I dunno who this may be. It's the central men now, I'm thinkin', aal right. Yes, it's them. There's three ave thim. Better put those things away if ye waant thim.

[*Enter Detectives* MCGRANAHAN, HARSH *and* SKUMM. *They are typical sleuths—very wide-eyed, very dull, very suspicious, and very secretive. Detective-fashion, they keep their hats on, even while bending over the dead. They swagger into the room, looking about as if each detail might contain a secret. They look at* LEACH *and* ARMSBY *copying, then approach the bed. As they do, they greet the newspaper men familiarly, who eye them askance, but return the salutation genially.*]

MCGRANAHAN: [*Turning back the sheet and eyeing the face of* ISADORE.] Well, we've caught him at last, eh? So he quit, eh? The poor nut! Crazy, I hear! [*He looks around loftily at the newspaper men.*]

SKUMM: [*Equally superior.*] Gas! Whaddy ya know! [*He looks at the gas jet and the rubber tube.* QUINN *nudges* ARMSBY, *who eyes him without smiling.*]

HARSH: [*As* MCGRANAHAN *pulls back the sheet.*] Pretty tough-lookin' mug, eh? [*They turn to the newspaper men, who are looking at the letter.*]

MCGRANAHAN: What's that? Find anything much to identify him by, boys?

QUINN: [*Who has a paper in his hand.*] It's a letter to his mother. We'll give it to you after. There're a dozen things about the place—letters on the walls an' everywhere.

SKUMM: [*Sarcastically, with a crude attempt at humor.*] I don't suppose there was any joolry or anything like that on him? [*He smiles wisely.*]

LEACH: [*Irritably.*] Why don't you search him? There he is.

HARSH: We will in a minute. Who was the first to find him, d'ye know?

ARMSBY: [*Pleasantly.*] The landlord, I think. We didn't get here first. He doesn't know it's Berchansky yet, though. [*Aside, to* QUINN.] Wait'll he hears he's lost that two thousand reward!

[QUINN *lifts his hands.* HARSH *goes over to* MCKAGG. SKUMM *goes to the head of the bed.*]

SKUMM: [*Surveying the scrawl about* OFFICER GAVAN.] Knockin' even before he dies, eh? Whaddy ya know! A swell chance he had to get away, with all o' us after him!

[*A new noise is heard on the stairs. Enter an Inspector of Police in uniform, a sergeant of detectives,* ELKAS, HAGAR ELKAS, *a fourth reporter who shows his badge to* MCKAGG, *and after them various onlookers and curiosity mongers from the building and the street, whom* MCKAGG *pushes back. The* INSPECTOR *and* SERGEANT *make their way to the bedside.*]

ELKAS: [*Excitedly, to* MCKAGG.] Vuz it Berchansky yet? Oi! Oi!

MCKAGG: Man, aare ye just findin' that out now?

THE INSPECTOR: [*Brusquely, turning to the crowd.*] Don't let all these people in here, Officer. Only the ones who have business here. Drive them out! Drive them out! [*He looks at the detectives, who salute him.*]

MCKAGG: [*Vigorously.*] Get back! Get back! What'll ye be afther waantin' in here, anyhow? [*He admits* ELKAS, HAGAR, *and the fourth reporter. The latter joins the three.*]

THE INSPECTOR: [*Surrounded by detectives.*] This is the man, is it? Well, that's one trouble over, anyhow. Who found him?

MCGRANAHAN: [*Sycophantically.*] The landlord here, chief—Elkas is his name, I believe.

ELKAS: [*Pushing forward.*] Here I am. It is Berchansky, you say? Vere do I get de reward?

THE INSPECTOR: Aw, don't get excited. There's no reward in this case. That was for catching him alive. Can't you see he's dead? [ELKAS'S *face falls.*]

ELKAS: Ach, my house! My gas! He owes me for t'ree veeks' rent!

THE INSPECTOR [*Paying no attention to* ELKAS.] Where's his old man? Anybody gone for him? We ought to get him here to identify him. [*Turning to* MCKAGG.] When'd they find him, Officer?

MCKAGG: About nine this mornin', chief. The landlord caalled me in.

THE INSPECTOR: What about his old man? Anybody gone for him?

MCKAGG: Aafficer Vallally wint an hour ago. [*A noise is heard.*] I'm thinkin' he's comin' now, sir.

MCGRANAHAN: [*Ingratiatingly.*] Not a doubt in the world, chief. There are letters from him all over the place—on the walls, everywhere. [*He points to the writing at the head of the bed.*]

THE INSPECTOR: Where are they? Let's see some of them.

[ARMSBY *brings one forward. The* INSPECTOR *takes it and reads. The noise at the head of the stairs increases.* BERCHANSKY, *accompanied by an officer and several plain-clothes men, appears in the doorway.* MCKAGG *makes way for them.*]

MCGRANAHAN: [*Softly.*] Here's his old man, now, chief.

[*The* INSPECTOR *turns to look.* BERCHANSKY, *very pale, very worn, pauses at the door a moment, then, pushed and led by the detectives, comes forward. A hush falls over the room.* MCGRANAHAN *turns down the sheet, which has been pulled up, and* BERCHANSKY *looks at the corpse in silence. A pause ensues.*]

BERCHANSKY: [*Heavily and sadly, folding his hands over his breast.*] Yes, dat's my son. Dat's my boy. [*Pauses, and looks around*] Gas? Vell, it's better den de oder. [*Pauses again, while the silence endures.*] Dat he should end so! [*He wipes his eyes.*] It is too bed! [*He shakes his head and looks around again.*] It is strange. Four years ago ve lived next door.

THE INSPECTOR: [*Coming alongside.*] You're sure it's your son, are you, Mr. Berchansky?

BERCHANSKY: Yes. Yes. I know. [*He turns as if to go.*]

ELKAS: [*Who has crowded forward, speaking with irritation.*] So he vuz your son, vuz he? Such a scoundrel! He owes me for t'ree veeks' rent, yet. An' *he* should come by *my* house! He tells me his name is Abrams. I should lose two t'ousand dollars! If I know, he vouldn't 'a' been here long. I t'ought he acted strange.

BERCHANSKY: [*Humbly.*] I vill pay! I vill pay—only not today, please. I heven't so much.

ELKAS: [*Angrily, while the police stare at him tolerantly.*] An' you! Vy shouldn't you bring your children up right? If you should bring him up right—if you should keep him off de streets, den he vouldn't do such a t'ing!

BERCHANSKY: [*Slowly, with suppressed emotion, as the police push* ELKAS *back.*] My friend, hev you children?

ELKAS: [*Defiantly.*] Yes!

BERCHANSKY: [*In a quavering voice.*] Den you should know. Vy pull at de valls of my house? Dey are already down!

**CURTAIN**

1. Theodore Dreiser in his Greenwich Village Apartment. Courtesy U Penn.

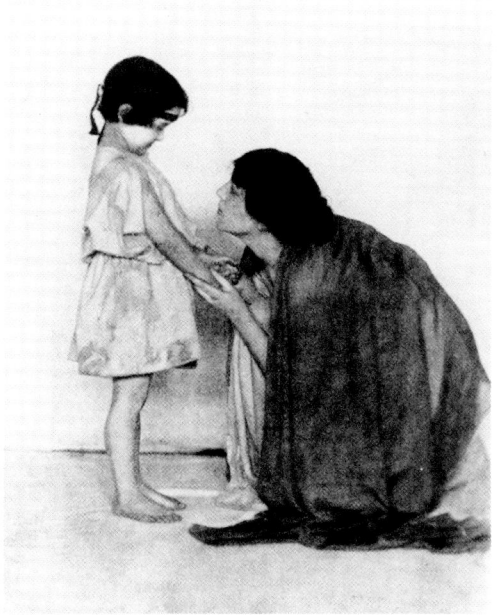

2. Above: Kirah Markham as Andromache in *The Trojan Women*. From Floyd Dell, "The Littlest Theater," *Harper's Weekly* 58 (29 November 1913), p. 23.

3. Right: Estelle Kubitz, Dreiser's typist for *The Hand of the Potter*. Courtesy U Penn.

## The Voice

Scene: A simple room with a round reading table in the centre, an open fire, right, and at the back two french windows, the one giving into a bedroom, the other out upon a balcony. Left, a baby grand piano.

The Voice: Pof! Pof! Pof! You see I make the same sound as of old.

The Woman (at the table) I hear you! Oh — I hear you. (She stops her sewing, leans her elbows on her knees, her face in her hands and stares into the fire.)

The Voice Then up the balcony in that other place I climbed, while your parents slept; and held you in my arms. Do you remember how I held you?

4. First leaf of the manuscript of *The Voice*.
Courtesy U Penn.

5. Climax of the Washington Square Players production of *The Girl in the Coffin*, with Arthur Hohl as John Ferguson & Kate Morgan as Hannah Littig. From the *New York Call*, 3 January 1918.

6. Sketch of *Laughing Gas* set by Donald Dohner. From Oliver M. Sayler, "Novel Stage Experiment," *Boston Evening Transcript*, 22 December 1916, p. 27.

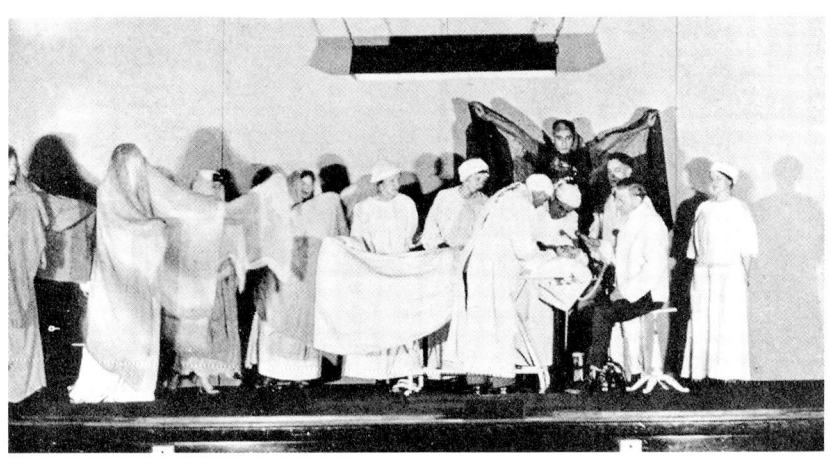

7. Photo of *Laughing Gas* set appearing in Constance D'Arcy Mackay's *The Little Theatre in the United States* (1917).

8. Newspaper accounts of the Swartz-Conners case were Dreiser's primary source for the action and characters in *The Hand of the Potter*. The details in this drawing that accompanied the story "Swartz, Slayer of Julia Connors, a Suicide by Gas" in the *New York World* (19 July 1912, p. 5) appeared in Isadore's suicide notes in the play.

9. Dreiser quoted the headline from this story in the *New York Herald* (17 July 1912, p. 7) in Aaron Berchansky's speech at the close of Act III in *The Hand of the Potter*.

10. Sketch of the characters in the Provincetown Players production of *The Hand of the Potter*, appearing in the *New York Call*, 11 December 1921, p. 4. Courtesy U Penn.

# TEXTUAL COMMENTARY

This Whitston edition of the collected plays of Theodore Dreiser presents the author's final intentions for the reading versions of all of his published plays plus the text of a one-act play he completed but did not publish. Using the methods of modern textual scholarship, the editors have assembled and collated the surviving forms of each of the published plays, selected one of the forms as copy-text, and then emended the copy-text to eliminate errors and other readings that appear to have been introduced without Dreiser's approval and to incorporate Dreiser's corrections and revisions.

## I. The Forms

Dreiser wrote the first draft of all of his plays in longhand on full or half-sheets of 8 1/2 x 11 paper. As he worked on this draft, he would make revisions in the text by crossing out words and sentences and adding others between lines or in the margins and, occasionally, by inserting pages on which he had redrafted what he had written earlier or added new text to be inserted in the earlier draft. After he completed a holograph manuscript of all or a portion of the play, he would turn it over to a secretary for editing and preparing a typescript. He then proofread the typescript, often making further revisions in longhand that were incorporated in a new, revised typescript.

Once revisions of the typescript were completed, Dreiser began the process of trying to sell the play to a publisher. And often, at the same time or shortly before he began circulating the typescript among publishers, he would send carbon copies of it to H. L. Mencken and others showing interest in the work for their review and comments. As a result, by the time he found a publisher, he generally had a file of suggested changes and/or revisions to the play that he could, if he wished, introduce into the work at the time he prepared setting copy for a printer or revised proofsheets of the typeset pages.

With three exceptions, a holograph manuscript that is complete, or nearly complete with only a leaf or two missing, is extant for each of the plays. The exceptions are *Phantasmagoria* and *The Court of Progress*, for which there are no manuscripts surviving, and *The Girl in the Coffin*, for which there is only a partial manuscript. Extant, also, are a typescript of *In the Dark* that has, in Dreiser's hand, an inscription reading "this mss contains directions for staging it"; three different typescripts of *The Dream*, among which appears to be one prepared as setting copy for the periodical version of the play; a typescript of *Phantasmagoria* with corrections in Dreiser's hand; a typescript of *The Court of Progress* inscribed "song version"; and an early, unrevised typescript version of the second scene of the fourth act of *The Hand of the Potter*. Finally, for *The Hand of the Potter*, there exist three pre-publication forms of typeset pages: a salesman's dummy corresponding to page 188, line 1, to page 193, line 24, of this edition that was probably made from the galley proofs, a full set of first page proofs, and a complete set of revised page proofs.

Also available to the editors were the published texts of seven of the one act plays that appeared in periodicals prior to book publication and book versions of all of the plays except *The Voice*. The periodical texts are *The Girl in the Coffin, The Blue Sphere, Laughing Gas,* and *In the Dark,* all of which were published in *The Smart Set; The Spring Recital,* which was published in the *Little Review; The Light in the Window,* published in *International;* and *The Dream,* published in *Seven Arts.* The book versions that appeared during Dreiser's lifetime were three impressions of the first American edition of *Plays of the Natural and Supernatural* containing *The Girl in the Coffin, The Blue Sphere, Laughing Gas, In the Dark, The Spring Recital, The Light in the Window,* and *"Old Ragpicker";* one impression of the first American edition of *Hey Rub-A-Dub-Dub,* that included *The Dream, Phantasmagoria,* and *The Court of Progress;* two impressions of the first American edition of *The Hand of the Potter* and a revised second American edition; and a British edition of the collected plays entitled *Plays, Natural and Supernatural.*

Finally, there are extant a number of forms related to productions of Dreiser's plays: a typescript of *The Girl in the Coffin* prepared for an intended 1915 production by The Modern Stage, based on the *Smart Set* printing; a typescript for a 1930 radio performance of *The Blue Sphere*; a marked up copy of the first American edition of *The Hand of the Potter* used as a prompt script for the Provincetown Players production and a typescript of the prompt script made for Dreiser sometime after the production; and a typescript used as the prompt script for the London production of *The Hand of the Potter*. Since these forms are not part of the history of the reading versions of the plays, they were not collated for potential emendations in the Whitston edition.

## II. Choice of Copy-Text

Although the holograph manuscripts have an authority no other forms can claim, the editors of the Whitston edition have decided not to use them as copy-texts for the published plays. As shown by the numerous emendations to *The Voice*, which survives only in manuscript, Dreiser focused his attention on what textual critics call substantives, the words themselves, and paid little attention to what the critics categorize as accidentals, things such as punctuation and mechanics, when he wrote his plays. Even when he made revisions in the manuscript or prepared fair copy from a rough draft, he frequently omitted needed commas and quotation marks, and used the wrong end punctuation. A former newspaperman, Dreiser was used to having his work copy-edited, and, perhaps as a consequence, throughout his career he relied on the secretary preparing the typescript to "clean-up" the text by supplying omissions and correcting errors in pointing and mechanics. To use the manuscripts as copy-text, therefore, would require the editors to perform the editorial function he had already given authority to the typist to perform. Moreover, because collations of those plays for which a manuscript and a typescript were extant revealed that Kirah Markham, Estelle Kubitz and other typists generally did not introduce changes in the typescripts of his plays that were intended to improve his style or "censor" his work, as some of the typists did for his novels and autobiographical writings, there does not appear to be a need to choose the manuscript to avoid non-authorial revisions of this nature.

The editors have also decided not to use as copy-texts the versions of the plays that first appeared in a periodical. Dreiser could have used tear sheets of these versions when he prepared setting copy for book publication, but it appears that he used typescripts instead. The differences between two of the typescripts for *The Dream*, one of which corresponds to the readings in the *Seven Arts* version and the other to the readings in the book version, provide support for this decision. Further support comes from the pattern of revision among the manuscript, periodical, and book versions of a number of plays for which there are no typescripts, such as *The Blue Sphere*. An examination of the variants among the three versions of this play reveals readings in the book version that are different from readings in the periodical version but the same as readings in the manuscript version. Unless Dreiser or a secretary compared the *Smart Set* version to the manuscript and restored manuscript readings on the tear sheets, which seems highly unlikely, the best explanation for this variation is that the periodical readings were made on one typescript and the book readings on a different typescript.

With the exception of *The Voice*, the copy-text for each play in the Whitston edition is the form that is closest to the setting copy Dreiser prepared for the book version of the play. For most of the one-act plays, this form is the text of the first impression of the first American edition because typescripts are not extant and the book versions were not derived from the periodical versions. In the case of *The Dream* and *Phantasmagoria*, however, the typescripts that appear to have been prepared at the same time as or immediately proceeding setting copy for the book version have been chosen as copy-text. Finally, for *The Hand of the Potter*, the versions closest to setting copy and therefore the ones used as copy-text are the salesman's dummy for page 188, line 1, to page 193, line 24, and the first page proofs for the rest of the play.

### III. Principles of Emendation

When they were extant, the manuscripts were the primary source of emendations in the copy-texts of the one-act plays. For the most part, the readings introduced from the manuscripts correct errors and sophistications in the words of the copy-texts that appear to have been introduced by a typist, an in-house editor or a compositor. The manuscripts were also useful in correcting spelling in the copy-texts, particularly in instances where a typist appeared to ignore Dreiser's preference for British spellings and his attempts to capture dialect through spelling. On the other hand, because Dreiser expected a typist to "clean-up" his manuscript in the area of accidentals, only a few of the many manuscript variants in punctuation and mechanics are introduced into the copy-texts.

Because the periodical and book versions of the plays were derived from different typescripts, no emendations to the copy-texts are made from variant readings in the periodical versions of the one-act plays. However, in the two one-act plays for which a typescript is the copy-text, variants in the first impression of the American edition were introduced when they appeared to represent changes Dreiser made in the text as he read and revised galley and page proofs.

The holograph manuscript is a primary source of emendations in the copy-text of *The Hand of the Potter*, as well, and similar to the manuscript readings introduced in the one-act plays, the majority correct errors and sophistications in wording and restore spelling preferences. In addition, a few emendations come from the typescript that survives for the second scene of the fourth act to correct errors in the copy-text that appear to have been made by an in-house editor. By far the most significant and extensive emendations, however, are the variant readings from the page proofs and first American edition, because they document the extensive revisions to the play Dreiser made in the galley and page proofs.

Three book versions of Dreiser's plays contained variants that were also rejected by the editors as potential emendations. In the 1926 printing of *Plays of the Natural and the Supernatural*, some copies contain a variant reading of the last speech in *The Girl in the Coffin*. Since the editors were unable to determine the authority for this revision, it was not introduced into the copy-text but is instead cited in a textual note. Also rejected were the changes in the revised second edition of *The Hand of the Potter*, which, with one exception, involved extensive deletions in the debate among the newspaper reporters in the last scene of the play. According to Dorothy Dudley in *Dreiser and the Land of the Free*, Dreiser made the deletions for the Provincetown Players, but as noted in the introduction, Dreiser was not in New York at the time of their production. Of course, he could have sent the changes in a letter, but a comparison of the deletions in the revised edition to those in the Players' prompt script shows that they are not the same. It seems more likely, therefore, that the changes were made because of the negative comments on the scene that appeared in reviews of the first edition. Perhaps Dreiser made the cuts himself. But given the nature of the cuts, which eliminate some of the final revisions he made for the first edition, it seems more plausible that they were made by an editorial assistant. Finally, none of variant readings in the British edition of the collected plays were considered for emendation. These, too, appear to be non-authorial as a few are misreadings introduced by English compositors and the majority are changes in accidentals that resulted from house-styling done to make the text conform to British practices in punctuation and spelling.

### IV. Record of Prior Publication of Plays

Listed below are the plays published during Dreiser's lifetime.

A. In Periodicals:
The Girl in the Coffin, *Smart Set* 41 (October 1913): 127-40.
The Blue Sphere, *Smart Set* 44 (December 1914): 245-52.
Laughing Gas, *Smart Set* 45 (February 1915): 85-94.
In the Dark, *Smart Set* 45 (January 1915): 412-25.
The Spring Recital, *Little Review* 2 (December 1915): 28-35.
The Light in the Window, *International* 10 (January 1916): 6-8, 32.
The Dream, *Seven Arts* 2 (July 1917): 319-33.

B. In Books:
*Plays of the Natural and Supernatural*. New York: John Lane, 1916.
Contents:  The Girl in the Coffin.
The Blue Sphere
Laughing Gas
In the Dark
The Spring Recital
The Light in the Window
"Old Ragpicker"

            Later Printings:  London: John Lane, 1916
                              New York: Dodd, Mead, 1922.
                              New York: Boni and Liveright, 1926.

*The Hand of the Potter.* New York: Boni and Liveright, 1918 (Released in 1919).
            Later Printing:   New York: Boni and Liveright, 1919.

*Hey Rub-A-Dub-Dub.* New York: Boni and Liveright, 1920.
            Contents:  The Dream
                       Phantasmagoria
                       The Court of Progress
            Later Printing:   London: Constable, 1931.

*The Hand of the Potter.* Rev. ed. New York: Boni and Liveright, 1927.

*Plays, Natural and Supernatural.* London: Constable, 1930.
            Contents:  The Girl in the Coffin.
                       The Blue Sphere
                       Laughing Gas
                       In the Dark
                       The Spring Recital
                       The Light in the Window
                       "Old Ragpicker"
                       Phantasmagoria
                       The Court of Progress
                       The Dream
                       The Hand of the Potter

# EMENDATIONS IN THE COPY-TEXTS

Presented below is the record of emendations made in the copy-texts, with the exception of those that have been regularized, to produce this Whitston edition. Typographical inconsistencies among the texts in matters of layout and signaling scene changes and dialogue cues have been regularized. Dreiser and his typists did not always consistently capitalize characters' names in the manuscripts and typescripts, nor did the compositors and proofreaders catch the inconsistencies when setting the plays in type. We have regularized the presentation of characters' names in capitals without recording each instance in the table of emendations. Similarly, punctuation of dialogue cues also differs among the copy-texts, with some cues ending variously with periods, colons, or no punctuation at all. We have therefore also regularized terminal punctuation of dialogue cues to end with a period without recording each emendation. For the following words, Dreiser's manuscript spelling has been adopted throughout without recording each emendation: *centre, tonight, tomorrow, today, goodbye, theatre, odour, color, smoothes, aeon, ice cream.*

Under a heading for each of the plays is a table listing the emendations made in the copy-text and textual notes providing explanations for some of the editorial decisions to emend or not to emend. Each entry begins with a page-line reference, followed by the emended reading with the source of the reading in parentheses to the left of the bracket. The rejected copy-text reading is presented after the bracket. An asterisk identifies a textual note, which offers further explanation. For example:

*2.16 *majolica* (MS) ] *highly decorated*

This entry indicates that on page 2, line 16 of this edition, the reading "*majolica*" has been adopted from Dreiser's manuscript; the book printing's "*highly decorated*" has been rejected; and an accompanying textual note offers additional explanation.

The sigla below designate the source for each emendation:

For the one-act plays:
 ed = the editors of this edition
 MS = the holograph MS
 HR = *Hey Rub-A-Dub-Dub*

For *The Hand of the Potter*:
 ed = the editors of this edition
 MS = the holograph MS
 TS = the typescript of IV.2 made of the holograph
 PP1 = the first page proofs
 A1 = the first American edition

1. *The Girl in the Coffin*

Copy-text: *Plays of the Natural and Supernatural*

| | |
|---|---|
| 2.15 | "mahogany" (MS) ] mahogany |
| *2.16 | majolica (MS) ] highly decorated |
| 3.11 | Where'd (MS) ] Where did |
| 4.9 | an' (MS) ] and |
| 4.10 | an' (MS) ] and |
| 4.32 | no loom (MS) ] a loom |
| 4.39 | an' (MS) ] and |
| 4.39-40 | no right (MS) ] a right |
| 5.8 | knowed (MS) ] knew |
| 5.9 | o' (MS) ] of |
| 5.9-10 | a holdin' (MS) ] holdin' |
| 5.10 | an' (MS) ] and |
| 5.12 | to where (MS) ] where |
| 5.18 | nobuddy (MS) ] nobody |
| 5.19-20 | she . . . door (ed) ] She . . . door. |
| 5.22 | nobuddy (MS) ] nobody |
| 5.36 | to the (MS) ] at the |
| 6.5 | o' (MS) ] of |
| 7.10 | an' (MS) ] and |
| 7.19 | tuck (MS) ] took |
| 8.10 | an' (MS) ] and |
| 8.12 | an' (MS) ] and |

| | |
|---|---|
| 9.27 | he . . . voice (ed) ] He . . . voice. |
| 11.24 | seen to take (ed) ] seen take |
| 12.13 | mornin', (ed) ] mornin' |
| 13.21-22 | straightening . . . him (ed) ] Straightening . . . him. |
| 19.38 | you, (ed) ] you |
| 22.5 | restaurants, (ed) ] restaurants |

**Textual Notes**

| | |
|---|---|
| 2.16 | *majolica*   Dreiser's specific reference to majolica pottery was replaced in both printings by the more general "highly decorated." Since his typist likely did not understand the term when transcribing the MS, we have restored Dreiser's original intent. |
| 24.27 | **She said I was to give you this.**   In the 1926 Boni & Liveright printing of *Plays of the Natural and Supernatural,* some copies contain a variant reading of the last speech: "She said I was to give you this. She said I was to say that she loved you and that it was all right." Since we do not know the authority for this revision, we have chosen not to include it in this edition. |

## 2. The Blue Sphere

Copy-text: *Plays of the Natural and Supernatural*

| | |
|---|---|
| *25.11 | PETERSON (ed) ] PETERSEN |
| 26.12-13 | mustache (MS) ] moustache |
| 26.21 | Ah, (MS) ] Ah |
| *26.22 | it (MS) ] he |
| 26.23 | it (MS) ] he |
| 29.20 | him. To (ed) ] him. ] ¶ [To |
| 29.21 | greeting.] (ed) ] greeting]: |
| *30.4 | smoky (MS) ] sinewy |
| *30.10-11 | shoveling . . . below (MS) ] shoveling |
| 30.21-22 | eyes. DELAVAN (ed) ] eyes.] ¶ [He |
| 31.14 | He hands (MS) ] hands |
| 31.22 | it (MS) ] him |
| 32.26 | don't (MS) ] doesn't |
| 32.34 | Ellsworth (ed) ] Ellworth |
| 33.3 | understand— (MS) ] understand. |
| 33.16 | MRS. DELAVAN (ed) ] HIS MOTHER |
| 34.25 | it. (ed) ] it! |
| 36.1 | 'em (MS) ] them |
| *36.32 | I (MS) ] we |

**Textual Notes**

25.11      PETERSON    Both the *Smart Set* and book printings spell the fireman's name as "Petersen." We have retained Dreiser's MS spelling of the name.

26.22      **that it was born!**    Both printings substituted the pronoun "he" for Dreiser's MS "it" to refer to the MONSTROSITY. Since Dreiser clearly wished to depersonalize the deformed child by referring to him as "it" elsewhere in the play, we have retained the MS term here and at 26.23 and 31.22.

27.1      THE SHADOW    In the MS Dreiser originally termed the ghostly entity "*The White Lady*," which has been crossed out in all but one place (28.22) and "The Shadow" substituted by another hand, probably Kirah Markham's. All printings of *The Blue Sphere* adopt "The Shadow." The same hand that inserted "*The Shadow*" also added the phrase, "*a gay, girlish figure*," which was transcribed as "*a soft, girlish figure*" in the *Smart Set* and book printings of the play. The MS shows numerous similar insertions and sophistications in the same hand. Because Dreiser allowed these revisions to stand in subsequent printings, they have been retained in this edition too.

30.4      *smoky*    Dreiser's typist apparently misread his handwriting, typing "*sinewy*" instead of "*smoky*." "*Sinewy*" appears in both printings.

30.10-11      *shoveling . . . below*    In the MS, Dreiser had inserted a phrase after "*the fireman*," crossed it out, and then inserted another. Dreiser's typist apparently could decipher only "*stopping in his shoveling*" and simply omitted the rest. We have restored all of Dreiser's revision.

36.32      **until I was right on**    In the MS Dreiser ascribed responsibility for the train's striking the monstrosity to Galloway, who exclaims, "I didn't see it until I was right on." In the *Smart Set* printing, the pronoun "I" becomes "it," thereby changing the meaning of the sentence; and in the book printing the pronoun is changed to "we," further distorting Dreiser's original meaning.

## 3. *Laughing Gas*

Copy-text: *Plays of the Natural and Supernatural*

38.13      *Michael Slade Memorial Hospital* (MS) ] *Michael Slade Hospital*

39.2      *Michael Slade Memorial Hospital* (MS) ] *Michael Slade Hospital*

39.11      *anesthetist;* (ed) ] *anesthetist,*

| | |
|---|---|
| 40.5 | gifts, (MS) ] gifts |
| *40.11 | cone (MS) ] cap |
| *40.12 | DRYDEN (ed) ] THE ANESTHETIST |
| 42.1 | VATABEEL'S (ed) ] VATABEEL S |
| 48.29 | hands. To himself.] (ed) ] hands; to himself]: |
| 49.14 | cone (ed) ] cap |
| *50.12 | God (MS) ] Gad |
| 51.6 | No (ed) ] no |
| *51.17 | My God! (MS) ] Oh, no!! |
| *53.4 | an arm (MS) ] one arm |

**Textual Notes**

40.11  *cone*  Dreiser originally inscribed "*breathing cap*" in the MS and then subsequently crossed out "*cap*" and wrote "*cone*." Elsewhere in the MS Dreiser repeated the revision, but his typist was inconsistent in transcription. Both the *Smart Set* and book printings print "*cap*" twice and "*cone*" thrice; we have emended the text to "*cone*" throughout.

40.12  **DRYDEN**  In the MS the character of Dryden was originally named simply "The Anesthetist." During the revision process, Dreiser gave him a name, but the MS bears only three instances of this revision. Both the *Smart Set* and book printings failed to carry through the revision consistently. We have silently regularized the character's name in this edition.

50.12  **God, yes!**  The vowel in the MS spelling has been inscribed twice: first as an "a" and then, with more pressure, as "o." Whether for reasons of propriety or ambiguity, Dreiser's typist apparently transcribed the word as "Gad," which both the *Smart Set* and book printings adopted. We have retained Dreiser's apparent intention in this edition.

51.17  **My God!**  Both the MS and *Smart Set* versions include this phrase, replaced in the book printing by the more genteel "Oh, no!!" To be consistent with Dreiser's intent (in 50.12 and one other instance, when Vatabeel remarks, "Great God!" in a speech added to the book printing, 49.21), we have rejected "Oh, no!!" as non-authoritative.

53.4  *an arm*  Dreiser originally wrote "*an*" in the ms, but a typist misread his handwriting as "*on*," and the error remained in the *Smart Set* printing as "on arm." The error was corrected to "*one arm*" in the book printing, but we have restored Dreiser's original intent in this edition.

## 4. In the Dark

Copy-text: *Plays of the Natural and Supernatural*

| | |
|---|---|
| *55.9 | SYPHAX (ed) ] SYFAX |
| *55.16 | THE GHOST WITH RED EYES (ed) ] THE GHOST WITH THE RED EYES |
| 56.13 | [*Subsiding* (ed) ] [*subsiding* |
| 57.6 | life (MS) ] Life |
| *57.19 | WOITEZEK (ed) ] JACOB WOITEZEK |
| 58.24 | STEPHANIK (ed) ] THE SHOE-DEALER |
| 59.1 | STEPHANIK (ed) ] THE SHOE-DEALER |
| 59.21-22 | feel creepy (MS) ] creepy |
| 59.27 | STEPHANIK (ed) ] GEORGE STEPHANIK |
| 60.7 | meanta (MS) ] meant |
| 60.10 | It (ed) ] He |
| 61.7 | *the while* (MS) ] *while* |
| 62.29 | somethin' (MS) ] something |
| *63.17 | I will pretend not to know. (MS) ] Me make me don't know. |
| 63.25-26 | da Anglais (MS) ] the English |
| 63.33 | Eleventh (ed) ] 11th |
| 64.28 | THE FRUIT DEALER (ed) ] FRUIT DEALER |
| 64.30 | hoythen (MS) ] heathen |
| 65.3 | scut (MS) ] hound |
| 65.10 | THE OLD WOMAN (ed) ] OLD WOMAN |
| 65.11 | yez (MS) ] ye |
| 65.13 | THE OLD WOMAN (ed) ] OLD WOMAN |
| 66.31 | intah (MS) ] into |
| 67.3 | iv (MS) ] of |
| 67.12 | Whadjah kill 'im (MS) ] Whadyu kill im |
| 67.16-17 | *mustache* (MS) ] *moustache* |
| *68.5 | *Officer-surgeons* (ed) ] *Officers, surgeons,* |
| *68.6 | *representation of* THE WRAITH *follows* (MS) ] *representation follows* |

**Textual Notes**

55.9     **SYPHAX**   The *Smart Set* and book printings spell the officer's name as "Syfax." We have retained Dreiser's MS spelling throughout.

55.16     **THE GHOST WITH RED EYES**   Dreiser was inconsistent in his naming of the ghostly entity in the MS, at times referring to it as the "RED-EYED GHOST," "THE RED-EYED DEMON," and "THE EVIL SPIRIT WITH RED EYES," variations that were preserved in the *Smart Set* printing of the play. For the book printing, he began to revise these variations to read "THE GHOST WITH RED EYES," but did not carry them through consistently. We have therefore

|       |                                                                                                                                                                                                                                                                                                                                                                           |
| ----- | ------------------------------------------------------------------------------------------------------------------------------------------------------------------------------------------------------------------------------------------------------------------------------------------------------------------------------------------------------------------------- |
| 57.19 | **WOITEZEK** The copy-text inconsistently signals Woitezek's speeches, sometimes as "WOITEZEK" and sometimes as "JACOB WOITEZEK." Elsewhere, the copy-text also inconsistently signals John Repiso's speeches as "REPISO" and "JOHN REPISO." We have regularized dialogue cues to follow the convention of referring to a character by his or her last name. |
| 61.17 | **OFFICER BOCOCK** Of the various police officers, Dreiser at first named only Officer Brady, referring to the others as the "First," "Second," and "Third" Officers. As he revised the MS, he gave them the names "Bocock," "Dingwalter," and "Train" but did not completely carry through the revision. The *Smart Set* printing follows the MS's inconsistency. The book printing regularized the renaming of these officers but did not attempt to give the other unnamed officers names. |
| 63.17 | **I will pretend not to know.** Both the MS and *Smart Set* printing follow this phrasing, which was replaced in the book printing with "Me make me don't know," an unsuccessful attempt to render Repiso's line as dialect. Since the line doesn't follow Dreiser's usual dialect practice, we have rejected it as unauthorized. |
| 68.5  | *Officer-surgeons* The MS reads, "Officer surgeons gather up the remains." Both the *Smart Set* and book printings distort Dreiser's MS by misreading Dreiser's compound noun and adding unnecessary commas, resulting in grammatical confusion: "*Officers, surgeons, gather up the remains.*" To resolve the apparent ambiguity, we have hyphenated his phrasing. |
| 68.5  | *representation of* **THE WRAITH** *follows* Both the *Smart Set* and book printings leave out Dreiser's MS "of the wraith," which renders the sentence's meaning unclear. |

## 5. *The Spring Recital*

Copy-text: *Plays of the Natural and Supernatural*

|         |                                   |
| ------- | --------------------------------- |
| 69.8    | FAUN (ed) ] FAWN                  |
| 70.19   | Didja (MS) ] Did you              |
| 71.13   | to playin' to (MS) ] playing to   |
| 73.6    | THE BOY (ed) ] THE BOY LOVER      |
| *74.5   | THE BUM (ed) ] THE GHOST          |
| 74.8    | sweetheart (ed) ] Sweetheart      |
| *76.29  | *flower tones* (MS) ] *tones*     |
| 76.30   | Still, (MS) ] Still               |
| 78.6    | Ah, (MS) ] Ah                     |

| | |
|---|---|
| 80.7 | THE BOY (ed) ] THE BOY LOVER |
| 80.24 | *Egyptians* (ed) ] EGYPTIANS |
| 80.29 | THE BOY (ed) ] THE BOY LOVER |
| 81.10 | THE CAT (ed) ] THE CHURCH CAT |

**Textual Notes**

71.34  **play a Chopin Nocturne or something of Grieg**  In the MS Dreiser left blank the names of all composers and song titles, relying on Kirah Markham to fill in appropriate names. As Markham explained in a letter to W.D. Swanberg, 26 Oct. 1963: "I did the designing of 'Plays of the Natural and Supernatural.' I even wrote the songs for one of them, something Mencken suspected instantly when he reviewed them for the Smart Set" (Dreiser Collection).

73.14  **Arch of church or arch of trees**  Markham revised Dreiser's song lyrics of the Six Hama-Dryads, and her revision appeared in both the *Little Review* and book printings of the play. Dreiser's original MS version of the song reads as follows:

>Ever, ever new delight
>Ever moonlight and the tree
>Silver rhythms flowing bright
>Perfumed rhythms flowing free.
>
>Out of lilac, out of oak,
>Hard by asphodel and rose
>Where the purpled rhythm broke—
>Where the purpled rhythm blows.
>
>Weaving, turning high and low,
>Where the rose toned rhythm fall
>Where the plangent metres call
>Where the dew wet odours flow
>Round and round and round we go.

Elsewhere (79.22), Dreiser simply left the lyrics blank, to be supplied later by Markham.

74.5  **THE BUM**  Dreiser greatly expanded this character's role during revision. In the MS, the Bum (called the Ghost) has only one line. As he developed the character, Dreiser apparently dropped the name "Ghost," replacing it with "Bum." Neither Dreiser nor his typist, however, caught the change of name when preparing printer's copy. We have therefore emended the name to accord with Dreiser's apparent intent.

76.29  ***flower tones***  Dreiser's typist neglected to transcribe the adjective *"flower."* When the play was published in the *Little Review*, the phrase appeared as *"dark notes and tones."*

## 6. *The Light in the Window*

Copy-text: *Plays of the Natural and Supernatural*

| | | |
|---|---|---|
| | 83.33 | Colonel (ed) ] Col. |
| | 84.5 | *children.*] (ed) *children*]. |
| *84.5-6 | | "What . . . spend." (MS) ] What . . . spend. |
| | 85.10 | KINDELLING (ed) ] TRURO |
| | 85.25 | KINDELLING (ed) ] TRURO KINDELLING |
| | 85.31 | God! (MS) ] Gad! |
| | 86.6 | God! (MS) ] Gad! |
| | 86.24 | LAURA (ed) ] MRS. KINDELLING |
| | 86.32 | LAURA (ed) ] MRS. KINDELLING |
| | 87.7 | LAURA (ed) ] MRS. KINDELLING |
| | 87.12 | LAURA (ed) ] MRS. KINDELLING |
| *87.14 | | Mother! Mother! (MS) ] (not present) |
| | 87.24 | suing (MS) ] sueing |
| | 88.11 | Why, no, (MS) ] Why no, |
| | 89.13 | *Surveying* (ed) ] *The butler, surveying* |
| | 90.5 | can't (MS) ] don't |
| *90.32 | | *pretends* (MS) ] *begins* |
| | 91.30-31 | at the time (ed) ] at this time |
| | 92.25-26 | Burton, [*to himself*] (ed) ] Burton [*to himself*], |
| | 93.8 | I'm (MS) ] I've |
| | 93.15 | *up the street* (MS) ] *up street* |
| *93.16 | | [*Not noting the exit.*] (MS) ] [*Noting the exit.*] |

**Textual notes**

| | |
|---|---|
| 84.5-6 | **"What . . . spend."** Unlike other speeches in the play, Dreiser surrounded this line in quotation marks, suggesting he intended it as a proverb. His typist dropped the punctuation marks in her transcription. |
| 87.14 | **Mother! Mother!** Dreiser had revised the passage, and his typist apparently missed these words. |
| 90.32 | **pretends to cry** In the MS Dreiser wrote, "pretends to be crying." Both the *International* and book versions read, "*begins to cry.*" Since in her next speech Laura "*begins sobbing dramatically,*" we have restored the MS reading to accord with Dreiser's initial depiction of Laura's manipulation of Truro. |
| 93.16 | **[*Not noting the exit.*]** The word "*Not*" appears in both the MS and the *International* printing of the play. Since the omission of the word distorts the meaning of the scene, we have restored Dreiser's original intent. |

# Emendations in the Copy-Texts 299

## 7. "Old Ragpicker"

Copy-text: *Plays of the Natural and Supernatural*

| | |
|---|---|
| 96.20 | mornin' (MS) ] morning |
| 96.28 | shenanigans (ed) ] Shinannigans |
| 96.31 | live (MS) ] lives |
| 97.4 | jackrabbit (MS) ] Jackrabbit |
| 97.4 | kin (MS) ] can |
| 97.9 | a (MS) ] 'a' |
| *97.11 | Whaddy yah (ed) ] Whadyyah |
| 97.16 | a (MS) ] ha' |
| 97.20 | o' (MS) ] of |
| 97.22 | kin (MS) ] can |
| 97.29 | 'im (MS) ] him |
| 97.32-34 | He give . . . Christmas! (MS) ] He give old Bealstock when he had the beat here last Christmas fifteen dollars! |
| *98.15 | stoogin' (MS) ] stagein' |
| 98.18 | 'im (ed) ] him |
| 98.19 | 'im (MS) ] him |
| 98.27 | t' give 'im (MS) ] to give him |
| 98.31 | all right (MS) ] alright |
| 99.20 | they're (MS) ] they are |
| 100.1 | THE OLD WOMAN (ed) ] OLD WOMAN |
| *100.10-11 | Now I'm . . . was. (MS) ] Now I'm a manufacturer like I was. |
| 100.30 | de (MS) ] the |
| 100.32 | THE OLD WOMAN (ed) ] OLD WOMAN |
| 101.5 | Madame (ed) ] madame |
| 103.4-5 | *He . . . ear.*] (ed) ] *he . . . ear*]. |
| 103.16 | Sure, (ed) ] Sure |
| 103.41 | it's marching, the boys you know, (MS) ] it's marching the boys you go, |
| 104.19 | an' (MS) ] and |
| 104.20 | force. To (MS) ] force . . . to |
| 104.26-27 | "OLD RAGPICKER" (ed) ] the RAGPICKER |
| 104.29 | Whaddy yuh (ed) ] Whaddyuh |
| 105.13 | what we want. (MS) ] it? |
| 106.5 | to care (MS) ] cold |
| 106.12 | school—all (ed) ] school,—all |
| 106.29 | Sure, (ed) ] Sure |
| 107.15-16 | Whaddy yah (ed) ] Whaddyah |
| 107.26 | Whaddy yah (ed) ] Whaddyah |
| 108.3 | un'erstan' (ed) ] unerstan' |

**Textual notes**

97.11   **Whaddyah**   The book version of the play incorporates several dialectical spellings for "what do you": "whaddy

|  |  |
|---|---|
| 98.15 | yah," "whaddy yuh," "whaddyah," and "whaddyuh." The MS originally spelled the term "whaddy y'." We have emended all one-word versions to accord with Dreiser's apparent preference for two words, which appears to be based on pronunciation.
**stoogin'** Dreiser wrote "stogin'" in the MS, a misspelling for the slang term "stooging," which became transcribed as "stagein'" in the published version. |
| 100.10-11 | **Now I'm . . . I was.** Dreiser probably intended Old Ragpicker's assertion to be a sign of his mental illness, but because the book printing omitted "Now I'm a gentleman again," the sentence appears to have an omitted "not," as in "I'm not a manufacturer like I was." We have therefore restored the omitted MS sentence to accord with Dreiser's original emphasis on Old Ragpicker's disconnect from the reality of his impoverishment. |

## 8. *The Dream*

Copy-text: Revised typescript for *Hey Rub-A-Dub-Dub* printing

| | |
|---|---|
| 109.2-8 | CHARACTERS . . . Thunder (ed) ] (not present) |
| 110.3 | *11:15* (ed) ] *11.15* |
| 113.18 | *street.*] (ed) ] *street*] |
| 114.1-2 | again. [*Begins to write.*] (ed) ] again [*begins to write*] |
| 114.7 | Counsellor. (ed) ] Counsellor, |
| 114.18-20 | [*He . . . out.*] (ed) ] [*he . . . out*] |
| 114.20 | do believe. (HR) ] believe. |
| 114.21 | *rest.*] There, it's thundering already. (HR) ] *rest.*] |
| 115.20 | *the other* (HR) ] *another* |
| *115.24 | SYPHERS (ed) ] THE PROFESSOR |
| 116.35 | but, (HR) ] but |
| 117.4 | *him:* (ed) ] *him;* |
| 117.9 | *shakos* (HR) ] *shakes* |
| 117.11 | *shakos* (HR) ] *shakes* |
| 117.13 | there. (HR) ] here. |
| 117.14 | soldiers. (HR) ] soldier. |
| 117.30 | [*He* (ed) ] [*he* |
| 118.9 | Once (ed) ] Once, |
| 118.10 | *in.*] (ed) ] *in*] |
| 118.25 | soldiers (HR) ] soldier |
| 120.1 | *door.*] (ed) ] *door*] |
| 120.20 | *blank* (HR) ] *black* |

**Textual Notes**

| | |
|---|---|
| 115.24 | **SYPHERS** Two holograph drafts of *The Dream* are extant. In the earliest draft, Syphers is referred to simply as "The |

Professor." When Dreiser revised the play, he changed the character's name to Syphers but only carried through the revision for the first few leaves, and the inconsistency was never caught in the subsequent printings of the play. We have carried through the revision without recording each instance in the table of emendations.

## 9. *Phantasmagoria*

Copy-text: Dreiser's revised typescript

| | |
|---|---|
| 123.5 | *all-in-all* (HR) ] *all in all* |
| 123.7 | separateness and individuality (HR) ] individuality |
| 123.27 | *spinning, changing* (HR) ] *spinning* |
| 124.2-3 | leers and . . . time. (HR) ] leers sinisterly. |
| 125.5 | strength! I . . . power! (HR) ] strength! |
| 125.6-7 | Follow me! Follow me! (HR) ] Do you follow me! |
| 125.7 | destruction! (HR) ] destruction among these others! |
| 125.25-26 | aside . . . And (HR) ] aside with me. What have we in common with these? Are we not his thoughts also—and |
| 125.28-29 | his . . . again! (HR) ] his thoughts also, but not of them. No, no, no! Not of them—no! He should sleep again. |
| 126.30 | I have made me this! (HR) ] I have made it! |
| 127.18 | *swirl,* (HR) ] *swirl* |
| 127.21 | *fancy.* (HR) ] *fancy. In charge of the legions of darkness,* AMBITION. |
| 128.12 | dreams, (ed) ] dreams |
| 128.15 | Lord, (HR) ] Lord |
| 128.17-18 | Sweet am I! But . . . Dream on. (HR) ] Sleep no more! |
| 128.19 | so! (HR) ] so, Lord! |
| *128.23-24 | but nothing—nothing! (HR) ] but—nothing—nothing! |
| 128.26-27 | Think not so! A dear dream! (HR) ] A dear dream! |
| 128.30 | it all is (HR) ] it is |
| 129.6-7 | Kind and . . . ever! (HR) ] So! So! It is best ever! Kind and tender thoughts! |
| 129.13 | Beauty (HR) ] beauty |
| 129.16-17 | even Beauty, Lord! What is Beauty (HR) ] even she, Lord, even she! If thou wilt, what is beauty |
| *129.26 | shadow! (HR) ] his shadow! |
| *129.27 | pale shadows (HR) ] pale, bright shadows |
| 129.28-29 | On Power! Come, Hate! (HR) ] Come, Hate! |
| 129.30 | with me! (HR) ] with me! [*He clanks his armour.*] |
| 129.34 | Beauty (HR) ] beauty |
| 130.22 | stay! (HR) ] stay! I am that I am. Oh, Beauty! Beauty! |
| 130.29-31 | his hands.] . . . Hail! Hail! (HR) ] his hands.] ¶ CHERUBIM AND SERAPHIM Hail! Hail! ¶ A CLOUD OF SERAPHIM [*Fluttering nigh.*] He dreams of beauty! We will not die! |

302    Collected Plays of Theodore Dreiser

| | |
|---|---|
| 130.32-33 | Beauty! We will not die! Hail! Hail! (HR) ] beauty! We will not die! |
| 131.1 | hovering, (HR) ] hovering |
| 132.31 | left (HR) ] Left |
| 133.1 | fury! (HR) ] Fury! |
| 133.3 | Woe! Tears—bring (HR) ] Repining! Woe! Bring |
| 133.9 | Darkness (HR) ] darkness |
| 133.11 | pity (HR) ] glory |
| 133.35-36 | his mood. [To DESPAIR.] (HR) ] his mood. |
| 134.5 | think (ed) ] thinks |
| 134.12-14 | behind! He . . . rumble.] (HR) ] behind! To harry, slay, lay waste! It is as it is! He knows thee not! [The destroying legions rumble.] He is for strife, strength, conflict! |
| *134.23-24 | wraith! [LOVE fades to a point.] (ed) ] wraith! |
| 134.26 | REASON steps (HR) ] It steps |
| 134.29-30 | He thinks not on thee—but on me! (HR) ] He thinks on me! |
| 134.30 | HOPE pales (HR) ] It pales |
| 134.34 | Beauty! His first thought! (HR) ] beauty! |
| 135.6 | Thought—Pain—with (HR) ] Pain—with |
| *135.22-23 | he be, even though he sleep, (HR) ] he be, |
| 135.23 | thought! (HR) ] thought. |
| 136.2 | entering in. (HR) ] entering. |
| 136.5 | entering in. (HR) ] entering. |
| 136.8 | [Returning and entering in.] (HR) ] [Returning.] |
| 136.22 | Oh, ho, ho, ho! (HR) ] Oh, ho, ho! |
| 136.25 | Writhing and fading (HR) ] Writhing fading |
| 136.30 | He (HR) ] It |
| 137.3 | He (HR) ] It |
| 137.6 | He (HR) ] It |
| 137.14 | heavily. (HR) ] heavily, the illusion of the halls of horror fades and disappears. |

Textual Notes

| | |
|---|---|
| 128.23-24 | **but nothing—nothing!**   In the typescript Dreiser blotted out the word immediately following "nothing," thus: "but [blotted]—nothing—nothing!" We have therefore carried through his probable intent by deleting the first dash. |
| 129.26 | **shadow!**   The typescript reads "his shadow!" The nearest antecedent is "Beauty," which is female, so the pronoun must refer to the Lord of the Universe. Someone, presumably Dreiser, deleted the pronoun in the printed version to clarify the ambiguity. |
| 129.27 | **pale shadows**   The typescript's "pale, bright shadows" is an apparent oxymoron, so we have followed the book version's deletion of "bright." |
| 134.23-24 | **wraith! [LOVE fades to a point.]**   The book printing adds the line, "She fades to a point." Since the book printing |

Emendations in the Copy-Texts 303

has replaced the pronoun "IT" with "REASON" and "HOPE" at 134.26 and 134.30, we have carried through Dreiser's intent by replacing "she" with "LOVE."

135.22-23  **he be, even though he sleep,**  The typescript reads, "Mad though he be, even now I feel his thought." The book printing revised the line to read, "Mad though he be, even though he sleep, now I feel his thought." Since the deletion of the "even" before "now" alters the meaning of the sentence, we have restored Dreiser's probable intent.

135.29  **AMBITION**  In Dreiser's typescript, AMBITION addresses the six Powers of Darkness as they return to the LORD'S brain, repeating his similar action of addressing them as they fly out from the LORD's brain earlier in the scene (132.11) and again at 136.20. In the book printing, it is the LORD who addresses each returning Power, creating a doubled speech at 136.9, where both the LORD and AMBITION utter "'Tis well!" We have retained Dreiser's copy-text reading, from 135.29-136.10, since it avoids the coherence problems created by the HR revision.

## 10. *The Court of Progress*

Copy-text: *Hey Rub-A-Dub-Dub* printing

| | |
|---|---|
| 139.2 | PODUNKUS, (ed) ] PUDUNKUS: |
| 139.4 | HASH, (ed) ] HASH: |
| 140.31 | *Plaster* (ed) ] *plaster* |
| 141.9 | *people.* (ed) ] *people,* |
| *141.27 | *papier-mâché* (ed) ] *papier-maché* |
| 143.24 | *catechize* (ed) ] *catechise* |
| 143.26 | *etc.,* (ed) ] *etc.* |
| 144.5 | *specimens* (ed) ] *speciments* |
| 149.39 | NOXUS PODUNKUS (ed) ] PODUNKUS |
| 150.21-22 | Bonehead V (ed) ] Bonehead V. |
| 150.23 | NOXUS PODUNKUS (ed) ] *Podunkus* |
| 150.35 | —[*Aside:* (ed) ] [*aside* |
| 152.20 | question. [*He* (ed) ] question [*he* |
| 153.5 | *each hand him* (ed) ] *hand him each* |
| 153.32 | NOXUS PODUNKUS (ed) ] PODUNKUS |
| 155.6 | *jew's harps* (ed) ] *jew'sharps* |
| 155.24 | *flip-flops* (ed) ] *flip-flaps* |
| 155.25 | *thunderous* (ed) ] *thunders of* |
| 157.13 | [*Jigging.*] (ed) ] [*Jigging*] |
| 158.9-10 | [*He is fed.*] (ed) ] [*he is fed*]. |
| 161.33 | [*He* (ed) ] [*he* |
| 161.37 | NOXUS PODUNKUS (ed) ] PODUNKUS |
| 162.5 | *Bonehead V* (ed) ] *Bonehead V.* |
| 162.11 | How?" (ed) ] How? |

304         Collected Plays of Theodore Dreiser

| | |
|---|---|
| 162.36 | NOXUS PODUNKUS (ed) ] PODUNKUS |
| 163.5 | soufflé.] (ed) ] souffle. |
| 163.30 | NOXUS PODUNKUS (ed) ] NOXUS |
| 166.2-3 | you. [The Moonshees stir.] (ed) ] you [the moonshees stir]. |
| 166.19 | exhaustion] (ed) ] exhaustion.] |
| 166.28 | Anti-White-Slavers (ed) ] Anti-White Slavers |
| 167.15 | Anti-White-Slavers (ed) ] Anti-White Slavers |
| 171.2 | calmed.] (ed) ] calmed. |

**Textual Notes**

| | |
|---|---|
| 141.27 | *papier-mâché*   Neither the typescript nor the *Hey Rub-A-Dub-Dub* printing follow the convention of assigning diacritical marks to foreign words. We have regularized the spelling of "papier-mâché" and "soufflé" without recording each instance in this table of emendations. |

## 11. *The Voice*

Copy-text: Dreiser's unpublished holograph MS

| | |
|---|---|
| 172.2-5 | CHARACTERS ... lover. (ed) ] (not present) |
| 173.3 | right, (ed) ] right |
| *173.3 | French (ed) ] french |
| 173.10 | hands, (ed) ] hands |
| 173.16 | me (ed) ] me, |
| 174.11 | phlegmatic, (ed) ] phlegmatic |
| 174.13 | soon? (ed) ] soon. |
| *174.14 | sweetheart (ed) ] Sweetheart |
| 174.14-15 | What are you making? (ed) ] What making? |
| 174.20 | work, (ed) ] work |
| 174.27 | come? (ed) ] come. |
| 175.8 | tired, (ed) ] tired |
| 175.12 | sweet (ed) ] Sweet |
| 175.19 | girl? (ed) ] girl. |
| 175.24 | it? (ed) ] it. |
| 176.12 | here? (ed) ] here. |
| 176.13 | bygones? (ed) ] bygones. |
| 176.15 | me? (ed) ] me. |
| 176.31 | mood, wasn't it? (ed) ] mood wasn't it. |
| 176.32 | sweetheart, (ed) ] sweet heart |
| 177.1 | you? (ed) ] you. |
| 177.25 | matter? (ed) ] matter. |
| 178.1 | besides, (ed) ] besides |
| 178.9 | see? (ed) ] see. |
| 178.20 | neck? (ed) ] neck. |
| 178.26 | Oh, (ed) ] Oh |
| 179.3 | foolishly! (ed) ] foolishly. |

# Emendations in the Copy-Texts 305

| | |
|---|---|
| 179.11 | me, (ed) me |
| 179.21 | true? (ed) ] true. |
| 179.22 | do you (ed) ] will you |
| 179.27-28 | Why do you come . . . form? (ed) ] Why will come . . . form. |
| 180.6 | body— (ed) ] body |
| 180.9 | flame, it is true, (ed) ] flame it is true |
| 180.19 | Edith! (ed) ] Edith. |
| 180.26 | Yes, (ed) ] Yes |
| 181.5 | it, (ed) ] it |
| 181.8 | "Harold" (ed) ] Harold |
| 181.17 | Harold! (ed) ] Harold. |
| 181.19 | see? (ed) ] see. |
| 181.22 | Oh, (ed) ] Oh |
| 181.22 | see? (ed) ] see. |
| 181.25 | all right (ed) ] alright |
| 181.27 | Please, (ed) ] Please |
| *181.29 | . . . (ed) ] (sentence incomplete) |
| 182.14 | can, (ed) ] can |
| 182.15 | see? (ed) ] see. |
| 182.19 | of— (ed) ] of |
| 182.27-28 | *Abelard and Heloise* (ed) ] Abelard and Heloise. |
| 183.1 | *The Story of a Lie* (ed) ] The Story of a Lie |
| 183.3 | poetry? (ed) ] poetry. |
| *183.6 | He opens a book and (ed) ] He opens a and |
| *183.9 | "Ave Atque Vale" (ed) ] "Atque, Atque, Salve" |
| 183.9 | read? (ed) ] read. |
| 183.22 | stop? (ed) ] stop. |
| 184.1 | anything, (ed) ] anything |
| 184.14 | Well, (ed) ] Well |
| 184.15 | Oh, (ed) ] Oh |
| 184.20 | All right, (ed) ] Alright |
| 184.21 | all right (ed) ] alright |
| 184.25 | Harold, (ed) ] Harold |
| 184.29 | Edith (ed) ] Edie |
| 185.10 | Oh, (ed) ] Oh |
| 185.13 | all right (ed) ] alright |
| 185.18-19 | *it, which she does,* (ed) ] *it which she does* |
| 185.27 | Why, (ed) ] Why |
| 186.9 | grieve? (ed) ] grieve. |
| 186.22 | live! (ed) ] live. |
| 186.28 | me? (ed) ] me |
| 187.6 | *turns,* (ed) ] *turns* |

**Textual Notes**

173.3      **French**   Like Dreiser's other holograph MSS, *The Voice* displays occasional spelling errors, slips of the pen, omitted apostrophes, and omitted periods coinciding with the end of a line. We have silently supplied omitted

| | |
|---|---|
| | apostrophes and end-of-line periods, and we have silently corrected obvious misspellings. We have not, however, modernized obsolete or alternative spellings. |
| 174.14 | **sweetheart**   Dreiser's spelling and capitalization of the term is inconsistent in this play, reflecting the differing stages of its composition. The MS follows Dreiser's usual practice of combining portions of earlier drafts with freshly-written leaves. On some pages, the endearment is written as two words and on others as a compound. We have regularized the spelling and capitalization to follow his usual practice of inscribing one lower-cased word. |
| 175.28 | **Lumiphere**   Dreiser's handwriting is difficult to decipher, but Daisy's surname appears to be "Lumiphere." |
| 181.29 | **If that were but the most . . .**   The sentence is incomplete in the MS. It coincides with the end of a leaf, so Dreiser apparently forgot to finish it when he was copying the MS. |
| 183.6 | *He opens a book*   Dreiser originally wrote "She opens it," and then revised the line to read, "He opens "Ave, Atque, Salve." He then crossed out the pronoun "it" and the phrase "Ave, Atque, Salve," inscribed the article "a," but neglected to supply a noun. We have supplied "book" as the most likely noun on the basis of the couple's conversation. |
| 183.9 | **"Ave Atque Vale"**   Dreiser has misremembered the title of the Swinburne poem. Edith is reading the opening stanza. |

## 12. *The Hand of the Potter*

Copy-text: Salesman's dummy for 188.1 to 193.24 and first page proofs for the rest of the play

| | |
|---|---|
| 188.4 | *his wife*  (ed) ] his wife |
| 188.6 | *sons.* (ed) ] sons |
| 188.8 | *trade* (PP1) ] *trade.* |
| *188.9 | *manicuress* (MS) ] *manicure.* |
| 188.10 | *sister* (PP1) ] *sister.* |
| 188.11 | GEORGE (PP1) ] GEROGE |
| 188.16 | *Attorney.* (PP1) ] *Attorney.* ¶ BALCH, *Assistant District Attorney.* |
| *188.17 | JURY. (PP1) ] JURY. ¶ MICHAEL PRESKOVSKY ¶ GEORGE TIMBERLAND [brace] *jurors.* ¶ ALBERT LATSON |
| 189.1 | OF THE POTTER (PP1) ] OF POTTER |
| 189.4 | *in the* (PP1) ] in the |
| 189.27 | *portières* (PP1) ] *portieres* |
| *189.28 | *door which* (MS) ] *door, which* |
| 189.31 | July (PP1) ] August |
| 189.35 | *are* (ed) ] *is* |
| 190.14 | They couldn't stand (PP1) ] *They couldn't stand* |

# Emendations in the Copy-Texts 307

| | |
|---|---|
| 190.24 | somet'ing (PP1) ] something |
| 190.28 | But (MS) ] but |
| 190.28 | t'ings (PP1) ] things |
| 190.30 | vedder (PP1) ] weather |
| *190.34 | New (MS) ] Now |
| *190.37 | talking (PP1) ] talkin' |
| *191.19 | *unloosens* (MS) ] *loosens* |
| *191.29 | *manners* (MS) ] *manner* |
| 192.3 | Rae! Dat (PP1) Rae, that |
| 192.3 | t'ings (PP1) things |
| 192.13 | New York . . . than that? (PP1) ] New York? |
| 192.28 | dat's (PP1) ] that's |
| 193.13 | anudder (PP1) another |
| 193.14 | Nutting (PP1) Nothing |
| *193.30 | Him (MS) ] H'm |
| 194.17 | —[*Pauses* (ed) ] —[*pauses* |
| *198.14 | mouths (MS) ] lips |
| 200.29 | *window* (MS) ] *windows* |
| 201.34 | *Gaily* (MS) ] *Gayly* |
| *202.31 | maybe (MS) ] maybe, |
| *202.40 | *His shoulder* (ed) ] *It* |
| 204.12 | KITTY (ed) ] KITTY NEAFIE |
| 204.23 | KITTY (ed) ] KITTY NEAFIE |
| 204.28 | KITTY (ed) ] KITTY NEAFIE |
| 205.3 | KITTY (ed) ] KITTY NEAFIE |
| 205.20 | *She* (MS) ] *she* |
| *206.21 | while (MS) ] awhile |
| *208.7 | *door and* (MS) *door,* |
| 211.4-5 | *He . . . again.*] (ed) ] *he . . . again*]. |
| 214.23 | ven (MS) ] vet |
| 215.1 | oilcloth (ed) ] oil cloth |
| 215.3 | MASHA.] (ed) ] MASHA. |
| 215.5 | Oilclawt (ed) ] Oil clawt |
| 215.7 | Oilclawt (ed) ] Oil clawt |
| 215.12 | oilcloth (ed) ] oil cloth |
| 216.1 | Nu!— (MS) ] Nu— |
| 216.20 | *trouser* (MS) ] *trousers* |
| *216.26 | awe-struck (ed) ] awe-stricken |
| 217.14 | Go (MS) ] Go, |
| 218.28 | can (MS) ] cen |
| 221.10 | *window sill.* (MS) ] *window sill* |
| 222.13 | GREENBAUM (ed) ] GEORGE GREENBAUM |
| 224.13 | *She stares.*] (ed) ] *she stares*]. |
| 225.32 | understend (ed) ] understand |
| 226.11 | put (MS) ] pull |
| 227.3 | *shuffling* (MS) ] *shuffiing* |
| 228.10 | Berchansky (ed) ] BERCHANSKY |
| 229.13 | she (MS) ] she's |
| 231.11 | *large,* (MS) ] *large* |

| | | |
|---|---|---|
| 231.13 | *The* (MS) ] *he* | |
| 231.15 | *sort* (MS) ] *sort,* | |
| *231.19 | *larger,* (ed) ] *larger* | |
| 231.33 | *is* (MS) ] *are* | |
| *232.13 | some vun (MS) ] some von | |
| 232.17 | heered vunce (MS) ] heered vonce | |
| 232.18 | ich vunce (MS) ] ich vonce | |
| 232.19 | sagt "verloren" (MS) ] saght "veloren" | |
| 232.21 | vunce (MS) ] vonce | |
| 232.22 | dreissig (MS) ] dreisig | |
| 232.22 | vierzig fuess (MS) ] verizig fuess | |
| 232.22-23 | (ich . . . gemeasured) (MS) ] [ich . . . gemeasured] | |
| 232.23 | vuss (MS) ] vus | |
| *232.26 | cuffered (MS) coffered | |
| 232.26 | some vun (MS) ] some von | |
| 232.28 | und she (ed) ] and she | |
| 232.38 | cuffer (MS) coffer | |
| 233.1 | vun (MS) ] von | |
| *233.2 | hab (ed) ] haf | |
| 233.5 | hab (ed) ] hop | |
| 233.7 | hab (MS) ] hop | |
| 233.11 | some vun shoudt (MS) ] some von shoult | |
| 233.12-13 | (she . . . dere) (MS) ] [she . . . dere] | |
| 233.16 | some vun (MS) ] some von | |
| 233.24 | das she (ed) ] dass she | |
| 233.24-25 | uberbekommen (MS) ] uber bekommen | |
| 233.36 | offered. [*He . . . inquiringly.*] (ed) ] offered [*he . . . inquiringly*]. | |
| 234.1 | FOREMAN OF THE JURY (ed) ] FOREMAN | |
| 234.24 | an' (ed) ] and | |
| 235.5-6 | THE FOREMAN OF THE JURY (ed) ] *The foreman* | |
| 235.17 | FOREMAN OF THE JURY (ed) ] FOREMAN | |
| *235.18 | *stirs* (MS) ] *stares* | |
| 235.28 | ask (MS) ] ast | |
| 235.30 | *She . . . weep.*] (ed) ] *she . . . weep*]. | |
| 236.13 | Berchantsky, an' Mrs. (ed) ] Berchantsky an' Mrs. | |
| 236.20-21 | it." [*The jury . . . astonishment.*] (ed) ] it [*the jury . . . astonishment*]. | |
| 236.26 | myself. (MS) ] myself | |
| 237.16 | anyone (MS) ] any one | |
| *238.15 | last saw (MS) ] had last seen | |
| *239.10 | two (ed) ] three | |
| 240.29 | THE CLERK (ed) ] CLERK | |
| 241.23 | anyone (MS) ] any one | |
| 241.27 | months (MS) ] months, | |
| 243.1 | him, whatsoever, (ed) ] him whatsoever | |
| 243.21 | this? [*He illustrates.*] (ed) ] this [*he illustrates*]? | |
| 245.12 | No. (MS) ] No; | |
| 247.8 | manicuress (MS) ] manicure | |

# Emendations in the Copy-Texts 309

| | |
|---|---|
| 247.15 | 22nd  (MS)  ] 22d |
| 251.19 | THE FOREMAN OF THE JURY  (ed)  ] *The foreman* |
| 251.24 | BUSH  (ed)  ] RUFUS BUSH |
| 252.23 | only  (MS)  ] only, |
| 253.19 | testimony. [*The*  (ed)  ] testimony [*the* |
| 254.2 | *Bible.*]  (ed)  ] *Bible.* |
| 254.10 | THE CLERK  (ed)  ] CLERK |
| 254.12 | THE CLERK  (ed)  ] CLERK |
| 255.9 | girls  (MS)  ] girls, |
| 256.9 | anyone  (MS)  ] any one |
| 257.6 | right—(MS)  ] right, |
| 258.24-25 | understend  (ed)  ] understand |
| 258.35 | THE FOREMAN OF THE JURY  (ed)  ] *The foreman* |
| 259.5 | *suggest*  (ed)  ] *suggests* |
| *259.8 | roof copings  (MS)  ] roofs, copings |
| 259.21 | old,  (MS)  ] old |
| 259.29 | *frowsy*  (MS)  ] *frowzy* |
| 261.7 | *pins*  (MS)  ] *puts* |
| 262.5 | *shoulder*  (ed)  *arm* |
| *263.21 | there.  (ed)  ] there? |
| 263.26 | *neck*  (MS)  ] *neck,* |
| 263.34 | look very  (MS)  ] look, very |
| 264.20 | ken't  (MS)  ] kent |
| 265.30 | SOFT,  (MS)  ] SOFT |
| 267.4 | *below,* . . . "HAGAR! HAGAR!"  (A1)  ] *below.* |
| 267.7 | *Silence.*  (A1)  ] *The voice dies away. Silence.* |
| 267.18 | *slams*  (A1)  *he slams* |
| *267.27 | windows  (MS)  ] window |
| 268.1 | handkerchief,  (MS)  ] handkerchief |
| 268.4 | pins  (MS)  ] pins, |
| 268.14 | tube  (TS)  ] tubing |
| 269.13 | FIRST (ed) ] THE |
| 269.26 | aal  (MS)  ] all |
| 269.31 | FIRST (ed) ] THE |
| 269.37 | dooty? [*He pokes . . . elbow.*]  (ed)  ] dooty [ *he pokes . . . elbow*]? |
| 270.14 | foine  (MS)  ] fine |
| 270.34 | aal  (MS)  ] all |
| 271.1 | Oh, I don't know.  (A1)  ] I don't know about that. |
| 271.18-19 | *They begin to write.*  (ed)  ] They begin to write. |
| 272.20 | manufactor  (MS)] manafactor |
| 272.33-34 | an' hair an'  (A1)  ] and hair and |
| 272.34 | walk an'  (A1)  ] walk and |
| 272.34 | shirtwaists so fine  (A1)  ] shirtwaists |
| 272.35 | an' you  (A1)  ] and you |
| 272.38 | Isadore Berchansky  (MS)  ] "ISADORE BERCHANSKY |
| 273.1 | tough  (A1)  ] queer |
| 273.2 | tough  (A1)  ] queer |
| 273.3 | as [*he . . . letter*] ye  (A1)  ] as ye |

| | |
|---|---|
| 273.4 | runnin' (A1) ] running |
| 273.6-8 | times . . . Oh, (A1) ] times. [LEACH *goes to the bureau and begins to smooth out the paper.* QUINN *opens one of the drawers.*] ¶ LEACH ¶ Oh, |
| 273.9 | that. I wonder (A1) ] that. ¶ QUINN ¶ Sure, the poor divil was clane out of his mind, an' half-starved, I'm thinkin', too, be the looks ave this place. ¶ ARMSBY ¶ [*Shaking his head.*] Well, it's too bad, anyhow, whatever he was. He couldn't help it, I suppose, do you think? He was clean crazy, of course. ¶ LEACH ¶ [*Recovering himself, and with a learned and explanatory air, taking off his glasses, and giving the letter to* ARMSBY.] Oh, I don't know that these fellows need so much sympathy. I wonder |
| 273.10-12 | are. . . I can't (A1) ] are, if at all. I can't |
| 273.14-23 | interest . . . then? (A1) ] get grown ones. Now, if it were a grown person it might not be so bad—I mean that people wouldn't feel so terrible about it. [QUINN *stops searching and looks up.*] What strikes me as the worst of all, though, about this is the way a man like that can be walking about the streets here in New York free, and not a person to touch him. His parents must have known. |
| 273.24 | Well, why (A1) ] Why |
| 273.25-28 | up then? . . . either. (A1) ] up? Think of a fellow like that being at large! ¶ QUINN ¶ [*Thoughtfully*] Well, ye can't always tell. |
| 273.30 | was, (A1) ] was— |
| 273.31-35 | Supposing . . . better. (A1) ] No one likes to break up their own home, ye know. They might 'a' thought he'd get better. |
| 273.36 | this (A1) ] that |
| 273.38-274.18 | QUINN . . . *holding.*] (A1) ] LEACH ¶ Yes, but then there was that other case against him, that other little girl in the dentist's office. They might have known from that. Why didn't they lock him up for good then? That would have saved this other kid's life. ¶ ARMSBY ¶ [*Pausing and looking up.*] True enough, only, as Quinn says, sympathy plays such a big part in these things. People feel sorry, especially a family if it's one of their children, and they get around the officials. It's pretty hard to lock up a man for good, or just on one charge. |
| 274.19 | *Superiorily.*] Oh, . . . right. (A1) ] *Superiorily.*] |
| 274.21 | Cornell (A1) ] Johns Hopkins |
| 274.22 | a pretty fine (A1) ] the finest |
| 274.23 | there (A1) ] in the world down there |
| 274.28 | *Irritably,* (A1) ] *Irritably* |
| 274.29 | Man, ye (A1) ] Ye |
| 274.30 | Cornell (A1) ] Johns Hopkins |
| 274.30 | It's (A1) ] Man, it's |
| 274.32-33 | [*He . . . write.*] (A1) ] [*He writes.*] |

# Emendations in the Copy-Texts 311

| | |
|---|---|
| 274.34-35 | What . . . think? (A1) ] What of it? |
| 274.35 | tired, though, (A1) ] tired |
| 275.11 | [*Stopping* . . . *coming* (A1) ] [*Coming* |
| 275.12 | staring (A1) ] and staring |
| 275.18 | an' (A1) ] and |
| 275.19 | ave (A1) ] of |
| 275.20 | an' doin' naathin' (A1) ] and doin' nothin' |
| 275.23 | ave (A1) ] of |
| 275.24 | an' (A1) ] and |
| 275.26 | naht (A1) ] not |
| 275.27 | an' no way ave (A1) ] and no way of |
| 275.27 | ave (A1) ] of |
| 275.28-276.37 | If . . . years, (A1) ] What else can ye make out of these papers if not that? Whaddy ye say about that letter to his mother? [LEACH *shakes his head.*] Ye were sayin' a while ago that he aaht to take grown women only, but grown women wouldn't have him, and besides, they're well able to take care of themselves in most cases. Ye wouldn't caall him exactly attractive to women, would ye? [LEACH *smiles.*] But what I'm tryin' to tell ye, me young friend, is this, and that is that there's another side to aal this—somethin' maybe that ye didn't find out at Johns Hopkins, but that ye can see right here in this room if ye have half an eye—an' that's this: I've been studyin' these cases years before ye were born, me young friend, |
| 276.40-41 | at aal (A1) ] at all |
| 276.41 | aal endowed (A1) ] endowed |
| 277.2 | nahtwithstandin' (A1) ] notwithstandin' |
| 277.3 | an' (A1) ] and |
| 277.5 | brain, . . . ayther. (A1) ] brain. |
| 277.9 | ave waan (A1) ] of one |
| 277.9 | accordin' (A1) ] according |
| 277.13 | right . . . sight. (A1) ] right. |
| 277.14-18 | have . . . forces (A1) ] do as they'd like to, or as they know they aaht to, perhaps, to save their own lives, but as they're made to do be forces an' instincts |
| 277.20 | Sometimes . . . we're (A1) ] We're |
| 277.28 | no, naht (A1) ] no. Naht |
| 277.29 | aalways shows (A1) ] shows |
| 277.38-42 | made . . . people. (A1) ] been in love with a woman—really in love, I mean—ye'd know somethin' more about that. The sex-instinct is the most powerful thing in nature. It drives people mad at times. It's caused wars. Maybe ye think that poor felly was like yourself—a hit with aal women—but—— ¶ LEACH ¶ Ah, cut that! ¶ QUINN ¶ Well, don't get mad—but maybe he wasn't. Maybe he was shut aaf to himself with quair instincts and longin's, an' no outlet of any kind. How do ye know how badly he was made up, or how he might have been tortured be what was |

|          |          |
|----------|----------|
|          | in him? Somebody has said somewhere that the felly with the full stomach never understands the felly with the empty waan, an' I think that's right. This poor felly lyin' here was probably sufferin' from an empty waan. He had his desires, an' he had no way of gratifyin' them. If these notes here mane anythin' at aal, that's what they mane to me, anyhow—that he was hungry for somethin' he never had, an' couldn't get and—— |
| 278.1-2  | Let's ... time. (A1) ] I don't want to be too hard on him. I know there are two sides to everything, but what are you going to do—let him run loose and kill little girls? ¶ QUINN ¶ What taalk have ye! Haven't I just been afther tellin' ye I don't? What I'm sayin' is that it would be better for aal if, instead of huntin' him like a wolf an' tryin' to kill him on sight, they'd catch him and make a study of him an' try an' find out what to do in such cases in the future—that's aal. |
| 278.4    | *Berchansky!"*] (A1) ] *Berchansky!"*] ¶ QUINN ¶ [*Continuing.*] There ye have it! Outside is this big city yelpin' at his heels like a wild animal—seein' only the waan side to him—an' yet look at that note to his mother! Ye wouldn't say that a man that could write that was aal bad, now would ye? He wasn't, I tell ye, an'—— ¶ LEACH ¶ Oh, I agree with that, all right. But what's the use of getting so excited about it? |
| 278.5    | Yes (A1) ] Say |
| 278.13   | *stairs* (MS) ] *stair* |
| 279.4    | There're (TS) ] They're |
| 279.5    | walls (TS) ] walls, |
| 279.5    | an' (ed) ] and |
| 279.22   | *stairs* (ed) ] *stair* |
| 281.18   | around (TS) ] around, |
| 281.20   | INSPECTOR (ed) ] INSPECTOR OF POLICE |
| 281.32   | Vy (TS) ] vy |
| *282.5   | valls (ed) ] walls |

**Textual Notes**

| | |
|---|---|
| 188.9 | *manicuress* The copy-text refers to Rae as a "manicure" here and at 247.8, and as a "manicuress" at 241.1. Since Dreiser is consistent in his use of "manicuress" in MS, the changes must have been made by Estelle Kubitz, his typist, or by an in-house editor at Boni & Liveright. |
| 188.17 | JURY In MS the third act opens with an exchange of greetings between Assistant District Attorneys Miller and Balch, the calling of the jurors during which Michael Preskovsky and George Timberlake are named, and a lengthy opening statement by Miller covering twenty-six |

# Emendations in the Copy-Texts

MS leaves. Apparently this material remained in the copy used to typeset the salesman's dummy.

189.28 *door which* Because the clause "which gives into the hall" identifies the door on which the mezuze hangs, it is clearly restrictive.

189.28 *mezuze* The Jewish luck-piece referred to is usually spelled "mezuza" or "mezuzah." The spelling used in the copy-text must have been suggested by Dreiser's typist or by one of the persons who read the typescript because Dreiser wrote "mazuzulum" in MS. The copy-text spelling is retained on the basis of Dreiser's reaction to a letter he received from Symon Gould dated 28 August 1919. After expressing his admiration for Dreiser's ability as a playwright, Gould pointed out "a few errors in detail" in the play, including the spelling "mezuze." "On page 16," he wrote, "you speak of the Jewish luck-piece 'mezuze'. This is wrongly spelt, as its pronunciation would sound like 'me-zooze' while the correct spelling should be 'mezuzeh' which would be pronounced 'me- zoo-zeh', phonetically in keeping with the Jewish word." In his letter of reply, Dreiser must have rejected Gould's suggestion, however, as Gould wrote on 11 September 1919: "While it would be presumption on my part to take issue with the galaxy of Jews you have mentioned as having made no comment with regard to the spelling of 'Mezuze' . . ., I still must maintain (and I have been supported by others to whom I submitted same) that I am correct in my contentions."

190.34 *New* The copy-text reading "Now" makes sense if one wishes to assume that Berchansky has a rare book, but "New" is clearly superior and has the authority of MS.

190.37 *talking* A comparison of the copy-text and PP1 shows that Dreiser paid careful attention to dialect when he revised galley proofs. It seems reasonable to suppose, therefore, that he was responsible for the return to the MS reading "talking" in PP1.

191.19 *unloosens* The MS reading is characteristic of Dreiser's style and acceptable grammatically. The copy-text "loosens" was probably a sophistication introduced by Dreiser's typist or an in-house editor.

191.29 *manners* The MS reading is superior to the copy-text "manner" because it captures Dreiser's intention of commenting on the conduct of a group instead of the specific behavior of Rae. In MS Dreiser first wrote "this modern looseness of the young." Then, at a later time, perhaps to clarify what he meant by "looseness," he deleted "the young" and interlined "tongue and manners." That he still had a group in mind when he made the revision is shown by his decision to retain the adjective "modern."

| | |
|---|---|
| 193.30 | **Him** An addition in MS, "Him" was probably misread by Dreiser's typist because the dot for the "i" is to the right of the "m," and the last loop in the "m" is squeezed. Both readings make sense, but, in context, "Him" is superior as it better captures Joe's surprise upon hearing that Isadore was helping sponge one of the men at a prizefight. |
| 198.14 | **mouths** Dreiser crossed out the copy-text reading "lips" in MS and wrote "mouths" above it. While it is possible that Dreiser returned to "lips" when he proofread the typescript, it seems more likely that his typist made the change on the basis that "red lips" is a superior reading. That Dreiser preferred "mouths" is supported by his having Isadore again refer to girls' mouths at 199.16. |
| 202.31 | **maybe** The comma in the copy-text changes the meaning of this passage. MS clearly indicates that Dreiser intended the adverb "maybe" to modify "out of." The comma makes "maybe" a modifier of "now." |
| 202.40 | **His shoulder** The MS stage directions in Isadore's soliloquy refer to his arm twitching. In later versions Dreiser changed these references to "shoulder jerks." Apparently he failed to notice the pronoun "it" refers to "arm" when he substituted "jerks" for "twitches" in this direction. |
| 206.21 | **while** The colloquial "after while" in MS seems more appropriate to the speech of an eleven-year-old than the formal "after awhile" in the copy-text. Since many of Dreiser's revisions in the various prepublication forms of the play indicate that he was attempting to make the speech of his characters more informal, one suspects that the sophistication was introduced into the text by Estelle Kubitz or an in-house editor at Boni & Liveright. |
| 208.7 | **door and** The comma instead of "and" in the copy-text reading is confusing because it gives the impression that the sewing machine is between the table and the bedroom door. According to the stage directions in Act I (see 189.17-26) the sewing machine is behind the table to the right, and the bedroom door is behind the table to the left. |
| 216.26 | **awe-struck** Dreiser wrote "awe struck" in MS. The copy-text reading may have been made at the time Dreiser's typist or an in-house editor added the hyphen. |
| 231.19 | **larger,** Since "each occupied by a grand juror" does not appear in MS, Dreiser probably added the non-restrictive clause at the time he decided to change the opening to Act III discussed in an earlier note and failed to add a comma when he made the addition. |
| 232.13 | **some vun** In MS Dreiser underlined the "u" in "vun" at 233.1 (see Emendations in the Copy-Text) to indicate to his typist how he wanted the German pronunciation of "one" spelled. |

# Emendations in the Copy-Texts 315

232.26  **cuffered**  Dreiser changed the "o" in "coffered" to a "u" in MS. That he preferred this spelling for the German pronunciation of "cover" is further supported at 232.38, where, in MS, he underlined the "u" for the typist.

233.2  **hab**  Dreiser's typist must have misread his "p" in "hap" for a "f," perhaps thinking he intended the word "half." Dreiser clearly intended "have," however, which, in MS, he spelled "hap" here and at 233.5, 233.9, and 233.12, and "hab" at 233.7. Later, when he revised "hap" to "hab," the copy-text readings at 233.9 and 233.12, he must have overlooked the need for similar revisions here and at 233.5.

235.18  *stirs*  Since this reading appears in a section of MS that is heavily revised, Dreiser's typist could easily have misread "stares" for "stirs." While both readings make sense, "stirs" is clearly superior as the juror would have to move (stir) in order to whisper to a neighbor.

238.15  **last saw**  The reading in the copy-text appears to be a revision by Estelle Kubitz. In MS Dreiser first wrote "had seen." Then, in pencil, he cancelled the words and wrote above them "last saw."

239.10  **two**  The copy-text reading is an error that Dreiser made when he revised MS beginning at 238.30. In his first draft Dreiser wrote at the bottom of leaf 236: "you had not seen your son in two weeks—that you had seen him three days before the murder. Now whom are [top of leaf 238:] we to believe—You—or this reporter?" Later, while he was proofreading this material with a pencil, he cancelled the material at the bottom of leaf 236 after "weeks" and wrote above it, "that was two days before the murder." Next, he added a new leaf (237) and wrote in pencil the text beginning with "Now what" at 239.2 and ending with "at that time you said" at 239.9. Finally, in order to make the new material fit the text at the top of leaf 238, he added the lines he cancelled on leaf 236 to the bottom of leaf 237. While restoring these lines, he failed to note that he had changed the number of days from "three" to "two."

259.8  *roof copings*  The copy-text reading appears to be an error introduced by Estelle Kubitz. In MS Dreiser wrote, "A small window (back centre) shows chimneys, roof copings,—a red, dry colorless prospects [sic]." Familiar with Dreiser's habit of omitting commas in series and noting the omission of "and" between "chimneys" and "roof," Kubitz probably thought that the object of "shows" was a three-part series and added a comma. At the same time, she could have added the "s" to "roof," although Dreiser may have added it when he proofread the typescript.

263.21  **there.**  The question mark in the copy-text appears to be an error resulting from Dreiser's revision of galley proofs. In MS Dreiser had Elkas ask "You in there?" When he changed the question to the statement "You are in there," he apparently overlooked the need to change the punctuation mark.

267.27 *windows* The copy-text "between the window" is illogical. The MS reading suggests that Dreiser was thinking of window panes when he wrote the directions. Compare "window" at 259.8 and "windows" at 259.9.

282.5 **valls** The authority for this emendation is a slip of paper inserted in a copy of A1 once owned by W. T. H. Howe, President of the American Book Co., and now housed in the Berg Collection of the New York Public Library. Written on the slip in Dreiser's hand are the last lines of the play, which read as follows: "'Vy pull at de valls of my house? | Dey are already down.' | Theodore Dreiser."

# APPENDIX 1

## THE ANÆSTHETIC REVELATION

The second issue of the first impression of *Plays of the Natural and Supernatural*, and all other editions thereafter, includes an added gathering entitled "The Anæsthetic Revelation," and paginated pp. 1-4. Dreiser had received a letter from Charles DeCamp on 16 September [1914] in which DeCamp evaluated several of Dreiser's one-act plays and remarked that the effect of *Laughing Gas* "was weakened by my knowledge (via Wm James) of the scientific explanation of this" (Dreiser Collection). Dreiser seems not to have acted upon DeCamp's remark until April 1916, when he sent a version of the gathering to Mencken, asking whether he had "any objection to this as a footnote to 'Laughing Gas'" (Dreiser to Mencken, [undated, before 13 May 1916]; Dreiser Collection). For a discussion of "The Anæsthetic Revelation," See Linda S. Boren, "William James, Theodore Dreiser, and the 'Anæsthetic Revelation,'" *American Studies* 24 (1983): 5-18.

## THE ANÆSTHETIC REVELATION

It seems, in connection with the play, "Laughing Gas," that some of the effects of nitrous oxide gas (laughing gas) have been observed before.

In a pamphlet published in 1874 at Amsterdam, New York, by Benjamin Paul Blood, entitled "The Anæsthetic Revelation and the Gist of Philosophy," Mr. Blood wrote:

"Of this condition (a state of intense illumination or philosophic perception), although it may have been obtained otherwise, I know only by the use of anæsthetic agents. After experiments ranging over nearly fourteen years I affirm—what any man may prove at will—that there is an invariable and reliable condition (or uncondition) ensuing about the instant of recall from anæsthetic stupor to sensible observation, or "coming to" in which the genius of being is revealed; but because it can not be remembered in the normal condition it is lost altogether through the infrequency of anæsthetic treatment in any individual case ordinarily, and buried amid the hum of returning common sense under the epitaph of all illumination: "this is a queer world." Yet I have warned others to expect this wonder on entering anesthetic slumber, and none so cautioned has failed to report to me of it in terms which assured me of its realization. I have spoken with various persons who induce anæsthesis (dentists, surgeons, etc.) who had observed that many patients at the moment of recall seem as having made a startling yet somehow matter of course (and even grotesque) discovery in their own nature, and try to speak of it, but invariably fail in a last mood of introspection. Of what astonishes them it is hard to give or receive intimation, but I think most persons who have tested it will accept this as the central point of the illumination: that sanity is not the basic quality of intelligence, but a mere condition which is variable and like the humming of a wheel, goes up and down the musical gamut according to a physical activity; and that only insanity is formal or contrasted thought while the naked life is realized only outside of sanity altogether; and it is the instant contrast of this "tasteless water of souls" with formal thought as we "come to" that leaves in the patient an astonishment that the awful mystery of life is at last but a homely and a common thing, and that aside from mere formality the majestic and the absurd are of equal dignity."

Sometime subsequent to this, but before 1896, judging by the dates of the volume in which his comment appears, the attention of William James, Professor of Psychology at Harvard, was called to this, for, in his volume, "The Will to Believe" (Longmans Green and Co.—1897) as a footnote to his essay entitled "Some Hegelisms," occurs the following:

"Since the preceding article was written (Some Hegelisms), some observations on the effect of nitrous-oxide-gas-intoxication which I was prompted to make by reading the pamphlet called The Anæsthetic Revelation and the Gist of Philosophy, by Benjamin Paul Blood, Amsterdam, N.Y., 1874, have made me understand better than ever before both the strength and the weakness of Hegel's philosophy. I strongly urge others to repeat the experiment, which, with pure gas, is harmless enough. The effects will of course vary with the individual from time to time; but it is probable that in the former case, as in the latter, a generic resemblance will obtain. With me, as with every other person of whom I have heard, the keynote of the experience is the tremendously exciting sense of an intense metaphysical illumination. Truth lies open to the view in depth beneath depth of almost blinding evidence. The mind sees all the logical relations of being with an apparent subtlety and instantaneity to which its normal consciousness offers no parallel; only as sobriety returns, the feeling of insight fades, and one is left staring vacantly at a few disjointed words and phrases, as one stares at a cadaverous-looking snowpeak from which the sunset glow has just fled, or at the black cinder left by an extinguished brand.

The immense emotional sense of *reconciliation* which characterizes the 'maudlin' stage of alcoholic drunkenness,—a stage which seems silly to lookers-on, but the subjective rapture of which probably constitutes a chief part of the temptation to the vice,—is well known. The center and periphery of things seem to come together. The ego and its objects, the meum and the tuum, are one. Now this, only a thousand-fold enhanced, was the effect upon me of the gas; and its first result was to make peal through me with unutterable power the conviction that Hegelism was true after all and that the deepest convictions of my intellect hitherto were wrong. Whatever idea or representation occurred to the mind was seized by the same logical forceps, and served to illustrate the same truth; and that truth was that every opposition, among whatsoever things, vanishes in a higher unity in which it is based; that all contradictions, so-called, are but differences; that all differences are of degree; that all degrees are of a common kind, that unbroken continuity is of the essence of being; and that we are literally in the midst of *an infinite,* to perceive the existence of which is the utmost we can attain. Without the *same* as a basis how could strife occur? Strife presupposes something to be striven about; and in this common topic, the same for both parties, the differences merge. From the hardest contradiction to the tenderest diversity of verbiage differences evaporate; *yes* and *no* agree at least in being assertions; a denial of a statement is but another mode of stating the same, contradiction can only occur of the same thing,—all opinions are thus synonyms, are synonymous, are the same. But the same phrase by difference of emphasis is two; and here again difference and no-difference merge in one.

It is impossible to convey an idea of the torrential character of the identification of opposites as it streams through the mind in this experience. I have sheet after sheet of phrases dictated or written during the intoxication, which to sober readers seem meaningless drivel, but which in the moment of transcribing were fused in the fire of infinite rationality. God and devil, good and evil, life and death, I and you, sober and drunk, matter and form, black and white, quantity and quality, shiver of ecstasy and shudder of horror, vomiting and swallowing, inspiration and expiration, fate and reason, great and small, extent and intent, joke and earnest, tragic and comic, and fifty other contrasts figure in these pages in the same monotonous way. The mind saw how each term *belonged* to its contrast through a knife edged moment of transition which *it* effected, and which, perennial and eternal, was the *nunc stans* of life. The thought of mutual implication of the parts in the bare form of a judgment of opposition, as 'nothing—but' 'no more—than,' 'only—if,' etc., produced a perfect delirium of theoretic rapture. And at last, when definite ideas to work on came slowly, the mind went through the mere *form* of recognizing sameness in identity by contrasting the same word with itself, differently emphasized, or shorn of its initial letter. Let me transcribe a few sentences:

What's mistake but kind of take?
What's nausea but a kind -ausea?
Sober, drunk, -*unk*, astonishment.
Everything can become the subject of criticism—
 how criticise without something to criticise?
Agreement—disagreement!!

Emotion—motion!!!
Die away from, *from*, die away (without from).
Reconciliation of opposites; sober, drunk, all the same!
Good and evil reconciled in a laugh!
It escapes, it escapes!
But—
What escapes—WHAT escapes?
Emphasis, EMphasis; there must be some emphasis in order for there to be a phasis.
No verbiage can give it, because the verbiage is the *other*.
*In*coherent, coherent—same.
And it fades! And it's infinite! AND it's infinite!
If it wasn't *going* why should you hold on to it?
Don't you see the difference, don't you see the identity?
Constantly opposites united!
The same me telling you to write and not to write!
Extreme—extreme, extreme! Within the *ex*tensity that 'extreme' contains is contained the *'extreme'* of *in*tensity.
Something, and *other* than that thing!
Intoxication, and *otherness* than intoxication.
Every attempt at betterment,—every attempt at otherment—is a—
It fades forever and forever as we move.
There *is* a reconciliation!
Reconciliation—*e*conciliation!
By God how that hurts! By God how it *doesn't* hurt! Reconciliation of two extremes.
By George, nothing but *oth*ing!
That sounds like nonsense, but it is pure *on*sense!
Thought deeper than speech—!
Medical school, divinity school, *school!* SCHOOL! Oh, my God, oh God—oh God!
The most coherent and articulate sentence which came was this:—
There are no differences but differences of degree between different degrees of difference and no difference.
This phrase has the true Hegelian ring, being in fact a regular *sich als sich auf sich selbst beziehende Negativität*. And true Hegelians will *überhaupt* be able to read between the lines and feel, at any rate, what *possible* ecstasies of cognitive emotion might

have bathed these tattered fragments of thought when they were alive. But for the assurance of a certain amount of respect from them, I should hardly venture to print what must be such caviare to the general.

But now comes the reverse of the medal. What is the principle of unity in all this monotonous rain of instances? Although I did not see it at first, I soon found that it was in each case nothing but the abstract *genus* of which the conflicting terms were opposite species. In other words, although the flood of ontologic *emotion* was Hegelian through and through, the *ground* for it was nothing but the world-old principle that things are the same only so far and no farther than they *are* the same, or I partake of a common nature,—the principle that Hegel most tramples underfoot. At the same time the rapture of beholding a process that was infinite, changed (as the nature of the infinitude was realized by the mind) into the sense of a dreadful and ineluctable fate, with whose magnitude every finite effort is incommensurable and in the light of which whatever happens is indifferent. This instantaneous revulsion of mood from rapture to horror is, perhaps, the strongest emotion I have ever éxperienced. I got it repeatedly when the inhalation was continued long enough to produce incipient nausea, and I cannot but regard it as the normal and inevitable outcome of the intoxication, if sufficiently prolonged. A pessimistic fatalism, depth within depth of impotence and indifference, reason and silliness united, not in a higher synthesis, but in the fact that whatever you choose it is all one,—this is the upshot of a revelation that began so rosy bright.

Even when the process stops short of this ultimatum, the reader will have noted from the phrases quoted how often it ends by losing the clue. Something 'fades,' 'escapes'; and the feeling of insight is changed into an intense one of bewilderment, puzzle, confusion, astonishment. I know no more singular sensation than this intense bewilderment, with nothing particular left to be bewildered at save the bewilderment itself. It seems, indeed, a *causa sui*, or 'spirit become its own object.'

My conclusion is that the togetherness of things in a common world, the law of sharing, of which I have said so much, may, when perceived, engender a very powerful emotion; that Hegel was so unusually susceptible to this emotion throughout his life that its gratification became his supreme end, and made him tolerably unscrupulous as to the means that he employed; that *indifferentism* is the true outcome of every view of the world which makes infinity and continuity to be its essence, and that pessimistic or optimistic attitudes pertain to the mere accidental subjectivity of the moment; finally, that the identification of contradictories, so far from being the self-developing process that Hegel supposes, is really a self consuming process, passing from the less to the more abstract, and terminating either in a laugh in the ultimate nothingness, or in a mood of vertiginous amazement at a meaningless infinity."

It is needless to say, I presume, that "Laughing Gas" was not suggested or inspired by either of these comments. My attention was not called to them until two months after my own work had been published.

THE AUTHOR.

New York, April, 1916.

# APPENDIX 2

## TEXTUAL CHANGES IN THE REVISED SECOND EDITION OF *THE HAND OF THE POTTER*

Presented below are the revisions made in the 1927 printing of *The Hand of the Potter* in the text of the debate among the reporters from p. 272, line 10, to p. 278, line 13, in the Whitston edition. Deletions are marked by strikeout. New readings are added in braces.

QUINN: Sure! You're not goin' to hold anything out, are you?

LEACH: [*Irritably.*] Not at all! Not at all! Who's holding anything out? Can't I see it first if I find it? [*Opens it.*] Look at this! [*Reads.*] "This is to my dear mother who I am always homesick for, and same to rest and pop, whose word I am taking by doing this. Go 'way! Maybe you think it's easy. Well, maybe it is. I don't know. It's the reds, not the blacks. Mostly red. They won't let me alone. I figure easiest of my own. I want to say if I don't die this way I'll take my medicine just the same. Fields, carriages, four trees. Don't cry. My last job was in pants manufactor at 61 Norfolk. He owes me two days' work. I ain't et in three. Please secure pay and give to my dear mother who is very poor and for truth my mind ain't right. Go 'way! My oldest sister has lots of money and Greenbaum and don't help as she should, or Rae either. Eleven buttons—four seams—and the bottoms turned up. I'm sorry to cause all this trouble to my neighbor in particular, but all he's gotta do is call a cop! Go 'way! Go 'way! Gavan is a liar! Tell mother I'm really guilty and she'll not cry her eyes out—heart. Poor mom! You think I'm innocent, even yet,

don't you? Mothers is wonders! Great! I am, too, only I ain't made right. Red, not black. We ain't made right—not all of us—all wrong. It's their pretty mouths an' hair an' the way they walk an' them shirtwaists so fine—that's it! Sorry. I got crazy like I often do, an' you can't blame me or nobody else. It don't do things right always. Can you blame a man when he ain't right?
Isadore Berchansky."

ARMSBY: [*Looking up.*] Tough, eh?

QUINN: You're right, it's tough. Ye never can tell about these poor divils, as [*he points to the letter*] ye can see by that. Here's the whole city runnin' him down an' he may not have been as bad as the people have been thinkin'. Life's a pretty stiff thing at times.

LEACH: [*Going to the bureau and smoothing out the paper he has found, preparatory to copying it.*] Oh, I don't know about that. I wonder sometimes just how crazy some of them are. I know a doctor who has made a study of these cases at Johns Hopkins, and he isn't so sure that they deserve so much sympathy. I can't understand it myself, wanting to attack a little girl like that{.}, especially when he might interest a grown girl. The public wouldn't feel one-fiftieth as terrible if he had tried to attack a grown one instead of this little kid. But a little girl! And to torture her! Hell, you might as well talk about having sympathy for a mad dog. What I can't understand, though, is how it comes that a man like that should be allowed to walk about the streets here in New York free—not a person to touch him. And he had tried to attack another little girl two years ago. Why shouldn't his parents have done something about him then? He himself says he should have been dead two years ago. Well, why didn't they lock him up then? What's the big idea, letting a fellow like that run at large?

ARMSBY: [*Thoughtfully and apologetically.*] Oh, I know, but then you can't always tell, either. Everything isn't on the surface in this world. His parents might not have thought him as bad as he was, or they might have been sorry for him. Supposing you had a brother like that—then what?

Would you want him locked up right away? People don't like to break up their own homes, especially parents. They feel too bad about it. At the same time, they're likely to think he'll get better. A single offense don't always prove a man's crazy, especially in a case like this. He might change.

QUINN: ~~You're right there. The public doesn't understand them yet. I've been readin' up on these cases for some time, an' from what I can make out they're no more guilty than any other person with a disease. Did ye know, ayther ave ye, that there's something they've called *harmones* which the body manufactures an' which is poured into the blood streams of every waan ave us which excites us to the m'aning ave beauty an' thim things—"sensitizes" is the word they use. Now if a felly is so constituted that he has more ave that an' less ave somethin' else—somethin' which balances him a little an' makes him less sensitive to the beauty of women or girls—he's likely to be like that. He can't help it. There's something in him that pushes him on in spite of himself. This felly's letter says so. I believe if the public knew more about these cases it might be able to catch some of these fellies earlier an' begin to treat 'em or put 'em away somewhere where they'd come out aal right. They're naht aal bad—that's one thing sure, as ye can see by this. [*He points to the letter* LEACH *has been reading and is still holding.*]~~

LEACH: ~~[*Superiorily.*] Oh, all right. Just the same, this business of sympathizing with people can be carried too far, I tell you. When I was at Cornell we made a study of some of these fellows. They have a pretty fine psychiatric laboratory there. We studied dozens of such cases. In every one we found that however feeble-minded a fellow like that might actually be, or queer, still, ordinarily you couldn't tell it, you know, and often he was able to do better if he wanted to. They look just like other people.~~

QUINN: ~~[*Irritably, and yet lightly.*] Ave course! Ave course! What taalk have ye? Man, ye don't mane to say ye went to Cornell to find that out, do ye? It's in a hundred books. Haven't ye ever read Havelock Ellis or Kraft-Ebbing?~~

~~They give thousands ave cases—thousands. [He takes the letter from ARMSBY and begins to write.]~~

LEACH: [*Testily.*] ~~Sure I've read 'em. Of course. What do you think? What makes me so tired, though, is your taking up for those fellows as though they were deserving of nothing but sympathy. I don't see that so much sympathy is to be wasted on 'em, really. How~~ {Yes, but how} about the little girl he killed? Her life was as good to her as his was to him. And I notice that fellows like that are nearly always shrewd enough to take care of themselves and get what they want. ~~Take this,~~ {This} Berchansky ~~there, now.~~ ~~[He nods~~ {[he looks} toward the bed{]}~~.]~~ ~~He~~ was clever enough to lure that little girl to that empty apartment ~~in some way. You can't say that that was so very fine~~. You can't have too much sympathy for them, I tell you. They ought to be watched, and at the first sign, shut up for good—that's what I say. ~~It's just as well that they are hounded in this way.~~ {And they ought to be hounded, too.} It has to be so. [*As he talks,* ARMSBY, *who has been prowling about looking for other things but now scenting an argument, draws near.*]

QUINN: [*Stopping his writing and coming directly under* LEACH'S *chin, staring up at him, argumentatively.*] Who's denyin' it, I'd like to know? ~~Me?~~ What ye say is aal true enough, and I'm naht sayin' that he shouldn't have been locked up long ago if they could have caught him—I think he should have—but what makes me tired in you an' others an' the papers is ~~aal~~ {all} this shoutin' about human tigers lurkin' on the East Side an' everywhere else, men without a spark ave anything but evil in 'em—plain murderers—an' doin' naathin' aal day long but lie in wait for little girls, to kill 'em. Ye'd think there was only waan side to the story. Ye'd think from the papers ave the past six weeks that this felly was aal wolf—naathin' but murder an' rape in his mind~~, a sane, calculatin' villain turned to this sort of thing for the fun of it only~~ —naht a poor, crazy ~~wastrel~~ {boy} like this, without a place to go an' no way ave gettin' himself anything ave any kind. If he was such a divil, what was he doin' workin' for a dollar a day—an' naht gettin' his pay, at that? Now, for aal ye've been to

Cornell—an' I don't doubt ye learned a lot there—there's another side to this, an' ye're just the waan to know it if ye've been there. People judge these fellies solely by their acts, when as a matter ave fact they aaht to take into account the things which make up their natures an' dispositions. This felly could no more help bein' what he was than a fly can help bein' a fly an' naht an elephant, an' that's naht at aal. ~~Nature is deeper an' stronger than anything we know. An' by that I'm naht sayin' that the human race hasn't the right to defend itself from this sort ave felly. It has, an' does. What I'm taalkin' about is aal this palaver in the papers about wolves an' divils. Why, man, by the papers ave the last six weeks ye'd think the streets were full ave demons in the shape ave men. Ye've seen 'em arrest at least a hundred men for even smilin' at a child or ahfferin' it a stick ave candy. And now look at 'im. There he is—hungry an' dirty an' thin an' hidden away in this pe-latial room, an' there's that letter to his mother tellin' her not to cry an' that he aaht to have been dead two years ago, an' that he's naht right. Ave course he wasn't right, the poor divil, an' perhaps no waan knew it better than his mother, ayther, an' that's why he writes to her.~~ [LEACH *shakes his head argumentatively.*] ~~An', me boy, while we're on this subject, let me tell ye just waan thing more; I'm an older man than ye by fourteen years an' I've seen a little somethin' ave life that maybe ye haven't seen yet, anyhow.~~ Don't be so cocksure in your judgments of who are the good an' who are the bad in this world {, me boy}. ~~Facts an' proofs are naht aal on the surface, by any means, as Armsby here was aafter sayin'. Ye were sayin' a while ago that he aaht to have taken a grown woman or girl. How do ye know whether any girl or woman would give him a single look or no, let alone a second waan? But supposin' ye were like him—hungry an' tortured by their pretty mouths an' their hair an' the way they walk an' their shirtwaists so fine—I believe that's what he says here~~ [*he looks at the letter*]—~~then what?~~ Are ye sure ye'd do so very different from what he did, driven by the things that were drivin' him?

LEACH: Oh, I don't know. I might not, of course.

QUINN: Ye're tootin', ye might naht, nor any other man in the same state an' place. ~~Now, I wouldn't have a single word to say ave this case if it weren't for all the noble palaverin' that's been goin' on in an' out ave the papers, in the churches an' everywhere else. Everybody seems to know exactly just what a low, horrible scoundrel he was without a spark ave decency in him. Well, it just so happens that I've been studyin' these very kinds ave cases for years, an' I know what I'm taalkin' about. Aal men are naht balanced or normal be their own free will an' say-so, any more than they're free an' equal in life, an' that's naht at aal. They're naht aal endowed with the power or the will to do an' select, aal the rules of the copybooks to the contrary nahtwithstandin'. Some are so constituted mentally an' physically that they can't do otherwise than as they do, an' that's what ye never can get through the average felly's brain, nor through the average newspaper's, ayther. Most people have a few rules, a pattern, an' everybody's supposed to be like that. Well, they're naht. An' naathin' will ever make 'em exactly alike, ayther—ayther aal good or aal bad, or a little ave waan or the other, accordin' to anybody's theory. Nature don't work that way. An' nature makes people, me young friend, me an' you [*he taps him on the chest*], an' every waan else, an' she don't aalways make us right ayther, by a damned sight. Some people don't aalways have aal they waant mentally or physically—if they did I'd be a millionaire today—nayther can they aalways do as they'd like to, or aaht to, aal theories to the contrary nahtwithstandin'. Sometimes they're made to do things—lots ave thim—by forces over which they have no control. [LEACH *stirs argumentatively*.] Man, ye're naht goin' to deny that? Sometimes I think we're naht unlike those formulae they give ye in a chemical laboratory—if ye're made up right, ye work right. If ye're naht, ye don't, an' that's aal there is to it—laa or no laa. An' another thing I'm tellin' ye, me young friend, an' I'd like ye to think it over from time to time, whether ye like it or naht—that Dennis Quinn said it—an' that is that laa is merely somethin' that forces people to do what they don't waant to do whether they will or no, naht somethin' that aalways shows 'em how to do it—ye get me? Remember that, me young friend. I'm tellin' ye. If ye~~

~~waant to come out exactly right in this world, which nobody does, ye waant to be pairfectly balanced, or nearly that—an' damn few are that. It's more luck than anythin' else, an' that's true, too. Now ye were sayin' a while ago that ye can't understand why a man like that should be attackin' a little girl, unless he were a low, vile creature, even if he wasn't balanced quite right—but I can. If ye'd ever made a study ave the passion ave love in the sense that Freud an' some others have ye'd understand it well enough. It's a great force about which we know naathing as yet an' which we're just beginnin' to look into—what it manes, how it affects people.~~

~~LEACH: Oh, I'm ready to admit all that. Let's cut this, anyhow. We haven't got time.~~

[*The voice of a newsboy sounds:* "Extro! Extro! All about Isadore Berchansky!"]

{LEACH: Say, fellows, let's cut this. We haven't got time.}

ARMSBY: [*Energetically.*] {You said it. We should better speed up on our copy.} Yes, fellows, you'd better cut the argument and make copies of this. Look around! Look around! The bulls'll soon be here! Then they'll be wanting to shut everything off.

[*He opens all the drawers and looks under the bureau.* QUINN *goes over to the body and feels in the pockets. He looks under the bed and picks up a collar, and starts to conceal it.* LEACH *examines more of the walls. A step is heard on the stairs.* MCKAGG *looks down.*]

# APPENDIX 3

## PRODUCTIONS OF DREISER'S PLAYS

### I. Productions of the One-Act Plays

Upon publication of Dreiser's *Plays of the Natural and Supernatural* in 1916, Montrose Moses closed his generally laudatory review in the May *Book News Monthly* by announcing that "the volume must not be taken too seriously as a contribution to the theatre. . . . I do not see how [the plays] could be whipped within the confines of the proscenium arch and the footlights."[1] Despite his authority as one of America's leading dramatic critics and as the author of the influential *The American Dramatist* (1911), Moses' dismissive comment proved remarkably shortsighted. Dreiser's plays soon interested a number of amateur and semi-professional theater groups that promptly performed the plays as part of their campaign to replace the stale conservatism of the commercial theater with artistic innovation.

By 1912 at least nine non-commercial theaters had been formed to foster the ideals of the "art" theater. Dissatisfied with the general vulgarity of commercial productions, such groups as the Chicago Little Theater (1912-17), the Wisconsin Dramatic Society (1911-15), and the Boston Toy Theater (1912-15) consciously sought to embody the "new stagecraft" ideals of Gordon Craig and Adolphe Appia. Craig insisted upon the primacy of the artist-director whose vision unified play, acting, setting, and lighting into an impressionistic whole; Appia subordinated realistic setting through simplification and emphasized emotional effects through the manipulation of light and shadow. Both sought to replace the standardized productions of the commercial theater with a performance that expressed a unified, synthetic artistic vision. In practice, the art theater ideal meant realistic sets were gradually abandoned in favor of impressionistic and expressionistic staging methods that emphasized visual experimentation rather than fidelity to the text.

The growth of the little theaters was truly astounding. In 1912 there were nine; by 1917, 50; by 1922, 300-400; by 1929 over 1000.[2] What was responsible for this explosion of non-commercial theater? Publicity played a significant role in the growth of the little theaters, for newspaper reviewers widely covered early productions and often accompanied their reviews with columns extolling the principles of experimental theater. In 1914 Samuel Hume, who had studied with Gordon Craig, presented his New Stagecraft Exhibition in Cambridge, Mass. Widely reviewed and praised, the exhibition toured during the next year to New York, Chicago, and Detroit, at each stop attracting crowds of theater enthusiasts (15,000 in Chicago alone). The exhibit consisted of a variety of stage designs, including "five hundred drawings and photographs, . . . twenty-one electrically lighted models, and . . . two working models of the sliding stage and the skydome."[3] To meet this interest in the new stagecraft, several books appeared, among them Sheldon Cheney's *The New Movement in the Theatre* (1914) and *The Art Theatre* (1917), Thomas Dickinson's *The Insurgent Theatre* (1917), and Constance D'Arcy Mackay's *The Little Theatre in the United States* (1917). In 1916 Sheldon Cheney founded *Theatre Arts Magazine,* which served as the principal organ for the movement. Universities began offering workshops in playwriting, among them the Harvard 47 Workshop (1913), the Dartmouth Laboratory Theatre (1913), and the Laboratory Theatre of the Carnegie Institute (1914). To meet the need for scripts, volumes of one-act plays soon began appearing from such publishers as Frank Shay, Mitchell Kennerley, and Brentano's Bookstore, as well as from the little theaters themselves.

This flowering of little theaters encouraged an increased interest in the one-act play as an art form. Little theaters favored the one-act play partly because the compressed form did not overextend the capabilities of the actors, most of whom were amateurs, and the plays, usually presented in a bill of three or four for a period of less than a week, enabled the actors to try a variety of roles. The generally small royalties for one-act plays facilitated their production by troupes constantly fighting to make ends meet. The small compass also invited experimentation in staging methods—especially in those theaters devoted to the new stagecraft—for the short form enabled the director to distill the dramatic intention into a unified whole. As the little theaters grew in numbers, they began to clamor for more plays by American authors, and many devoted themselves entirely to American authorship.

Dreiser thus found himself in the right place at the right time to write plays and see them produced. Upon publication, Dreiser's plays immediately attracted notice from those interested in the progressive theater. After Dreiser's third drama, *In the Dark*, appeared in the January 1915 *Smart Set*, Mencken wrote Dreiser that he had received a letter from the novelist and playwright Harry Leon Wilson "lavishing high praise on your plays. Not the first, by any means. They have made an unmistakable hit, and it is worth noticing that the persons best pleased by them have been writers."[4] After publication of *Plays of the Natural and Supernatural* in 1916, little theater directors began negotiating with Dreiser for production rights, despite the difficulties posed by their form. The austere, even inflammatory content of *The Girl in the Coffin* and the fanciful experimentation of the other dramas demanded a resourcefulness that few theaters could muster. As Nellie Dawson of the *New York Globe and Commercial Advertiser* remarked, with pointed reference to *Laughing Gas*, "The most skilled play producer of our day would hardly know what to do with characters like Alcephoran (power of physics), and Demyaphon (nitrous oxide)."[5] Yet in December 1916 a producer with the requisite skill did emerge, not in the theatrical center of New York, but in that unlikely bastion of Midwest conservatism, Indianapolis.

In November 1916 Carl Bernhardt, who had recently taken over the reins of the Little Theater Society of Indiana, wrote to Dreiser to enquire about production rights to *Laughing Gas*. Dreiser agreed, and on 7 December 1916 the Society became the first theater to perform a Dreiser play. Founded in 1915 to encourage "the experimental and repertory presentation of both approved and untried dramatic works," the Society may have been attracted to *Laughing Gas* in part because it was then promoting the works of Indiana playwrights and had just concluded a bill of "dialogued excerpts" from local authors.[6]

Bernhardt, a theatrical licensing agent for the Bobbs-Merrill Company, had formerly worked with Arthur Hopkins and Robert Edmund Jones on their production of *The Devil's Garden* in December 1915 and from Hopkins had learned to incorporate abstract expression into realistic sets.[7] He undertook *Laughing Gas*, he told the *Indianapolis Star* in a pre-production interview, as an experiment in the new stagecraft: "This play of Dreiser's involves a number of technical questions, not only of stage lighting, but actually of play construction, for it approaches the dividing line between motion pictures and the technique of the legitimate stage."[8] The play was something of a *cause célèbre*, for the presentation of *Laughing Gas* would mark the first time in America that a theater would attempt to personify simultaneously the workings of both the conscious and the unconscious mind. Other theaters had staged mental states before—most notably Arthur Hopkins' production of Eleanor Gates' *Poor Little Rich Girl* (1913)—but as Bernhardt pointed out, Hopkins "was able to divide his action into reality in one act and unreality in another."[9] The Little Theater Society would depict both states simultaneously by employing an impressionistic set, designed by Donald Dohner and Harrison Brown, and symbolic shades of lighting, designed by Piatt Orlopp, to suggest the interplay of the conscious and the unconscious.

A production faithful to Dreiser's intention would also require the simultaneous portrayal of two planes of existence: the "realistic" plane, in which the surgical team carries out the operation, and the "dream" plane, in which Vatabeel's thoughts are intercut with the comments of the incarnate forces that control him. The central production problem, then, was how to depict both states without losing the effect of interconnection, since the dream characters determine Vatabeel's actions and perceptions, which in turn are prompted by the actions of the surgical team. In an extended review for the *Boston Evening Transcript* (accompanied by an impressionistic sketch of the set by Donald Dohner), Oliver Sayler perceptively noted the problem and described Bernhardt's solution. The key, as Sayler saw it, was Dreiser's notion of rhythm, symbolized by the regular pulsations of the anesthesia machine (the incarnation of the Rhythm of the Universe), which unified the conflicting forces of Dreiser's "equation."

> In "Laughing Gas" there is need for the two main rhythms—of the natural and the supernatural. The natural rhythm is the rhythm of sheer realism—the casual everydayness of the group of surgeons and nurses around the operating table. The supernatural rhythm is taken up and carried forward by the

figures in the shadow world. In close connection with this is the mechanically contrived rhythm of the universe which backs up and gives body to the shifting, changing rhythms of shadow voices and shadow bodies in motion. Rising, individualized, from the shadow rhythm, are the two clashing rhythms of the two leading shadow figures—Demyaphon, the negative spirit, and Alcephoran, the positive spirit, the conflict of which provides some of the most intense drama of the play.[10]

Bernhardt's successful staging of this conflict between the material and spiritual plane was, Sayler noted, of signal importance to American drama. A central premise of the art theater movement was that realistic drama was at a dead end, for the theater could not (and should not) compete with the motion picture, which excelled at realistic depictions. To succeed as art, Sayler argued, drama had to move toward symbolic expression to convey what the film of the time could not: an "appeal to the emotions and the imagination through the abstractions of mood and feeling, and to portray these moods and feelings as the background for the action of the play rather than to particularize that background in the guise of either a literal or symbolic representation of *locale*."[11] *Laughing Gas* was the first successful integration of this abstraction of mood and feeling—and America's first staged expressionistic play—and to Sayler would serve to "give encouragement to others to push on through the breach and enter into the rich possibilities of an entirely new field of expression through the drama."[12]

Reception of the play was mixed. Sayler, a devotee of the Russian Art Theater and an advocate of the new stagecraft, noted in his unsigned review for the *Indianapolis News* that "The achievement in the effective production of 'Laughing Gas' is nothing less than revolutionary. Like all great achievements, it seems easy now that it has been accomplished. . . . [The production] is one of the three or four creative discoveries of the little theater movement the world over."[13] Hector Fuller, writing for the *Indianapolis Star*, remarked that the production was a "sensation" but he was less appreciative of the experimental nature of the play. His comment is perhaps illustrative of the general play-goer in 1916 in its preference for more traditional fare that instructs while amusing: "Fantasy, I suppose, some may call 'Laughing Gass' [sic], but others will place it in the category of horrors, and will ask themselves what possible useful purpose can be served by dishing up the tortures of a man on the operating table. Ugh!"[14]

Yet, as Sayler prophesied, this experimental production of *Laughing Gas* encouraged others interested in the new stagecraft. Bernhardt wrote to Dreiser to inform him that at the last performance (16 December 1916) "the director, scenic artist and electrician of *The St. Louis Little Theatre* put in their appearance. They seemed to think it interesting enough to have come on from St. Louis to see and asked about the royalties. I told them I thought you would want a fairly large royalty now that we had demonstrated that the play could be put on."[15] Dreiser's royalty may have been too large (or *Laughing Gas* too demanding for their resources), for the St. Louis Players Club did not stage *Laughing Gas* but instead chose the more manageable *The Girl in the Coffin*, which they performed one month later, on 29 January 1917, to favorable reviews.[16] In October, the St. Francis Little Theater Club staged *The Girl in the Coffin* in San Francisco, and the same group gave a production of "Old Ragpicker" in January 1918.

On 2 November 1917 Edward Goodman, the manager of the Washington Square Players, expressed interest in staging *The Girl in the Coffin*. By 1917 the Washington Square Players had arrived at the pinnacle of their success, and Dreiser was no doubt aware that a successful production would validate his work. After 10 days of negotiation over the amount of royalty, Goodman accepted Dreiser's terms of "$100 down and $50 per week for eight weeks."[17] Beginning 21 November Dreiser regularly attended rehearsals of the play, which opened at the Comedy Theater on 3 December. Playing with *The Girl in the Coffin* were three other one-act dramas by American authors, Zona Gale's *Neighbors*, Samuel Kaplan's *The Critic's Comedy*, and J. Garcia Pimentel and Beatrice de Holthoir's *Yum Chapab*, a pantomime.

Dreiser's diary shows him wavering between excitement, despair, and forced nonchalance as he awaited the production. When he attended the first rehearsal, he noted cryptically: "Go up at 2:45. Find Goodman in charge. Actors on stage. Am introduced. Take seat in front and watch fairly capable first reading. I think these actors may do. Come out at 4:30."[18] By 28 November Dreiser was assisting in the rehearsals, but occasionally he bungled: "In trying to make one actress get the idea of Mrs. Shafer I make her cry and have to let her go for day. Bert [Estelle Kubitz] roasts me for my 'brutality.'"[19]

By 2 December, the dress rehearsal, Dreiser had the jitters. "Rehearsal very bad. I don't like size of coffin, too small and too obscure. Stage setting not bad. Mr. [Arthur] Hohl doesn't look the part of Ferguson, somehow. I feel disgusted, but it goes big. Much applause. Helen Westley, Marion Powys and several others come down to where I am, crying."[20] Although he acknowledged the effective pathos of the production, Dreiser was so skittish that he refused to attend the opening. He did, however, walk past the theater and noted: "See first fire-sign ever carrying the name of a play of mine. . . . Bert and I stand and look at it and she wants to know if I get a thrill out of it. I don't—alas!" While Kubitz went on to the play, Dreiser stayed home alone before meeting friends at the Knickerbocker to hear the verdict. His fears failed to materialize; he learned the play was a hit: it had "18 curtain calls and many cries for the author. Glad I wasn't there."[21]

Dreiser's friends did not exaggerate the audience's response nor the merits of the production. The *Brooklyn Daily Eagle* noted that "There were loud cries for the author, but Mr. Dreiser did not respond," after opening its review with the unequivocal statement, "If the Washington Square Players do not produce another play this season they will have justified their existence by the presentation of Theodore Dreiser's powerful and intensely human little drama."[22] Burns Mantle praised the play as "a dramatic etching done in bold strokes by an artist with a steady hand and a sincere belief in himself and his knowledge of human nature. A fine, true drawing—as true in its psychology as it is photographic in detail."[23] And Channing Pollock proclaimed, "The other three new pieces at the Comedy are insignificant in comparison [to *The Girl in the Coffin*]. . . . The bill, as a whole, is worth seeing—chiefly on account of Mr. Dreiser."[24]

What the reviewers mostly appreciated—and what the Players wished to suggest through their choice of plays—was the realism of situation and dialogue, which in 1917 was still not common in commercial plays. Charles Darnton of the *Evening World* wrote that "Mr. Dreiser's play is . . . so sane and true and real that it has the grip of tragedy. The characters talk and look and act like people who have felt the hard grind of labor all their days."[25] Louis Sherwin of the *Globe and Commercial Advertiser* praised the "sheer emotional force of the play, the truth of the characters, the genuine artistic beauty."[26] The *Dramatic Mirror* singled out Arthur Hohl's performance as Ferguson for its "powerful character analysis."[27] And Burns Mantle, in a second review for the *Minneapolis Sunday Journal*, anticipated the few demurrers by noting that the play would "probably not . . . be included in the lists of plays indorsed by the leagues of uplift, but [it is] sound drama and effective."[28] Indeed, the most condemnatory review appeared in the *Nation*, which denounced the play as "pretentious" and as "a drab bit of realism." The reviewer clearly preferred more "wholesome" fare and blasted the production because its portrayal of the consequences of marital infidelity "insinuates a dangerous doctrine while ostensibly bent upon a minute study of a humble life." The play therefore "has little meaning either for life or for art."[29] Despite the overwhelmingly positive response to his play, after the dress rehearsal Dreiser, with his fear of crowds, apparently never attended another performance and consequently missed seeing the audience applaud his work.

Two other productions of *The Girl in the Coffin* suggest the range of little theater approaches to the play. On 16 January 1918, Sam Hume of the Detroit Arts and Crafts Players wrote to the John Lane Co. inquiring about the royalty for four performances of *The Girl in the Coffin*.[30] After several weeks haggling over the amount of royalty, *The Girl in the Coffin* appeared on 21, 22, and 23 March with Philip Moeller's *The Beautiful Legend of Pokey, or the Amorous Indian* and Lord Dunsany's *The Golden Doom*.

Founded in 1916, the Arts and Crafts Players soon became the foremost exemplar of the new stagecraft. Hume began his tenure with the Society by modifying the architects' plans for the theater, then about to undergo construction, to create what Sheldon Cheney called "one of the best little theatre stages in the country."[31] Hume's modified plaster sky dome, then the second such installation in the United States, his "permanent adaptable setting," and his innovative lighting system enabled the Players to showcase the new stagecraft in its productions. *Theatre Arts Magazine*, then edited by Cheney, popularized the Society's productions, enabling other theaters to follow Hume's example.

When *The Girl in the Coffin* appeared in March, with Hume as Ferguson, the reviewers, who had come to expect great things from Hume's theater, were not disappointed. Ralph F. Holmes in the *Detroit Journal* called it "A masterpiece of thought and writing" and "a masterpiece of acting and production on the part of the players." Holmes, who followed the Players' activities closely, believed *The Girl in the Coffin* to be the best play the Players had yet staged. Under Hume's direction, Dreiser's occasionally verbose writing became for Holmes "a set of speeches that rank with the most moving I have ever heard from an American pen."[32] The *Detroit Free Press* concurred, writing that *The Girl in the Coffin* "proved one of the best things Mr. Hume and his players have offered in two seasons." The reviewer also praised Hume's use of "an honest-to-goodness coffin as one of the 'props,'" despite the superstition of other managers who had shied away from the play in the past.[33]

With its strong labor theme and realistic style, *The Girl in the Coffin* naturally interested those of a radical bent. On 19 December 1919 Dreiser received a letter from Wayne Arey who was busy forming The Workers' Theater Guild, a socialist organization dedicated to bringing serious drama to the workers in an effort to improve their lives. Its inaugural performance would be under the auspices of the Workers Defense Union, Arey wrote in a second letter, and the Guild would offer three plays—Susan Glaspell and George Cram Cook's *Suppressed Desires*, St. John Ervine's *The Magnaminous Lover*, and *The Girl in the Coffin*—to raise "a fund for the political prisoners and the deportees"—apparently a reference to the incarceration of socialist activists.[34] The Guild received much favorable press from the socialist *Call*, which devoted a series of seven articles to promoting Arey's cause and the idea of a workers' theater in general. The company was composed of professional actors who were disenchanted with the commercialism of Broadway productions—Arey had been a member of Holbrook Blinn's Princess Players repertory company (1913) and had appeared in *Blue Grass* (1908), *Vic* (1914) and a film version of *King Lear* (1916) before turning to labor activism.

Like many of the activist theater schemes, Arey's lofty intentions were difficult to implement. The bill of plays appeared at the Provincetown Playhouse during an interim between the Provincetown Players' productions. The expected swarm of workers eager to be uplifted failed to materialize. The price of a ticket—one dollar—was probably a bit steep for the target audience of workers. In addition, other papers, with the exception of the *Call*, were not enthusiastic about the production. J. Ranken Towse of the *Evening Post* called the bill as a whole "lamentable beyond words," while the *New York Times* merely noted that the plays "have all been seen before."[35] Louis Gardy, the *Call*'s enthusiastic champion of proletarian theater, indulged his anger in a lengthy column blasting the hypocrisy of those socialists who talk about a workers' theater yet who do not show up to support it: "the finest proletarian group of actors in New York played to much less than a hundred auditors one night this week."[36]

## II. *The Hand of the Potter* and the Provincetown Players

Although Dreiser was unsuccessful in finding someone to stage *The Hand of the Potter* before it was published, he refused to give up his dream of seeing the play on the boards. After he had moved to Los Angeles in November 1919, he enlisted Edward Smith to act as his agent in New York. "I feel that something ought to be done soon if at all since much of the interest manifested by Hopkins and others is still keen," he wrote Smith on 25 November 1920. He outlined the previous attempts to stage the play and suggested that Smith might be able to interest, among others, Emanuel Reicher, Augustin Duncan of the Theater Guild, the Friars Club, the Columbia University Theater Guild, or the Provincetown Players, provided the latter group "take an outside theatre and do it." Indeed, so confident was he of the play's appeal that he wrote, incredibly, "There are actors in plenty, good ones, who if they knew of such a chance would be delighted to act for nothing, for the opening performances or test at least." He had learned, however, from his dealings with Hopkins the necessity of tailoring a play for stage presentation. "One thing be sure and do," he wrote.

> If you talk to any one at all be sure and explain that the scene in the first act where Isadore grabs the child and carries it into the bedroom is to be left out. It is not necessary to the drama. Sufficient horror or thrill will be achieved if he but lay a hand on her with the evident intention of seizing her as the curtain descends.[37]

Smith replied that he was willing to assist, declined Dreiser's offer of a fee for his services, and suggested that the 1921-22 season would offer better chances, since "Ten new theatres are building. Plays will be needed."[38]

Smith's efforts paid off. On 4 October 1921 Dreiser received a telegram from George Cram Cook of the Provincetown Players asking for permission to stage *The Hand of the Potter* and "to make cuts if absolutely necessary." Four days later he wired terms: 5% of the gross for a 2 to 7 week run at the MacDougal Street Playhouse, and more if the play went uptown. In his exuberance he noted that "This gave O'Neill six thousand dollars last winter"—a reference to the Broadway success of *The Emperor Jones*—and that he had a "wonderful Isidora and Kitty Murphy [sic] . . . Whole cast first class." Informing Dreiser of O'Neill's profit was a mistake, for Dreiser characteristically tried to jack up the terms and demanded a $500 guarantee. On 12 October he received an urgent telegram noting the impossibility of his request, since the MacDougal Street Playhouse, if filled to capacity every night for two weeks, would only gross $2800, netting Dreiser $140.[39] Dreiser agreed to the original terms, and *The Hand of the Potter* made its debut on 5 December 1921.

The 1921-22 season found the Provincetown Players with so many productions playing concurrently that they overextended their resources and created division among their members. As a result, *The Hand of the Potter* did not receive the "first class" production Cook promised. When Adolph Klauber offered to bring *The Emperor Jones* to the Selwyn Theater for a series of special matinees beginning 27 December 1920, the Players were faced with a crisis: to remain amateur or to turn professional. Financial temptation won, and *The Emperor Jones*, after moving to the Princess Theater, began a 200 performance run before embarking on a two year tour.[40] Helen Deutsch and Stella Hanna point out that this phenomenal success of *The Emperor Jones* led the players "to identify success with a move to Broadway"; the Players therefore tried "to force plays into success by moving them uptown instead of letting the plays force them into the move." For instance, when the 1921-22 season opened with Susan Glaspell's *The Verge* on 14 November, the Players announced it for "an uptown showing even before the first curtain" at the Macdougal Street Playhouse. But *The Verge* was poorly received, and when the Theater Guild offered "to take it over for a series of special matinees at the Garrick" Theater, the Players eagerly accepted to salvage what "success" they could.[41] These matinees began 6 December and concluded 16 December; *The Verge* therefore ran concurrently with *The Hand of the Potter*, which strained the Players' resources considerably for, in addition to the expense and logistics of mounting three productions simultaneously, the most accomplished actors were playing in *The Emperor Jones* and *The Verge*. Moreover, many of the best actors had been lured away by the commercial theaters, which left Cook with a largely inexperienced cast for *The Hand of the Potter*.

Dreiser quickly noted Cook's evasiveness concerning the cast and asked Mencken to attend a rehearsal and "tell me how the thing goes."[42] To Smith he was more specific, asking for the names of the actors playing the Berchanskys as well as the actor portraying Isadore "and what his record is." "I make some allowance for Cook who is a very temperamental person himself," he wrote, "but he certainly has troubled less to tell me about the cast in hand than anyone I have ever worked with before."[43]

Dreiser's fears were justified. Of the 26 members of the cast, only two—Harold McGee and Harry Gottlieb—had previously played with the Provincetown Players, and their roles were minor: McGee as Miller, the District Attorney, and Gottlieb as Rufus Bush (called Thomas Bush in the production), a witness at the Coroner's Inquest. Apparently, the only experienced actor in the group was John Paul Jones (playing Isadore), who had previously played the minor role of John Wilkes Booth in Lester Lonegran's production of *Abraham Lincoln* in December 1919. As Smith, who attended the opening performance, accurately but uncharitably wrote,

> Cook has done the usual Greenwich Village group thing. He has sent all the competent players in his organization up-town in his wife's play and recruited your caste [sic] from hangers-on and nobodies. You can be sure that the Provincetown players are organized for the advantage and greater glory of Glaspell, Cook and O'Neil [sic], and that outsiders will not be permitted to outshine these worthies. For instance, they got Gilpin, a masterly negro actor, to play O'Neil's hero in "Emperor Jones," and they procured Margaret Wycherly to do the first part in Miss Glaspell's new play. But T. Dreiser is not entitled to even one third rate actor for his tragedy.[44]

Although the cast was distinctly amateur, the Provincetown Players did try to overcome the inherent weaknesses of the script through some judicious cutting.[45] Most of the cuts in the first three acts, with one exception, were fairly minor omissions of repetitious dialogue and did not substantially alter Dreiser's intent. To lessen the shock of Isadore's attack on Kitty Neafie (and to avoid offending the audience), the Players omitted the pantomime scene that closes Act I in which Isadore carries Kitty into the bedroom and emerges with her limp body—the scene Dreiser referred to when he asked Smith to arrange production of the play. Instead, the act closes with the curtain descending during Kitty's scream, at which point she utters, "Hail Mary, Mother of God—" as a "quick curtain" falls.

Act IV, however, was substantially altered. In the first scene the Players omitted some of Isadore's hallucinations but retained his soliloquy; curiously, they also omitted, perhaps inadvertently, the details which supply the motivation for Isadore's sudden ability to master his impulses and refrain from attacking Hagar. In the text Isadore hears a voice calling "HAGAR! HAGAR!" and a newsboy calling out the headline "*Extro! Extro! Isadore Berchansky—!*" These details are absent from the Provincetown script, as is the line, "Get out, I tell you, before I do sompin! Get out! You don't know me! Can't you see? Quick! Quick!" What remains is an inadequately motivated scene in which Isadore appears to miraculously regain his reason and resists attacking Hagar—without apparent purpose. Smith noticed the incongruity, and in his extensive report of the opening performance he asked Dreiser, "I wonder why you brought that extra little girl into this act. I wonder why you did not go through with the rape if you felt you needed another shock."[46]

The second scene of Act IV was substantially condensed, to the credit of the play. Much of the initial exposition between reporters and police was omitted, and the Players did a real service to the play by cutting over three quarters of the extensive debate between Leach and Quinn. As the reviewers of the book publication had noted, in this scene Dreiser needlessly preaches what had already been developed. While the scene remains anticlimactic, it is not as tediously dull as it had been formerly.

The performance of the play was the subject of considerable controversy that confirmed Dreiser's impression that he was being persecuted by a conservative press. However, Dreiser's residence in Los Angeles complicated matters, for he had to rely on letters and clippings and could not survey the critical response himself. One can imagine Dreiser's shock when he received a three page, typewritten, single-spaced letter from Smith informing him that the opening night was an unmitigated disaster and that he should "Give thanks, oh brother, that you were three thousand miles away." Claiming that what followed was the "full truth," Smith proceeded to describe, scene by scene, what he perceived as "the final abasement that may come to an author." The setting was "grotesque from end to end." The actors were completely unsuited for their roles—the fourth act soliloquy in particular "slopped around like a drunken sailor in the hands of an inexperienced, unsubtle, clumsy actor." The second act portrayal of the Berchanskys' grief, rather than moving an audience to pity and tears, caused "Some of the audience near me [to laugh] outright." Smith continued the bad tidings for two more pages before concluding that "Anything done for the American theatre in our age must be actor and producer proof."[47]

In contrast to this blast, Hutchins Hapgood described the same performance as having "the exhilaration of real tragedy. It is cool, simple, so lacking in all literary pretentiousness, so pure in outline, so impersonal, not at all *shocking*." He described the presentation as "very good, the acting, for the most part, adequate," although "it needed a great actor to bring out the full possibilities of the father."[48] Dorothy Dudley, who recorded her impressions during intermissions, was in raptures. "The first scene, just over, was amazing. To hear, for the first time, *American* spoken on the stage! . . . Rae, Joe, Esther, are good. The father, quite wonderful. . . . It is magnificent." And in marked contrast to Smith's concluding comment, she felt that "The play was very nearly actor-proof, except in the last scene."[49]

With responses such as these, Dreiser was understandably confused. As he wrote Smith, "Can't judge, from your two letters, as to the exact situation. Have had several letters and telegrams which would indicate that the presentation had impressed a few people." He enclosed a copy of Hapgood's letter and noted, "Liveright wired that he thought the play was impressive and that it should go uptown"; he then asked Smith whether he "knew any manager who would interest himself in the [uptown] staging of the thing."[50] Smith, of course, was aghast at Dreiser's suggestion and promptly wrote another letter in which he condemned Hapgood's judgment and wondered whether Dreiser would have preferred "I'd written you the polite reassurance of my admiration" rather than the facts as he saw them.[51]

In the meantime Cook was singing the play's praises. He wrote with characteristic vagueness and equally characteristic self-promotion that "A rather distinguished crowd of professional stage-people came to a matinee yesterday afternoon. They were enthusiastic about the acting, about the play, and about the Provincetown Players for doing such a play." He noted that although "the house has been only half full," "We are sold out for tonight and tomorrow night. We are going to nurse it along through a third week here in Macdougal Street, and then try to get it into the 2nd Avenue Theatre."[52]

Complicating these reports were the various reviews that began trickling in. Although many objected to the content of the play, most early reviewers admired the performance of the actors. For example, the reviewer in the *New York Globe and Commercial Advertiser*, while concluding that "the play should not have been written, and certainly it should never have been produced," praised the acting as "admirable." Nathaniel Freyer's performance as Berchansky was "Best of all"; Esther Stockton's was "an extraordinary achievement"; J. Paul Jones' performance as Isadore "was almost too realistic and unsparing of details, and the terrible performance leaves a haunting memory." Moreover, contrary to Smith's assessment, the reviewer believed "the production showed signs of unusual care."[53]

The most laudatory review came from the socialist *Call*, which thought the acting "extraordinarily good" and that "Few professionals could hope to attain the sincerity and tragedy of Freyer." The reviewer praised the characterization, the "fidelity" and "restraint" of Dreiser's realism, and his sympathetic portrayal of insanity, which led the reviewer to note: "If the Birth Control societies are in need of propaganda material, 'The Hand of the Potter' offers all they could ask."[54]

But on 18 December 1921 a condemnatory blast by Louis V. DeFoe appeared in the widely-read *New York World* that warped both the Players' and Dreiser's perception of the trend in reviews. DeFoe began his review by stating that the critics had agreed to ignore the play:

> The unanimity with which the best friends of the Provincetown Players have ignored their descent to the revolting specimen of pathological drama on which they are at present engaged at their theatre in Macdougal Street may be taken as a charitable way of expressing disapproval of what, from any point

of view, is a gross misuse of a stage supposedly dedicated to the best interests of dramatic art. But silent contempt in this case is mistaken charity, considering the flagrancy of the offense.[55]

The remainder of the review is an artful assassination of the play, the Players' judgment, and Dreiser's abilities as a playwright. As a consequence of this review, and what followed, Dreiser never came to appreciate the true reception of *The Hand of the Potter*.

Dreiser received DeFoe's review and, his persecution complex aroused, quickly seized upon the review as representative of the critical reception. To Margaret Johnson Withey he wrote, "As for my play,—well, I have reports to the effect that the critics ignored it. . . . The noble DeFoe, in the New York World admits as much. He practicall[y] says that the critics conspired to ignore it."[56] Edna Kenton sent him a letter that confirmed his sense of persecution. "With the exception of The Call, the Jewish Daily Forward . . . and The Nation, [the critics] appear to have unanimously agreed to ignore it,—not to review it at all," she wrote. "There is scarcely any question as to that. DeFoe, of the World, . . . spilled the truth." Kenton buttressed her argument by enclosing a list of eight newspaper reviews with perfunctory excerpts that stressed the unfavorable response; she concluded, "No other daily notices."[57]

Kenton's list, however, was both selective and misleading. By 30 December at least 19 reviews had appeared—not 11—and the reviews were, for the most part, balanced assessments.[58] Albert P. Lewin, writing for the *Jewish Tribune* typifies the general trend: the production "has many flaws, but it is distinguished by a quality rare in American literature and drama—the quality of compassion." Lewin identified the difficulties presented by a windy third act and concluded, "in spite of these weaknesses, the play has moments of intense poignancy, of almost painful suspense, and that deep compassion which gives it a significance it might otherwise lack."[59]

The letters Dreiser wrote after he received Kenton's complaint suggest that he took Kenton's summation as truth. He repeated her charges in letters to Smith and to Mencken, who responded, "I take no stock in La Kenton's conspiracy tosh. It sounds very Greenwichy. . . . The real truth is that the Provincetown Players devote more attention to posturing as martyrs than they do to producing plays."[60] Mencken, in this instance, was right: the Provincetown Players did not adequately prepare *The Hand of the Potter*'s production, for their commitments to *The Verge* and their preparations for the coming production of O'Neill's *The Hairy Ape* seriously overextended their capabilities. Dreiser was not the victim of a conspiracy by moralist reviewers; he was the victim of a mediocre production of a controversial play and misguided reports from sycophantic friends.

*The Hand of the Potter* was a typical Provincetown production. While the play has been castigated for what most critics perceive as a short run, its three weeks on the stage was in fact typical; with the exception of *The Emperor Jones* and *Diff'rent*, which were moved to uptown theaters, all Provincetown plays ran, on average, 14-21 days.[61] True, *The Hand of the Potter* was a financial failure, losing the Provincetown Players $1500 and alienating "subscribers, critics, and friends," as Cook wrote,[62] but losing money was a common occurrence in a theater devoted to staging experimental works. Rather than being "a flop," as W. A. Swanberg flatly asserts, or what Carl Bode terms "a theatrical disaster,"[63] *The Hand of the Potter* was a mediocre production by a theater troupe from whom, after the Broadway success of *The Emperor Jones*, the audience had come to expect better things.

### III. Conclusion

The foregoing stage history of Dreiser's plays suggests that, for a while at least, Dreiser's work seemed dramatically compelling to those dedicated to experimental theater. *The Girl in the Coffin* in particular appealed to those troupes interested in overcoming the artificiality of commercial productions. What most attracted theaters to this play was its evocation of pathos, its realistic characterization, and especially its employment of naturalistic detail in its staging. As one reviewer marvelled, "the [Detroit] Arts and Crafts Theatre dallied with disaster . . . in using an honest-to-goodness coffin as one of the 'props' in Theodore Dreiser's play, 'The Girl in the Coffin.'. . . [T]he very fact that it was a necessary part of the staging has caused producers of one-act plays to fight shy of this particularly keen and good little drama."[64]

At the same time, the difficulties in securing a production of *The Hand of the Potter* testify to the resistance of the theater-going public to controversial subjects enacted on the stage. Reviewers tended to fall into two camps: those who condemned the play because they were troubled by its frank portrayal of sexual deviance that did not accord with their sense of stage propriety; and those who welcomed the play as an attempt to enact a new vision of tragic drama. As Ludwig Lewisohn, reviewing the production for *The Nation*, explained, Dreiser

> substitutes the concept of tragic guilt for that of sin; he sees that guilt arises out of the life-process itself and selects its guilty but sinless victim.... He alienates the ordinary spectator by repudiating the notions of sin and expiation through punishment. It is Isadore Berchansky's undeserved punishment that he is what he is. The tragic guilt that he must bear issues from implacable and anterior sources. Why should we strike at him because the hand of the potter slipped?

Reviewers condemned the play, Lewisohn concluded, because Dreiser's conception of tragedy "invalidates their absolute moral judgments; it cracks the foundations of their punitive justice; it shows up the blank folly of hate, war, revenge."[65]

It is not Dreiser's realistic plays, however, but his supernatural plays that have had the most influence on subsequent playwrights. Elmer Rice attributes *Plays of the Natural and Supernatural* as one of the influences upon *The Adding Machine*.[66] And Thornton Wilder was reportedly influenced by Dreiser's expressionistic depiction of synchronous movement. Richard Goldstone, who knew Wilder well, suggests that *The Blue Sphere* in particular provided Wilder with a method for depicting "scenes of continuous and even simultaneous action" that Wilder would employ so masterfully in *Our Town*. Moreover, Wilder was absorbed by two themes expressed in *The Spring Recital* and *Laughing Gas* and developed them fully in *Our Town* and *The Skin of Our Teeth*: "the ecstasy of being alive, as seen through the eyes of those who no longer have life, and the repetitive, cyclical history of mankind."[67] Though now largely forgotten by students of American literature and theater, Dreiser's campaign to introduce his work to the theater did affect others, who built upon the path he helped to blaze.

## IV. Record of Productions

A complete list of productions follows. Dates are opening dates; as is so often the case with little theaters, the plays ran, in most cases, for less than a week

*Laughing Gas*
1. December 1916. Indianapolis.
   Little Theater Society of Indiana.
   Director: Carl Bernhardt.

*The Girl in the Coffin*
1. 29 January 1917. St. Louis.
   St. Louis Artist's Guild.
   Director: A. H. Brueggman

2. 9 October 1917. San Francisco.
   St. Francis Little Theater Club.
   Director: Arthur Maitland.

3. 3 December 1917. New York.
   Washington Square Players.
   Director: Edward Goodman.

4. 21 March 1918. Detroit.
   Arts and Crafts Players.
   Director: Sam Hume.

5. 24 January 1920. New York.
   Workers' Theater Guild.
   Director: Wayne Arey.
   (moved to Princess Theater 9 February 1920, for 1 week)

6. 11 July 1941. Institute, WV.
   West Virginia State College.
   Director: F. S. Belcher.

"*Old Ragpicker*"
1. 30 January 1918. San Francisco.
   St. Francis Little Theater Club.
   Director: Arthur Maitland.

2. 1 June 1923. New York.
   Cellar Players.
   Director: George Bamman.

*The Hand of the Potter*
1. 5 December 1921. New York.
   The Provincetown Players.
   Director: Charles O'Brien Kennedy

2. September 1928. Berlin, Germany.
   Drei Masken Verlag.
   Director: Gustave Hartung.

3. 5 May 1938. London, England.
   Portfolio Players.
   Director: Hector Abbas.

*The Blue Sphere*
1. Broadcast over radio WABC, New York
   4 June 1930.
   Director: Georgia Backus.

### NOTES

[1] "Plays by Theodore Dreiser," *Book News Monthly* 34 (May 1916): 414-15; rpt. in Jack Salzman, *Theodore Dreiser: The Critical Reception* (New York: David Lewis, 1972), p. 267.

[2] See Thomas H. Dickinson, *The Insurgent Theatre* (New York: Huebsch, 1917), pp. 227-3; and Jack Poggi, *Theatre in America: The Impact of Economic Forces, 1870-1967* (Ithaca: Cornell University Press, 1966), p. 107. "Non-commercial theater" loosely describes three distinct areas of emphasis comprising the movement. Some theaters referred to themselves as "independent theaters" to stress their economic independence from the commercial stage; others called themselves "art theaters" or "experimental theaters" to underscore the artistic excellence or experimental nature of their productions; most, however, preferred "little theater" as the term most expressive of both financial and artistic independence. Common to all was a desire to present plays of artistic or social merit considered unprofitable by commercial managers. For further discussion of the distinctions between types of theaters, see Poggi, pp. 99-101; and Kenneth Macgowan, *Footlights Across America* (New York: Harcourt, 1929), pp. 7-9.

[3] John Seelye Bolin, "Samuel Hume: Artist and Exponent of American Art Theatre" (Diss., University of Michigan, 1970), p. 66.

[4] Mencken to Dreiser [after 14 Jan. 1915], in Thomas P. Riggio, ed., *Dreiser-Mencken Letters: The Correspondence of Theodore Dreiser and H. L. Mencken, 1907-1945*, 2 vols. (Philadelphia: University of Pennsylvania Press, 1986), 1: 187-88.

[5] Dawson, "Plays by Mr. Dreiser," *New York Globe and Commercial Advertiser*, 26 February 1916, p. 8; rpt. in Salzman, p. 256.

[6] The Little Theater Society of Indiana became the Civic Theatre of Indianapolis and exists today as the "oldest continuously-operated production theatre in the United States." Housed in the Showalter Pavillion at the Indianapolis Museum of Art, the Theatre holds scrapbooks dating from 1914. Included in the 1914-1919 scrapbook are a program and clippings concerning the *Laughing Gas* production. *Laughing Gas* played at the Masonic Temple on 7, 9, and 16 December; included on the bill were *Polly of Pogue's Run*, by W. O. Bates; the anonymous 13th century *The Farce of Pierre Patelin*; and *The Lost Silk Hat*, by Lord Dunsany.

[7] Clipping, Civic Theatre of Indianapolis scrapbook.

[8] Hector Fuller, "In Front of the House," *Indianapolis Star*, 26 November 1916, p. 45.

[9] Fuller, "In Front."

[10] Sayler, "Novel Stage Experiment," *Boston Evening Transcript*, 22 December 1916, p. 27.

[11] Sayler, *Our American Theatre* (1923; New York: Blom, 1971), pp. 209-10.

[12] Sayler, "Novel Stage Experiment."

[13] Sayler, "Little Theater Marks Epoch in Producing 'Laughing Gas,'" *Indianapolis News*, 8 December 1916, p. 27.

[14] Fuller, "Little Theater Bill Unusually Pleasing," *Indianapolis Star*, 8 December 1916, p. 6.

[15] Bernhardt to Dreiser, 18 December 1916; Dreiser Collection, Van Pelt-Dietrich Library, University of Pennsylvania.

[16] The correct name of the group is the St. Louis Players Club, which performed *The Girl in the Coffin* in two private showings, 29 January at the Artists' Guild, and 30 January at the Knights of Columbus Hall, St. Louis. Playing with *The Girl in the Coffin* the first night was Shaw's *The Man of Destiny*; Hall Gibson's *The Bridal* replaced the Shaw play on the second night. For reviews of the production, see Carlos F. Hurd, "'Girl in the Coffin' Has Dramatic Power," *St. Louis Post-Dispatch*, 30 January 1917, p. 9; and "Works of Dreiser and Bernard Shaw Given by Players," *St. Louis Globe-Democrat*, 30 January 1917, p. 7.

[17] Dreiser, *American Diaries, 1902-1926*, ed. Thomas P. Riggio (Philadelphia: University of Pennsylvania Press, 1983), p. 202.

[18] *American Diaries*, 21 November 1917; p. 216.

[19] *American Diaries*, p. 222.

[20] *American Diaries*, p. 226.

[21] *American Diaries*, pp. 227-28.

[22] "An All-American Bill at Comedy," *Brooklyn Daily Eagle*, 5 December 1917, p. 7.

[23] Mantle, "Washington Sq. Players Win New Laurels in a Bill of American Plays," *New York Evening Mail*, 12 December 1917, p. 11.

[24] Pollock, "The Washington Square Players," *Greenbook Magazine* 19 (February 1918): 213.

[25] Darnton, "The New Plays: Washington Square Players Give Fine New Bill," *New York Evening World*, 7 December 1917, p. 25.

[26] Sherwin, "The New Play: Theodore Dreiser and Others at the Comedy," *New York Globe and Commercial Advertiser*, 4 December 1917, p. 12.

[27] "Washington Square Players," *New York Dramatic Mirror*, 15 December 1917, p. 5.

[28] Mantle, "Theodore Dreiser's 'Girl in the Coffin' Done by Uplifters," *Minneapolis Journal*, 23 December 1917, Amusement Section, p. 1.

[29] F., "The Washington Square Players," *Nation* 105 (13 December 1917): 675.

[30] Hume to John Lane Co., 16 January 1918; Dreiser Collection.

[31] Cheney, *The Art Theatre* (New York: Knopf, 1917), p. 90.

[32] Holmes, "Dreiser Plays Proves Masterpiece and Best of Arts and Crafts Work," *Detroit Journal*, 22 March 1918, p. 11.

[33] "Arts and Crafts Scores Success," *Detroit Free Press*, 22 March 1918, p. 8.

[34] Arey to Dreiser, 19 December 1919 and 8 January 1920; Dreiser Collection.

[35] Towse, "The Drama: The Theatre-Workers' Guild," *New York Evening Post*, 10 February 1920, p. 11; "Guild Gives Little Plays," *New York Times*, 10 February 1920, p. 10.

[36] Gardy, "In Which the Dramatic Editor Loses His Temper and Says Some Things Which May Sound Fresh," *New York Call*, 29 January 1920, p. 4.

[37] Dreiser to Smith, 25 November 1920; *Letters of Theodore Dreiser: A Selection*, ed. Robert H. Elias, 3 vols. (Philadelphia: University of Pennsylvania Press, 1959), 1: 302-04.

[38] Smith to Dreiser, 1 December 1920; Dreiser Collection.

[39] Cook to Dreiser, 4 October 1921 and 8 October 1921; Will [?] to Dreiser, 12 October 1921; Dreiser Collection.

[40] Helen Deutsch and Stella Hanau, *The Provincetown: A Story of the Theatre* (New York: Russell & Russell, 1972), p. 71.

[41] Deutsch and Hanau, pp. 84-85.

[42] Dreiser to Mencken, 23 November 1921; *Dreiser-Mencken Letters*, 2: 453.

[43] Dreiser to Smith, 4 December 1921; Dreiser Collection.

[44] Smith to Dreiser, 8 December 1921; Dreiser Collection.

[45] On 8 January 1942 Cleon Throckmorton, who designed the set for the Provincetown production, wrote Dreiser to ask for the prompt script of *The Hand of the Potter*. Dreiser replied on 27 January that he couldn't find the stage version of the play, but he apparently had a script prepared from a copy of the book in which the cuts were marked. Both the text with the marked cuts and the typescript are extant in the Dreiser Collection.

[46] Smith to Dreiser, 6 December 1921; Dreiser Collection.

[47] Smith to Dreiser, 6 December 1921; Dreiser Collection.

[48] Hapgood to Dreiser, 9 December 1921; Dreiser Collection.

[49] Dudley to Dreiser, 14 December 1921; Dreiser Collection.

[50] Dreiser to Smith, 15 December 1921; Dreiser Collection.

[51] Smith to Dreiser, 21 December 1921; Dreiser Collection.
[52] Cook to Dreiser, 17 December 1921; Dreiser Collection.
[53] J. H., "The Provincetown Players" *New York Globe and Commercial Advertiser*, 6 December 1921, p. 18.
[54] "Theodore Dreiser's 'The Hand of the Potter' Is Remarkably Acted by the Provincetown Players," *New York Call*, 8 December 1921, p. 4.
[55] Defoe, "A Misuse of the Theatre," *New York World*, 18 December 1921, Metropolitan Section, p. 2M. See also G. D. E., "'The Hand of the Potter'—And Criticism," *Michigan Daily Magazine*, 22 January 1922, pp. 5, 7-8.
[56] Dreiser to Withey, 29 December 1921; Dreiser Collection.
[57] Kenton to Dreiser, 30 December 1921; Dreiser Collection.
[58] Our count is based on the reviews listed in *Theodore Dreiser: A Primary and Secondary Bibliography*, ed. Donald Pizer, Richard W. Dowell, and Frederic E. Rusch, 2nd ed. (Boston: G. K. Hall, 1991), pp. 130-32; and Kenton's letter, which lists additional reviews by Nellie Dawson for the *New York Globe*, by Channing Pollock for the *Brooklyn Eagle*, by an unnamed reporter for the *Brooklyn Times*, and by Abraham Cahan for the *Jewish Daily Forward*. The Dreiser Collection also contains one additional unlisted review: "'Hand of the Potter' Is a Grim, Pitying Study in Crime," *Greenwich Villager*, 10 December 1921, p. 1. After 30 December, at least two other reviews appeared—by George Jean Nathan for the *St. Paul Pioneer Press* and by G. D. E. for the *Michigan Daily Magazine*—making a total of 23 reviews, a number which suggests neither critical neglect nor overwhelming enthusiasm but rather a mediocre reception. (For comparison, the Washington Square Players' production of *The Girl in the Coffin* garnered 25 reviews.)
[59] Lewin, "Play Things," *Jewish Tribune*, 16 December 1921; clipping, Dreiser Collection.
[60] Dreiser to Smith, 3 January 1922; Dreiser Collection. Dreiser to Mencken, 14 January 1922, *Dreiser-Mencken Letters*, 2: 462.
[61] For a calendar of productions by the Provincetown Players, see Robert K. Sarlós, *Jig Cook and the Provincetown Players: Theatre in Ferment* (Boston: University of Massachusetts Press, 1982), pp. 168-80. Deutsch and Hanna reprint cast lists for each production (pp. 199-313).
[62] Cook to Dreiser, 6 January 1922; Dreiser Collection.
[63] Swanberg, p. 258; Bode, ed., *The New Mencken Letters* (New York: Dial, 1977), p. 68.
[64] "Arts and Crafts Scores Success," p. 8.
[65] Lewisohn, "Drama: Year's End," *The Nation* 113 (28 December 1921): 762-63.
[66] Rice, *Minority Report: An Autobiography* (New York: Simon and Schuster, 1963), p.198.
[67] Goldstone, *Thornton Wilder: An Intimate Portrait* (New York: Dutton, 1975), pp. 118-19.